ON
MARRIAGE

Theodor Gottlieb von Hippel. Eighteenth-century portrait by an unknown artist, formerly in possession of the Prussia Museum in Königsberg (destroyed in World War II).

ON MARRIAGE

Theodor
Gottlieb
von Hippel

BICENTENNIAL EDITION

Translated and edited
with an Introduction by

TIMOTHY F. SELLNER

WAYNE STATE UNIVERSITY PRESS   DETROIT

Original title: Über die Ehe

English translation copyright © 1994 by Wayne State University Press,
Detroit, Michigan 48202. All rights are reserved.
No part of this book may be reproduced without formal permission.
Manufactured in the United States of America.
99 98 97 96 95 94   5 4 3 2 1

Library of Congress Cataloging-in-Publication Data

Hippel, Theodor Gottlieb von, 1741–1796.
[Über die Ehe. English]
On marriage / Theodor Gottlieb von Hippel : translated and edited
with an introduction by Timothy F. Sellner.—Bicentennial ed.
p.   cm.
Includes index.
ISBN 0–8143–2495–9 (alk. paper)
1. Marriage.   I. Sellner, Timothy F., 1938–   II. Title.
HQ731.H5613   1994

306.81—dc20   93–31782

Designer: Joanne E. Kinney

To My Wife

CONTENTS

ACKNOWLEDGMENTS

I WOULD LIKE to express my sincere gratitude for valuable help received from the following:

Professors John L. Andronica, Mary L. B. Pendergraft, James T. Powell, and Robert W. Ulery, Jr. of the Department of Classical Languages, Wake Forest University; Christa G. Carollo, Stefanie Tanis, and Professor Wilmer D. Sanders of the Department of German and Russian, Wake Forest University; Professors Cyclone Covey and James Barefield, Department of History, Wake Forest University; Professor Joseph Kohnen of the Centre Universitaire de Luxembourg; and Keith E. Gibeling and Thomas G. Schuster of Wake Forest University.

I would further like to thank the University of Colorado Libraries, the Yale University Libraries, the Washington University Libraries (St. Louis), the Indiana University Libraries, the Staatsbibliothek Preußischer Kulturbesitz, and the Graduate Council of Wake Forest University for their help.

INTRODUCTION

I

1774 WAS A BANNER YEAR in the history of German letters. That year a young German poet and dramatist by the name of Johann Wolfgang von Goethe, known only in German-speaking lands as the author of a rousing "Storm and Stress" drama published the year before, issued in two slim volumes an epistolary novel which was to establish the international reputation of German literature for the first time since the troubadours. In a matter of a few short years, any reference to the unfortunate hero or heroine of *The Sorrows of Young Werther* became, in the words of one writer, "as certain of being understood by European readers as one to Hero and Leander or to Héloise and Abelard."[1] By the time the "Werther-mania" of the late eighteenth century had subsided, imitations of the work numbered in the hundreds and Goethe's novel had been translated into virtually every major and minor European language.

That same year another work appeared in the German-speaking states which caused a similar sensation and also enjoyed an extended publishing history, running to four separate editions during the author's lifetime and seven printings by 1841. The work saw seven additional printings after that time with other publishers, three of them in the twentieth century, the latest in 1979. Nevertheless, while such a publishing history clearly reveals a public fascination with the work rivalling *Werther* in longevity, if not in initial intensity, the work has never been translated into any other language, and thus, unlike its literary counterpart, its influence has been confined almost completely to German-speaking readers. This book bore the title *Über die Ehe* (On Marriage), and while the nearly universal interest in the topic and the author's lively treatment of it were the chief reasons for its popularity, vigorous and widespread speculation concerning the author, who had published the work anonymously, contributed in large part as well. Virtually no author of the day was above suspicion, including Goethe himself,[2] and later, several members of the foremost intellectual circle of Königsberg in East Prussia, including even the old bachelor Immanuel Kant, were considered as likely candidates.

Two years after its first publication, in 1776, a second and enlarged edition appeared, indicating the immediate popularity of the work and adding further fuel to the fire of debate concerning the author of the treatise and the controversial ideas contained in it. Part of the appeal of the work was its uniqueness; *Über die Ehe* was a far cry from the beloved (at least by parents of newlywed couples) but heavily didactic and moralistic treatises written by clergymen in the interest of preserving the moral integrity of the family by reiterating perhaps one last time the Church's teachings on marriage.

Thus the work was not by any standard of eighteenth-century measurement what we of this century would call a "marriage manual"; there is almost nothing in the work concerning how to enjoy or preserve a happy marriage, how to please one's mate, or how to save a marriage which, again in twentieth-century parlance, is about to "go on the rocks." While the treatise did contain shorter chapters addressed to young men and women (as well as to widowers and widows), conspicuously absent were the traditional enumeration and description of the qualities to be sought and avoided in the selection of a Christian spouse, and the work contained little in the way of practical advice for the raising of children.

Thus the author laid no claim to supporting the established churches in their advocacy of Christian marriage based on the dual pillars of biblical morality and Church doctrine—although he did regard marriage as a holy institution, and included a chapter on that subject. Rather, it was the author's intention to examine as thoroughly as possible—according to the principles of enlightened inquiry—a human institution whose true function had long been obscured by centuries of both heathen and Christian religious practice, demeaning public prejudice, and meaningless superstition. Here marriage was no longer viewed as if through the eyes of the Church alone, but examined as to whether the institution worked to the advantage or disadvantage of the marriage partners, the state, and the human race as a whole. No longer did God speak to an uneducated and unenlightened human race solely through Holy Scripture and Church doctrine, the Creator had now begun to reveal His will to a mature humanity through the two great catchwords of human progress during the Enlightenment, *reason* and *natural law*. Now, like all other human institutions recently laid open to the probing eye of the scientist and mind of the philosopher—now it had become marriage's turn.

The chapter headings of the work testify to the intention of the author to investigate his subject thoroughly: the first chapter is entitled "Complaints Concerning Prejudices Against Marriage" and deals with the reasons why people choose not to marry or to marry later in life; chapter 2 attempts to define the purpose of marriage and its significance for all parties concerned; chapter 3 has for its heading "Why Marriages Are Considered Holy" and discusses whether the sanction of the Church is a necessary prerequisite for marriage; the fourth chapter treats the question of faithfulness in marriage, first as regards men, and then women; chapter 5, entitled "On the Question of Authority in Marriage," treats one of the most important, but obviously more ticklish, topics in the work, and it is this chapter which understandably engendered the most controversy with every edition. The remainder of the book consists of the above-mentioned three chapters, addressed to young men, young women, and to widowers and widows, followed by a concluding chapter.

While the topics were of almost universal interest, this does not adequately explain the book's widespread popularity through the years, especially among less educated readers for whom such a treatise, filled as it was with biblical allusions, legal terminology (often in the original Latin), and copious quotes from classical authors, would have presented a formidable challenge. Moreover, the work was written in a quirky style which jumped helter-skelter from point to point and often attempted to prove its thesis by means of sheer accumulation of examples rather than by logic. Two elements keep this work from being a dry and pedantic disquisition and make it as enjoyable to read today as it must have been two hundred years ago: namely, its wealth of worldly wisdom, and above all, its humor. The nature of this humor can best be described as "puckish" in the true sense of the word. Yet while Shakespeare's famous fairy in his *Midsummer-Night's Dream* utters the well-known phrase "What fools these mortals be"[3] out of disdain for the nonsensical goings-on of the human beings with whom he is forced to come into contact, the author of the treatise on marriage, denied the supra-human perspective of a Puck, often seems to be expressing instead a quiet despair at the frailties of his own species by means of his tacit agreement with the haughty fairy: "Indeed, what fools we mortals be."

Yet while the author was attempting to vivisect a venerable and, by many accounts, comatose institution with the scalpel of reason, his findings, particularly regarding the conduct of young women before marriage and the role of the housewife, often reflect the popular prejudices, inequities of the law, and conservative position of the Protestant and Roman Catholic Churches of the day. Thus the author—and despite the controversy surrounding his identity, there seemed little doubt that it was a man—chided young unmarried women for being coquettish, fickle, and superficial, and in his chapter on authority in marriage he unequivocally assigned the role of master in the household to the male. He began this latter chapter with a modification of the ancient legal maxim "By-law has precedence over town law, town law over provincial law, and provincial law over Imperial law," and then defined the husband of the household as the administrator of that by-law (household law). The reason women are considered unfit by nature to rule (even in the household) is, he concluded, their frequent state of pregnancy. Yet as we shall soon see, the author was later to change his opinion radically regarding the role of women before and after marriage.

No new editions of *Über die Ehe* were published during the 1770s or 1780s, and the public's fascination with the work and the identity of its author subsided almost completely except for a brief revival between 1778 and 1781. When a lengthy novel with the puzzling title *Lebensläufe nach aufsteigender Linie* (Biographies on an Ascending Line) appeared in the bookstores in 1778, it seemed to many people to possess all the stylistic earmarks of the book on marriage, causing more than a few to conclude—correctly as it later turned out—that the authors of the two works were one and the same person, although speculation still persisted as to who that might be.

Finally, in 1792, sixteen years after the publication of the second edition of the book on marriage, a third edition of the then almost forgotten treatise was offered for sale to the public. This edition was ostensibly merely an enlarged version of the previous work (it was longer by over a hundred pages) in a somewhat more elegant format—that is, it now contained two illustrations by the most important German, and likewise one of the best known European book illustrators of the period, Daniel Chodowiecki, whose illustrations for Goethe's *Werther*, incidentally, had become the accepted standard for *Werther* illustration. Moreover, this edition was printed using Latin letters instead of the German script (*"Fraktur"*) customary at the time. The reason for this is open to question, but it appears to have been an attempt to attract an international readership for the book.

Nevertheless, these changes were minor in comparison to the alterations in the text, and many a reader familiar with the first two editions must have sat up with a jolt the first time he or she encountered one of the sentences in the new edition dealing with the behavior of women before marriage and their status within the marriage bond—for here the author had completely reversed his position. The fault for women's frailties was laid squarely at the feet of the men, and what must have been even more shocking, the author seemed now to be advocating complete equality between the sexes within marriage and even within the state—that is, equality to the point of granting actual rights of citizenship to the female sex!

That same year, 1792, there appeared another work bearing the German title *Über die bürgerliche Verbesserung der Weiber* (recently translated as *On Improving the Status of Women*[4]) which actually *did* go so far as to advocate granting the right of citizenship to women, and then went on to praise at great length women's natural ability in disciplines to which they had previously been denied admittance: not only barbering and tailoring, but also politics, academics, and most particularly, for this discipline is still the topic of heated debate today, the ministry. This work also appeared to be by the same author as *Über die Ehe*.

One year later the public was offered still another edition of the treatise on marriage, this time expanded from 426 to 501 pages and thus containing countless additional examples and arguments in support of the position the author had taken in the third edition. Once again the public's interest was piqued and the debate concerning the book's authorship began anew. Finally, upon the author's death in 1796 and as a somewhat fortuitous consequence of the settling of his estate, the mystery was solved: the author of all three works was revealed to be none other than Theodor Gottlieb von Hippel, close personal friend of the philosophers Kant and Johann Georg Hamann, and governing mayor of the city of Königsberg, the largest and most influential city in all of East Prussia. Some who had suspected Hippel all along must have smiled with deep satisfaction at this news, for in fact his name had been bruited about in connection with each of the works, despite Hippel's consistent denials of authorship. Others wondered why a man such as Hippel, known throughout the entire state of Prussia as a highly capable, industrious, and ambitious civil servant, characterized more by his aloofness and arrogance than his wit, would undertake to write such a book—or even how he *could*, since he had never been married a day in his life! Moreover, an astounded readership began to ponder as well just what might have prompted the author to change his position regarding women so radically during the period between the second and third editions.

And indeed, the changes went far beyond the addition of new material in the later editions. For example, Hippel no longer began the chapter on authority in marriage with the quotation on household law mentioned above; the quotation was now prefaced by the following statement: "If it is the role of the man to exert authority in the household, then it is the function of the woman to do the ruling; if the husband is Director of the Household Judicial System, then she is Director of Police." While it is difficult to find a suitable modern equivalent for the two German terms (*"Präsident von der Hausjustiz"* and *"Polizeipräsident"*), it seems clear that Hippel intended the two functions to be viewed as dissimilar in nature but equal in importance. This new relationship also received its sanction from the aforementioned household law, which represented a radical alteration in Hippel's position in the sense that this law formerly established the authority of the man to rule in the household alone. Thus the man does not have authority over the woman in marriage, nor the woman over the man. And who has the final say in household matters (and matters of state as well)? Hippel answered the question in true Enlightenment fashion: "Reason, and reason alone."

As to the question whether pregnancy or any other alleged weakness of the female sex renders it unfit to rule, Hippel managed to reverse his position in an ingenious way by placing his previous assertion that pregnancy made women unfit to rule in the mouth of an unenlightened male chauvinist who wished to claim authority for men over women in the marriage bond. Thus, when this unrepentant chauvinist repeated Hippel's *own* previous assertion concerning pregnancy, Hippel was now able to greet him with a barrage of arguments utterly refuting his former theory, including the fact, for example, that their Excellencies (the men of rank and power) spend months at a time taking cures at the spa without giving the slightest consideration to the exercise of their authority while they are away from the seat of power.

Hippel's definition of the ultimate purpose of marriage remained the same throughout all four editions, although it was elaborated upon from edition to edition. It is not, as the state and the Roman Catholic Church have taken it to be, that of procreation; nor is it, as the Protestants have often been wont to consider it, a kind of safety valve for the sex drive in the sense of Paul's words: "It is better to marry than to burn."[5] Hippel instead views the purpose of marriage as did the Romans in their notion of the *arctissimum vitae commercium,* or, as Hippel defines it, as *"die genaueste Lebensvereinigung"*—as the closest possible intertwining of two lives. The precise interpretation of this concept will necessarily vary from marriage to marriage, but in every case it is to be determined by the married couple alone. Thus there will be marriages consisting only in the union of two bodies, marriages in which both bodies and souls are united, and those in which the only union is that which takes place between the souls of the two partners. Marriage is what the couple wishes to make of it; anything is permissible which does not harm either of the two married persons or any third party. Thus extramarital affairs, for example, the bane of eighteenth-century society and severely condemned by Hippel in chapter 4, are unacceptable because of the harm they cause at least two of the three people involved. By means of this new understanding of the ancient concept of marriage, Hippel was attempting to free the institution from its burdens and limitations and establish a more enlightened definition of humankind's most fundamental union.

The reasons which prompted Hippel's radical change in attitude will perhaps never be revealed completely, although recent scholarship has come a long way in explaining to the late twentieth century what forever remained inexplicable to Hippel's contemporary audience. These derive at least to a certain extent from the circumstances of his very active life and the peculiar nature of his character, for there probably has never been another writer in the history of German letters whose life has so abounded in contradiction. Hippel's life in many respects represented the very antithesis of his writings. He was a rationalist who abandoned the principles of reason when he felt they interfered with the search for truth, and a devout Christian who struggled his entire life with the reality of death. He once wrote that he considered liars detestable and a lie one of the most heinous crimes,[6] yet he published his works in the strictest anonymity, and his almost pathological insistence on the preservation of that anonymity forced him occasionally into outright denials when he was confronted by those who suspected his authorship. He gleefully pilloried secret societies in his writings, all the while remaining an active member of a Masonic lodge. His most famous work is a treatise on marriage, and he recommended the institution to all who would listen, but he himself remained a bachelor all his life. Although confident, almost dictatorial, in his manner, he often complained to his closest friend, Johann George Scheffner, of hypochondria, melancholy, and fits of weeping. He upbraided others for their greed, yet when called upon by his friends to account for his own stinginess he pleaded utter bewilderment as to how he had acquired his immense fortune.[7]

Hippel was both the quintessential man of the eighteenth century and a writer whose work speaks to readers today with astonishing, almost uncanny, relevance. A thorough examination of the complete body of his writings reveals him as a novelist and poet of great wisdom and touching sensibility; as a political thinker who accepted only those forms of government which guaranteed liberty, equality, fraternity, justice, peace, respect for the individual, and intellectual, moral and material progress; and finally, as an emancipator whose ideas still challenge the late twentieth century to rethink its deeply held notions concerning the relationship between the sexes.

II

Theodor Gottlieb Hippel was born on 31 January 1742 in the small town of Gerdauen, a day's ride over an often bleak and dreary landscape from Königsberg, the capital of East Prussia. He was the third child of Melchior and Eleanore Thime Hippel and the first to live longer than a few months. His birth was followed by that of his brother, Gotthard Friedrich, on 3 May 1743. Hippel's father served as principal of the local school most of his life, although in his autobiography, begun in 1790, Hippel maintains that his father and grandfather were ministers, and implies that they had also married daughters of ministers.[8] This expansion of the truth doubtless derives from Hippel's exalted view of the life of the clergyman, a topic to which he dedicates several pages of romanticized depiction in his

autobiography.[9] The household in which he was raised was characterized by a strict adherence to the tenets of the Pietists, a sect within the
Lutheran Church which in general stressed rigorous self-examination
and zealous devotion, and which in Hippel's East Prussian homeland
had also assumed a kind of mystical yearning for death and the glories
of Heaven. Although the family had noble antecedents, by Hippel's
grandfather's day the prefix *"von"* had been dropped from the surname
and, Hippel's autobiographical reflections of later years to the contrary,
the family lived in relative poverty and without particular distinction in
the isolated hamlet. Hippel's natural sensitivity and high intelligence,
carefully molded by the strict pedagogical methods of his father and
the rigorous religiosity of his mother, engendered a certain precocity
and a sense of superiority over his younger brother and playmates
which further increased the isolation and loneliness of his childhood
years. His youth was a particularly unhappy time for Hippel, and
doubtless the basis for his lifelong unsuccessful search for happiness
lay in the painful events of his childhood years in Gerdauen. One
striking example is provided by his bitter autobiographical recollection
of having been forced repeatedly to play the role of the bridegroom in
the marriage games staged by the local princess for the benefit of her
youthful playmates. Hippel was made the butt of laughter because of
his boorishness in these charades, made doubly humiliating through
Hippel's acute sense of social inferiority. He later wrote he "could
almost go so far as to maintain" that these incidents were the reason
for his having remained a bachelor all his life.[10]

Having received an excellent preparatory education from his father
and the local pastor, Hippel—although not yet sixteen years old—was
ready by the summer of 1756 to enter the University of Königsberg. It
was expected that he, like his brother after him, would study theology
and later enter the ministry. The strongly philosophical bent of the
theological lectures at the university, as well as the more cosmopolitan
and less restricted life of the bigger city must have severely weakened
Hippel's resolve—probably never strong to begin with—to study theology, for by 1759 he had largely given up going to lectures and was
considering yielding to his inclination to become a poet.

In May of that year, however, a circumstance intervened which
was to have a significant effect on Hippel's later social and intellectual
development. Probably through the influence of his father, Hippel was
offered the position of tutor to the children of the Dutch Counselor
Theodor Polykarp Woyt, a student friend of Hippel's father and one

of the richest and most influential men in Königsberg. Hippel's acceptance of this position necessitated that he reside in the house of his employer, and here the young provincial student experienced at first hand the splendor of the life of the upper classes and the power at their disposal to maintain it. Doubtless there arose in the young subordinate the desire to emulate their way of life and someday to rise to a position of rank and wealth himself. Late in the year 1760, a nephew of Woyt and friend of Hippel, Hendrik von Keyser, was commissioned by the governor of East Prussia to present a valuable amber collection to the Empress Elizabeth in Russia. As fortune would have it, von Keyser had just won eight hundred rubles in a lottery and invited Hippel to accompany him on the journey, offering to assume much of the latter's costs by means of his recent windfall. This episode was to prove so important to Hippel's later development that he dedicates the entire second half of his unfinished autobiography to it, describing it as the period of the "manumission of his soul."[11] Hippel spent nearly six weeks in Russia, fully half of which was taken up by travel to and from St. Petersburg, and was introduced to the members of Russian society at the very highest levels. His admiration for a later ruler of this vast land, Catherine the Great (formerly a German princess from one of the humblest of German states), and the reforms she introduced remained with him for the rest of his life and finds profuse expression in the last two editions of *On Marriage* and in *On Improving the Status of Women*.

Like many of his Prussian countrymen before him, Hippel was offered a military commission with the promise of a glorious career in the service of this foreign state, yet in spite of the highly flattering nature of such an offer to the then nineteen-year-old tutor, after much soul-searching he came to the conclusion that his roots in his Prussian homeland and Lutheran religion were already too deep for transplanting and that he would do best to seek his fortune on his native soil.

His return from Russia ushered in a difficult period for Hippel. His former employer had taken his sudden departure for Russia amiss and dismissed him, leaving him destitute; his friends had left the university and von Keyser still remained in Russia. And perhaps worst of all, Hippel's decision to abandon the study of theology had incurred the wrath of his parents, who from this point on refused to support his university studies. In desperation, Hippel took a position as tutor to the daughter of a wealthy family in Wesselshöfen. There matters went from bad to worse. He promptly fell madly in love with his charge, creating an impossible situation by virtue of the significant difference in the social status of the two lovers. As soon as the relationship was discovered, Hippel was removed from his position and forced to renounce both his love and the source of his income. The effect of this unfortunate episode on Hippel was profound; in a letter to Scheffner he later remarked that he had been in love only once in his life, and that every time he thought of it, he "got the shivers."[12] In every edition of the book on marriage Hippel includes a brief dramatic scene between a suitor of modest social standing and a prospective father-in-law inordinately proud of his pedigree who disapproves of the union between the suitor and his daughter for reasons of pure snobbery. Hippel utilizes this passage as a vivid example of the folly of marriages of convenience, and the poignancy of the words uttered by the poor suitor leads us to believe they are not far different from those once spoken by the author himself. Once again, Hippel had been made to feel deeply the insignificance of his status in the face of those possessing nobility, wealth, and power, and from this point on, in the words of a contemporary biographer, Hippel "seized upon the idea of someday becoming [her] equal in both wealth and social position."[13] He now began to pursue his career with a relentlessness and singleness of purpose not previously discernable in his character. Worldly success, wealth, and reputation seemed to have become his only goals, and in 1762 he returned to the university to take up the study of law, a discipline which he now viewed as a more useful vehicle for the attainment of these ends.

For several years, Hippel suffered the most severe deprivations in order to finish his degree. Finally, in 1765, he took the oath of office at the Königsberg city court, enabling him to practice law in the city. As his nephew later described it, his "penetrating intellect, his logic, his sonorous voice and his precise, often admired declamation"[14] won cases and clients for him right from the beginning. He soon enjoyed an excellent reputation and tried a number of significant cases for wealthy and noble families of the surrounding area. Always on the lookout for open positions where he might advance more quickly, he was nevertheless unsuccessful in his pursuit of greater financial reward and prestige, to a degree that he began to complain bitterly to his friend Scheffner of the "ingratitude of his fatherland" and his intention to leave it. Realizing the danger of such an attitude, however, Hippel enjoined Scheffner at the same time not to reveal his dissatisfaction to others, since such matters were a bit like "rejected proposals of marriage, whereby the snubbed suitor invariably becomes the butt of ridicule himself."[15]

Hippel had been a member of the Masonic Lodge "The Three Crowns" since 1761, and he pursued his lodge duties with enthusiasm, later going so far as to assert that whatever he had learned about the world and the human race he owed to his membership in the Masons.[16] Also from this period stem his earliest poetic works, of which the first, his *Rhapsodie* of 1763, was a long poem giving vent to his sentiments after the unfortunate love affair of two years before. This was followed by two comedies in the French vein, a satire of 1765 entitled *Der Mann nach der Uhr, oder der ordentliche Mann* (The Man o' the Clock; or, the Man of Order) in which the excessive love of order and punctuality of Kant's (and later his own) friend, Joseph Green, are pilloried, and *Die ungewöhnlichen Nebenbuhler* (The Unusual Rivals) of 1767. In 1772 he published a collection of Christian hymns with a strong Pietistic inclination, a number of which have become a permanent part of Protestant hymnody in Germany. During these early years Hippel also penned a number of short discourses on Freemasonry, and as early as September of 1767 he had already mentioned that he was working on a "treatise on marriage," although at least one biographer places the beginning of Hippel's work on marriage even earlier.[17]

And indeed, there is evidence that Hippel was concerned with the marriage question, at least from a personal standpoint, throughout the sixties and into the early seventies. His letters to Scheffner reveal the magnitude of his dilemma during these years, for while Hippel was obviously lonely in his unwedded state and genuinely wished to marry, the eligible young women he encountered appeared so frivolous and superficial to him that he gradually began to turn in upon himself and dedicate his entire energy to the advancement of his career. At the age of twenty-seven he already seemed resigned to a life of bachelorhood. "You celebrated a wedding once, but I have no hope of ever celebrating one. There aren't any girls here for me, and it appears that my grave inscription will be even less imposing than that of Old Man Gellert [a German writer]: 'He lived without a wife and died.' Well, come what may! My best years are already past.—The morning is over, noon is upon me, and maybe I will never get to see the evening, maybe my afternoon nap will be a long, long sleep for me,"[18] he wrote to Scheffner about this time. The single exception to Hippel's incipient misogyny was Scheffner's wife "Babet," whom Hippel often praised and never failed to greet in his letters, and whose critical judgment he valued highly. It was thus without a doubt Hippel's own personal circumstances, coupled with the scandal created by the public behavior of several Königsberg wives of Hippel's own acquaintance involved in unseemly divorces and remarriages, and perhaps even the disregard for the marriage bond exhibited by the King himself,[19] which prompted Hippel to undertake a satirical-philosophical treatise on the subject of marriage in which he could at the same time discourse on the follies of the female sex and proffer his own version of the ideal woman and mate. This "treatise" later formed the basis of the first two editions of the book on marriage.

Finally, the beginning of the seventies ushered in an almost unbroken string of rapid promotions within the Prussian bureaucratic system and an equally swift ascension in social prominence for Hippel. On 30 October 1771 he was named Advocate in the Königsberg High Court of Justice, and a few months later was selected as the Prussian Commissioner to carry out Frederick the Great's annexation of several regions of Poland. For his excellent work in the fulfillment of this task Hippel was recommended for the position of judge in matters dealing with shipping, the coastline, and the collection of amber, a promotion immediately ratified by the King. Since, however, this position would have removed him from Königsberg and any chance of a career there, Hippel pulled every string possible to have the promotion revoked. He was eventually successful in this attempt, and on 29 July 1773 was promoted once again, this time to the position of Royal Counsel in Criminal Matters, a post which matched Hippel's unique talents and personality traits far better than the earlier proposal.

In 1778 he was called to the position of City Counselor, which also gave him a seat on the municipal council. With this promotion Hippel left the service of the Prussian state and entered the municipal government of Königsberg. On 26 August 1780 the King named him to the post of Director of Criminal Affairs. During this period Hippel suffered constantly from overwork and stress, resulting in periodic outbreaks of hypochondria and a painful disease of the eyes which was later to have tragic consequences. Nevertheless, his reputation as a highly capable and hardworking public servant continued to grow among those of influence in the city. By 1778, Hippel was in a position to purchase a large house in the city—considered by many to be the most beautiful in Königsberg and later dubbed "Hippel's Palace" by its citizens[20]—for the considerable sum of eleven thousand talers, a venture which reveals more clearly than anything else just how far Hippel had come since the days of his employment as a tutor for the pittance of forty talers a year.

Hippel's letters from the period 1770 to 1780 reveal another episode which appears to have fundamentally affected his attitude toward women after the first two editions of the book on marriage. In 1770 he mentioned for the first time the name of a woman with whom he had entered into a relationship; this liaison quickly burgeoned into a sort of "idyll," in Hippel's own words, which was to afford him and his consort many "happy hours." Apparently this relationship continued for a decade or so without any hint in the letters of a proposal of marriage on Hippel's part. Finally, on Christmas Day, 1780, Hippel reported to Scheffner that he had broken off the relationship. The reason became apparent when he wrote the following April that in the meantime the woman had committed suicide, leaving an infant to be cared for by her irresponsible seducer, a man who was only interested in pawning as many of her possessions as he was able to obtain for himself. It is possible to view this episode, as does Hippel's most recent biographer,[21] as another example of Hippel's misadventures in matters of the heart, but it is also important to note that by 1780 he had most probably already resolved to remain a bachelor all his life,[22] so that the unfortunate incident was hardly a matter of his having been deserted at the altar. Moreover, his letters express such anger and pity at the fate of the woman he cared for at the hands of a ruthless opportunist that it was apparent he had come to understand as never before the vulnerability of women and their frequent victimization by men because they lacked the protection of the law and the rights of citizenship. The attainment of protective laws and the rights of citizenship for women was later to become one of the most significant new themes introduced into the third edition of the book on marriage. In order to console himself and dispel his loneliness, Hippel shortly afterward legally adopted his nephew, the only son of his pastor brother and the latter's late wife, and attempted to give the boy the benefits of an education which only the city and a man of means could offer.

Hippel continued to write during this busy period as well, and in the course of three years (from 1778 to 1781) published in four volumes the genealogical novel *Lebensläufe nach aufsteigender Linie*. The work was immediately popular, and is the main source of Hippel's present literary reputation as a sentimental novelist after the manner of

Laurence Sterne. Much of the controversy surrounding the anonymous author of the work centered around his revelation in the novel of some of the basic tenets of Immanuel Kant's philosophical system before the latter had published any of his major works. To be sure, these ideas had been known for some time through Kant's university lectures, but his annoyance at their premature revelation was considerable. Moreover, when the authorship of the *Lebensläufe* was finally revealed at Hippel's death, Kant, to his even greater irritation, felt called upon to defend himself against the charge that it was *he* who had plagiarized from Hippel, since the latter's work had appeared prior to his own![23]

In November of 1780, the First, or Governing, Mayor of Königsberg, who also bore the title of Director of Police, died ending a twenty-eight-year administration marked by corruption and inefficiency. The Second and Third Mayors, knowing well the Herculean task which awaited the new Governing Mayor in restoring order and confidence in the government, refused to be considered for the position. The City Council appealed to Berlin for a solution to their problem, with the recommendation that the position of Director of Police be separated from that of Governing Mayor due to the many responsibilities of the office of Director. The government in Berlin not only ignored this suggestion completely, but urged the immediate appointment of a new Governing Mayor who could fill both positions capably. Once more the Council failed to come to a conclusion, whereupon Frederick and his advisors in Berlin lost all patience with their Königsberg subordinates and ordered them to appoint the youngest member of the City Council, Theodor Gottlieb Hippel, as the new Governing Mayor and Director of Police, and to grant him the title of Counselor of War as well. The entire Council was stunned, and no one more so than Hippel himself. Shortly after his election he wrote to Scheffner:

> With a heart heavier than lead I report to you that I am [now] Counselor of War and Governing Mayor.—I have known about it since Wednesday morning at 10, and my patent has already arrived. God, if you knew what I have suffered since Wednesday until yesterday evening, you would pity me. . . . Worst of all is that on top of everything else people actually envy me! . . . I do not possess the soul of a mayor. But what am I to do? Send it back? Prostitute myself even further? I have kept silent and not thanked God, and thus I go to meet my fate."[24]

Nevertheless, with a steely will Hippel immediately set about the reform of the city in an effort to model his own administration after the enlightened state government of his King (and lifelong idol) Frederick the Great. He struggled tirelessly the first few years against the corruption and inefficiency of the bureaucrats under him and the vested interests of the various factions of the city administration, and by the late 1780s the once rusted machinery of the state was once again running smoothly. There was not a single aspect of municipal life, from the care of the poor to the organization of the fire department, which had not undergone significant improvements at the hands of Königsberg's perpetually vigilant Governing Mayor. Such competence hardly escaped the notice of the Prussian court in Berlin, and even the death of Frederick in 1786 and the accession of his nephew, Frederick William II, brought no change in the favor in which Hippel was viewed there. During his short stay in Königsberg in 1786, the new king decorated him personally for his services to the state, and that year Hippel was also named City President, a titular office which he held until his death.

From the end of the seventies Hippel had been a permanent fixture at Kant's afternoon *"Tischgesellschaften"* ("table gatherings"), to which the philosopher of language Hamann and various other Königsberg intellectual lights from all professions were invited regularly. By this time the now famous philosopher and his former student had become fast friends, and Kant as well as Hippel cherished the long discussions, both at table and in private, about matters philosophical and practical. Although much of what was discussed more than likely found its way in one form or another into the writings of *both* writers, it would be a mistake to assume that Hippel is merely a follower and interpreter of Kant, or, as some have maintained, that the reverse is actually the case.[25] Hippel attended Kant's lectures only very irregularly as a student over a period of years, and even a cursory reading of a work such as *Über die Ehe* is enough to convince anyone that Hippel is anything but a systematic philosopher. Systems are "lazy servants of the mind," he once wrote,[26] and he gave up reading Kant's *Critique of Pure Reason* after only a few pages, remarking that because of the "incomprehensibility" (*"Dunkelheit"*) of Kant's style the work was "beyond him."[27] Furthermore, while Hippel pays homage to Kant the philosopher in the book on marriage, the work also contains a number of caustic references to decidedly chauvinistic observations on women the philosopher apparently had made during the course of table conversations at which Hippel must have been present.

In the year 1790, the citizens of Königsberg were surprised to learn that their Governing Mayor had been ennobled and from then on would be entitled to the perquisites of that estate, including the right to affix the prefix *von* to his surname. Although Hippel had long since earned this rank, and in fact his ancestors had actually been members of the lesser nobility, he was only able to renew the patent by means of lengthy secret negotiations with the court of the Holy Roman Emperor, Joseph II, in Vienna. This action came as an even greater shock to many of his friends, since Hippel had for years espoused democratic ideals. Although most biographers view Hippel's apparent yearning for aristocratic prerogatives as motivated by his lifelong ambition and a vanity grown excessive through the years of his mayoralty, in his autobiography Hippel himself attributes this action solely to his concern for the members of his extended family who would later benefit from his singular good fortune and bear the name von Hippel proudly because of it.[28]

By 1790 the pressure to reform the government of Königsberg had abated, and the early nineties were witness to Hippel's literary flowering, which produced the ripe fruit of a lifetime of reflection on a number of important topics, in particular that of marriage and the role of women in the state. In 1791, Hippel abandoned the autobiography he had started the year before in order to concentrate on a new edition of the book on marriage, published in 1792. This was followed the same year by *On Improving the Status of Women*, wherein his advocacy of a more just treatment of women and greater rights for them in marriage is extended to the state as a whole. In 1793, the last edition of the book on marriage appeared, representing the culmination of his thoughts on the woman question, although his posthumously published collected works contains a short series of sketches entitled *"Über weibliche Bildung"* ("On Female Education"), ideas presumably jotted down after 1793 for a planned second edition of *On Improving the Status of Women*.

The reasons for Hippel's change of heart in the sixteen years between the publication of the second and third editions of the book on marriage cannot be determined precisely. Certainly the aforementioned tragic *affaire de coeur* played a role, as did the fact that during his years as a lawyer Hippel was constantly compelled to deal with laws and regulations which worked to the detriment of women and served to maintain their guardianship status both inside and outside the marriage bond. Perhaps even more significant is Hippel's obsession, clearly manifest from the first days of his mayoralty, with improving every institution within the state by applying the tenets of right reason to the administration of human government according to the model of the two "great" rulers whom he had venerated since his early years, Frederick of Prussia and Catherine of Russia. And finally, while the French Revolution had given many the hope that the liberty and equality advocated by the Enlightenment would at last attain universal legal sanction, the French Constitution of 1791, the most "enlightened" document of the age, wherein the application of right reason to the administration of human government was thought to have achieved its fullest expression, had itself failed to grant equal rights to women, though it spoke grandiloquently of "universal suffrage." Concerning the effect the events in France had on Hippel there is no doubt whatsoever, for he frequently casts a critical eye in that direction in his writings. This is likewise true for the new ideas coming across the border from the West, and it is obvious that Hippel was aware of the state of the debate in France, and had read the works of Helvétius, Montesquieu, D'Holbach, Condorcet, and Tallyrand on the subject of women's rights. Far more important than any of these was Rousseau, however, for the latter's work—Hippel's writings show nothing but disdain for the *man*, although he knew him only through his *Confessions* and by reputation—was of great inspiration to Hippel during those sixteen years, and much in his work reveals an indebtedness to Rousseau's *Discourse on the Origin of Inequality among Men*, and to *The Social Contract* in particular. Thus Hippel gradually came to believe that the institution of marriage—the most basic social contract existing between the sexes and, like humanity itself, capable of continual improvement through the instrument of human reason—could not be perfected until true equality between the sexes themselves had been achieved.

Hippel's last major work is a two-volume novel of more than a thousand pages entitled *Kreuz- und Querzüge des Ritters A bis Z* (Crusadings of the Knight A to Z), published in 1793–94; a satirical novel after the manner of *Don Quixote*, it takes as its target the lodges and secret societies of the day.

Yet in spite of the blossoming of his literary productivity, Hippel's last days were not happy ones. After 1791 he suffered difficulty in breathing, probably as a consequence of a previous bout of tuberculosis. His old eye illness recurred about this time, first requiring the incessantly active Hippel to spend days lying in a darkened room, and ultimately resulting in the loss of his right eye. His adopted son, Theodor Gottlieb von Hippel the Younger, first as a teenager inclined to romantic dallying and then as a university student, rebelled against the stern and austere Prussian upbringing of his pedantic uncle. By June of 1795 it had come to a complete break between the two, and although the uncle continued to support his charge financially, it was not without continuous demands for a full account as to how the latter's time and money were being spent. During this period Hippel also broke with his lifelong friend Scheffner (whose ideas of women's emancipation were not as progressive as Hippel's), mainly as a result of Scheffner's severely critical remarks concerning the book *On Improving the Status of Women* after Hippel had sent him a presentation copy.

In 1793, Hippel had been called to Danzig by his old friend Baron von Schrötter, who had been named President of the government of all East Prussia, to supervise the incorporation of that city into the political organization of Prussia, the result of the Second Partition of Poland by Russia and Prussia in 1793. Although Hippel had accomplished this task as well with distinction, the disruption for nearly an entire year in his carefully regulated way of life had also exerted a deleterious effect on his health. His constitution had become permanently weakened, and the personal tragedies of the succeeding two years merely accelerated his demise. He died in Königsberg on 23 April 1796 of, according to the official reports, "dropsy of the chest."[29] As had been his wish, Hippel was buried in the cemetery for paupers whose restoration he himself had supervised as mayor. The inscription on his gravestone had also been requested by him: *"Hier ist All' eines"* ("Here it all comes down to the same thing").[30]

In spite of his lengthy illness, Hippel's death occurred rather suddenly, and his failure to destroy any of his papers was the cause of the singularly unfortunate way his name was sullied in the years immediately following his demise. Amid the jumble of papers comprising his literary estate were found several hundred pages on which he had jotted down personal observations and quotations—occasionally amounting to entire conversations—that he had read or heard which had caught his fancy and he had felt might be useful. It is clear from these and the general format of his writings that part of his method of composition was simply to incorporate such information wholesale into his writings, often with only slight changes in form and never with any acknowledgement as to their source. Apparently, these notes contained much in the way of uncomplimentary character sketches of his friends, as well as statements made to him in casual conversations whose dissemination their authors would have found embarrassing. Furthermore, his friends found traits in his fictional characters which could only have been drawn from members of his own circle, and these traits were not always flattering. In addition, others who considered themselves his friends felt betrayed at not having been drawn into the secret of his anonymous authorship. The result was that Hippel's character was denounced as ruthlessly and as systematically by his friends as if they had been lifelong enemies. His enemies, moreover, now saw the chance to avenge themselves on the man who had sometimes high-handedly dismissed their individual interests in favor of what he perceived to be those of the state. As his nephew later described it, shortly after his uncle's death "vermin of every sort descended upon him, as upon every corpse. The dead lion could not defend himself, and there was no protecting hand nearby, for he was cursed with the lot of all those who remain unmarried. No loving hand pressed closed the eyes of the dying man, none spread the veil of goodwill and brotherly love over the deceased and his memory."[31] His friends, even Scheffner, vied with each other in reviling Hippel, and unfortunately some of this meretricious material found its way into the biography of Hippel in von Schlichtegroll's *Nekrolog* for the year 1796,[32] and into print elsewhere.

The first attempt at a rehabilitation of Hippel's name was not undertaken for almost forty years,[33] by which time many records had been lost and the facts blurred by the passage of time. His nephew's investigations prior to the editing of Hippel's collected works and their publication in 1828–39 also did much to correct the impression given by von Schlichtegroll. Hippel's own autobiography ends with his return from Russia, and while his letters to Scheffner could provide the most valuable source of information regarding his later life, those from 1786 to the end of his life appear nowhere in the collected works. Moreover, while some of Hippel's papers had apparently already disappeared by the middle of the nineteenth century,[34] the remainder, especially those which had found their way into the archives of the city of Königsberg, were probably burned in the fire which swept through the city after the air raids of August, 1944. Thus it would have been necessary for any biographer of Hippel to assemble materials from other sources in order to verify or dismiss many of the charges laid against his name. It was not until the publication of Joseph Kohnen's monumental biography in 1983[35] that any scholar attempted to separate truth from allegation on the basis of such external evidence. With Kohnen's work we have probably come the closest we shall ever come to an understanding of the baffling and paradoxical nature of Theodor Gottlieb von Hippel.

As a final note, it might be mentioned here that the nephew whom he so diligently raised did in fact—in spite of Hippel's continual misgivings—bring honor to the family name after his uncle's death. Theodor Gottlieb von Hippel the Younger became in turn a lawyer, State Counselor, Counselor of Justice, and finally Commissioner of State. He later refused an offer to join the President's cabinet, preferring instead to undertake important diplomatic missions for the state. After Prussia's humiliating defeat by Napoleon and subsequent occupation by French troops in 1806, he performed his most notable act of patriotism by composing in 1813 the famous call to arms *"An mein Volk"* ("To My People") for the King and thereby inspiring thousands of subjects to answer their sovereign's call to drive the hated French from their homeland. The creation of the Iron Cross is also said to have been his work.[36] In the realm of *belles lettres*, the younger Hippel came to deserve the everlasting gratitude of the world for his repeated beneficent interventions on behalf of his lifelong friend, the unstable genius E. T. A. Hoffmann (known to the English-speaking world as the literary source for Jacques Offenbach's *Tales of Hoffmann* and Tchaikovsky's *Nutcracker Suite*, as well as for his influence on Edgar Allan Poe), always precisely at the point when one of Hoffmann's frequent indiscretions or his calamitous financial state threatened to terminate his artistic production altogether. But perhaps one thing would have gladdened the old man's heart more than anything, for within a year after his uncle had died and been revealed as the author of the book on marriage, young Theodor Gottlieb took his uncle's advice and stepped up to the altar. The twenty-two-year-old took the hand of the fifteen-year-old daughter of a Polish general and they enjoyed a long, happy marriage blessed with many children.

III

"And determined to marry I would be, were it not for this consideration, that once married, and I am married for life. That's the plague of it!—Could a man do as the birds do, change every Valentine's day (a *natural* appointment! for birds have not the *sense*, forsooth, to fetter themselves, as we wiseacre men take great and solemn pains to do), there would be nothing at all in it," writes the rake Lovelace to his friend Belfort in Samuel Richardson's mid-eighteenth-century novel *Clarissa*. He thereupon submits his proposal for introducing a system of one-year marriages—a system which, as he believes, would be a mean of annihilating, absolutely annihilating, four or five very atrocious and capital sins.—*Rapes*, vulgarly so called; adultery, and fornication; nor would *polygamy* be panted after. Frequently would it prevent *murders* and *duelling*; hardly any such thing as *jealousy* (the cause of shocking violences) would be heard of; and hypocrisy between man and wife be banished the bosoms of each. Nor, probably, would the reproach of *barrenness* rest, as now it too often does, where it is least deserved.—Nor would there possibly be such a person as a barren woman.[37]

While Lovelace is perhaps extreme in assigning *all* of the above sins and crimes to the institution of marriage as it has traditionally been conceived, it is no doubt true that by the middle of the eighteenth century the institution had forfeited much of its stature and allure. The enraptured public which doted on the passionate but unconsummated love affair between Werther and Charlotte and idealized it into the very model of the erotically tinged spiritual union of two sensitive human souls seems willfully to have overlooked the fact that Charlotte was engaged when Werther first met her and married for fully half the novel thereafter. According to one source, "Divorce and wifeswapping were as common in Berlin as in the most corrupt times of ancient Rome,"[38] and there seems little doubt that the vices and disregard for the marriage bond which Hippel felt constrained to condemn, namely adultery, fornication, illegitimate children, polygamy, arranged marriages, marriages contracted for money or status, and marriages postponed by family interests until the groom was too old to be a competent husband or father were very real problems of the day, both in Prussia and elsewhere. It is hardly a wonder, then, that Hippel considered it necessary to make the very first chapter of his book an appeal to the hesitant and the truly disinclined male to consider the merits of the married state.

But it had long never really been a matter of choice at all. While it is true that in Socrates' time the question as to whether to marry or remain single was open to a man of the privileged class in the most civilized societies,[39] for the man of the peasant class and the woman of any rank the choice was not his or hers to make, and in many cases, particularly those involving possessions and real property, the choice of one's mate was made by others as well. The wishes of the man were subordinated to those of the family or clan, and the woman, as a possession herself, was naturally given no say in the matter. In pre-Christian times in Europe, marriages were contracted among the peasantry for the purpose of perpetuating the extended family unit or tribe and providing workers for the sustenance of the group.

Nevertheless, among the men of the primitive Germanic tribes there had existed from time immemorial a respect bordering on reverence for the virtue, loyalty, and powers of divination possessed by their womenfolk which Tacitus, for one, wished to see duplicated among their supposedly far more civilized counterparts in Rome.[40]

With the advent of Christianity and the rise to power of the medieval Church, however, this primitive Germanic attitude gradually began to take on a different aspect. By means of the twin doctrines of the *proles procreanda* and the *fornicatio vitanda* the Church came to see the institution of marriage as consisting in the propagation of the human race and the avoidance of sins of the flesh; while considering marriage one of the seven sacraments, it simultaneously forbade any of its own clergy from partaking of this sacrament. The various ascetic movements during the period, moreover, only served to contribute to the notion that the desires of the flesh were impure, which had for a result first, the conclusion that the woman, as the object of this sensual desire, was possessed with demonic sexual attraction, and second, that marriage itself was unclean. Such a degraded view of woman and of marriage can already be discerned clearly in the most revealing source on the status of marriage among the peasantry during the Middle Ages, the proverb, where of those following the rubric "woman" or "marriage" nearly half betray strongly negative connotations. "There are only two good days in a marriage: the day of your wedding, and the day your wife dies"; "Whoever has things too good in life, let him but take a wife"; and "A blind man is happy because he can't see his wife; a deaf one even happier, because he can't hear his,"[41] are but three examples of these ancient pearls of "folk wisdom" coined almost exclusively by the male sex as an expression of their own experience and for the edification of their compatriots.

And doubtless many marriages were miserable affairs for both parties concerned, for in addition to the fact that marriages often began inauspiciously, without love or choice, neither did the possibility exist to end a bad marriage by divorce. Little wonder, then, that the Humanist scholars of the new Renaissance movement in Italy and then in Germany concerned themselves with this pressing social problem in a number of short treatises written in Latin during the fifteenth and early sixteenth centuries. Aside from a brief passage in Boccaccio in praise of women, however,[42] nothing appeared in the vernacular of any European country until Albrecht von Eyb's *"Ehebüchlein"* ("Little Book on Marriage") of 1472, which, because of its elegant but simple

German style and widespread dissemination by means of the newly-invented printing press, proved a highly popular inspirational and instructional treatise, running to 12 printings by 1540. Von Eyb, a canon of the Church, had been trained in the tradition of Humanistic legal scholarship in Italy, and thus was, like Hippel, both a lawyer and himself unmarried. It is evident from the actual title of the work, *Ob einem Manne sey zunemen ein eelichs weyb oder nicht* (Whether a Man Ought to Take a Wife or Not), that by this time the rise of the middle class had rendered it possible for the man, at least, to decide for himself whether he wanted to marry. Casting an eye as well to contemporary problems in marriage, the author also covers the topics of faithfulness in marriage, barrenness in women, the raising of children, the lack of harmony in marriage, and what the husband should do when his wife is shrewish or talks too much. Von Eyb ends his treatise on marriage by answering his titular question in the affirmative, and with a section each of praise for marriage and for women. While his approach to the purpose of marriage is not far different from that of the medieval Church, it is possible to understand his dedication of the book to the city fathers of Nuremberg as an attempt to shift the responsibility for marriage from purely ecclesiastical towards secular authority.[43]

About this time there appeared in England several discussions on marriage which were essentially translations from the Latin of briefs on matrimony intended for the use of parish priests. The best known of these is John Mirk's fifteenth-century *Instructions for Parish Priests*. In 1493, Henry Parker published a short elaboration on the Ten Commandments, entitled *Diues & Pauper*, in the sixth "Precept" of which he proffered his thoughts on the subject of marriage. Parker's work, which argued for marriage and recommended the institution to the hesitant, is the first and only known serious examination of marriage printed in English before about 1528.[44] These works were followed by four other longer treatises which altogether went through eleven recorded editions between 1528 and 1546. These were William Harrington's *The commendacions of matrymony* (printed first without date, then later in 1528); Richard Taverner's *In laude and prayse of matrymony* (1530?); David Clapham's *The Commendation of Matrimony* (1540); and Miles Coverdale's highly popular *The Christen state of Matrimonye* of 1541. Coverdale's work is actually a translation of *Der christlich Ehestand* by Heinrich Bullinger, a Swiss reformer; Taverner's and Clapham's works are translations from the Latin. All four of these works derive their basic arguments from the Scriptures, and discuss essentially the same aspects of the marriage covenant as did Albrecht von Eyb: namely, the cause and purpose of the sacrament of matrimony, and the conduct required by it.

Drawing his motifs from the proverbial literature, John Heywood, in his *A Dialogue of Proverbs* of 1546, recounts the complementary tales of two lovers, one of whom marries a poor woman for love, the other an ugly woman for her money, as illustrations of the principle that one is ill-advised to enter into the state of marriage too hastily. Heywood's narration in proverbial form actually constitutes a compendium of proverbs on matrimony from both the sacred and secular spheres, from which he draws conclusions as to the function of marriage, the advisability of marrying, the role of the woman, the qualities of a good wife and other questions of interest to the reader on the subject. In quoting proverbs, however, Heywood is in fact merely offering the opinions of his own and an earlier day; especially, for example, as with his quotations from Paul on the role of the woman and his paraphrase of Proverbs 21:9 in describing the worst fate which can befall a man in marriage: "It is better to dwell in a corner vnder ye housetoppe then with a braulinge woman in a wyde house."

In attempting to rehabilitate the image of marriage, the Humanists, as well as Luther and the Reformers, came to view the spiritual and bodily rebirth of post-lapsarian man in terms of the spiritual and bodily union of the man and woman in marriage. But while they made their opinions known in a variety of tracts and proclamations, probably the most popular of such writings in the sixteenth century was Johann Fischart's work *Das philosophisch Ehzuchtbüchlin* (Little Book on the Philosophical Cultivation of Marriage) of 1578.[45] This work, although for the most part a translation of several of Plutarch's works on marriage, along with a translation from Erasmus and a compilation of classical and German anecdotes, fables, and proverbs on the subject, also contains enough commentary from Fischart himself to give us an inkling as to his own ideas on the subject and reasons for publishing his translations. For, in contrast to the earlier writers of the period, Fischart attempts to gainsay the negative proverbs and common misconceptions of marriage by laying the blame for the sad state of marital affairs on the evils and weaknesses of humanity. Thus we encounter in Fischart for the first time—as later with Hippel at the end of the Enlightenment—the antipodes of nature and reason, whereby the former is to be viewed as consonance with God's will and the definition of *virtus* practiced by the ancients, while reason stands in its service.[46] For Fischart, it is upon these two pillars alone that a solid and lasting marriage can be built, and the key to the adherence to both principles is moderation in all things, especially in household matters. Thus while Plutarch advises women not to take their husbands' dalliances too seriously, Fischart condemns this yielding of reason to the senses as immoderate. Yet Fischart is utterly the man of his century when he writes that the woman's place is in the home and then draws the "natural" comparison of wives to snails or tortoises, which are so closely bound to their "homes" that they carry them around with them at all times.[47]

Fischart's work also includes a series of passages in praise of women and wives, and it was this motif—along with its counterpart, that of the corruption inherent in the female sex—which was to become the chief theme for the writers on marriage from this time until about the middle of the eighteenth century. One early champion of women was François Poullain de La Barre, whose seminal 1673 work, De l'égalité des deux sexes (recently published as The Woman as Good as the Man, Or the Equality of Both Sexes[48]), praises the talents of women for almost every activity at that time not open to them, even the offices of civil government. Unfortunately, Poullain says little specifically about the marriage state, however, and when he does it is in a descriptive, rather than a prescriptive sense, as for example when he refers to the difficulties women experience in marriage: "What Complyance do not Wives use, that they may live peaceably with their Husbands? They submit to their Humours, do nothing without their Advice, lay constraint upon themselves in many things for fear to displease them, and even deprive themselves of honest and lawful Recreations, to free them from Suspition."[49] He does acknowledge, however, that in the France of his time men have "resigned the government" of the household to women, an interesting observation which must be kept in mind when we consider Hippel's deliberations on the question of authority in marriage.[50]

Another early advocate for women was a certain Jacques Chaussé, about whom little is known other than his self-depiction as Sieur de la Terriére and that he flourished from about 1685 to 1687. In the former year he published in Amsterdam a three-hundred-page work entitled Traite de l'excellence du mariage, de sa necessité, et des moyens d'y vivre heureux (Treatise on the Excellence of Marriage and Its Necessity, as Well as on the Means of Achieving a Happy Life). More revealing, however, than the long baroque title of this work, is the subtitle, Où l'on fait l'apologie des femmes contre les calomnies des Hommes (Wherein Is Contained a

Defense of Women Against the Calumnies of Men), indicating the low esteem in which women (and marriage itself) were held by the men of his time. In the five parts of this work, Chaussé defines the beneficial aspects of marriage; condemns incontinence in all its forms; treats the qualities which could reasonably be required of a man in order for him to be considered fit for marriage; and responds to the objections often raised against marriage. He concludes by attempting to suggest the means for achieving a good marriage and a happy life. Nevertheless, Chaussé's method of argument is to offer proof from Classical authors and Scripture for each assertion he makes, and thus his work cannot be considered other than as fundamentally aligned with the approach to the marriage question as it had traditionally been viewed by the Church and society.

With the advent of the Enlightenment, the biblical grounding for the institutions of Western civilization began to come under close scrutiny, however. John Locke began his groundbreaking work, *Two Treatises of Government* of 1690, by positing the question as to whether it is permissible to trace the relationship between princes and their subjects to that between Adam and Eve, which was supposedly ordained by God after the Fall of Man. Locke determined that not only does the prince *not* derive his authority from that of Adam, but that Adam himself, if the biblical narration is to be properly interpreted, received no sanction for his *own* rule from the episode: "God, in this Text [Gen. 3:16], gives not, that I see, any Authority to *Adam* over *Eve*, or to men over their Wives, but only foretels what should be the Woman's Lot, how by his Providence he would order it so, that she should be subject to her husband, as we see generally the Laws of Mankind and customs of Nations have ordered it so."[51] The relation between a ruler and his state, Locke later concluded, is that of a social contract, an agreement entered into for mutual benefit of each party which can be abrogated by either party if the other fails to live up to the terms agreed upon at the outset of the bargain. Locke's ideas received wide circulation, and it was not long before they were applied once again to the marriage relation, this time in a bitingly satirical and often bitter treatise published in 1700 under the title *Some Reflections upon Marriage*. This treatise, published anonymously, was reprinted in a third edition in 1706 with a Preface revealing that the author was in fact a woman; the fourth and final edition was published in 1730. The author, Mary Astell, was, like Hippel, unmarried and an outsider when it came to the most intimate aspects of the marriage union, and yet an astute and objective critic when comparing the status of the institution in her own day to the potential it possessed for bringing happiness to humanity. The problem, as she perceived it, was that men had failed, by virtue of their despotic rule over women, to fulfill their part of the social contract implied in the marriage relationship. The lot of the women around her she viewed as nothing more than wretched:

> To be yok'd for Life to a disagreeable Person and Temper; to have Folly and Ignorance tyrannize over Wit and Sense; to be contradicted in every thing one does or says, and bore down not by Reason but Authority; to be denied one's most innocent desires, for no other cause but the Will and Pleasure of an absolute Lord and Master, whose Follies a Woman with all her Prudence cannot hide, and whose Commands she cannot but despise at the same time she obeys them; is a misery none can have a just Idea of, but those who have felt it.[52]

If marriage is such a blessed state, she asked, why are there so few happy marriages? Men marry for wealth, love, power, or physical desire; women have a choice only to refuse or accept what is offered them. The man marries and continues to interact with the outside world, the woman marries to have children and to offer her life as a sacrifice for the world to come—here through her children and after death by means of her virtuous life as a wife. The woman has much the harder bargain, Astell lamented,

> because she puts her self entirely into her Husband's Power, and if the Matrimonial Yoke be grievous, neither Law nor Custom afford her that redress which a Man obtains. He who has Sovereign Power does not value the Provocations of a Rebellious Subject, but knows how to subdue him with ease, and will make himself obey'd; but Patience and Submission are the only Comforts that are left to a poor People, who groan under Tyranny, unless they are Strong enough to break the Yoke, to Depose and Abdicate, which I doubt wou'd not be allowed of here. For whatever may be said against Passive-Obedience in another case, I suppose there's no Man but likes it very well in this; how much soever Arbitrary Power may be dislik'd on a Throne, not *Milton*[53] himself wou'd cry up liberty to poor *Female Slaves*, or plead for the Lawfulness of Resisting a Private Tyranny.[54]

Since Astell, unlike Locke, did not accept the right of the oppressed in this case to sever their bonds by revolting against their oppressors (nor did she think this likely or even possible), there remained but two solutions: either men must begin to treat women more humanely and to rule not out of their own selfish desires, but "for the good and improvement of their subjects,"[55] or women would be better off not entering into contract with men—that is, better off not marrying at all.

Astell rarely talks of "rights," and when she does, it is only to question whether the man ought not give better evidence of his right to rule and the prerogatives he assumes,[56] and yet her treatise is a highly important contribution to the development of improved relationships between the sexes in marriage. It is in almost every respect more modern than all that preceded and much of what followed it for the next fifty years. For if Astell's views of marriage are perhaps more jaded than her female contemporaries, we have here for the first time a *woman's* depiction of the fate to which she was consigned by virtue of her sex, a fate corroborated by countless novels and dramas from the post-Restoration period in England.[57] Astell reveals to us the status of marriage at the beginning of the Enlightenment as clearly as Hippel later will do at the end, and we encounter in her writings for the first time a theme—expounded upon at great length by Hippel—which was later to have a profound impact on the direction marriage was to take in more modern times: namely, the notion that women (in Astell's case, only women of intelligence and independent means) were capable of leading a fulfilling life outside the home and even perhaps outside the marriage relationship itself. Astell's life and writings reveal to us the possibility that some women, at least, were now able to choose not to marry and it was for the purpose of providing a sort of gathering place for such independent women that she suggested in another treatise, entitled *A Serious Proposal to the Ladies for the Advancement of Their True and Greatest Interest*,[58] the creation of a "religious retirement" where women not only could temporarily withdraw from the world, but where they could also be equipped by means of education to return later to society and play useful roles therein. Perhaps the most important accomplishment of Mary Astell's treatise on marriage, however, by virtue of her oft-repeated analogy between the marriage relationship and that of the prince to his state, was to encourage interest on the part of later reformers in bringing marriage within the purview of the state for the first time since the classical period. This renewed interest was later to culminate in Hippel's plea at the end of the century for the granting of legal rights not only in marriage, but within the state itself.

The idea that the single path leading toward improvement in the status of women both inside and outside marriage lay in the direction of education did not originate with Astell. A school in France and later one in Germany[59] had already been established to put into practice the ideas advocated by the French Archbishop and educational reformer Fénélon in his 1687 work, *Traité de l'education des filles*. Fénélon had been appalled that the young women of Paris, educated to subservience and delicacy, were often unable to perform some of the simplest tasks of daily life and showed utter indifference to anything but fashion, flirting, and frivolity. Dissatisfied with the mediocrity of the cloister schools in which young women were then educated, he recommended in his treatise the establishment of schools for girls where the more practical aspects of household management could be taught, but also—and this is Fénélon's great contribution—where a knowledge of the laws of the land, the legislative process, and the statutes regarding inheritance might be imparted to young women contemplating marriage. Anticipating Rousseau and in flagrant disregard for the fashions of the time, he likewise recommended that women adopt a simpler and more natural mode of dress and use of cosmetics. As with Locke before him and Rousseau and Hippel after him, for Fénélon reason, conceived of as a law of nature (natural law), has rule over all human endeavor, and virtue is thought to be the natural result of the proper application of that law.

This was also the basis upon which the moral weeklies in newspaper form, which first began to appear about this time, were founded. The forerunners for such periodicals were Addison's and Steele's *Tatler* and *Spectator*, of which several issues are dedicated to questions of education, marriage and domestic life.[60] In issue number 141 of the *Tatler*, Steele went so far as to assign the future fortune or misfortune of society to the methods by which young women were educated for marriage and the raising of children. While these and other periodicals adhere strictly to the traditional notion of the wife as bound to hearth and home, they nevertheless sought to combat the most serious threats to marriage which had been arising gradually within the middle class as well as the nobility since the beginning of the previous century: marriages contracted without love for the sake of possessions or children; mistresses kept by men for the sake of sexual fulfillment; artificiality and frivolity in dress and behavior, particularly on the part of women; and an educational process according to which young women were taught to shine at balls, in salons, and at the tea table, and nowhere else. Especially offensive to these weeklies was the prevailing idea that love between marriage partners was repulsive, and in part their attempts to raise the level of young women's education derived from their belief that harmony in marriage can only be truly achieved when the man and woman have similar interests. Hippel was certainly not unaware of these early attempts at reform; the English forerunners quickly found their imitators in Germany and remained popular among the upper two classes until well past the middle of the eighteenth century.[61]

Regarding the question discussed by Locke as to whether and to what degree wives should be subject to their husbands, a certain Thomas Salmon published a long work in 1724 under the title *A Critical Essay Concerning Marriage* in which he devoted an entire, if rather brief, chapter to this very subject. It was Salmon's intention to dispute the contention made by Lord Halifax in his highly popular *The Lady's New Year Gift; Or, Advice to a Daughter*, where the latter had uttered the then-famous line that marriage was "too sacred to admit a liberty of objecting to it"—that is, however lamentable the state of marriage might be for his daughter in particular and women in general, it could not be changed from *without*, but would have to be adjusted to from *within*. Salmon countered Halifax by citing the famous German legal philosopher Samuel Pufendorf on the matter of equal rights within and without the marriage bond:

> All human Persons, whether of one Sex or of the other, are naturally equal in Right, and no one can claim the Sovereignty over another, unless it be obtained by the free Act of one of the Parties; for tho' in Strength of Body and of Mind we are allowed to have the Advantage of the fair Train, yet this Superiority is not of it self sufficient to justify us in setting up for their Masters and Governors. Therefore whatever Right a Man holds over a Woman, inasmuch as she is by Nature his Equal, he must acquire either by her Consent, or by the Sword, in a just war: Yet since it is most natural that Marriages should be founded on mutual Good-will, the former Way seems more proper for the winning of Wives, the other for the procuring of Slaves.[62]

Pufendorf, a contemporary of Locke, had attempted nothing less than to derive from the laws of nature and human behavior a system of jurisprudence which would be of universal and permanent applicability. Here we find articulated, along with the notion of equality between the sexes and perhaps for the first time in a treatise on marriage, the notion of equal *rights* within the marriage bond, which Locke's concept of the social contract had at most merely implied. Unfortunately, the time was not yet ripe for change in the marriage relation through actual acknowledgement of these rights, and Salmon appears to have ended his discussion satisfied simply to have proved his point.

By far the most influential intellectual figure in the latter half of the eighteenth century was Jean-Jacques Rousseau, and one might certainly expect him, as the author of the *Contrat social* and the popularizer of Locke's ideas in the political sphere, to have applied such ideas to the institution of marriage as well. But Rousseau's ideas on marriage, grounded in his belief in the supremacy of nature as law and teacher, depart but little from the traditional view of the wife even though he comes at the institution from an entirely new direction. Perhaps this new approach is itself at fault, however, for when Rousseau examines the consequences of the differences between the sexes as determined by nature, he discovers them to be threefold: first, that it is the part of the man to be active and strong, that of the woman to be passive and weak; second, that it is the place of woman to please man; and third, that the stronger sex may appear to be master, yet actually be dependent upon the weaker. This comes about as a law of nature, he concludes, because "by giving woman the capacity to stimulate desires greater than can be satisfied, nature has made man dependent on woman's good will and constrained him to seek to please her as a condition of her submission."[63] These ideas are developed in his didactic novel *Émile* (1762), in which Rousseau discusses the proper kind of wife for his young charge in the last brief part of his lengthy tome. Since Rousseau saw the feminine domination of increasingly effeminate males as the chief malady of his age, his Sophie, the ideal mate for Émile, was made by nature to please and be dominated, to make herself agreeable to her husband and to avoid provocation. Yet woman was not meant by nature to be a slave languishing in utter ignorance, for her lively mind gives proof of her educability, and the man who treats his wife as a slave is depriving himself of the particular charms of her company, and will not be as happily married as he could. Therefore the woman's education is to serve her in the fulfillment of the practical arts of the home, but should also enable her to be a fit companion for her educated· husband—that is, she should be permitted and taught to think, judge, and love by herself, in order that she might better cultivate her mind for the delectation of her husband. The proper study of womankind—thus Rousseau sums up his thoughts on Sophie's education by seeming to rephrase Pope's famous dictum—is man.[64]

Following directly in Rousseau's train, a certain Monsieur De Cerf-vol writing a decade later in his two-volume work on the "science of marriage,"[65] writes to a Sophie of his own that the subordination of woman in marriage "consists less in obedience than in the deprivation of power." "The man is the head of society," he maintains, "and not the woman. The latter is thus his assessor, whose qualities and intelligence he should respect, whose council he should reflect upon and take. She has the right to representation, and the right to resist unjust laws; but she does not have the right to create new ones."[66]

It was thus entirely within the spirit of the times created by Rousseau, then, that Hippel penned the first two editions of his work, and we find in them the same glorification of nature and traditional view of the subordination of women—although there is no mention of Rousseau himself. Paradoxically, it is only in the last two editions that we find numerous references to Rousseau by name. It appears that, for all the Rousseauian flavor of the first two editions of the book on marriage, Hippel in fact only came to a thorough reading of the philosopher of the age during the time between the second and third editions of his treatise. Moreover, while the third and fourth chapters of Hippel's *Status of Women* consist of a long and highly original anthropological discourse on the question as to how the superiority of the man over the woman first came about (which in approach is reminiscent of Rousseau in his *Discours sur l'origine de l'inégalité parmi les hommes* [Discourse on the Origin of Inequality Among Men] of 1755), and while Hippel continues to preach the gospel of a return to nature and the original state of society advocated by the Swiss reformer, in the latter two editions of *On Marriage* he manifests exceeding annoyance at Rousseau's retrogressive ideas on marriage in general and his treatment of his mistress of many years, Thérèse Levasseur, in particular. In spite of the admiration for Rousseau he expressed openly at times in his works, Hippel considered it unthinkable that Rousseau should neglect to marry his common-law wife of so many years, give all their children to the foundling home virtually at birth, and then claim in that masterpiece of egocentric sentimentalism, his *Confessions*, that he had made the decision to do this alone and that he considered it best for all concerned.[67] "It was not Rousseau the philosopher, but Rousseau the crank who—with Thérèse serving as his muse, as she did so often—declared the man to be the natural despot of the woman," Hippel writes in the first chapter of his treatise.

The turbulence caused by the prevailing currents and countercurrents of opinion on the woman question in the late eighteenth century rose to gale force in the period shortly after the French Revolution. The works of Olympe de Gouges and the Marquis de Condorcet[68] in particular did much to bring about the inclusion of the question of rights for women in the debate regarding the rights of man being waged by the framers of the new French Constitution. Nevertheless, the final version of 1791 did *not* in fact grant the rights of citizenship to the female sex, and what later became the two manifestos of the movement for the emancipation of women, Mary Wollstonecraft's *A Vindication of the Rights of Woman* and Hippel's own *On Improving the Status of Women*, both published the next year, represent the angry response to this exclusion from citizenship within the state penned at a safe distance from the guillotine and from prison, the final destination of the two French reformers. Both later editions of Hippel's *On Marriage*, then, constitute the most profound plea for a more humane treatment of women within the *marriage bond*, and the first systematic attempt to argue for an extension of civil rights for women to this institution of the state as well.

Hippel begins his treatise, as the title to the first chapter suggests, by lamenting the fact that individual families and the state itself place so many hindrances on the man that he is not able to marry until such time as he is no longer capable of fulfilling his role as husband and father. But Hippel's discursive style of writing, modeled without a doubt on that of his favorite essayist, Montaigne, allows him latitude to discourse on a wide variety of topics not limited by the title of the chapter he is composing. Chapter 1 thus also broaches the theme of marriage as a barometer of morality in the state, as well as the benefits to the state from the institution of marriage, and he likewise questions the traditional notions of the morganatic marriage and Church-imposed celibacy. Almost without realizing it, he launches into a spirited defense of the role of the bachelor in the state, only abandoning this pet topic when he becomes aware of the fundamental inconsistency involved in advocating bachelorhood in a book designed to promote marriage. He frequently encourages women to overcome their slavish adherence to fashion, flattery (coquetry) and the perquisites of rank, although he quickly points out that men appear to be more strongly addicted to these vices than women. Anticipating in an almost uncanny way some fashion trends of the late twentieth century, at one point he even ponders the question as to whether it is necessary to differentiate between the sexes by means of clothing at all. Hippel considers women's obsession with such frivolities as those mentioned above the strongest of the fetters which then held them down, and would like to see the former two eliminated immediately. The obsession with rank presented a more difficult problem, however, given the stable nature of the social structure, and here he stresses the need for acting with patience over time. If he had his wish, Hippel would rather see an aristocracy based on merit, which would allow women to rise as far as their considerable abilities would take them. Writing to a largely aristocratic audience at the time of the French Revolution, however, he felt compelled to couch his democratic ideals in terms which would not be perceived as advocating abolishment of the existing social hierarchy. Yet to change the status of women alone threatened no *specific* class or social structure, only the hierarchy dictated by the dominance of men in general, and at the end of the chapter Hippel takes up his lance for the cause of women in marriage with greater fervor than anyone before or for a hundred years after him. Hippel here appeals to men for nothing less than an improvement of the status of the entire opposite sex, beginning with the granting to women a greater say in the choice of a marriage partner, continuing with the abolishment of the system of sex-guardianship under which women had languished for centuries, and ending with the recommendation of a "declaration of majority" for women, under which they would receive full civil and human rights as befitted adults capable of making decisions for themselves. The theme of this appeal runs as a thread throughout the book, visible behind each of Hippel's arguments, now in the forefront, now in the background, but never dropped from the beginning to the end of the work.

In the second chapter, Hippel makes use of the literary technique of the fabricated author in order to answer the question concerning the true purpose of marriage. He presumably adopts this technique— whereby a certain celebrated legal authority delivers a lecture on the above-mentioned topic to a hall filled with both fledgling and experienced lawyers, referring to Hippel himself only as "our respected author"—as a means of presenting a rather large body of legal material without revealing his own profession as a lawyer, and thus preserving his anonymity. This alteration in the mode of narration also affords Hippel the opportunity to poke sly fun at the members of two professions he had come to regard with some misgivings, namely lawyers and physicians, while the shortcomings of theologians, who in the meantime have risen in respect in his eyes, are utterly ignored. After some consideration of the merits of both arguments, Hippel concludes that the purpose of marriage is neither, as the Roman Catholic Church has always maintained, that of procreation, nor is it, as the various Protestant sects have claimed, the sanctioned fulfillment of the sex drive; rather it is that of providing mutual support for the partners and can best be defined as "the closest possible intertwining of two lives," as he translates the Latin legal phrase. He closes the chapter

45

with a discussion about the physical aspects of the marriage relation, and, oddly enough, it is in regard to this topic that Hippel reveals a restraint bordering on prudity in the later editions which is hardly apparent in the first two. In the earlier editions, for example, the narrator broached the subject of the frequency of sexual intercourse with an italicized "How often?" as the supposed "fiftieth question" he had dealt with years earlier in a legal brief; by the time of the last two editions, the august legal scholar has decided that the matter can only be discussed in proverbs and language so highly stylized and delicate that the reader of Hippel's century unfamiliar with the earlier versions must have been even more puzzled than his twentieth-century counterpart, who can at least be assisted in his comprehension by means of a footnote.

In chapter 3, Hippel attempts to explain why marriage is considered a holy work in the eyes of both the Roman Catholic and Protestant Churches. Although a man of deep religious conviction himself, he studiously avoids attempting to *prove* the sanctity of marriage by copious biblical citations (as had almost all other writers on the subject before his time)—his entire essay is to be conducted along rational lines, and when he quotes Scripture it is merely to embellish a point by providing further examples. He begins by noting that we are born as human beings, but "reborn" (i.e., educated) as citizens. Marriage is therefore a holy work and sacred to the state and the world because it is within marriage that human beings' education to citizenship begins and receives its strongest impetus. Women are thus the first educators of the human race, although both the mother and father have a role to play in the education of the child. Hippel then continues with a synopsis of his views on education, which dovetail with those of Rousseau to the extent that they view education as a process of unfolding and nature as the supreme guide in this process, but strongly diverge on the issue of the education of women. For Rousseau, the woman is to be educated more or less separately from the man and merely to the end of pleasing and serving him; for Hippel, the two sexes should be educated together although not in the exact same way, and each with an eye toward their later roles in marriage *as well as* in service to the state. Before this true "rebirth" comes about, Hippel believes, much will have to change in the education of human beings, and one thing is clearly implied by Hippel's theories of education: for women to be able to educate their male and female children better for citizenship, they will have to be educated for citizenship themselves.

46

In the first part of the fourth chapter, Hippel means to consider the problem of unfaithfulness among men, and in the second part among women—to judge by the titles at least. In fact, however, more than half of the second part is once again addressed to men, indicating that while he previously had dealt with infidelity among women with more severity than among men, he believes it is actually the way women are treated by men, privately and through the state, which is the cause of infidelity among women and the prevalence of unhappy marriages. The state encourages unfaithfulness among women by refusing to allow them any diversion and activity through employment, and the men themselves privately encourage their wives to unfaithfulness by their own frequent affairs and their injust and foolish behavior in the home.

While this is the general tenor of his remarks, this chapter frequently deviates widely from its course, and polygamy, childlessness, impotence, and divorce are topics which receive some attention, along with several tips, directed at both sexes, for keeping the savor in marriage after many years of life together. He even recommends to an impotent man the very modern technique of inducing sublimation in his wife in order to keep her happy and faithful to him—a decidedly tongue-in-cheek Hippelian resolution to the problem! Be this as it may, the burden for the restoration is placed clearly on the shoulders of men, who, if marriage as an institution is to be saved, ought to practice "becoming and being at home that which [they] are expected to be and become elsewhere in life."

It is in dealing with the difficult topic of authority in marriage in chapter 5 that Hippel differs most significantly from those who have gone before him. Approaching this topic circumspectly, he describes the relationship between husband and wife as resembling that between the Director of the Household Judicial System and the Director of Police; as between a regent and his prime minister; and later, as between the soul and the body. Perhaps a not impertinent modern comparison based on Hippel's analogies would be that based on the relationship between the judicial and legislative branches of the American government. Whichever metaphor we choose, however, it seems clear that Hippel understands these areas of influence as equal in authority but different in function. True authority in the household belongs neither to the man nor the woman alone, but to *reason*, because both parties rule together to the extent that they rule with reason.

Yet Hippel realizes full well that such a situation does not yet prevail in most marriages, men ruling with an iron hand in many, women with a gentler, but no less authoritative, one in a few. To the men he proposes the voluntary relinquishing of much of their authority based on their supposed strength, to the women he counsels patience (and not revolution) in the face of a situation in which change will only come about slowly, if it is to come at all. Hippel closes the chapter with a brief discussion along the lines of the much longer investigation of chapters 3 and 4 of *On Improving the Status of Women* as to how the male achieved dominance over the female in earliest times when mankind was beginning to leave its natural state. His point in doing so is clear: only by *first* achieving her lost equality in the marriage relation can woman hope to re-attain the rights she later lost in the greater realm of the state as well.

Chapters 6 and 7 are addressed to young men and young women respectively, and are intended to give each sex insight into the true nature of the other at a time when relationships between them were unduly complicated by parental circumspection, frequent forced separations, and coquetry on the part of both sexes. Hippel speaks here neither in the moral platitudes of a preacher nor with the finger-wagging severity of a Dutch uncle, but as a wise older man who has spent the better part of his adult life observing human behavior and recording it. To be sure, he occasionally lapses into condescending forms of address, and less frequently, into outrageous statements arising out of personal crotchets which readers will find (and in his own century they must have found) impossible to take seriously—his comments on male singers constituting perhaps the best example of this kind of tongue-in-cheek contention. Yet what Hippel writes about the two sexes, much of it admittedly blatant generalization, nevertheless has the ring of truth to it, and reflects Hippel's belief—and here he shows himself to be firmly in the camp of the Platonists as opposed to the Aristotelians[69]—that reason is universal in human nature and that each of the two sexes, while they are not alike, can be brought by means of education in the use of reason to fulfill its potential in the marriage relation and in the state. But this fulfillment has not yet come about, and Hippel is nowhere more explicit than in these chapters that *both* sexes are degraded by a relationship in which it is the woman's single duty to please, the man's to dominate. In Hippel's view, it is in fact men, whether they realize it or not, who are the true losers under such circumstances, in that their roles as both husbands *and* administrators of the state are compromised by their exclusion of women from an equal voice within marriage and the state at large.

48

It is in these two chapters, moreover, that Hippel utilizes his gift of humor most adroitly and to the best effect. Here he is able by means of his wit to scold and praise, expose folly and bring to light true virtue, and to prompt the reader to action. For however much Hippel would entertain us by wit and levity, the function of humor in his treatises is in truth a highly serious one, consisting in providing the sugar coating on the large and bitter pill of change and the relinquishing of power.

It is interesting to observe that Hippel's remarks to widowers and widows in the eighth chapter concerning the problems encountered by remarried parents in attempting to consolidate separate families take on a very modern aspect if we simply draw the analogy between what was perhaps the most serious threat to marriage in the eighteenth century, namely the death of a spouse, and that of the late twentieth, divorce. In both cases the question of remarriage is paramount, and Hippel here takes a very unpopular stand on the issue by urging the surviving spouse—especially the widow—*not* to remarry. He offers in support of his suggestion the argument mentioned above concerning the children of previous marriages, as well as the highly convincing conjecture that all married couples would treat each other better while they were both alive if they knew they were permitted to marry only once in their lives. Such a solution would obviously have a profound influence on the high divorce rate of the twentieth century as well, but Hippel is perhaps right in perceiving his answer as far too radical and theoretical to find acceptance among the general population as a whole, and particularly among those for whom it would be intended. And anyway, as he himself is compelled to acknowledge, the men of his time seemed to prefer widows to unmarried girls, many good marriages have resulted from the remarriage of widowers and widows, and nothing reveals the popularity of marriage quite so well as the frequency with which both men and women enter into a second, or even a third, marriage!

In his conclusion, Hippel undertakes to explain why he chose to write in a humorous vein in his treatise and why it was necessary to write figuratively at times. In the proverbial fashion typical for him, he gives the reader a "standard" whose proper application will enable both those already married and those contemplating marriage to avoid most of the mistakes committed in marriage if—and this is the essence of his message throughout the book—if the fair sex is viewed from the point of view of this standard: namely, that "there is an Old Eve to go along with the Old Adam." By this utterance Hippel means many things, none of which will go unperceived by the careful and attentive reader of his treatise.

And finally, after many postscripts which belie Hippel's assertion that he actually won the "bet" with a woman described in chapter 6 on the issue of whether a woman could ever write a letter without a postscript, Hippel takes leave of his reader. The reader has been a fellow traveler throughout his long journey, and although in such a relationship it is the author who does all the talking, Hippel admits it is the listener who always has a harder time of it. The road *has* been hard, but not without its pleasures, and Hippel thanks the reader for his company while simultaneously warning him of other traveling companions who might later suggest smoother roads and more agreeable destinations. And the reader, for his own part, likewise takes leave of Hippel, who, because of his anonymity, has not been as well known to his fellow traveler as he might have been—although Hippel sincerely hopes the reader will forgive him for his lack of candor in this regard. And just who was this man? Like many men in high office and perhaps many bachelors as well, an essentially lonely man known well by almost no one during his own lifetime, whose life will always remain a paradox, and yet whose *writings* at least remain as a bold testament to his lasting friendship with readers of any century and to ideas which will remain valid as long as men and women "marry and are given in marriage."

IV

The flurry of activity which characterized Hippel's efforts to be heard on the woman question during the years 1792 and 1793 was not without cause, for it was during this time that the state of Prussia was undertaking a complete revision of the old "Code Fréderic" which had been in effect since the early years of Frederick the Great's reign.[70] An early attempt at recodification had been begun in 1784[71] and work had continued until 1788, at which time the result had been published for critical inspection by eminent legal scholars. Then, in order to achieve as wide a circulation of ideas among the educated public as possible, prizes had been offered for the best answers to certain particularly troublesome questions in the new law. Hippel himself, along with a law professor and several other upper-level bureaucrats, had won a gold medal in one of these competitions,[72] indicating his early interest in the reform of Prussian law. Finally, in 1791 an official lawbook was published for use in the states then under Prussian rule.[73] It was intended that this lawbook, with which Hippel nevertheless takes issue at several points in the present work, would go into effect on 1 June 1792. Soon after the work's publication, however, it proved necessary to postpone this date until an unspecified future time. Unknown to the general public, the compilers of the new lawbook had encountered resistance to the more liberal aspects of the work from their monarch, Frederick William II, who had revealed himself as not nearly so enthusiastic about the principles of the Enlightenment on which the new lawbook was based as his predecessor and uncle, Frederick the Great. With the official suspension of work on the lawbook on 18 April 1792, the situation seemed hopeless for the reformers.

Yet in spite of the obstacles, Privy Councillor Carl Gottlieb Svarez (1746–98) in particular refused to give up on the project. Hoping that he could sway the king and his legal advisors by bringing his own arguments before practicing lawyers and other members of the educated populace, he published in 1792 a selection of extracts from the lawbook with the title *Unterricht über die Gesetze für die Einwohner der Preußischen Staaten* ("Instruction in the Laws for the Inhabitants of the Prussian States"), which soon became well known by every lawyer throughout the kingdom.[74] This effect entirely fulfilled Svarez's hopes, and it was not long before the lawbook itself, which proved infinitely less cumbersome to interpret and apply in everyday legal practice than the manifold edicts of the king, was being used everywhere in the courts of Prussia in spite of its lack of legal validity. With the Second Partition of Poland in 1793, moreover, Prussia acquired a large section of that country which then had to be brought under Prussian legal jurisdiction. The need for a codified Prussian law had thus become greater than ever, and the king and his advisors finally agreed to a reissuing of the lawbook, albeit with a few compromise alterations and a new title.

It is highly likely that Hippel was aware of much of the controversy surrounding the lawbook early on, for in May of 1791 he ceased work on his autobiography rather abruptly and turned his attention once more to the plight of women, this time with the express intent of influencing directly (albeit anonymously) the drafting of legislation aimed at improving their status. His efforts were unsuccessful, however, for several reasons. First, while Hippel was able to have the third edition of *Über die Ehe* ready by around Easter (April 8) of

1792,[75] and the entirely new book, *On Improving the Status of Women*, sometime later that year, Svarez was given only a scant *six weeks* in which to revise the entire lawbook—now bearing the name "Prussian General [or Territorial] Code"[76]—after the king ordered its reissue on 17 November 1793. Thus, even though Hippel was able to publish his own ideas soon enough for them to have an effect, because of the time constraints under which Svarez was forced to work the new Code contained hardly any changes from the 1791 lawbook, especially as far as the laws on marriage were concerned.[77] Second, and more important, there existed a fundamental disagreement between Hippel and the framers of the Prussian Code as to the role of marriage within the state, even though both parties viewed the institution through the eyes of reason. While Hippel is certainly aware of (and frequently discusses) the function of marriage in producing large numbers of citizens for the state, he is nevertheless far more concerned with freeing marriage from this practical responsibility with which it had been saddled by the Church and the state and imbuing it with a social, and even spiritual, justification. The Prussian state, on the other hand, faced with the task of populating a large and sparsely settled land as quickly as possible in order to increase Prussia's influence through economic and military means, chose to view marriage as no more than the chief means to this end, and formulated its laws accordingly. Thus, while for Hippel the purpose of marriage was to provide mutual love and support through life's journey for each of the two parties, for the Prussian state it was for the purpose of producing children.[78]

Such a conception of marriage led the Prussian Code to establish regulations for married couples with regard to their life together which Hippel preferred to see as acts of kindness arising naturally out of the relationship of a loving couple to each other. Consequently, the Code contains such ordinances as: "Married couples are *obliged*, as far as it lies within their power, to offer mutual assistance in all difficult situations"; "They *must* live together"; "even in times of difficulty they *must not* leave one another" (emphases mine).[79] Even the so-called "conjugal duty" is regulated by the Prussian Code in such a way as to recall the strictures of the Old Testament and Islamic law.[80]

In the absolute monarchy which was the Prussian state, the monarch was a "father" to his people. This patriarchal relationship was continued in the marriage laws of the Code, and the concept of sex-guardianship so despised by Hippel formed the basis of the new Prussian Code just as it had that of the lawbook and the Frederician Code. Consequently, the man continued to be the head of the household and the legal guardian of his wife, and the children (whether unmarried or not) who still lived under his roof. His decision was foremost in matters affecting the common household. The woman shared his dwelling, name, and rank, and was obliged therefore to manage the household, but without his approval was not permitted to ply a trade or perform any service outside that household. According to the new Code, the husband was justified in opening his wife's mail, and, depending upon the rank of the parties involved and the circumstances, acts of violence on his part directed against her were not necessarily grounds for complaint in the courts.

The man was her full and legal guardian, empowered (and also obligated) by the Code to represent "the person, honor, and property of his wife in and outside the courts."[81] Thus she was not permitted to initiate any legal procedure without his full consent. In fact, she could not even enter into a legal contract by herself if this contract necessitated the fulfillment of any obligation on her part. In certain cases, however, she was permitted some contractual control of her own property. Thus, if a woman entered marriage already possessing property or money of her own, she and her spouse could elect (either before or after the ceremony) to maintain their property separately or to share and share alike—but such a decision was required to be announced publicly beforehand for the benefit of possible future creditors. In the event a couple chose the first option, the woman was then permitted to enter into legal contracts involving her own property. In no case, however, was she permitted to exercise legal powers of decision regarding the property which she and her husband *acquired jointly* during the course of the marriage. This was of particular disadvantage to the divorced woman, and was only partially offset by the alimony paid to the woman in cases where she had been divorced by her husband. Widows had it somewhat better with regard to marital property, in that they (as well as widowers) had full rights to their own property, as well as to one-third of the spouse's property before inheritance (one-quarter in cases where no heirs had been designated).

In general, the laws governing divorce can be said to derive from the theory of marriage which underlies the Prussian Code. An edict of Frederick the Great of 1783 had already set the tone for the work which was to follow: "[We] must not be so free in allowing divorce that it comes to be misused; neither should we make divorce too difficult, otherwise the growth of the population will be impeded."[82] (Frederick is implying by the second half of his edict, of course, that a newly-divorced couple will remarry and perhaps each have the children they could not or would not have had in the previous marriage.) In the new Code, then, unfaithfulness constituted grounds for divorce for *either* spouse—and thus almost a century before her counterpart in England or France, the woman of Prussia received not only a moral, but also a legal, right to faithfulness on the part of her husband. Hippel doubtless applauded this attempt at an early abolition of the so-called "double standard" in principle, for his work fairly seethes with outrage against the prevailing morality of his time which not only condoned, but often promoted unfaithfulness in marriage. Nonetheless, when the Code goes on to permit the unfaithful husband to challenge the writ of divorce if he is able to prove unfaithfulness also on the part of his wife, and when the motivation for this regressive step is plainly stated as deriving from the axiom that "extramarital affairs on the part of the man are not as significant as on the part of the woman,"[83] then, paradoxically, we find Hippel among the assenters on this side of the issue as well, for he defends this very axiom at some length in his book on marriage. This sort of contradiction abounds in Hippel's life and work; we as readers are free to accept or reject his point of view, and it is only on rare occasions that a consciously intended elusiveness prevents us from perceiving his stand immediately on any aspect of the woman question.

If the laws of marriage had all been cast by the framers of the Code with an eye toward increasing the population, then those regarding divorce and child custody were no exception. Divorce on the grounds of mutual or individual "irreconcilable incompatibility" was permitted for the reason that it was assumed no (more) children would be born within marriages suffering under such circumstances. In such cases, the person who initiated divorce proceedings was considered to be the one "at fault." The party not at fault could choose either lifelong alimony or a sixth (in some cases a quarter, depending upon the social class of the parties involved) of the property of the party at fault as recompense. The initiation of divorce proceedings was thus made far more difficult for the woman, unless she had brought property of her own to the marriage, in the sense that she was not permitted to possess legally or inherit any of the property which she and her husband had acquired together during the course of their marriage. In cases of divorce, children were assigned as a rule to the party not considered at fault. Where neither party was declared to be at fault, however, the children were given to the father after the attainment of their fourth year of life. Daughters could be assigned to the mother by the court in certain cases, but the mother had no legal right to such a judgment. As did the English code of laws, the Prussian Code even permitted a father declared at fault to lay claim to the privilege of supervising the education of his sons, providing he had not been declared an unfit father under the terms of the divorce.

Given the severity of the sex-guardianship into which women entered upon marriage even after the publication of the new Code, one might come to the conclusion that it was better for them not to marry at all. That almost all who had the chance did marry is testimony to the fact that if anything, matters stood worse for those who chose or were compelled to accept the only other realistic alternative, namely continuing to reside in the home of the parents after the attainment of the age of majority. This unfortunate situation arose because the Prussian Code—quite in contrast to natural law, which viewed parental duties as synonymous with paternal guardianship and as ending with the raising of the child to its majority—elected to continue the period of paternal guardianship far beyond that required for normal upbringing, and in the case of women, extended it to the time of their marriage or, if they remained unmarried, to the death of the father. Thus, as Hippel states, those women who married were "freed" by their husbands—yet it must be added that while the married woman's state of dependency became far less severe than before, the legal significance of her marriage really amounted to nothing more than the transfer of her sex-guardianship from one man to another.

When it comes to enumerating the duties of each sex in the raising of children, the Code unabashedly assigns the provision of a dwelling, food, and clothing to the father, and to the mother the fulfillment of their other bodily needs as long as these should last. The logical consequence of this assignment of duties is the almost unenforceable regulation—with which Hippel in the present work, incidentally, fails to concur—that healthy mothers had to breast-feed their children themselves. Strongly indicative of the highly paternalistic nature of the Code is the further regulation that the precise time when the children were to be weaned from the mother's breast was to be determined by the *father*, even though the Code encouraged the latter as a practical matter to solicit the advice of a physician in such instances.

The education of the children remained totally the province of the father, and while the Code of Hippel's day permitted the girls at least to follow the religious confession of the mother, an amendment of 1803 gave the choice of the religious confession for the children over to the father as well. Moreover, in what is perhaps the most flagrant inequity of the entire Code, the father was actually empowered to give one or more children up for adoption without the approval of their mother!

Taken as a whole, the *"Allgemeines Preußisches Landrecht"* was not bad legislation—in fact, in some respects it served as a model for other legal codes of the day. While it took feudalism and serfdom for granted, it nevertheless sought to protect the individual against public or private oppression. It abolished unnecessary courts, expedited legal proceedings, and mitigated punishments. Moreover, it made appeal to the king accessible to all. Even in regard to its treatment of women, it was in many cases superior to other codes of the period, as, for example, the French *Code Napoléon* of 1804.[84] And although Hippel was unable, with the publication of his later works on women, to influence the framers of the Prussian Code as he had hoped, given the circumstances prevailing at its creation, it is doubtful that in any case they would have given complete credence to the ideas of a man so far ahead of his day. When the time was finally right at the beginning of the twentieth century for a change in thinking on the rights of women, Hippel's ideas were resurrected and placed at the forefront of thought within the movement for emancipation, where, along with others, they served well.[85] Yet while it could be maintained that women have now attained their rightful *legal* status within marriage in the Western world, there is much evidence from the daily life of our time that such legal progress has not been realized in a practical sense, and thus it is with this disparity in mind that Hippel's ideas are once again being offered—two hundred years after they last appeared—as a contribution to the ongoing development and refinement of the most significant relationship into which human beings are privileged to enter.

NOTES TO THE INTRODUCTION

1. Stuart Pratt Atkins, *The Testament of Werther in Poetry and Drama* (Cambridge: Harvard UP, 1949), 1.

2. Theodor Gottlieb von Hippel, *Über die Ehe*, ed. Wolfgang Max Faust (Stuttgart: Deutsche Verlags-Anstalt, 1972), 101; and Joseph Kohnen, *Theodor Gottlieb von Hippel: eine zentrale Persönlichkeit der Königsberger Geistesgeschichte. Biographie und Bibliographie* (Lüneburg: Verlag Nordostdeutsches Kulturwerk, 1987), 93.

3. Act 3, Scene 2.

4. Theodor Gottlieb von Hippel, *On Improving the Status of Women*, trans., ed., and with an Introduction by Timothy F. Sellner (Detroit: Wayne State UP, 1979).

5. I Corinthians 7:9.

6. Theodor Gottlieb von Hippel, *Sämmtliche Werke*, ed. Theodor Gottlieb von Hippel, 14 vols. (Berlin: Reimer, 1827–39), 12: 58. (The editor is Hippel's nephew.)

7. Hippel, *Werke*, vol. 12, 31–32.

8. Theodor Gottlieb von Hippel, *Biographie; zum Teil von ihm selbst verfaßt*, ed. Ralph Reiner Wuthenow (Gotha: Perthes, 1801; Hildesheim: Gerstenberg, 1977), 73.

9. Hippel, *Biographie*, 58–64.

10. Ibid., 75.

11. Hippel, *Werke*, vol. 12, 45.

12. Ibid., vol. 13, 23.

13. Friedrich von Schlichtegroll in Hippel's *Biographie*, 273.

14. Hippel, *Werke*, vol. 12, 206.

15. Ibid., vol. 13, 143.

16. Kohnen, *Hippel*, 41.

17. Franz Erdmann, "Theodor Gottlieb von Hippel: *Über die Ehe*. Eine literarhistorische und sprachliche Untersuchung," diss., U of Breslau, 1924, 10.

18. Hippel, *Werke*, vol. 13, 44.

19. Frederick the Great lived separately from his wife after the first six months of their forced marriage; moreover, ladies were rarely seen at his court in Potsdam. Rumors thus circulated throughout his reign that he was a homosexual. Johann Georg Zimmermann, the "First Physician to his Brittanic Majesty at Hannover," who was called to Frederick's deathbed in 1786 and gave an account of Frederick's final illness, defended Frederick's manhood by describing his problem as deriving from a "small mutilation" (he insisted it was *not* emasculation) resulting from surgery on a gangrenous wound of the genitalia which Frederick had developed following a bout of venereal disease the year of his marriage (*Select Views of the Life, Reign, and Character of Frederick the Great, King of Prussia*, tr. Major Neuman, vol. 1 [London: Hookham, Carpenter, & Newbery, 1792], 45–48, 61–67). Shortly after the king's death Hippel became involved in a literary dispute with the pompous and sycophantic Zimmermann, publishing in 1790 a satire entitled *Zimmermann der I. und Friedrich der II.*, in which he defended the Enlightenment against the anti-rationalist Zimmermann's manifold criticisms of its effects in Germany (see note 38, below). The negative references to solitude [*"Einsamkeit"*] in *Über die Ehe* are also directed at Zimmermann, who had published multi-volumed works on the subject in 1756, 1773, and 1781.

20. Kohnen, *Hippel*, 84, 141.

21. Ibid., 89.

22. Hippel, *Werke*, vol. 13, 84–85.

23. Immanuel Kant, *Gesammelte Schriften*, ed. Royal Prussian Academy of Sciences, 24 vols. (Berlin and Leipzig: De Gruyter, 1910–66), 12: 360–61.

24. Hippel, *Werke*, vol. 14, 203.

25. On the matter of Hippel's independence of thought, see Kohnen, *Hippel*, 33, 159.

26. Hippel, *Werke*, vol. 12, 45–46.

27. Ibid., vol. 14, 223.

28. Ibid., vol. 12, 33.

29. *"Brustwassersucht"*; see Kohnen, *Hippel*, 206.

30. Kohnen, *Hippel*, 208.

31. Hippel, *Werke*, vol. 12, vi–vii.

32. Adolf Heinrich Friedrich von Schlichtegroll, *Nekrolog 1796*, vol. 2 (Gotha: Perthes, 1796), 171–346; *Nekrolog 1797*, vol. 1, 123–416.

33. In an article by Theodor Mundt in *Zeitgenossen*, 3rd. ser. (Leipzig: Brockhaus, 1832), bks. 1–2.

34. Arthur Warda, "Der Anlaß zum Bruch der Freundschaft zwischen Hippel und Scheffner," *Altpreußische Monatsschrift* 52 (1916): 276.

35. Joseph Kohnen, *Theodor Gottlieb von Hippel, 1741–1796; L'homme et l'oeuvre* (Bern: Peter Lang, 1983).

36. Kohnen, *Hippel*, 191.

37. Samuel Richardson, *Clarissa; or the History of a Young Lady*, ed. Angus Ross (New York: Viking, 1985), letter 254, 871–74.

38. A statement made by the above-mentioned Johann Georg Zimmermann (who attributed the cause to the Enlightenment) in his *Über Friedrich den Großen und meine Unterredungen mit Ihm kurz vor seinem Tode* (Leipzig: Weidmann, 1788), 32, 78–79; quoted

in Hamilton H. H. Beck, "Framing the Debate: Hippel's Response to Zimmermann's Attack on the Enlightenment," *Eighteenth Century Life* 14 (1990): 30.

39. See for example, Plato, *Laws*, 721b–d and 774a–b. In his *ideal* state Plato would require the man to marry between the ages of thirty and thirty-five, however, or be subject to a yearly fine and loss of status.

40. Tacitus, *Germania*, secs. 18–20.

41. Quoted in Fischart, Johann, *Johann Fischart's Ehzuchtbüchlein, nebst dem Ehstandskapitel aus dem Gargantua, für Volk und Familie bearbeitet*, ed. Richard Weitbracht (Stuttgart: Metzler, 1881), 25, 85, 27.

42. Boccaccio, *Decameron*, day 4, tale 1 ("Sigismunda and Guiscard").

43. Albrecht von Eyb, *Ob einem manne sey zunemen ein eelichs weyb oder nicht*, ed. Helmut Weinacht (Darmstadt: Wissenschaftliche Buchgesellschaft, 1982), xxvii.

44. John Heywood, *A Dialogue of Proverbs*, ed. Rudolph E. Habenicht (Berkeley: U of California P, 1963), 35.

45. Hugo Sommerhalder, *Johann Fischarts Werk* (Berlin: De Gruyter, 1960), 97.

46. Ibid., 101–3.

47. Fischart, *Ehzuchtbüchlein*, 111.

48. François Poullain de La Barre, *The Woman as Good as the Man; Or the Equality of the Sexes*, trans. A. L., ed. Gerald M. MacLean (Detroit: Wayne State UP, 1988).

49. Poullain de La Barre, *Woman*, 88.

50. Ibid.

51. John Locke, *Two Treatises on Government*, treatise 1, sec. 47.

52. Mary Astell, *The First English Feminist; "Reflections Upon Marriage" and Other Writings by Mary Astell*, ed. Bridget Hill (New York: St. Martin's Press, 1986), 90.

53. In his pamphlet, *The Doctrine and Discipline of Divorce: restored to the good of both sexes, from the bondage of Canon Law, and other mistakes to Christian Freedom, guided by the Rule of Charity. Wherein also many pieces of Scripture have recovered their long-lost meaning. Seasonable to be now thought on in the Reformation intended* (1643), John Milton had advocated divorce on grounds of incompatibility, in opposition to the Roman Catholic Church's position that adultery be the only grounds considered. Nevertheless, he felt it still remained up to the husband to decide whether he and his spouse were hopelessly mismated, and to take care of the business of divorce fairly. On this point, see William Riley Parker, *Milton; a Biography*, vol. 1 (Oxford: Clarendon, 1968), 239–48.

54. Astell, *Feminist*, 101–2.

55. Ibid., 55.

56. Ibid., 112.

57. As for example, William Wycherley's *The Country Wife* (1674) and *The Plain Dealer* (1674); William Congreve's *The Old Bachelor* (1693) and *The Double Dealer* (1693); and John Vanbrugh's *The Provoked Wife* (1697) and *The Provoked Husband* (1698).

58. This work first appeared in 1694. All of the third edition of Part I (1696) and selections of Part II from 1697 are reprinted in Astell, *Feminist*, 133–79.

59. Françoise d'Aubigné, Marquise de Maintenon, known as Madame de Maintenon, the second wife of Louis XIV of France, established a school for girls based on Fénélon's principles at the Abbey of St. Cyr in 1686 with funds from an endowment given by the king. In 1698, the German translator of Fénélon's writings, August Hermann Francke, opened a girls' school in Germany which was never as successful

as its French counterpart and was forced to close its doors for the last time only a few years after Francke's death in 1727.

60. In issues 15, 98, 189, and 248, for example, the *Tatler* deals with pedagogical questions; in numbers 5l, 61, 71, 141, 185, 192, and 212 matters dealing with women and the family are treated; and in the *Spectator*, numbers 268, 433, and 525 contain discussions of marriage and the woman question.

61. The best known and most influential of these were the *Diskourse der Mahler* (begun 1721); the *Patriot* (begun 1724); Johann Christoph Gottsched's *Die vernünftigen Tadlerinnen*, the first German women's periodical (begun 1725); and the *Maler der Sitten* (begun 1746).

62. Thomas Salmon, *A Critical Essay Concerning Marriage* (London: C. Rivington, 1724), 77–78.

63. Jean-Jacques Rousseau, *Émile; Selections*, trans. and ed. William Boyd (New York: Teachers' College, 1962), 132.

64. "*Toute l'éducation des femmes doit être relative aux hommes,*" Rousseau, *Émile*, part 5, book 5 (Boyd translation).

65. De Cerfvol, *La gamologie; ou, De l'éducation des filles destinées au mariage; ouvrage dans lequel on traite de l'excellence de mariage, de son utilité politique & de sa fin, & des causes qui le rendent heureux ou malheureux* (Paris: Duchesne, 1772).

66. De Cerfvol, *La gamologie*, vol. 2, 32–33 (my translation).

67. Jean-Jacques Rousseau, *Confessions*, Book 8.

68. Olympe de Gouges, *Déclaration des droits de la femme et de la citoyenne*, 1789; Marie Jean Antoine Nicholas Caritat, Marquis de Condorcet, *Lettres d'un bourgeois de New-Haven à un Citoyen de Virginie*, 1787; and *Sur l'admission des femmes au droit de Cité*, 1789. This latter work has appeared in English as *The First Essay on the Political Rights of Women*, trans. Alice Drysdale Vickery (Letchworth: Garden City, [1912]).

69. For a long time prior to Hippel's writing, a dispute had raged on the matter of feminine equality between the Platonists, who pointed to Socrates' defense in the fifth book of *The Republic* of a kind of rational equality—that is, equality based on the primacy of reason in both sexes—and the Aristotelians, who based their position that the woman was naturally subordinate due to a difference in certain moral qualities between the sexes on Aristotle's arguments in his *Politics*, book 1, chap. 13. For further information regarding the nature of this dispute, see A. R. Humphreys, "The 'Rights of Woman' in the Age of Reason." *Modern Language Review* 41 (1946): 256–57.

70. An early English version of this code is: *The Frederician Code; or, a body of law for the Dominions of the King of Prussia. Founded on Reason, and the Constitutions of the Country. Translated from the French* (Edinburgh: A. Donaldson, 1761).

71. *Entwurf eines allgemeinen Gesetzbuchs für die Preußischen Staaten* (Berlin and Leipzig, 1784).

72. *Allgemeines Landrecht für die Preußischen Staaten von 1794; Textausgabe*, ed. Hans Hattenhauer (Frankfurt am Main: Metzner, 1970), 21.

73. *Allgemeines Gesetzbuch für die Preußischen Staaten* (Berlin: Königliche Hofbuchdruckerey, 1791), 4 vols. The index was published a year later by G. J. Decker and Sons.

74. *Allgemeines Landrecht; Textausgabe*, 27.

75. Letter to Joachim Christian Grot, 21 March 1792. Hippel, *Werke*, vol. 12, 225.

76. *Allgemeines Landrecht für die Preußischen Staaten* (Berlin: G. C. Nauck, 1794), 4 vols. Volumes 2 and 4 were published by G. J. Decker and Sons. This code has recently been reprinted (see note 72, above), and the Introduction to this reprint contains an important account of the events and personalities contributing to the origin of the "Prussian General [or Territorial] Code."

77. *Allgemeines Landrecht, Textausgabe,* 29. The two changes in the marriage laws were both relatively minor: while the 1791 edition had extended the legitimacy of the morganatic marriage to every member of the nobility and the higher rank of civil servants, the 1794 edition limits it once again to men of the nobility wishing to marry under "extraordinary" circumstances who have previously obtained permission directly from the king; and while the earlier version had granted to institutions for the poor rights to the estates of bachelors who had died without heirs, the later version rescinded this right. Since Hippel discusses both these laws in the present work (chapter 1), advocating the extension of the morganatic marriage (by which he appears to mean the "love match") to virtually everyone and suggesting that bachelors once again be given the right to dispose of their estate as they wish, one might take these two instances as proof that Hippel's writings did have some effect on the framers of the *Landrecht.* It appears from the evidence, however, that these two laws were changed at the behest of the king himself (*Allgemeines Landrecht, Textausgabe,* 28).

78. While this was deemed the main purpose of marriage, it was not the exclusive one. Consequently, it should be added here that while the section on marriage (First Title, Second Part of the *Landrecht*) clearly states at the outset that the chief purpose of marriage is the "begetting and raising of children," it takes pains to add the clearly worded declaration that valid marriages can also be contracted on the basis of "mutual support alone." See chapter 2 in the present work for Hippel's lengthy commentary on these two views as to the function of marriage.

79. Marianne Weber, *Ehefrau und Mutter in der Rechtsentwicklung; eine Einführung* (Tübingen: Mohr, 1907), 332. Much of the information which follows in the text on the Prussian Code of 1794 has been drawn from this work.

80. Ibid., 332.

81. Ibid., 333.

82. Ibid., 336.

83. Ibid.

84. Ibid., 33l, 334–35, 337–40, 342.

85. For example, in 1909, during the period of the most intense activity within the movement for women's suffrage in Germany, a pamphlet of thirty-nine pages was published by Felix Dietrich Verlag consisting of short selections from Hippel's *Status of Women* with the added subtitle: *A Contribution to the Woman Question.* This work, edited by Achim Winterfeld, was brought out as part of Dietrich's new series "Culture and Progress," a continuation of the publisher's previous series entitled "Social Progress, Pamphlets on Political Economy, Social Politics, the Woman Question, the Administration of Justice, and Matters of Culture." In addition, Clara Zetkin, editor of the Social Democratic women's newspaper *Die Gleichheit* ("Equality") from 1891 to 1916, gives Hippel full credit for his contribution to the theoretical background of the feminist movement in her book *Zur Geschichte der proletarischen Frauenbewegung Deutschlands* ("On the History of the Proletarian Women's Movement in Germany"), 2nd ed. (Berlin: Dietz, 1958).

ON
MARRIAGE

"The Joys of Parenthood," by Daniel Chodowiecki. Copper
engraving from _Almanach und Taschenbuch für häusliche und
gesellschaftliche Freuden_ (1796–99). Courtesy of the Deutsche
Verlags-Anstalt, Stuttgart, Germany.

"Domestic Happiness," by Daniel Chodowiecki. Copper engraving from _Almanach und Taschenbuch für häusliche und gesellschaftliche Freuden_ (1796–99). Courtesy of the Deutsche Verlags-Anstalt, Stuttgart, Germany.

"A SON OR A DAUGHTER?" the father asks the midwife the first time his wife is delivered of a child. The second time he can already read it on her face, and she lets him finish his question if it is a girl, otherwise by the time he gets to the word "or" she has already called: "A son!"—"Not to forget the four Kreuzers for the church as a thank offering," says the country parson. And the father gives ten if it is a boy. "For the good of the church," he says. But let it be a girl and he collects loose change from everywhere in his pockets, even though it is also for the good of the church. "Here," he sighs, "are four Kreuzers. May God send us a good rain, the crops certainly can use it."

A fourteen-year-old girl asks the midwife, "Is it a little boy?"—"Yes, Mademoiselle."—"What an adorable child," she says, and quickly takes it into her arms. The reason she leaves it in the crib when the midwife says "A girl" is because she is fourteen years old.

"Why such a beginning?"—Good friend, ask me rather: why this whole treatise? In fact, everything depends upon this beginning; if it is good, then more is good; if it is bad, then I wouldn't give a Kreuzer for the entire piece. An author is a spiritual father and *writes* sons and daughters, just as a physical father conceives them—although to determine the sex of a book is so difficult that the critical midwives often spend years arguing about it. Anyway, just so the good Reverends know that they are not getting a single Kreuzer from me as a thank offering, let me say that for this child, no thanks is required. And with that, God be with you!

1

COMPLAINTS CONCERNING
PREJUDICES AGAINST MARRIAGE:
A REMEDIAL DREAM

℮

IT IS A MATTER of agreement among almost all learned and common men that the riches of states must be determined by the size of their populations and not by ephemeral silver and gold; not only in great matters, but also in small ones, not only the state, but also in private households, it is human beings who make the difference. The father of the lower class who avails himself of the help of his grown children is on relatively equal footing with a head of state when he goes into battle with his countrymen and not with mercenaries. But it is also not too difficult to determine nowadays why, in spite of the obvious truth of what we have said above and the clear instructions contained in those magnificent words which lend themselves so well to an essay on marriage, "Be fruitful and multiply," so many stones of stumbling and rocks of offense[1] are placed in the path of this holy work. Certain biases which have become second nature after the manner of motherhood now make people incapable of playing the role they could play or should have played, and it is precisely these biases which are more at fault in the present depopulation than Egyptian bondage; than the imposition of taxes by the state; than the vanity of women afraid to lose their beauty through pregnancy; than the public enemy of luxury; or than the concern not that times are bad, but that they might become so. It is simply the way of the world that people

68

always look in the distance for things which are right before their eyes: they go hunting when all they need to eat is close at hand, and search everywhere for the horse they are already sitting on.

The law determines a person's majority and fitness for marriage and childbearing (the Germans derive the words "puberty" and "virility" from the male,[2] although the other sex is certainly not the only injured party in the matter); Nature determines these qualities even more precisely, and Nature and philosophy have never been at odds with each other. (*Nunquam aliud natura, aliud sapientia dicit.*[3]) It would in fact be desirable if people were not too early and at an immature age enrolled in the noble school of matrimony, and I am not of the opinion that marriage, like confession, should not be put off. Yet this goal cannot be attained by means of matrimonial laws of some sort, only by education; not by leaps and bounds, but only gradually. Forcing Nature is tantamount to stopping the course of the sun, asking the earth to rest for a while, obliging angels to dance on the head of a pin, or raising the dead. The more refined a people, the more quickly its individual members become mature, and the more quickly their lives are over. They cannot wait for time to pass and end up spending their lives in great haste, often acting like little children who run on ahead and then back again, doubling the distance and either reaching their destination dead tired or not at all.

For the Romans, a youth of fourteen was already considered capable of becoming a father, and a girl in her twelfth year of saying "yes" and giving proof of her assent. Only in the case where she married before this time was she held to be *quasi uxor*,[4] a wife in part or by permission only. The Romans took the existing conditions under consideration and were of the same opinion as Nature, although their learned men of law only rarely eluded the reproach of being somewhat too hasty in theory and slow to put it into practice. Nowadays our laws are of a different opinion. Now we are not only thought to be capable of marrying and having children at a later time—although this in itself might hardly be considered important and could perhaps be explained by the severity of our climate—but even when a person has reached the legal age he is still far from being allowed to be what he really is. An unnatural mode of behavior has come into vogue which now actually passes for a virtue of sorts. Its burden rests chiefly on the man, and amounts to the fact that he is not permitted to marry until such time as he is hardly capable of it any longer. People are not joined to people, but instead horses and carriages to coaches-and-four, Ducats

69

to hard Talers, a house in the country to one in the city. Everyone else picks fruit when it is ripe; a young man, however, needs not only to be forty-three years old, but to have a yearly income of two thousand Reichstalers, be of noble birth with no less than sixteen quarterings, wait until his father has died so that he can move into his house, own twelve parade horses, have traveled widely (this is most important), maintain five liveried servants and—whatever else one must have and have done before he is allowed to court a girl.

If we were to infer marriageability from the desire two people have for each other just as we infer eternal life from the soul's longing for immortality, then good laws on education have a long way to go in a very short time if they are ever to bring about an increase in the population. Yet the laws concern themselves to such an extent with the question of Mine and Thine that they have no time to consider the person. In new states, where the common man is less constrained and the more distinguished individuals have lesser needs, people multiply like willows at the side of a brook.

The word *father* is a grand word, the most important in the state. Whoever is not a father does not deserve the title "citizen" either; indeed, it is being generous to say he even halfway deserves to be called a human being. Young men, why do you wish to listen to the voices of men when you could be hearkening to divine ones? Why do you desire man-made statutes when you already possess a natural law? Why the letter of the law, when you already have it in spirit? Do not look to those tablets of the law which often hang so tyrannically high that the eye cannot perceive them, but look for the lost piece of silver in your own house. And when you have found it, call your neighbors together, marry and be married, baptize and be baptized, and believe in your future happiness.[5]

Whoever is healthy in mind and body has everything he needs; whoever wants to *be* happy and not merely *appear* so has it very easy: he only needs to know what he can do without. And what do you want with poetic evils, when you already have so many prosaic ones?—"But how will I be able to bring up my children?"—Dear friend, do you already have children?—"No, but I hope to"—Good, then place your hope then in the Giver of every good and perfect gift.[6] He has already given you what is best, and will not deny you in lesser things.

One of the most brilliant men ever to see the light of day makes education into such a heavy burden that, in spite of the sincere respect which my dedication of this page to him is intended to show, I feel compelled to contradict him completely.[7] "We should," this enlight-ened man states, "give humans to the human race, social beings to society, and citizens to the state. Whoever is not capable of these three things together should not be a father—and this does not exclude even the poorest man." The state must educate *citizens*; we, however, educate *human beings*, and that is easier than we imagine, easier than our prejudices would have us believe, for is it not a ridiculous state of affairs when those things which we do not absolutely need cause us the most grief and worry? The best education has our happiness for its goal; much in the way of money, possessions, or anything else which can be modified by the word "much" is not required, for it is only the eyes which want much—our actual needs are moderate and satisfied by little. We are slaves of the most disgraceful sort, for we are not only slaves of people, but of things as well. The Romans debased people by placing them under the rubric of "things"; we shake our heads about this and raise inanimate objects to the level of idols without ever showing the slightest grief or shame when we become their slaves. Most of our foods taste good to us because we have observed fashionable people ruin their digestion with them. How far we have strayed from the river banks of Nature! The mother nurses her child only the first year, because during the second she is already nourishing another invisibly; the father feeds it the second and third years, and by the fourth it is ready to feed itself under normal circumstances.

Come closer, you poor fellow! Don't kill the drive which Nature has placed into your heart! Come closer, and if you aren't suffering from a chronic state of hysteria—be happy that you can leave that to richer folks—step up to the altar! If your little boy knows nothing more than that God is in His heaven, a soul is in his body, and the Devil is in Hell, what more does he need? If he hasn't the arm for pitching hay, then he can gather strawberries. Give him what you can; assign him to Mother Nature and her treasury of incalculable wealth—she will most certainly honor his draft. Be assured that your widow's mite[8] will mean more than the overflowing hands of the rich. And just what is it that fashionable people (note what word they use to describe themselves) *do* allow their children to be taught by their wet-nurses? Upon careful scrutiny you will find that it is nothing more than fairy tales and foolishness in all sorts of languages and dialects: for example, knife and spoon on the right, fork on the left; not to blurt out "Daddy!" in the presence of their father, but to say, "Most gracious Papa, be so kind as to listen"; not to say to their mother, "Mama, you are the best mother in the world," but rather, "Most gracious Mama, you are dressed up like an angel!"; when they meet people of their own rank to be the first to say, "How do you do?", and if they are of higher rank, to inquire in proper terms after His Lordship's or Her Ladyship's health; to leave a visiting card even if the people are visible through the window and by means of a Roman fiction[9] would have others believe the gentleman and his wife have gone to the country, and other such nursery nonsense as this.

In my opinion, Diogenes became richer when he realized he could also ladle water with his hand.[10] If the state leaves its citizens in such unfortunate circumstances that they cannot educate their children, is it not then the duty of the state to look after their education itself? What a loss for the state if it loses a thousand people, all of whom are capable of becoming citizens, in order to maintain a hundred overeducated citizens who after the third and fourth generations will no longer be able to beget anything even remotely resembling themselves! Whoever fails to understand what I am driving at here will get no quarrel from me, and anyone who takes offense at my becoming long-winded at this point and not elsewhere ought not read this book.

Nothing is more unnatural than to prepare at great length for something that is over in a short time. Whether or not I agree with that roguish author who maintains that Jupiter would not have come to his divine decision to bestow a human honor on Danae if the latter had not been imprisoned[11] (while Dulcineas languishing under the burden of foul denunciations are strengthened by love and desire as fire by the wind[12]), everything must have its limits—something that cannot be said for indolence which leads to indifference or a mountain of hindrances which would exhaust even the healthiest of young men. A thief who is accustomed to breaking and entering will doubtless pass by an open door, but this does not make him any less of a thief, and most people, while they are not thieves, are still less interested in that which is there for the taking than in chasing interminably after that which flees their presence. All we can do here is to keep them from getting out of breath, since that would be tantamount to clipping their wings so they might fly better, or making two quite different institutions out of love and marriage.

The wisdom teeth (*dentes sapientiae*) we are said to get in our twentieth year are not, it seems to me, a requisite for marriage. Even if it were true that before our fortieth year we are not truly able to use our abilities to our own advantage, but that up to this point we only use our intelligence for others—how does the marriage bed lose by this? It is not necessary for a person to have a plan set in stone in order to marry, and sometimes the best thing in marriage is to think from hand to mouth. Criminologists maintain that hardened criminals have possessed their evil natures for years—why should love not have rights equal to these? I know of more than one state where most of the officer ranks from field marshal all the way down to ensign are held by noblemen, and I also know of one where this is exclusively the case.[13] Thus nothing is more certain than that families are extinguished by this means down to the very last letter of their names.—"Do you mean in time of war?"—Even when there are no wars, my impatient friend! (He can hardly be blamed for interrupting me with his question, since he has five sons in the army and thus not a single one who will be able to marry during his marriageable years.) If you had a cripple among them, you could be happy; at least he would pass on the memory of your name. Nowadays we don't marry for the sake of marriage, but only to celebrate the memory of those who have married in the past. *Pia recordatio!*[14]

It is the chief duty of the parents, or those to whom the Fourth Commandment applies (which, like the Fourth Petition,[15] allows for a broad interpretation), to provide their children with opportunities for love to blossom. Love is the tuning fork of the heart and sets limits to ambition and every other kind of greed or vice (which are one and the same thing). Love makes us agreeable and sympathetic; it makes people into human beings. It is experimental morality, just as there is now experimental physics. Yet our statutes, whether of a religious or civil nature, allow us no pleasure without profit in matters of love. Thus parents are forced to consider means for marrying their children off as soon as possible—or, in other words, to make a virtue of necessity.

"Whoever wishes to have children should no longer be a child himself," it is said, and indeed, is there a more serious business than this in the entire world? And should one not then be given the designation *venia aetatis*[16] right when one marries? In fact, it might not be at all improper to require people over fifty to apply for the status of *venia aetatis* before they could even consider marrying so close to the evening of their years. At the present, however, we have laws which are a disinterested party when it comes to protecting old age from folly, and yet which conjure up difficulties to hinder marriages between people in the prime of life. It almost seems as if the legislators wished by means of such laws to guard against the sins committed in their own youth and thereby render an expiatory sacrifice to the state, an act which helps the latter as little as it costs the former to give. After the bachelor party, we can no longer play the role of the youth; yet one can sooner take on the role of a theologian, judge, or doctor than that of a father—one simply *is* a father. It will take a master-stroke of legislation to emancipate our children; but who needs an Anastasius or a Justinian[17] when Nature herself begins to speak?

Aristotle states that a person should marry in his thirty-fifth year, and according to Plato, not before his thirtieth,[18] but *should* and *could* are two different things. The ancient Germans also believed that a man ought to be thirty years old, but they were the *ancient* Germans, and we no longer are. Now whoever attains the age of thirty is an ancient German in another sense of the word, since everyone assumes that he will remain unmarried the rest of his life.

"How did you manage to contract podagra, captain?" asked Von M——, a military hero grown gray with the honors of age, and the Leonidas[19] of our time. "In my time that malady was reserved exclusively for His Excellency the King." The more enlightened the times, the earlier young men and women become sexually mature, and likewise it is the sex drive itself which in turn comes to determine the degree to which any given age is enlightened; it alone animates us and gives us courage; it is the salt which gives flavor to all human endeavor.

Narses, the famous general of the Emperor Justinian, will, I hope, forgive me the assertion that nothing noble has ever been wrought or thought by eunuchs, or ever will be, if for no other reason than because of a law recently passed in France which demands the death penalty for those performing such mutilations. Eunuchs are said to make faithful servants. Yet who is a faithful servant without having wished at times to command? And if he has never wished to command, how much credit does he deserve for his faithfulness? It is said that there never has been a castrato who was a heinous criminal; if that is true, we ought to ask ourselves whether a castrato in fact even has the wherewithal to become a criminal at all. A person with only half a body will also be lacking in soul; according to Mosaic Law, such a person was not permitted to "enter the congregation of the children of Israel,"[20] and the designation "human being" could never be more than a bastard title for him. The suffering of a eunuch is greater even than that of the cross-bearer Job, who at least was able to beget sons and daughters after he had borne his trials. And the death of a eunuch—if one can even use this word to refer to the living dead—is never glorious or honorable, even if in the service of the fatherland, since his life has no value placed on it. He cannot adopt, for adoption in truth is merely a fiction, a beautiful art regulated by the rules of Nature. In short, he must limit himself to his singing, as the capon to his pretty feathers.

We might, of course, gain some advantages if people were to marry later in life, but I am not of a mind to enter into that topic at this point. People say the Israelites were small in stature because they married so early; nevertheless, I see no disadvantage in smaller citizens; they are at least better than none at all. Small soldiers, it seems to me, could be used to advantage: tall enemy soldiers would either shoot over their heads or have to bend down in order to shoot at them; in either case the former would come out ahead, and in any case they are equal as cannon fodder. Furthermore, more of them could be placed into a single grave than if they were the descendants of Anak.[21] There is probably also some truth to the assertion that small people are stronger and more capable of enduring the hardships of war than large people, since their strength is more concentrated. In many northern climes, where the summer sun has a greater effect, everything ripens in a couple of months.

Is it not a pity when a young man offers his first full glass to a prostitute because he has no alternative, while leaving the dregs for a girl with a good reputation? Who can then blame the girl if she in turn begins looking around for a fresh bottle herself?

One candle easily ignites another, and it could be assumed that geniuses would only be produced by a father in a still unweakened condition; the first children, at any rate, have since the beginning of time always been the best. It is no wonder that illegitimate children as a rule have the best minds—they are the result of an ingenious hour, the legitimate ones often of an hour of boredom. The former are dithyrambs, the latter didactic poems. The description by one of these so-called "natural" children of his circumstances often has something so blunt and honest about it that we cannot help but acknowledge the truth of what he says. "I consider it an honor," he says, "to be a *natural* child, since there are so many *unnatural* ones around." Moreover, the shape of the body is more beautiful in first children, a fact likewise demonstrated in illegitimate children, and which legitimate children as well have shown and can demonstrate again if a father and mother in their best years keep their love holy and the anticipation of future criticism does not destroy the contents of their cup of bliss.[22] Thus the rights of the firstborn and the sacrifice of firstborn children were based on good physical and moral principles. The result of a couple of wizened old faces gazing lovingly at each other is not very likely to be a well-proportioned child, while the son who is conceived in a tranquil hour by a faithful father in his best years, at peace with himself and the world, will bear the traces of this complete happiness in his physical form and be the very image of his creator in body and soul, strength and nobility. And just so I do not get into trouble with the mother of this vigorous young man: it will be apparent that she too has contributed to his formation from the very essence of her being, and that a priest and a priestess are necessary for this festival of marriage if it is to prove pleasing to God and a blessing for the world. I am not fond of caricatures, but in this case I would almost call the child a caricature of his father and mother.

If this is the appropriate time, let me also make the observation here that it is the father's and mother's interest in their child which determines whether it will turn out well, especially in cases where the parents are not too closely related to each other, since it is precisely here that—praise be to Nature!—a certain monotony is destroyed and a new type comes into being which she herself everywhere visibly favors. It is said that seed sown in the same field from which it sprang grows poorly in comparison to seed brought in from another field, and can it be denied that marriages between close relatives as a rule also fail for the same reason—namely, that such people have too much opportunity to take a peek at one another's cards, so to speak, and to get to know each other not only face-to-face, but also heart-to-heart, whereby it is almost inevitable that the glory and goodness of one's heart and the worth of one's soul, which were first admired at a distance, lose their appeal at close range the longer one is exposed to them, until they finally dissolve in a sort of blue haze and disappear entirely?

From time immemorial it has been the custom to allow the *human being* to suffer for the good of the *citizen*, but it will forever remain barbaric to kill feeble and sickly children under the pretext that they might perhaps with difficulty become human beings, but never proper citizens of the state—and what is more, then to sanction this action legally, as if one were doing a service to the Molech[23] of the state thereby. Nevertheless, the advantages which in ancient and modern times have accrued to the firstborn for precisely the reason mentioned

76

above are proper and justified, for even though parents tend to love their youngest children the most,[24] wiser people have seen fit to tie their hands somewhat in this respect by granting advantages to the firstborn at the time of inheritance. In France of old the eldest son inherited the property, the second became a soldier, and the third a priest. If you wish to reckon further, you will find that not only in France but everywhere the youngest children—the children of duty—usually die in homes for the infirm. The causes of this are obvious. Also among the Israelites of ancient times the firstborn was the head of the family and, before the establishment of the Levitical priesthood, simultaneously its priest. It is for this reason that Jacob, himself so richly blessed by God, called his firstborn "my might, and the beginning of my strength, the excellency of dignity, and the excellency of power."[25]

Is it not absurd that a man whom the state honors and who has the right to make decisions regarding the property and lives of an entire family must in this particular matter subject himself to the judgment of another person within that household—for example, his father, mother, or aunt? In order to point out how broad is the range of difficulties a person desiring to marry must overcome, the word *recruiting*[26] is sometimes used, which in this sense means to go at the matter hammer and tongs. In this analogy, the recruiting officers are generally the *Pastores* and *Advocati loci*,[27] occasionally joined by the town poets (the latter of whom are distinguished from the former after the manner of loose cookies from firm cake); no less significant a presence is that of our good friends the family doctors, who are able to determine quite precisely whether one's pulse beats to the time of wedding bells or not. "To woo is not always to marry," states a well-established proverb; thus even if the young lady recruit says "Yes" right away, a day must nevertheless be determined on which the matter will be considered more carefully and in detail. At this time the family comes together and the matrons receive not only a place and voice in the discussion, but also, by virtue of the fact that whether asleep or awake they have dreamed for years of nothing but this very day, the respect of everyone concerned.

Often the "Yes" is given without prejudice to a prior right or claim—that is, conditionally—and often an *offer* is made not unlike that which subjects are required to make to their rulers if they wish to sell their wares to them. It is upon these offers, then, that engagements, with or without conditions, are later based. And when the father and the mother and all who are legally included in this designation have registered their approval, either tacitly or explicitly, the *earnest money*, usually in the form of a ring, has been given, and (no less important) when, after a round of bridal parties, the family has filled its collective stomach and emptied its purse in equal proportions, and when the banns have been published and all the *deadlines* met, and everyone in the family has bought new clothes and a couple of bridesmaids have been fitted out in their finery, then and only then does the *training* commence. I use these terms intentionally because while I obviously consider the parents to be the debtors in this matter, the bridegroom becomes the creditor if the girl decides to marry him. It is for this reason that married children are referred to as "children under counsel."[28] But one still wonders why, in the face of all these formalities, the bridegroom does not lose all desire to marry whatsoever, even when the sunrise of his recruitment promised him an agreeable sunset and the first answer he received was a true certificate of investiture and not a mere acknowledgement of his application. Nonetheless, during this period he generally conducts himself without reproach and uses the time to become acquainted with his lady's chambermaid in order to attain practice in a matter which has the peculiar quality of being performed best without any practice at all. True, it is said of Jonathan Swift that in attempting for so many years to control certain desires he eventually lost the capacity to satisfy them, and that this was the reason he offered to his Banassa and his Stella[29] a love of the merely Platonic sort wherein the spirit is willing but the flesh is weak[30]—but then other causes might have made our good Swift into a Platonist just as well.

I don't know if any of my readers know Herr von H—y.

"No, my dear Herr von B—ss, my daughter is not for you," ran his fatherly decree.

"But my dear Herr von H—y," answered Herr von B—ss.

"As I said, nothing can come of it," the latter replied.

"Let me speak openly."

"I shall follow your example myself."

"You are poor . . ."

"I, poor? As long as this patent of nobility still has letters on it, and . . ."

"Laura loves me, Herr von H—y."

"Love is the least of my concerns. It is honor, my good sir, which brings about marriages."

"I have the greatest respect for honor, for our happiness and even our wealth depends upon the good will and respect we enjoy from our fellow men, but . . ."

"'But!'—The proof of my own 'But' comes from the *Corpus juris Romani*. Or turn to Matthew 8, verse 5 in the Bible and there you have it! That's the verse about the centurion at Capernaum. In fact, I can cite you two *loci;* one in the Bible where the centurion has his soldiers come to attention or present arms before the Lord, '. . . and I say to this man, Go, and he goeth; and to another, Come, and he cometh . . . ,' and where the Savior shows a great deal of respect for the military; and then another one that fits here, too, namely *L. 42ff.: de rit. nupt. non solum quid liceat, sed etiam quid honestum sit* ('not only what is right, but what is fair, not only what is good, but what can be seen by men')."

"I am a cavalier."

"But you can never be accepted into the Order of the Knights of St. John.[31] Your blood, while blue, is deemed to be several shades too pale."

"Your daughter will die of a broken heart."

"Then she will at least die on a bed of honor."

"And I . . ."—With that he went away, and it is known that he later went in desperation to Paris, where he squandered his fortune as the slave of a famous actress.

When a building falls, innocent people are frequently injured in the disaster. When businessmen say in cases of bankruptcy that the whole house has fallen, they are thus using a very apt expression. What a shame, then, that our Parisian still has six sisters. Poor girls! If your brother had only been able to take you under his wing you wouldn't have been exposed to the unnatural necessity of having to live without love. Even if she has no money, a pretty girl who is lucky enough to have lived in a good house where she was permitted to develop her talents will certainly be able to find a suitor who will be willing to be transformed into a husband. Add up yourself, dear reader, just how many citizens the world is deprived of because of this particular incident: give each girl six children, and multiply six by six. Figure in Laura and her good young man that makes forty-five people![32]

"Laura?" Herr A—— cries out, "How did the author come upon this name, which is etched into my heart with golden letters like Calais into the heart of Queen Mary?[33] Must all Lauras be unhappy, then,

79

and make others unhappy as well? Cruel and inhuman father of such a kind and gracious daughter!"

This cruel and inhuman father—just so I do not lead my readers a second time to Paris, a place to which no German usually travels a second time or is even able to—wished that his future son-in-law would, under the name "and Company," help him add another hundred thousand Talers to the double hundred thousand he already has, and at the same time make hundreds of widows and orphans wretched, all of whose names now appear in his ledger-books. And what of Herr A——? Is he dying of shame himself? I am well aware that all authors are empowered with a jurisdiction of the highest sort which has the authority to decide in cases of life and death, much in the way that art and literary critics do. Nevertheless, even though I hold the power of the *jus vitae et necis*[34] over Herr A—— in my hands, I will let him survive in order to show him that he is in fact in good hands. For you see, Herr A—— is Laura's *cicisbeo*,[35] and Laura is being unfaithful to her husband.

But what should I say about Herr B——? And Herr C——? and Herr D——? And all the other gentlemen through the entire alphabet? It almost seems as if failed love-affairs are responsible for the fact that the circle has never been squared, the breadth of the ocean has never been measured, and sea-water has never been transformed into fresh water. The fact that the Greeks and Romans produced greater geniuses than we have is due to their manifestly more rational way of marrying and the fact that the former did not have to learn Greek or the latter Latin. And since we are finished with the German A B C's, let me use a different one to illustrate what is already a matter of common knowledge: α ran away with a clerk because her father would not give her to a councillor; β is unfaithful to her husband because her mother forced her into an unequivocal but insincere "Yes" which her heart belied; and γ has no children, a circumstance easily explained by the fact that she has never slept with her husband. Can you hold back the rain, or extend the life of a blossom even a single hour? Can you preserve the apple forever from the bite of the worm? Just as little will you be able to lock up your daughter when she wishes to go out. Like promissory notes, girls maintain their vigor and validity only a certain period of time after they have attained their maturity, and Nature cannot be forced. Whoever can become a father or mother should not, at least as far as this particular matter is concerned, be subject to his or her parents' wishes. The parents should at most give advice or recommendations, they should possess the *votum consultativum* or, like the senior pastor in some countries upon the appointment of a chaplain, the *fidele consilium*, and be consulted out of propriety (which is often more severe than the law itself) and not of necessity.[36]

I know a state in which parents are induced by no less than fifteen legal sanctions to disinherit their children if they enter into a marriage against the parents' will. I personally would not only abolish the fifteenth, but the other fourteen sanctions as well and let the parents have free reign over the wealth which they earned themselves and which was not inherited by them under the condition that they pass it along to their children. The bequeathing of property by parents to children is viewed as a mutual testament from one generation to the next which the law has established once and for all on behalf of the interested parties; Nature in this case was not a motivating factor. Parents, it is true, have already given their children more than wealth—namely, a life and an upbringing—yet why do we wish to ruin the splendid duty of thankfulness by legalizing it, anyway? Why block the natural path of a child's noble heart by means of coercive commandments; and why hinder the most natural progression in the world by inappropriate and ill-timed restrictions?

Nevertheless I find it even more questionable to *require* the parents, in cases where the above-mentioned sanctions do not apply, to leave to their children what they have earned themselves. Nature, left on her own without this harsh obligation, will not fail to act in consonance with herself, and if we allow the parents to be unfettered in this matter we will not only produce more obedient children, but better ones as well. It seldom bodes well when a child early on is able to count on inevitable riches, and all those barbaric promissory notes reading "I promise to pay *a dato* one week after the death of my father . . ." will then become a thing of the past. I have gleaned the impression, perhaps not altogether incorrectly, that with respect to this point parents regard their children as their enemies while at the same time awaiting their grandchildren, as the enemies of their enemies, with great joy and anticipation. In the meantime, however, before these inheritances from generation to generation come to an end, we could at least limit the power of parents to annul marriages which are contracted without their approval. Among unworthy children the latter evil is always more frequently encountered than the former; good-natured children who have known the happiness of domestic life and the patriarchal joy of the family bond will not of themselves interrupt this pleasure by means of a discordant note caused by the choice of a matrimonial partner disapproved of by the parents.

Nobody in the world can more enthusiastically endorse our obligation to honor our parents than I; but if we also imbue the souls of our children with high moral principles, if we show them that everything, even love, must subject itself to the dictates of reason, then their desires too will keep pace with this reason and never become stronger than their moral principles. Reason can seldom serve as the *doctor* for love—but if it were to become its *father confessor* instead, could not a great deal of good advice be passed along and received in such a relationship? Parents take the place of reason for their children while they are young, and it depends on the direction they give to its burgeoning powers whether their children will later bring them joy and comfort, or pain and ingratitude.

I am far from maintaining that a child conceived in a secret marriage must be viewed by the parents as a sign from heaven; but it is also only fair and just that reason, when it has come of age, be given its rights and that the hearts of the parents, which are often as hard as the metals they now serve, then begin to soften. It is, moreover, likewise fair and just that the parents consider how good it is for them that they themselves are not led around forever on a leash by the state and that it treats them as citizens, rather than as children. Just as there are treasures which are not worth guarding, so there are also treasures which are beyond guarding. Secret engagements become public ones when a Certain Something is added to them, and it is a shame as well as a sin that remnants of the *dominium quiritarium*,[37] which extended paternal power beyond the bounds which Nature had assigned to it, can still be found today. Children obey their parents out of necessity only for a few years, and then out of gratitude—such is the extent of paternal control. If a string is strung too tightly, it will snap; it is no different with sons and daughters. Yet in spite of this, I consider even more questionable that Prussian law which stipulates that, in cases involving refusal by the parents or grandparents to allow the marriage of a child, the court should be called in to pass judgment on the legitimacy of this refusal.[38] The court must not interfere in matters between parents and children except in cases involving true criminal offenses. Coercion in matters of love, which brings to love some public and private prejudices assumed on behalf of the child, breeds amorous intrigue, and that is the plague of marriages.

Marriage is a burden, and if we are to undertake any burden we ought to receive encouragement and not have obstacles placed in our way. We would all prefer to carry only what we already have on our shoulders than have another burden added to it. But this is also proof positive of the fact that people can do more than they believe they can, that they have more than they need, and that, because their own accounts are in such disarray, they often borrow capital and pay interest when they ought to be lending it and drawing interest. If a person is happy to pay rent, why should he buy his own house? We are pilgrims in this world—no wonder we love change so much! Even a person who owns a house often entertains the thought of acquiring a new one, and if not, at least he moves from one room of his house into another. Everybody wants to have an estate by the time he is sixty, as a sign that Nature has run her course. We say of a sick man that he is confined to his room; and perhaps this is the reason German has appended to the word *Frau* ["woman"] the otherwise rather unsuitable word *Zimmer* ["room"].[39] If a man could receive the advantages of marriage without the duty of standing day and night at a woman's side in all sorts of wind and weather, then nobody would hesitate to get married. The state should direct its attention to nothing so much as the abolition of all prejudices which can hinder marriage, for marriage itself is a state in miniature. As things go in the majority of its homes, so they go in its cities, and the capital city often provides a truer picture of the provinces than the ruler's court does of the entire state.

In point of fact, marriage has from the beginning been the barometer of morality—how things stood with marriage determined whether the stocks of morality rose or fell. Here as well the political demographer can extract unknown numbers from known ones and find plenty of material in the marriage statistics of his own country for his sage speculations, to which the statistics from the subdivided categories of the nobility, the intellectuals, the middle class, and the peasantry will lend a ready hand. Go into whatever prison you want—you will find for the most part unmarried men. If you add up the number of criminal acts committed each year, the greater part of the perpetrators will fall under the rubric "single." A single man only looks out for himself; a married man has people who love him, people who embrace him before he is touched by the electric prod. In general, men who remain unmarried are godless, but women who never marry are pious. It is said that single people live longer, but this is open to question, for a bachelor purges and purifies himself, he blocks and parries every wrinkle, so that because of this mask we fail to estimate his age correctly. But when he dies—who cares about his death, and who even knows that he has died?

The ancient Romans had certain inducements to marry, and one can still find in many parts of Germany specific minor penalties set aside for those who do not marry after they have been citizens for a few years. In olden times it was customary to sacrifice a rooster to Aesculapius, the god of health; in the Hildesheim region of Germany married couples are required, if they have no children, to give to the *pastor loci*, as a substitute for the baptismal fees, one rooster yearly, called a "patience rooster," because His Reverence is supposed to have patience with their weakness. And in several places in Germany, "Many children, many blessings"[40] is an old proverb. It cannot be denied that it is the obligation of the state to bring about an increase in the number of its citizens, and children are the most useful tribute which a citizen of the state can pay; but is it not then unbelievably harsh to try to bring someone by means of coercion and penalties to undertake something which requires rather love and desire, if it is ever going to thrive? To be sure, there have been unmarried men and confirmed bachelors who for years were afraid of the obedience school of Hymen, the god of marriage, and gadded about on the leash of Priapus like Ubiquitarians[41] until, worn down in body and soul, and no longer filled with loathing at the thought of being henpecked, they wound up bending before the terrible domestic power of an aging prima donna. Could a worse punishment have been inflicted on these wretched people by sending them to Purgatory? What is more, these female tyrants took great care to see that not much in the way of money or goods was left over in cases of bachelors who were truly deserving of punishment. On the other hand, the remaining innocent unmarried men fell into the hands of the law and its officials, people who customarily catch only the doves and let the vultures fly where they may. In general, rewards are far and away more effective than punishments, since the latter call forth only acts of servitude, and never those of love.

It could actually be said that the punishments we have inflicted upon these bachelors, sitting proudly aloof within the confines of their own preserves, have harmed them less than their relatives, for by depriving them of the right to make a will we merely took away their possessions at a time when they no longer needed them anyway. A good German writer once said, "An unmarried man is like the savage who cares nothing for the future—he chops down the tree in order to pick the fruit." But is that the usual case with all unmarried men and bachelors? Without morality and reason they would doubtless act this way; nevertheless, there have always been those philanthropists among them who thought not only of their own houses, but of the wide field of mankind as well. And was their virtue not more pure and selfless than if they had done everything merely for those whom they know and love? If monks who are forced to remain unmarried constitute the strongest support for the Church, then it follows that unmarried men who do not experience this coercion and who often, out of love for the fatherland or for the good of others, choose not to follow the way of the flesh are more loyal to the state and the world.

Without doubt, it was really the cloisters and the churches which were intent on venting their anger on bachelors—the evil which we see in ourselves we tend to punish more severely in others. Moreover, the cloisters did extraordinarily well by these punishments for bachelors in taking over their possessions for having violated the lay sacrament of marriage, until the monarchs became high priests themselves and began confiscating the bequeaths of the bachelors after their deaths and those of the cloisters even though they were still very much alive. The good monks also have at their disposal, if the D—— begins to plague them too severely, an *argumentum ad hominem*[42] as to why they are so very much in favor of marriage for the laity—an argument which, whenever it comes to making a virtue out of necessity, enables them to be effective and useful shepherds to the latter. I do not wish to cry out in the words of that demagogue who, at the outbreak of the French Revolution, took the lantern-liberty[43] of maintaining that "among the clergy nothing is natural—everything is excessive and eccentric." But who can deny that in the celibacy of the priests the law of God is subordinate to that of the Church, and that we defy humanity itself when we contradict Nature? To marry oneself to the Church is tantamount to committing a moral sin of silence.[44] The Church is not bone of our bones or flesh of our flesh;[45] one cannot call it *female*, since it was not made of a male. This Church-imposed celibacy is also the straightest path to hierarchy and fanaticism, as far as the two are separable, or can at least be made to appear so. And the wealth of the cloisters—what else is it than dead capital, as dead as the pounds which those foolish and lazy servants put away in a handkerchief or buried in the ground?[46]

85

But, you might ask, what if we permit the celibacy of laymen without penalties for bachelorhood—will not marriages begin to decrease, and the state, whose real treasury is its people, have to renounce its possessions? Are there not other divine coffers besides the holy cloisters and the unholy royal treasury where the bachelor can be encouraged by law to sacrifice part of his treasure with more propriety? One law book,[47] differing from the others through the natural circumstance that, while conceived within a monarchical system of government, it was still more or less approved by the people even if it did not really originate with them, has recently declared itself against bachelorhood and in the nineteenth and twenty-first paragraphs of the second part, nineteenth Title, which deals with institutions for the poor and other charitable foundations, stipulates that the local relief fund has inheritance rights with respect to the estates of such male persons as have died after the age of forty without ever having married, and moreover, that if the deceased had designated living relatives in an ascending line, or his siblings and their children, as his heirs, the relief fund is entitled to a tenth, in other cases to a sixth, of his estate. It is beyond the scope of this treatise for me to air my opinions to any great extent on the subject of institutions for the poor; nevertheless, it is certain that excessive alms increase the number of poor people, and a too-generous right of reversion, which enables us to live off the fortunes of others, undermines our activity within the state, if it does not suffocate it entirely. Moreover, it is dangerous to give credence to a matter of conscience by means of legal enforcement. If the state would deign to refrain from excluding the poor *bonis modis*[48] from civil affairs and show them ways and means to attain a self-respect in proportion to their increased powers within the state, then the so-called poor would not, as is unfortunately often the case now, so easily give up their rights to citizenship and would no longer constantly be exposed to the danger of having to give up even the honor of being called members of the human race. But, be that as it may, why should bachelors be the ones to enrich the coffers of the poor houses and orphanages? Were they the only ones who in the view of our government and lawmakers played a significant role in certain cases of oppression within our society? Are they responsible for the guilt of the state? Was it because of them that this or that social class has not been able exercise its powers? Or would not they themselves sooner have increased the number of poor people if during those years when they were incapable of supporting a wife and child they had entered into marriage while living in a state which calculates its people, to be sure, but not the means necessary for fulfilling their needs?

Granted that among the lower classes unmarried men do not have the best reputation; on the other hand, however, are not great men, who are destined more for the world than the home, hindered in the performance of their great calling by the burdens of marriage? Whoever has children believes that he has adequately come to terms with that worthy drive to perpetuate and immortalize his name; those who are not married do not get off so easily, and whenever wise men say of them that they are better taken care of than anyone else when it comes to posterity, then these wise men have drawn their conclusion from the noble solicitude and selflessness exerted by bachelors in order to become immortal. They strive after it by treading the strait and narrow path, that of the mind, while the multitude attains the crown of life along a broader and more comfortable road. Free from the fetters of domestic life, they are oblivious to good and bad rumors about themselves, have no need to give consideration to wife or child or the well-meaning concerns of their spouses, and thus have more time to be a friend, judge, and benefactor to the state—and what is more, to the human race.

Seek, and you will find in your genealogies that it was bachelors who either founded or secured the fame and fortune of their families.[49] Socrates and Plato loved without being in love; Leibniz[50] and Kant were bachelors; and would Rousseau have been a Hans Jakob so often if he had not been Thérèse Levasseur's husband?[51] Even the poet himself has never been inspired by love, only by the idea of it.[52] We must remain awake if we wish to relate our dream to others. Health and well-being are the muses who give us divine inspiration and raise us above ourselves. Sampson had strength and Solomon wisdom; both lost what they had because of love.[53] Even if the above-mentioned Prussian law had exempted soldiers, academics, and civil servants, would it not still be a dangerous thing to penetrate into those mysteries and affairs of Nature she has reserved for herself alone? Truly, the procreation and reproduction of the human race are mysteries of the highest order! What a serious and important business comes from the play of children! From the way of all flesh a spirit in the likeness of the divine image![54] Instinct, that decisive factor by means of which Nature accomplishes such great things in us and all other creatures; that remarkable business which everyone knows and no decent person talks about raises us above all positive inducements and punishments designed to promote what such inducements and punishments sooner discourage than promote. No one can serve two masters without ruining his relationship with one or the other.[55] Are laws stronger when they are also made by men, and not by God alone? Do they need the sanction of a king, where divine authority is present? Do we not gladly do that which is not absolutely required of us, and perform with unwilling hearts that which is required? The obligations we have as *human beings* must not be imposed upon us as citizens as well; and whoever imagines that he is aiding in the cultivation of duties of love by imbuing them with the image and superscription[56] of coercion is degrading that which he wished to elevate in the first place and causing us to perform an action unwillingly we otherwise would not have hesitated to do gladly. Who would not infinitely rather fall into the hands of God than of men? Behold—in the face of every sort of moral decay, Providence has continued to vindicate itself in the matter of the propagation of the human race and to demonstrate its superiority and wisdom to every political accountant and auditor! It will not let its darling and heir of Nature, man, or any of his royal family, perish and die out in the Flood, but in spite of all the human race's overt or covert failings, it will maintain and preserve them unto eternal life.[57] Nature has provided for her institutions too well for them to be in need of political assistance. Without these institutions, and in spite of what the legislators did, we would long have been searching everywhere in vain for the remains of the human race outside of a few natural history museums!

Is not the great sign of Him who pointed to His disciples with the words, "These are my brother, my sister, my mother . . ."[58]—is this sign not a blessing for bachelors? Who would think of preventing an unmarried man from giving his fortune to the *person of his choice* not only after his death, but during his lifetime as well? And if such were the case, who would then stand in his way if, after having attained his fortieth year, he were to suffer a stroke, decide to put his affairs in order and take a wife who, even if the Angel of Death were to pass him by this time, would nevertheless cause him to die a little bit each day? And what would his innocent family have done to inherit an aunt like this? Why should the family suffer merely because it is *not* poor? Is there some advantage to being poor? And why should bachelors alone be subject to the curse of the law, and not old maids? Are they not more often responsible for the lack of marriages than bachelors? When they were young, did they not extinguish in others the desire to marry by their coyness, coldness, and their self-conceit? Is it not advisable to let each person do as he pleases with his own money—the protection of which being one of the main reasons why people form together into a state and acknowledge its authority—and let him remain steadfast in the conviction that, if he but strives to improve the moral stature of his fellow man, everything else will be granted to him?

It is not the object of this book to speak in favor of bachelorhood. Nevertheless, that well-intentioned Prussian law has made it *nolens volens*[59] advisable to speak on behalf of this prerogative, since it seems harsh to attempt to punish a class of people who are often already denying themselves the foremost joys of life merely for the sake of the state. If a bachelor has relatives, then he has children; if he has love for his fellow man, he has more heirs than he can count. In addition, the man who chooses not to marry will automatically play a role in the education of others' children, for there is something so sublime and rewarding in raising children that it merits praise as little as a good wine. And is it not remarkable how naturally everything works out in this case as well? What the bachelor loses in the joys of educating his own well-raised children he gains in direct proportion to the sorrow he avoids when children upon whom he has less influence turn out poorly.

Even without laws and relief funds for the poor there are ways to promote marriage—it is merely a matter of making it pleasant and easy. Allow me, if you would, to fall asleep and then relate a dream to you; let whoever prefers some other approach imagine that I am talking in my sleep. I dreamed there existed a state in which women had no rank whatsoever. I dreamed that this circumstance could befall an otherwise good country and continue to bear its bitter fruit a thousandfold[60] until the fair sex succeeded in the improvement of its status and attained a rank in society on the basis of its own merit. According to the gracious authority of the law of this country, the women could do little more without assistance and guardianship than get up in the morning and go to bed at night. To be sure, the businesswoman had the honor of being an exception to the rule, but this hermaphroditic status only pertained in matters of business, where—in order that here, too, nothing should infringe upon the rights of the male sex—she was nevertheless constantly accompanied by an overseer who in the short or long run knew what it took to make himself an integral part of the firm and, if he was especially fortunate, offer himself as a partner in marriage. All other women, with the exception of regents and the wives of regents, whom the proud male sex felt itself justified in treating as carefully considered exceptions, remained minors up to the day of their gentle and blessed death. Yet even in my sleep I am so far from giving assent to a form of "justice" which here as elsewhere has the appearance of a soiled garment that I am now prepared and even duty-bound, if the fair sex will permit me, to champion its cause and break a lance on its behalf.

The regulation in many states which prevents women from drawing up a bill on a customer; the honor bestowed on them by not permitting them to pay for something when they have vouched for its purchase with mouth and hand—these and other such legal gallantries by means of which they are raised to the level of dignity of aged children their whole life long argue convincingly against the law, but not against the opposite sex itself. For not only the weak instrument, but also the strong one; not only women, but also the soldiers in many countries, enjoy the same or similar "prerogatives"; and would not an open declaration that one is not permitted to keep one's word humiliate and degrade anyone thus privileged in his own eyes and in the eyes of any upright person in the country? God is gracious, and therefore also just. And when laws exhibit such displays of favoritism (itself actually more a province of the gospel than the law) and beneficence, it is tantamount to making an *honest* effort to act *dishonestly*—and this sort of thing happens more often than we would care to imagine!

"Because of the pension Your Majesty is granting to *one* person you are taking the bread out of the mouths of fifty people," a forthright government accountant once told his sovereign, a ruler who was accustomed to ignoring the ramifications of his decisions. The law itself must not respect the person any more than the judge does; and in fact the judge too is in the service of the law. Since that disciple is perfect who is like his master,[61] do not such biased laws give the disciple, even if he is no Judas, the unconditional authority (*cum libera*[62]) to act unjustly and to base his conscience and better judgment not on reason but directly on the law books in order to cover the multitude of his sins? Woe to that law which creates discord! What are we trying to say? That when women *do* arrive in heaven after the sufferings of a life of guardianship, whose consequence—in utter contradiction to Nature's intention—was that during their earthly period of testing they had no will of their own and were almost never permitted to act freely, or at least in such a way that the credit for what they accomplished did not constantly redound to their husbands' or guardians' assistance, or however these Susanna-seducers,[63] or perhaps legal Cicisbeos is the right word, should be called—that they will then be able to rest assured that their actions will not be so precisely monitored in that next world as they were in this one?

This is how I would honestly and justly defend you, O noble and beautiful half of the human race! But allow me instead to continue my dream and suggest to you with heavy heart that you abandon, without the help of your guardians' assistance, the status which the men only grant to you for the sake of show, and render thereby the most important proof that you do not require a leash of any kind. I do not wish to bring up the situation in the orient, which is like a heaven for young women and where one is not judged by one's status; where the nobleman marries the commonest girl and the daughter of a king believes that she has every right to a *husband*, even if he might not be the son of a *king*. At this point I will only make brief mention of one state which in recent times has actually exchanged its classes and ranks for the rights of humanity—although, as often happens with sacrifices, perhaps here and there it went further than necessary.[64] This state was your Canaan, where if not milk and honey, then good taste and fine fashion flowed daily and copiously.

How is it then? Can it be said of you that you do not possess enough self-control to refuse gifts which are bestowed upon you in a way that is almost insulting? Voltaire would rather have had bad things said about his writings than nothing at all, and has it not now come to the point where people are really referring to your husbands when they talk about your rank? To be sure, there have been orators and public speakers who have taken up your cause and sung your praises; but do they not do the cause more harm than your actual opponents? As a consequence of their feeble grounds for proof, their habit of blowing everything up out of proportion and of choosing far stronger words than necessary, they wind up denigrating the very thing they wished to elevate. Their pathetic ideas pander to their words and the means they use scorn the ends they wish to achieve. Whatsoever is more than truth and inner feeling cometh from evil.[65] Neither is it my desire here that the Duke of Orleans be addressed from now on as Monsieur de Capet;[66] rather it is the intention of my non-binding dream legislation for the peasant woman and the woman of the middle, noble, and ruling classes still to be differentiated from one another, only no longer by fire and sword. It is a hundred to one that education, attitude, and even personal wealth will secure us from too great a break with the past, even if occasionally the attraction of two people for each other will graft a splendid branch onto a wild trunk and cause a noble sprig to bear fruit on an otherwise barren tree. What a profit the world would derive from this relinquishing of rank if the common man were to pitch his instrument an octave higher and the nobleman his an octave lower, and by means of this home remedy a more enduring and noble race of men were to issue forth, in which understanding, ability, and integrity were inherited characteristics! We must not give up depending mainly on the chain of natural causes until it is apparent to us that it is fully integrated into our own destiny; and if in this regard my suggestion above should not constitute an effective cause for change in itself, then perhaps we would at least ascribe to it the value of a potential motivation for bringing mankind closer to that golden age where intelligence and virtue will have the deciding voice and clear majority on their side without having to resort to the use of bribery. The pace of evil is fast, that of the good is measured; and if you, my good ladies, wish to attain your last and most important goal and free yourselves from that Egypt where you languish, if not in a house,[67] then at best in a palace of bondage, consider then that only the mild and warming sun is able to burn off the morning mist and promote desired growth; that, before any tree can bear ripe fruit, it must first germinate, sprout, grow, and blossom; that the kingdom of God does not call up drummers and fiddlers every time a new regimen is to be instituted, and that it is not announced by heralds and harbingers, but proceeds quietly like Nature herself, only attaining its ultimate goal when the proper time has arrived.

It is true that you have titles because of your husbands; yet what good is the name, when the person who bears it belies its power? Are you really Madame President or Frau Dr. Sch—— just because you are called that by virtue of being married to Herr President or Herr Dr. Sch——? True, not one in a hundred men really deserves his title of honor; yet it is other men who serve as representatives for these conceited children, and their sex still retains its advantage. But I would say, honor to whom honor is due! When King Antigonus saw Cleanthes in Athens again after a long absence and asked him, "Are you still working as a miller?" he received as an answer: "Yes, King, I work as a miller in order not to abandon the study of worldly wisdom."[68] This is a splendid suggestion for wives: namely, to strive for an unceasing preoccupation with the education of their children and the salutary supervision of the household, and by abandoning all artificial adornment in favor of that philosophy of life unique to their sex to bring themselves honor and the reward of true wisdom!

Truly, in spite of all the injustice we have found it good to wreak upon the other sex, we still have left them one area—provided they dedicate themselves to it faithfully and do not act like those misers who cannot enjoy what they have for thinking about what they have lost—in which they find themselves on the road leading straight to Canaan. It is too bad, though, that wives and mothers carry out this task carelessly and, as one of the ancients once remarked, only take their children into their arms after they have been suckled, bathed, and cuddled by others—and then merely as playthings to relieve their boredom. In matters concerning the household they allow themselves, like Epicure's gods,[69] to be worshiped without paying the slightest attention to anything else that is going on. The oppressed sex would already have attained everything they now desire if they had secretly taken advantage of the opportunity for change while educating their male children, but their pure hearts do not need a written constitution to tell them that one must honor the rights of others even if these others permit themselves to do precisely the opposite.

Not cute and adorable, but well-raised children are a blessing to a marriage; not an immense, but a well-ordered household is one which women especially can earn for themselves, for they possess such an unmistakable propensity for imparting information and administering discipline that if they were employed in the public schools they could work wonders. A certain church[70] was at one time of the opinion that vows of marriage are made to populate the earth, and those of chastity, heaven; yet the time will come, and is in fact already at hand, when people will equate devotion to God with the remembrance of Him in their every action; when we will convince ourselves that God demands not that we adhere to the letter of the law, but rather that we seal off the sources of evil; and that freedom is adherence to the laws, and populating the earth is tantamount to populating heaven. The more souls there are for the earth, the more there are for heaven, and a statesman who aids in bringing about an increase in the population has rendered a greater service to heaven than a high-ranking clergyman, since the latter is weighed down merely by his cares for those souls who are already to be found in the church registeries, while the former assists them in entering into the visible world. In this sense, the clergyman could perhaps be considered as a kind of genius who, if he were gifted with the power of expressing his thoughts, would create the most sublime lyric poetry; the statesman, on the other hand, is the worldly-wise and diplomatic Homer. It is on the basis of this idea of populating with souls that the concept of the spiritual value of the state can be defended—a value which every monarch embodies for his own country, and rightly so, if he does not fail to heed the implicit and explicit dictates of his own conscience (a faculty no less capable of cultivation than one's understanding or will). "*Here* is your Patriarch," said Peter the Great as he beat on his breast, thereby divesting the Holy Synod of the Russian Orthodox Church for all time of the courage to renew their request to name a Patriarch themselves—and in truth, he was more to his state than Patriarch and Emperor, he was its creator and father!

The Romans gave so many advantages to men who had children that they ruined a good idea through excess and wound up bestowing privileges on some men who from the outset were incapable of handling them. The "Three-child-right" (*Jus trium liberorum*), applied to those in Rome who had three children, and in Italy and the provinces four and five respectively, is as familiar to us as its abuse, wherein it was granted to the gods as well.[71] Among the Hebrews, childlessness and the privileges accorded to those with many children were circumstances which chiefly affected the women. For the sake of this civil honor Leah and Rachel overcame their jealousy, and their handmaidens were compelled to bear them children by their own bodies,[72] very much in the way one is permitted to swear by the soul of another person. The expression "to bear children for a wife" so that the latter "can build a family through the maidservant"[73] was so well-chosen that even coming from the mouth of Sarah it was able to bring about a solution to the problem.[74]

It cannot be denied that the Hebrews were closer to the heart of things when they bestowed that honor on women with regard to their children which the Romans ascribed to men. Since women perform the greatest amount of work in this business, and since in their case one can be sure that they are in fact mothers, while in the man's case paternity can only be determined as a matter of probability, then it is only just to reward them for their children, especially in cases where they are helping not only to educate, but to support their children as well, by providing not *luxury*, but *security*. Whoever fulfills his duty for the world deserves thanks, whoever loses his life for his country can never die![75]

In the Old Testament, to have many children was viewed as a blessing from God and was a wish which good friends exchanged with each other. The common man calls his wife "mother" as soon as she has borne him more than one child. For him, this title means more than "wife"—and in this he is right, it does mean more! The abolition of the women's present inappropriate status and the restoration of their legitimate one will doubtless do more to populate a country than any other means, and will likewise have a salutary and restorative effect on the women themselves. The individual who knows and can apply reason and freedom, the two highest gifts of Nature, cannot be any happier than this; or do you, noble sex, prefer to imitate the words of the man suffering from dropsy who reproached his doctor for making him so thin? But if you become healthy by doing so—why not? Who would not give up his army of servants, who are always getting in the way of each other anyway, rather than by virtue of all this service become the servant of another? Who would not rather be without worldly goods than by means of their burdensome possession be lowered to the level of an object himself? Who would not rather live moderately than be served his last meal before execution with the words: "Tonight thy soul will be required of thee"?[76] One can have many praiseworthy traits and yet be without virtue; one can pay off many debts and still be poor; one can achieve great honor and still be despised; one can be a great lord and at the same time a wretched slave. I suggest that anyone who finds this puzzling take the shortest route to the court of any ruler. There he will find more examples than he could possibly imagine or ever require for proof of my assertion that our happiness is not always what we think it is.

Painters, it is often said, are in a ticklish situation when it comes to dealing with the fair sex: if they paint the lady as she is, then she considers herself not a little insulted; if, on the other hand, they flatter her, they leave themselves open to the charge that they have failed to capture her likeness. Which is better, to be flattered or to have one's likeness captured? If women were restored to their legitimate status, then that extravagance which now makes so many marriages impossible would disappear by itself and we men would follow the woman out of love and on principle. That wise simplicity consisting of a noble heart bound together with firm and correct principles and with an unadulterated perception of the true and the good would return to the world, in even more beautiful form than when it left, and the "left-handed" marriage (*ad morganaticam*[77]) could become the rule, whereas it now exists as an exception, and a problematical, if not utterly objectionable one at that. Problematical? Exactly—because human beings, and among them especially our own sex, have a propensity for exceptions to rules; because "left-handed" marriages, as they presently exist, destroy trust and unity in families and raise so many discordant voices that the continual cry to "Cast out this bondwoman and her son"[78] only adds fuel to the fire, and the persecuted love merely burns brighter than ever before; and because the unfortunate girls on the "right hand" find their worth decreasing and feel themselves obliged to seek refuge in trickery, whereby they descend to a point lower on the moral scale than those on the left hand have already descended in civil status. What a miserable end for the right hand! One more "because," and let it be the last: because wherever a thorough treatment is not too difficult to obtain it is always preferable to a palliative.

Let me just say a word here in praise of our lawmakers, who, instead of dozens of exceptions, of which not a single one is unproblematical, strive to state one main rule and provide entrance to their law through a single gate instead of ten side and back doors. Metals become strong by being hammered; too much hammering makes them weak again. The Ten Commandments give an example of good form in law books in that they are not weakened by any exceptions, but are as strong as Nature, decisive as a great man, and as easily understood as the Lord's Prayer.

It is ridiculous for women to assume the status of their husbands; nevertheless, it is perfectly just for them to have a share in their possessions in case they later become widows, and it is much easier to forgive parents who leave nothing to their children than men who take no thought of the possibility that their wives might become widows someday. It is not exactly known how the words "widows and orphans" came to be so closely associated with each other,[79] but the orphans, in my opinion, do not merit as much attention as has been lavished on them. It is outrageous, for example, that contracts entered into by minors should be considered valid only to the extent that they constitute a benefit for the minor or minors involved. This legal favoritism is an incessant source of corruption for the youth and merely accustoms them to acting deceitfully. Justice and favoritism— how can these co-exist? How can we praise laws which give us such a poor example to follow? Children who are not cripples are able to find a place in society relative to their wealth and talents, and it is not absolutely necessary that the son become a councillor just because his father was one. A widow, however, is almost always a cripple, and what is more, she cannot leave the place assigned to her through her marriage without exposing herself to scorn. Consider, thoughtless husband, that a good heart shows a kind of gratitude even toward inanimate objects which, although it may fall short of true thankfulness, nevertheless betrays a gentle affection for them. You place your beloved tobacco-box after use into the cabinet as if you were laying it to rest; if you do this for a piece of dry wood, how much more are you obliged to see that after your death your wife does not suffer want? A husband who fails in this duty does not deserve to live eternally in the memory of his widow, regardless of whether he has a right to or not.

Daughters cast off the family names of their fathers happily and without any difficulty whatsoever, often for a despicable mess of pottage[80] of a husband, and in fact would have thought little or nothing of giving up all claim to their names from the time of their childhood on. If my neighbor were named Heidefeld, then his daughter would perhaps be called before her marriage "Fräulein Minnie from the House of Heidefeld." If, still unmarried at the age of fifty and about to enter the local convent, she wished to take on the name of, say for example, Amadeus Creuzberger, then we should let her have this pleasure, as they did with Mademoiselle de Gournay who, beautiful as she was, considered it an honor to bear the name of Montaigne, the author with the open bowels.[81]

An unmarried young woman is a consonant which cannot be pronounced without a man; how obviously unjust, then, are those laws which establish that a woman must take a husband who is fully her equal by birth. A misalliance is in most cases an intolerable alternative.[82] The Romans had *contubernium, matrimonium, connubium,* or *nuptiae, conjugium,* or *matrimonium in specie,*[83] and all these paths led to the same goal, as do the wedding and the wedding-night. The Germans, who in general feel more comfortable dealing with objects than words, unite all these concepts under the rubric "marriage" and grant its advantages also to people who are otherwise limited in their civil rights, in the sense that the childbed, the marriage bed, and the deathbed all force each one of us to admit—to the honor of the race—that we are nothing more or less than *human.* The Romans themselves also recognized that too many exceptions weakened the rule, and Antonius Caracalla granted to foreigners the *jus connubiorum,*[84] thus bringing many practices under one heading. Because of the Roman way of doing things, however, not everything could be so easily subsumed under this one rubric; the *Lex Julia et Papia*[85] circumscribed the rights of senators and their children by preventing them from marrying freed slaves. Let us hope that the Germans, then, who render such innocent obedience to Roman law, will not needlessly exaggerate this favor by honoring laws just because they are laws, and not because they are just. As we do in so many other cases, in the case of marriage as well we should cling to that authority of Nature which no one can despise or neglect without debasing himself thereby.

At present, a nobleman is considered to be bestowing his favor on a girl of the middle class by offering her his hand, or, if it happens that a couple of his fingers have been shot off, his three remaining fingers in marriage. I am well aware of the consequences which the privilege of birth has brought about in the cases, for example, of jousts, duels, and hereditary ecclesiastical positions; I also know that reasonable laws would put an end to all this foolishness. True, monarchs have reason to permit their most honorable subjects to have their say, for they are the bulwark of the monarchy; nevertheless, my suggestion poses no threat to the nobility as such, which can prove very useful in republics and is absolutely necessary in monarchies. I can tolerate it, if the moths can, when a piece of parchment is preserved for generations within a family, because even if I know that the glorious deeds of the ancestors very often dispose the descendants to the inglorious act of twiddling their thumbs, good examples have from time immemorial been the motivation for similar noble actions. That very king who said of princes that *"les bâtards y valent mieux que les légitimes"*[86] was himself much predisposed to certain families and the nobility in general—and rightly so, since he accomplished more through the mere dropping of names than other regents through threats down to the third and fourth, and promises to the thousandth generation.[87] Let people count their ancestors, but let us not then be too severe with regard to the mothers. True, the children do follow the line of the father, although the daughters not in the same strict sense as the sons. However, to say more would be to belabor the point regarding this subject and others I only wish to touch upon briefly here. In this little work of mine I am really only interested in providing texts on which anyone who feels so inclined could deliver a proper sermon.

It is true to say that by this method flattery will be dethroned; yet when the tyrant of the land has been cast out, his like-minded minister deserves the same fate. Whoever holds the ladder is just as guilty as the one doing the stealing, and flattery is as unnatural as rank among women. Why should we crawl when we can walk; why beg when we can demand? Is it not the case, given our patented prejudices, that the only means now of being reconciled with a girl is to make her more annoyed? Whoever asks for forgiveness after having kissed a girl receives none; he is only forgiven when he places his hand even closer than before. The pins the women use to defend themselves are of no avail when we choose to storm the barricades. They have learned this means of fortification from the roses; but roses are picked anyway, and so it goes with the girls: they signal *"chamade"*[88] as soon as the outer fortifications have been breached and the enemy is preparing to press the attack. The law has given the unmarried girl grounds for complaint when she is kissed against her will, but in no case I can remember has anyone made use of it, due to the requirement stipulating the presence of witnesses. And in any case, such regulations have come down to us from a time when, according to the report of Valerius Maximus,[89] a father killed his freed slave because the latter had once kissed his daughter. But there is a vast difference between that heathen time and the present, when we are accustomed to saying that "an innocent kiss comes never amiss." Our friends the lawyers have likewise found it good—and what have they not found good—to consider the case in which a man is said to have been seduced by a woman, and have provided for punishment in this situation as well. In England, where the letter of the law causes people to be put to death, a law such as this is excusable. The natural thing—but for all our desire to mete out punishment the one least often considered—would be to banish a man who had let himself be seduced from the members of his own sex altogether. As a matter of fact, this banishment from one's sex would not be without its uses in other cases of men and women who had exceeded the boundaries of their sex. I do not know which would be more shameful—if a woman were exiled to the men, or a man to the women. Holy Nature, your ways are always goodness and truth, and how fortunate it is for us that you take such unceasingly maternal care not to give up your rights, but rather, in the face of all the abominations which take place in your holy abode, you strive to keep them from becoming obsolete!

At the present time, that is, before the male sex ceases to represent the world as content, and the opposite sex as form; now, before it has become clear what the fair sex can and will become, it *appears* at least that a girl would be gaining something if, by means of a change in the law, she could actually attain the status of "manhood." The reproach "Elizabeth was a king, now Queen James is on the throne" ("*Rex erat Elisabeth, nunc est Regina Jacobus*") was not directed at Elizabeth, but James, and it took a judge's decree to give Lord-Lady d'Eon back to the members of her own sex.[90] Yet do these circumstances prove anything more than that prejudice struggles against Nature like flesh against the spirit, and that prejudice, in order better to deceive, is able to take on the appearance of Nature much in the same way that the Evil One is accustomed to assuming the guise of the Angel of Light?[91] Deception is a sweet wine without vigor; and it is only people who are conscious of their own individual lack of worth who seek to impart an importance to themselves which passes for genuine among those with little knowledge of human nature, the way false coin does among those with little knowledge of money. The clergyman calls his personal business the "affairs of God," the statesman his own self-interest the "enlightened self-interest of the state"; and generally those who make themselves out to be notable members of the male sex are those who would be least likely to be considered as such by others.

If the suit of the man clothes the other sex better than it does us, does the fault lie anywhere else than in the cut of the suit? And where has Nature stipulated that men and women should be differentiated by means of their clothing? Did not Minerva come fully armed with lance in hand out of the brain of Jupiter?[92] The good and honest Duchess of Orleans,[93] who at least on the basis of her correspondence deserves less to be called "half German, half French" than she does a great and exclusively German lady, had the not unusual wish to be a man rather than a woman. "My whole life," she admits frankly, "I have preferred handling muskets and daggers to dolls, and I would have given anything to be a boy; in fact, that nearly cost me my life, for when I heard that Maria Germain had become a man through jumping, that set me as well to such frightful jumping about that it is a miracle I didn't break my neck a hundred times over."[94] If things had become truly serious, however, this estimable chatterbox would, I fondly hope, have cast away her muskets and daggers and left off with her jumping. Nonetheless, can one completely blame a woman of feeling who complains bitterly of the fetters which so undeservedly bind her sex, or if she struggles against institutions and arrangements which have been established by the male sex without her knowledge or consent? The French National Assembly, which claims so loudly to represent the rights of man, seems up to now to have forgotten that women also belong to the race we call "mankind," and this in spite of the fact that the women from the halls and salons, at least, have played such a significant role in the ennobling of the metal of the state.

If I were not dreaming right now I would perhaps entertain you with still other suggestions. How would it be, for example, if the fair sex were set free from the house of bondage of fashion into the land of freedom; if it were freed from slavish imitation to true originality and women no longer spent money on clothes for the sake of other women, but for themselves; if some female fashion despot, often only a princess of the stage and nothing else, were no longer to prescribe fashion rules for the entire and otherwise already fair sex, but if each woman were to become a law unto herself in this matter? Why a uniform besides that necessary for military service, which is not a woman's affair anyway? Why slavish conformity, when Nature is so infinitely variable in everything she does? Is there not in every refined soul an image or pattern of perfection in body and spirit? To develop and attain this should be the goal of a woman's desire if she is to deserve the name of the "fair sex." In fact, the women are all the more certain of attaining this goal, for the reason that they are much less predisposed to imitate than we are, or to do so in such virtuoso fashion.

It would show a lack of refinement on my part if in such a book on marriage as this I were to come to speak of clothing and fashion only a single time, and I hope to find an opportunity to pick up this thread at a later time. Let it be said, however, once and for all: the criticism which the fair sex has had to bear because of its supposed vanity in matters of dress applies to men to a far greater extent than to women. For, aside from the fact that we find pleasure in this vanity; that we extol it; that without it we would in fact be a great deal worse off; it is indisputable that the vanity of the fair sex with regard to clothing had nothing to do with the invention of, let us say, the bonnet,[95] but only with determining its cut. I will take up this matter again shortly.

The attempt to increase the number of marriages by utilizing the home remedy of allowing the woman to have more than a *votum negativum* in the choice of her marriage partner may well turn out to yield positive results. If he had been asked for his hand in marriage by an honorable girl, would even one bachelor out of ten refuse her? And is it not—I say this in order to comfort these honorable girls—and is it not more than mere rudeness to fail to answer a letter or to reply when one is greeted? Ah, how unfortunate it is that in some cases those people never meet who would so gladly have gone through life together! It would also further marriage if the royal "We, by the Grace of God" would not attempt to militate against luxury by dint of force and law, but by forceful example; if the upper classes were to seek to climb a step higher, to raise themselves to the level of human beings, and to find within themselves that which they now pursue so fervently in the external world.

And finally, a prescription: an improvement in the status of women, which would undoubtedly serve as the consummation of this entire important matter. How many a widow has not by means of better organization and management in the household restored *in integrum* (in fact, raised from the dead!) the level of nourishment which had seriously declined during the regime of her late husband?[96] And how many pursuits and occupations are there which the fair sex is not called by Nature to take over entirely? It was not Rousseau the philosopher, but Rousseau the crank who—with Thérèse serving as his muse, as she did so often—declared the man to be the natural despot of the woman.

True, the man is stronger in body than the woman—but is he also stronger in soul? Many a sturdy peasant girl would refute this statement not merely by shaking her head if she were challenged to a contest of strength by any one of the thousands of fops from our phalanxes of dandies. And even when we are speaking of the royal prerogatives of the stronger of the two sexes, are we not referring more to the soul than the body? Both sexes have a common purpose, and if each of them retains its unique qualities and preserves them in the worthiest manner possible, then even these varying qualities can become a means for achieving this common and universal purpose with all the more certainty. Do not the man and woman, in a certain sense at least, appear to make up but a single person?[97] And is it thus not chiefly the neglect and the resulting delicacy of the opposite sex which has thrust that burden on the entire human race under which it suffers so miserably? Why does the male of the race, the Adam, forget that it has a helpmeet[98] in the female, the Eve? What gives the man the right to regard the woman as not much more than a (moral) empty room or a geometric body which has dimensions, to be sure, but not the honor of possessing that which we call matter and impenetrability? At most we grant to the women such a small mass and rarefied density

102

that in the world of politics, for example, they only occupy a very tiny space.

When it comes to the enlightenment of the human race, there are those who would proceed analytically, while others wish to work synthetically. Some say the crown should finally declare its grown children to be of age, others want the children themselves to sue for this declaration of majority; and thus in the first case the reformation would begin at the top and proceed downwards, in the second it would go from the bottom upwards. Let us bring the opposite sex into this plan; let us give this *people of God* human and civil rights, and the *kingdom of God* will come closer than ever before, for whoever was weakest and least among us shall be greatest in the kingdom of God.[99]

The female form serves as the image for all manner of virtues and for virtue in general. "True," a misogynist once remarked on hearing this statement, "but that's just because of the weakness of all human virtues." My dear fellow—why then didn't they choose *our* sex to represent virtue? Is it not a lofty goal to be, according to the saying of a certain wise man, "weak as a human and content as a god"? Women gladly permit our sex the honor of representing learning by the figure of a man, as long as they themselves represent wisdom.[100] The Empress Catherine the Great of Russia (I would happily call this true autocrat the "Emperor Catherine" if she herself were not so dear to Nature and the truth) has espoused the cause of her sex through wise legislation, and freed it from that unworthy guardianship under which it almost universally languishes. In truth, she shows what a woman can become; yet as certain as it is that she possesses a nobly independent soul, it is equally certain that she does not wish to attain divinity at the cost of humanity. There she stands, the foremost of her sex—she takes the torch from Prometheus[101] in order to kindle the fire of life in that colossus first formed by Peter the Great; she tramples barbarity and superstition underfoot; she calls down truth and justice from heaven so that she may place them both on the throne next to her and, as the genius of half the world, utter the words "Let there be!" and it will be so. She has the wisdom and strength to obtain rights for a sex whose empress she is in a very special sense, rights which that sex has been deprived of up to now, while other princes, at present smiling at the suggestions of my dream, in private show an even greater degree of submissiveness toward persons of her sex who are not even worthy of her talents.

Thus, upon my awakening, ends my dream with a final short comment. Good morning, dear reader! If out of a feeling of kinship you have fallen asleep as well, then you might wish to get up and move around a little. Let us go take our breakfast in that special tavern of truth, a lecture hall. During your meal there you will either wake up—or fall even more soundly asleep.

2

THE PURPOSE OF MARRIAGE: AN ACADEMIC LECTURE

℮

A LAWYER, GENTLEMEN, is as different from a moralist as a surgeon from a general practitioner. Just to begin my lecture properly with the first letter of the alphabet, let us say that the lawyer is from Athens, the moralist from the world, and if a golden-tongued orator were to call the former the city oracle (*oraculum totius civitatis*), then a silver-tongued one might as easily call the latter the oracle of the world (*oraculum totus mundi*). To be a lawyer, if I may put it this way, takes a person who is a keen observer of the way the wind is blowing; to be a moralist, that is, a lawyer of the world, takes a great deal of *understanding*. The lawyer teaches us to avoid injury and damages; the moralist teaches us, if not to be happy, then at least to become worthy of happiness.

Your forefathers, gentlemen, possessed, as Ulpianus[1] has said, a true philosophy; its power extended over their legal scholarship when other less practical worldly philosophers had only a cloak and a beard.[2] Let nobody among you be a pettifogging lawyer, a fisherman in the troubled waters of the law, a *"Legulejus,"*[3] as I am accustomed to calling an unphilosophical lawyer, but rather seek to follow the friendly advice which, as far as circumstances will allow it, I am going to give here.

Observations, gentlemen, are something which people who are not schooled in philosophy can make as well as we can, but which really amount to nothing more in the end than a kind of quackery, a sign hung out for all to see with the words on it: "master craftsman and

105

citizen."[4] Observations often run counter to systems, and systems to observations, as flesh to the spirit; and yet they should be like body and soul or the higher and the lower faculties, for in fact they are kin to one another. If one has a brandy which is fundamentally good, then it can easily be redistilled and concentrated by means of an iron kettle; if applied to scholarship as well, this method will yield double the wit and double the learning.

We no longer have many of the things we once had; nonetheless, no one can yet dispute, for example, the rights we possess over our neighbors which we are empowered to make use of in the sale of land—a frequent enough occurrence the past few years. And in fact, as lawyers, we do make every effort to mine the gold ingots of philosophy and circulate the coin among the common man; moreover, we are the living logic in the face of some whose logic, while claiming to possess life, has already forfeited it. Those of you gentlemen who are already veterans in our profession will be acquainted with my method and forgive me the pointers which are contained here; but to those who are, I don't wish to say *"tirones,"* or recruits, but rather *salva venia dupondii*,[5] that is, young soldiers, I must announce in my welcoming remarks that *ratione formalis*[6] these lectures cannot be called either pandects, as if they contained everything, or digests,[7] as if everything were symmetrically arranged, or to put it better, as if everything were being examined under a magnifying glass. There will be frequent references to *Authenticae*, however, in case someone wishes to look upon our textbook as a series of *Novellae*.[8]

As a matter of course, gentlemen, any teacher needs to have in his academic edifice a great portal for the first onrush of ideas, for everything that is to come, and leave a back door open for a good friend; or, to put it another way, while cultivating elegant and learned *reason* he should also seek to develop *common*, but also healthy and practical, *sense* as well. The former is necessary for the reflective, the latter for the active and more habitual side of our lives. The former is for use at school, the latter for home use. Wolff, who incorrectly assessed the extent of the realms of possibility and impossibility,[9] was born to bring the Germans to their appointed destination, and we would already be there now if we had but followed his lead. The Germans all have a bit of the mathematical about them, as well as a tendency to prolixity, and both of these have their advantages. They all incline to order, and in their native works little treasure-troves are everywhere to be found; they have a genius for systems, and if the

English are accustomed to placing large and small coin into the same purse, we, on the other hand, proceed more precisely and separate each kind of coin from the others. We are drawn to institutes,[10] the English more to pandects. The French should not even be permitted to enter into this discussion, since in this regard everything they do is for the fair sex alone and for precisely this reason they spend more of their time trivializing the important and exaggerating the trivial. In matters of taste we probably ought to stick with the speckled sheep, since the French are already tending the white, and the English the black ones.[11] Nevertheless, for this to take place, some of the terms we Germans use in the theoretical sciences will have to be culled out and provided with more precise definitions, a process whose result would be that the common man in our states would then be able to express himself so distinctly that his language would immediately reveal his German nationality. With time it could even be said of the man on the street that the Englishman writes newspapers, the German is a philosopher, and the French washer-woman of today can become the Dauphine of tomorrow.

Like Alexander the Great before him, Herr Kant, our German Plato and Aristotle rolled into one, did not bother to loosen the Gordian knot, he merely cut it in two; no matter, the oracle has been fulfilled.[12] Since his philosophy speaks of matters which the founder of the Christian religion never really cleared up himself (although the New Testament, understood correctly and purged of its human institutions, does contain hints of pure theoretical and practical reason), Herr Kant is thus a Christian such as few philosophers before him, and his pure teachings will one day, after they have been transferred from books to real life, strengthen and invigorate mankind and provide a basis on which it can build. Nevertheless for us lawyers, gentlemen, it would not be the most comforting thing if these Christian teachings were to become the order of the day, for if the Kantian and assorted other Sermons on the Mount were to descend into the valley of everyday life, things would begin to look very bad for us. Aside from the so-called "external practice of the Christian faith,"[13] the Founder of the Christian religion directed his attention chiefly at us lawyers,[14] and without doubt we will be the first ones over whom that Christian philosophy will exercise its dominion. Be that as it may, I hope, at least, that this will be a blessing for the whole of society and that no other philosophical system will come along like that of which one of the ancients once said: "Not only does it not tolerate any light itself, but it deliberately puts out the eyes of its students"—a statement which, just between you and me, people are all too often able to make about jurisprudence and justice as well. Many laws make for many judges, and at least three times as many legal advisors; and since many of the laborers in their vineyards have no wish to be left without their penny,[15] so much wrangling, quarreling, and contention, so much ado about Mine and Thine must take place for the sake of the profession that in the end nobody can tell the man from the master. Our courts are like megaphones, which magnify the sound, to be sure, but which render the words incomprehensible in the process. Full barrels do not resound when struck, only empty ones do, and the worthless wheel is always the loudest. Nevertheless, in order to vindicate the honor of the legal lectern, I would like our friends the philosophers—whose ancestors were the Greeks, just as ours were the Romans—to know that they are not writing for us, but for posterity, and that whoever does not rise above his own time is but a mediocre mind. We lawyers, on the other hand, are completely absorbed in keeping up with our own contemporaries. The philosophers, moreover, appeal only too often from the court of reason to that of the imagination, and only later do they submit the review of the case to the court of common sense (the court of appeals could also be called the court of the hypotheses, that of the review, the court of the proof). Thus, by the time the case reaches this court of common sense, which one might also designate as the people's court, it has already taken on the guise of a *res judicata*.[16] We lawyers, however, have a code of laws to lay our heads on, a code of laws on which the judges in all three courts of appeal likewise repose and, when the severity of the code is diminished by the soft pillow of interpretation, often sleep pretty well. The really wise person, by the way, acts as if he only sees himself (according to the well-known proverb "know thyself"![17]), while in fact observing and studying the actions of others and, if necessary, the whole of humanity. Whoever is but worldly-wise, on the other hand, acts as if he is concerned with others and only looks out for himself. To put it another way, wisdom is the gunpowder, and learning merely the shot; the eyes receive their credentials from our understanding, the nose from our will. At any rate, these random thoughts, like all random occurrences beyond our power to control, ought not be allowed to distract us from the legitimate issues we have been called to discuss. So—easy come, easy go!

Those few young people at our institutions of higher learning whose activity is more than mere heat lightning know full well what they simply need to memorize and what they are required to reflect upon more deeply. They learn thoughts, but they don't learn to think; they learn philosophy, but not how to philosophize; they learn laws, but not justice. Thus, since the day is pleasant and no storm clouds are visible, let me repeat the request I have made so often in the past: namely, that my lectures not be viewed as a paradigm for making judicial judgments in general, but rather as an inducement to pass judgment merely on the ideas of our respected author and on me. It will not be my aim to introduce any general standard of measurement; each should use his own instead. I must say at this point, however, that for the first three hours I will be watching my listeners carefully and am confident that I will be able to assess their intellectual orientation quite quickly and determine whether any of these saplings will be able to survive in the orchard of jurisprudence or not. Right now, all of you are listening to my request and taking notes on everything I say; however, a great mind will write everything on a small piece of paper, a mediocre one on a quarto sheet, whereas a dull-witted fellow will fill an entire folio leaf—a practice I would not like to see carried over into our chambers of law for anything in the world.

We think that the writing we do has more significance than that of other honorable and learned people—but where is the legal document in which a person cannot find whatever he wants, or which, like an empty room, does not permit itself to be furnished with objects both useful *and* decorative? By this means any law, equipped with some splendid interpretative "furniture," becomes like putty in our hands, and it would hardly betray much talent for the profession of lawyer or judge if a person were not able to summarize the entire law for good or ill on a single sheet of paper and then to find without much ado precisely what he was looking for: the stone of the worldly-wise, alias the Philosopher's Stone, or the rope with which to hang the thief. A law which has been written down is of great significance to us lawyers, and on the whole we have almost come to view our fondness for writing as a fundamental principle. Thus the French, who—*quod bene notandum* [18]—prefer their intellectual capital in the form of ready money, have done a commendable thing in limiting this propensity for writing to their official legal proceedings, and in fact it was the English who first provided the example in this regard. Now if only a propensity for talking doesn't begin to creep in and become a greater evil than the one it replaced!

A certain kind of preliminary judgment in matters seems such a natural thing for mankind that it would perhaps be useful to reflect a bit further on the subject. This preliminary judgment is tantamount to the plan according to which the final judgment will run—one could call it the interlocutory decree upon which the final pronouncement will be based. This preliminary judgment carries with it no sentence or punishment; but among us men, for example, is not our first bow, the cut of our hair, and our clothing the preface to the person? And judge for yourself—is not a good book with a bad Preface, assuming both book and Preface are by the same author, a very rare thing? We tend to forget the soonest what we have perceived most clearly from the beginning. To remember something is a matter of wounding the memory; to flaunt one's knowledge of facts is thus to display one's scars. There is, however, as great a difference between a person who has forgotten a matter he once knew and one who never knew it as between a learned man and an unlearned one. In this respect there are resurrections from the dead to be observed daily, and often what is sown in dishonor is raised in glory, and what is sown in weakness is raised in power.[19]

Now, concerning the main point and present topic of my lecture—well, we are still at the wedding ceremony. For when during the course of my tenure the lectures I had been giving on the Tenth, or equivalent Title of the First Book of our Institutions[20] began to earn me much applause, I took it upon myself at this traditional sign of approval to pose various additional questions regarding the subject—questions which our beloved author, whom I have guided through frequent detours onto my own path, would never have thought of even in a fit of inspiration. The institution of matrimony bears the designation "holy" and thus possesses the authority to challenge the competency of the court with respect to the latter's objectivity. Nonetheless, *turpe est jure consulto sine lege loqui* ("Whoever would preach must have a text").[21] Moreover, a legal scholar expresses himself best when he speaks like a law book. Thus, in order to couple topics together as much as possible in this lecture, I will introduce two at once: "Whoever has taken a vow of obedience must not possess anything of his own," and "If two masters command, the greater one must be obeyed." As you know, concerning this Title I have posed fifty questions, which correspond in number to the fifty books of the Justinian Decisions. But you also know that with respect to the forty-eight already dealt with I have walked in the day and not avoided that way which is called righteous;[22] or, to put it differently, I have not let the escort which accompanies the Title out of my sight.

The Lord High Chancellor of Prussia, Von Carmer, once inspired Frederick the Great—a man who could be called "The King" in the same sense that the ancient world called Rome "The City"—to bring everything, whether large or small, under a central authority, and it was the world-famous royal decree of 14 April 1780 which established this center of all centers.[23] I freely admit, however, that if I were to build on this foundation my lectures and the very subject itself would take on a very sorry aspect, if not come to a singularly unfortunate end. We would become hopelessly lost in such a plan and never find our way back home again. In any case, the legislation which eventually came about was not as unfortunate as the royal decree had led us to fear, and although the ensuing peace is not to be completely trusted, we are, thank the Lord, still what we were. And a present-day lawyer, especially when he is far removed from Jove and his *fulmine*,[24] wearing a Roman cloak with canonically worked buttons, a German vest, a pair of breeches bearing the stamp of his native state, who has had his shoes and stockings made in his home town and whose hat, finally, was fashioned in the countryside—such a lawyer, who is everything to everybody, can and must in a situation like this strive to distinguish between Christians, natural religionists, state religionists, and whatever else they are called, since most of them end in "-ian" or "-ist" anyway; and it is precisely this which I am willing to undertake with respect to the forty-ninth question, namely the one that follows the forty-eighth and deals with the purpose of marriage.

What, then, is the purpose of marriage? In order to take up this question in an orderly manner, I would like once again to introduce a second, related question and begin by examining in appropriate detail the question as to what *is not* the purpose of marriage, and then to discuss what it *is*.

If we consider what is not the purpose of marriage, then I would begin by admitting that man, as the clergy are wont to describe him, is "abandoned unto himself"; or, as the lawyers say, he is in a "natural condition." I do not know what expression physicians use, but they might well say that man is "in the keeping of Nature," for Nature can but do her best in every case, and most especially in ours. We lawyers are *scribes*; the doctors *prescribe*, but more often in the sense of *scribble* or *scrabble*. Nonetheless, one ought not to carry one's torch against the wind if it is not to go out, and whoever cannot judge himself will not be much changed by the judgment of others. Yet I am not here to talk about our friends the physicians, but about the non-purpose of marriage, and I admit gladly and freely that the begetting and raising of children is and remains an important function of marriage and that, if one of the parties is unfit for procreation or, what is more, unfit to raise children, the marriage can begin to assume a very melancholy appearance. Unfitness—and you gentlemen know this as well as my own humble self—is grounds for divorce even today. But this word only means—and rightfully so—unfitness as regards one's conjugal duties, and, all things considered, it would be good if we did not set the limits any farther and cause the fig tree to wither because there is nothing on it except leaves.[25]

Voltaire, gentlemen, was the greatest master of irony, jest, and satire, and the witty king Frederick the Great never tired of admiring Voltaire's wit in his conversation and writings—and yet Voltaire was never able to write a successful comedy. He could describe, but not personify; and what he once told someone who wanted to travel to Italy applied to him as well: *"Vous quittez les hommes pour les tableaux."*[26] Thus there exist wonderful young men who are much loved among the women and yet cannot become fathers; and on the side of the ladies there are also sweet and charming young women who are as little suited to be mothers as Voltaire to write comedies.

To add a footnote to the above: in the words "conjugal duties" are contained the true sense of the idea of a right, for the reason that rights and duties, as is only fitting and proper, cohabit as it were in a lawful marriage and cannot abide a separation from bed and board;[27] what Nature hath joined together, the state cannot put asunder.[28] And as a postscript to this well-intentioned observation let me add the sincere suggestion to take things in marriage no more seriously than I have with this Title of mine, and to put many and various things into that traveling bag which Christian married people must carry with them to their—may God grant it be a blessed—end. What is more common in this vale of tears than to take smoke and sparks for flames, or mere oddity for powerful and vital originality? And in fact it might not be such a bad idea to go with the times and try to reconcile ourselves to an author, for example, who moves us less than he is moved himself; or who, although he cannot make us into sympathetic readers, at least deserves the honor of having revealed himself to us as one who can sympathize; or who, although unable to inspire life in his material, appears to us as one who has been inspired by it himself; or who, without being capable of making the material so lifelike that we ourselves see and feel, nevertheless takes the trouble to attribute his own feelings to us.

On the other hand, if we wanted to throw the baby out with the bath water and go so far as to let a person's fitness or unfitness for raising children be decided by a pedagogical court of some kind—who then would ever pass the test if, for example, one particular pedagogue required that children be taught their A B C's already in their eighth month by rewarding them with candy, while another insisted on raising them in a wild and undisciplined fashion without knowing how to read or write, on letting them play outside both day and night, and on training them in athletic skills to the point where the result is often tantamount to the soul of a dwarf abiding in the marble palace of a king? I will bet you a hundred to one that in this case as in every other, the best solution is to let the tares grow with the wheat until the day of harvest,[29] to avoid choosing methods which have no hope of succeeding, and not to demand partridges as alms.

Should people perhaps simply join together for the sole purpose of producing children?[30] Or, to put it another way, should people attempt to join a woodcarver's guild, for example, and not consider themselves full-fledged members until they have produced a masterpiece, or if that piece should prove unacceptable ("the nose is too small") depart with their *"conditione tua non utar"*[31] in hand? Should they rent before they buy, and if the house is not suitable continue their search, or if it is satisfactory, buy it straightway (*brevi manu*[32])? No, gentlemen—even though such an arrangement could give rise to many a *cause très célèbre* which would be used by that sort of "honorable" judge who knows how to make the simplest story so interesting that one has difficulty, just as with a very complicated novel, keeping track of the main point, and for all the elephantine descriptions finding the thread of a plot in reality no more complex than that of "The Three Billy Goats Gruff"—in a civilized state people cannot simply join together for this purpose. In truth, there exist everywhere good marriages to which no children are born and in which no children are raised.

But, you might say, should not marriage at least be recommended—depending upon the circumstances, of course—as an effective remedy for temptations of a certain sort, since we read in the Holy Scriptures that it is "better to marry than to burn"?[33] Wrong again, gentlemen, for the reason that whatever serves as a means should be prevented from becoming an end in itself. I do not deny, however, that there would be many who would declare themselves both for and against this proposal, and in a situation where two clever debaters were arguing the point an objective third party would derive about as much insight into the matter as from listening to two thieves fight over their booty. Yet certain points of honor can at times come up which academicians especially are not capable of thrashing out peacefully, and although the Prussian Court of Honor is presently attempting—more well-intentioned than effectively—to abolish the duel as a means of settling such arguments, I would gladly confess that my own opinion has been confirmed by more than one academic duel as well.

As is my custom, I intend merely to give you five barley loaves and two small fishes concerning this matter; may you thus receive them with thanksgiving and fill many baskets over and above that which will be eaten.[34] Euripides married for the sake of chastity, and in addition there are many who become eunuchs through marriage. Yet we seem to be concerned here only with the satisfaction of an instinctual need, while the matter of actual procreation lies on the distant horizon. At any rate, however, whoever imagines he is truly creating a child is not taking into consideration the fact that man is made up of both body and soul. Just because we are not preaching does not mean that we have no need to conduct ourselves in a dignified and reverent manner in church. If it were really possible for a human being to be cobbled together in an hour of drunken pleasure, then it would in truth hardly be worthwhile later on to take much trouble with him or to go through heaven and hell while raising him. In the creation of human beings we are dealing with natural mysteries of the very highest order which unquestionably have something of the divine about them. The marriage bed is an Adytum and married couples Mystagogues;[35] it is not without good reason that we draw the curtain before them. My friends, just count the number of male and female babies, for example—what do you think would happen if only male or only female babies were born?

Gentlemen, I believe you understand pretty well what I am driving at and will certainly be able to find the thread which binds all these ideas together, even though I am only providing mere indications and outlines so as not to detract from your opportunity to consider them at leisure. If you felt inclined, by the way, to undertake an Argonaut's crusade after the Golden Fleece in one of Mongolfier's balloons[36]—an invention Franklin was so good as to describe as a still unmannerly child—my humble advice to you would be to leave your

Muschenbroeks, Hallers, and Blumenbachs[37] at home and seek out better pilots. There are things between heaven and earth which we can no more imagine than our parents did electricity, a novel phenomenon by means of which some of the old sleight-of-hand artists sooner set their tongues to wagging than satisfied their curiosity. "Could that not be the spark of life?" they thought. But—*manum de tabula!*[38]

A human being who merely follows his instinctual drives puts himself below the level of the animals, for they have no other law and nothing to guide them; but we, whom God has given understanding and free will, are to have dominion not only over all other living things,[39] but also over ourselves. Those who can rule themselves are the real born rulers. Whoever is intolerant in marital matters denies not only his own body the comforts of hearth and home, but his immortal soul as well; only in the world of fairy tales can we always be a winner and never draw a blank in the lottery of life. And to deny ourselves something just so that it will bring us all the more pleasure later on is nothing more than rationalized Epicureanism!

That, then, would be a simple and succinct answer to the first question I posed: namely, that as to what is *not* the purpose of marriage. I have couched my *arsin*, my negation, in philosophical terms, and one thing we would have to grant the philosophers is that when they go about proving what a particular thing is not, they never leave the matter at mere empty negation, for otherwise such a definition might tempt us to define philosophy itself as a thorough comprehension of everything we do not know. It is not necessary to call to mind here the fact that one cannot prove a negative thing, or that infinitely more can be said about something that is not than something that is. Even in everyday life you will observe that people are much more eloquent when saying "No" than when they say "Yes." But while I would like to grant paternal permission at this point for everyone to say what he has in mind and on his heart about this matter or anything else, I am afraid the time would be too short for such an undertaking. Thus I will now turn to the second part, or the second half, of my lecture and ask: what is, then, the purpose of marriage? Love is blind by nature, good fortune resides with Providence, and mankind has made justice blind. I plan to make no other use of this sad truth, however, than to leave a great deal of material from this section in the dark as well, for too much light tends to be disastrous in matters of love. To be blind does not mean, if we are speaking of love, good fortune, and justice, that one is stone-blind, but merely that one has weak eyes. In this regard attempts have already been made to remove the blindfold from justice entirely and grant her ocular freedom[40]—but is it not too early for that? I would almost suggest giving her gloves into the bargain. In any case, and in a word: the purpose of marriage seems to me to be to provide *mutual support* for the partners. Seems to me? Parenthetically I would note that I do not take everything I believe for certain, and that I use the word "certain" to refer to personal judgments and "true" when referring to matters of a general nature. To be certain about something could be compared to buying *contant*, that is, with cash, and to believe something to making a purchase on credit. What scholars are certain of could be written on half a sheet of paper; what they believe could not be borne by an entire caravan of camels. I have kept this legal expression "camel's freight" (*multorum camelorum onus*) in order to avoid referring to a certain other animal.[41] This expression "mutual support" can be interpreted just as narrowly or broadly as that of the "closest possible intertwining of two lives," the so-called *arctissimum vitae commercium*, and can naturally also refer to the sharing of bed and board; the marriage vows, however, must be clear regarding this point and should not be treated like those of a certain church of which it is said: "Let whoever is able, keep the vow of chastity, whoever must, the vow of poverty, and whoever fears censure the vow of obedience."[42] Because of the constancy of our own self-love we love change; nevertheless, we must love our neighbors (and our spouse is our nearest neighbor of all) as ourselves.[43]

I know that the philosophers have many reservations about the expression "the closest possible intertwining of two lives" because this notion still has too much of the poetic about it. Perhaps they have a point, for in a certain sense Nature can be viewed as the positive, philosophy and studies related to it as the comparative, and poetry with its trappings as the superlative. But a philosopher who is no poet will have a hard time discovering anything, for poetry is the true algebra, a fact which could be verified simply by examining the great discoveries in the field of philosophy. The poetic mind is brought to an awareness of certain ideas by means of the imagination, and it is the philosopher who then refigures them and provides proofs of their correctness. One significant aid in the discovery and invention of new things is the willingness to try the opposite of what is generally taught and learned. You gentlemen will recall at this point that I once defined taste *in concreto*[44] in terms of reason, and in your recollections, although not all of them are appropriate in this particular case, will likewise not fail to note one fact at least which is very appropriate indeed: namely, that whoever finds the most appropriate expression of an idea, or if I may put it this way, whoever finds the body to fit the soul, deserves to be called a brilliant writer.

I have said "the closest possible intertwining of two lives" and "mutual support." Whoever includes the begetting of children in this, let him do it; whoever assumes other limits to these expressions, let him likewise assume them. For these notions are so full of tolerance that not only all of the "-ists," but also all of the "-ians"—the latter of which are far worse than the former—will be able to exercise their own ideas of conjugality freely. Let us pause for a moment at this word "exercise" and, since we have the honor of being *milites togati*, that is, soldiers in uniform, examine—out of obedience to this command to exercise our ideas and respect for the principles of legal strategy—the difference between the strict observance of natural law and the understanding of this law in the writings of famous legal scholars, although, truth to tell, there is room for many peaceable sheep in the same pen. According to the strict interpretation of natural law, if God so wills it, then everything and anything is permitted providing it does not injure or dishonor those who have bound themselves together or a third party. As far as the gratification of instinctual drives is concerned, that is the end of the matter. Now of course there are people of refinement who condescend to call it—and rightly so—the lowest rung on the ladder to perfection when others choose to understand by the words "the end of the matter" merely the gratification of that one particular instinctual drive *quaestionis*,[45] although it is rather difficult to see how those standing on the supposed higher rungs qualify as great beacons of light merely by comparing themselves to those in total darkness below them. Thus, natural law, as understood by its great teachers, exists *in arctissimo commercio* (that is, is most closely intertwined) with the teaching of morality and has for its goal the greater perfection and commonweal of the human race, and this particular interpretation of natural law consequently requires an even more difficult examination of all candidates for marriage. Finally, then, the constitution of the state places upon the head of this beloved and belauded institution of marriage a double crown of limitations by viewing human beings not merely as citizens, but as *Christians* as well. Here I have come to the point, however, where I can no longer simply stroll, or go somewhere merely for the sake of going; now I must begin to point out the way. I can no longer merely sow, but must reap and gather my harvest into barns.

Marriage stands under the protection of the law and is an exclusive and lifelong union whereby certain rights and responsibilities are introduced into the relationship between the two partners and any children which might be born of their union. You will remember, gentlemen, what I have given you in the way of random thoughts regarding a "legal definition" of marriage, namely that based on Roman law, according to which marriage is defined as the legal binding of a male and a female into an association which is both exclusive and as intimate as possible—the Romans used the phrase *legitima conjunctio maris et foeminae individuam vitae consuetudinem continens*—and this definition remains still in such close agreement with my own that it is a pleasure to read. Within the idea of an association which is both exclusive and as intimate as possible, the begetting of children burns, as it were, with a bright fire; and what is the need of a special reference to this important purpose of marriage in particular, since it is a well known legal principle with us that husband and wife are one flesh,[46] and that men and women do not ogle each other merely for the sake of the Lord's Prayer? This is the reason, moreover, why even Heineccius[47] cannot restrain himself from calling marriage, in spite of the serious legal implications involved in sequestering women's property, one of the most pleasant forms of trusteeship there are (*bellissima sequestrationis species*[48]), although this subject obviously still remains a very touchy one. In order to forestall adolescent seductions and the attendant decline in morality, the leader of the Israelites, Moses, forbade marriage between persons who, according to an old custom among his people, were permitted to see each other unveiled, and thus between parents, children, sisters and brothers, step-parents, and parents-in-law along with their children; likewise a man was not to marry his brother's widow, if this brother had not died without children;[49] and it is not worth the trouble, gentlemen, to comment further on a matter of which you are fully convinced yourselves.

According to Plato the wise, love is nothing other than the wish for the most intimate association with the object of one's affection;[50] and in fact not only Her Supreme Highness, Nature herself, but also German and canonical law, the Council of Trent, the Augsburg Confession,[51] and the law of the Protestant Church derived from it are of one heart and one soul with Roman law in this regard, and my *arctissumum vitae commercium* is but another bird of the same feather. As soon as a couple is married, it should depend on them just how they wish to determine the limits within their marriage. Moreover, they must also be at liberty to make changes during the course of time, for wisdom comes with maturity. And with time and maturity, some marriages will develop into marriages of the body, and others into marriages of the soul, whereby either one of these, as well as the union of both (double knots are stronger than single ones) constitutes a proper marriage. And even if in other cases people might prefer to see the limits of this highly acclaimed notion of mutual support sooner circumscribed than extended, Christian marriage partners, at least, would have nothing against helping each other—and not merely because they are bound by oath to do so—to satisfy a physical drive which in fact often tends to irritate more than really trouble us.[52] I once made it quite obvious in a *responsum juris*[53] that eunuchs can marry like everyone else; and while I do not quite believe that any of my listeners would so "bring into captivity" his own flesh[54] for the sake of justice, as Origen[55] did for the sake of piety, nevertheless I would now like to make a brief but concentrated extract from this *responsum* of mine, if not in the interest of making an original contribution to the study of jurisprudence, then at least to fill up the remainder of the lecture hour.

In the antechamber of our *responsum*, or legal opinion, constructed as it is according to the most pleasing proportions, the democratic motto "Many eyes see more than a single one" has been granted an honor it does not deserve, for five hundred weak eyes cannot see as well as one pair of healthy ones, and if one really wishes to see things clearly it is probably better even to close one of *them*. In the antechamber, however, we do not usually examine things so carefully.

Already three theological faculties have compiled a massive treatise in the defense of our friend Origen, and although a fourth faculty, hostile but equally honorable, later inflicted some damage on this imposing structure, all we need to do at this point is hang up the tapestries once again, repair the battered roof, and brick up several of the fireplaces to prevent them from causing a draft. The theologians, by the way, always have made use of tapestries, while the lawyers prefer to whitewash their own learned edifices. It was among these three faculties that we counted the most eyes, because three theological faculties in combination with a legal faculty such as ours would be capable of seeing more than four theological faculties alone. An example of this will be given below.

In the main chamber of our legal opinion I examined the purpose of marriage, and I can omit this at present, since you gentlemen are now aware of my impartial opinion already. The example I have in mind has to do with a general who was obliged, because of an unfortunate injury he had received in battle, to seek a legal opinion of the kind we are discussing. His bride was a very reasonable woman who made no secret of the year of her birth and who on the day she received her proposal had just turned forty-seven years "young," as we say. For the purposes of the test case she was designated as "Fräulein X" and he as "Herr Z," although neither one wanted any more from the whole matter than to enjoy the company of and fret over the other, and, since they were both related, to render a distant cousin, who had been fortunate to avoid the necessity for such a *responsum*, and had been married since his seventeenth year and done nothing more since that time than to reside in the country and tend to his bees, as rich in goods and property as he had been in children. (A note in passing: if the founder of a certain society of ill repute[56] had sought, like our trusty general here, a *responsum* in the form of a papal bull for his spiritual family, then without a doubt every priest would now be the husband of a wife and be grazing his flock not among the thorns and thistles of Scholasticism, or in forests of symbols, but in the free and open meadows of the gospel.) I raised the question as to what we would do if fifty such "X's" and as many "Z's" would request a similar judgment. But this objection seemed sooner to be transformed into another reason for accepting the couple's petition. "If they all pay their own postage on the petitions, then there is no problem."—"But the state loses fifty healthy "X's"!—"And gains fifty cousins thereby."—"Whatever you say, gentlemen." While we were thus breaking lances with each other, another of those present, whose powers of reason either go up in smoke or boil away when he becomes angry, declared those canonical scruples to be fallacious which forbid anyone from entering the priesthood whose case was similar to that of General Z. To that I replied quite casually, "What kind of a vow of chastity would that be?"

"He that is wounded in the stones," I continued, in order to take the offensive, "or hath his privy member cut off, shall not enter into the congregation of the Lord."[57] Only healthy animals could be sacrificed in the Old Testament,[58] and do we cut off the hands of those who serve the Church to keep them from stealing from the Poor Box? I realize that there are hardly any Origins to be found among our own clergymen—still, nothing in the world would make me want to have one of them as my father confessor either. This brought us to the subject of Dr. Martin Luther, and it was our unanimous opinion that he had done well to initiate the priesthood into the secrets of marriage; it was only the fact that he himself chose as well to go this way of all flesh that caused a bit of a stir. I then jumped up and said: "My highly esteemed colleagues, we can certainly open the doors, but let's not tear them from their hinges. If I knew that sooner or later one of you would have need of such a *responsum*, I would swear upon my honor that I would forbid myself any share of the payment received for such a judgment, and would declare myself willing to do without my easy chair as well as the new tablecloth which was to decorate our conference table and be paid for from the ten percent of our salaries we have been laying aside for so long."—"But while his son is still in the cradle and in order to make life easier for him, shouldn't a father perhaps act upon his parental authority and . . .?"—"No, just as little as he should take his son's life when he is still in the cradle."

In the final reply to the parties concerned—itself not devoid of much fundamental wisdom—the very subtlest distinctions were drawn between moral and physical eunuchs, between spados[59] and eunuchs, and between those who were made eunuchs of men and those who have made themselves eunuchs for the kingdom of heaven's sake.[60] We were so good as not to classify Herr Z himself, and decided as it were to look the other way in order to circumvent the opinion of the legal scholars, who have chosen to permit the marriage of spados under certain circumstances and forbid it among castrati under any and all conditions. The keystone of our argument was that since Fräulein X was completely aware of the conditions surrounding the agreement into which she was about to enter, and that she wished to marry not out of carnal lust, but merely for the sake of her cousin's well being, the *Traditio* ought to be considered as *symbolica*[61] and, since the letter of petition had been submitted with the postage prepaid, it could be decided in all good conscience to grant their request to marry—although not share the marriage bed, which had to be kept holy. Nevertheless, for their sake and that of others, the situation of the two was to be kept a secret until the Day of Judgment.

In the preface to their *responsum*, our friends the theologians had viewed everything in the brilliant snow-light of reason and, almost as if all three faculties had received confession from one another, had declared the evil of love, for which St. Francis once utilized the snow-bath as a remedy, as the cause of such petitions and thus fashioned their *responsum* accordingly. But we were of the opinion that where no cradle is possible the marriage bed ought not to be permitted either, whereby we based our appeal only on the aforementioned definitions regarding the notions of mutual support in everyday affairs and the closest possible intertwining of two lives in drawing the legal limits of our description of the purpose of marriage and giving our blessing to the splendid statement contained in I Corinthians 7:29: "they that have wives [should] be as though they had none." An emergency rudder is a means by which one replaces as best as one can a rudder or tiller lost to the sea.

The theologians were talking about Origen, we lawyers in fact about Abélard,[62] although to be honest both of them were rather unexpected guests at this gathering; they also disputed as to whether the prophet Daniel was a eunuch,[63] and as the final Amen to their investigation drew on faithful Abraham, unto whom God was able to raise up children out of stones,[64] as well as on the psalm according to which God, if he so pleased, could "give children even to those living alone"[65]—children who in the natural course of things might well later be able to wish their newly-wed parents a pleasant and peaceful night of rest.

We for our part, in order to erect a firewall against such arguments and in deference to the aforementioned cousin, wished him a good harvest as an indemnification *vis-à-vis* the state, even though we were compelled to maintain in the end that we would have come to an agreement sooner regarding the *responsum* if Z had requested permission to marry only with intent of legitimizing any children he might have had by Fräulein X *before* the war.

Since we are not in the habit of issuing a *responsum* without a beard, that is, without footnotes, we referred further to the Justinian Codex, Books 4 and 5, Chapter X, entitled *De frigidis et maleficat,* adding here and there offscourings in the form of citations in the Latin and following all the while in the footsteps of canon law, and made Z and X into brother and sister by allowing the sharing of board but not of bed, thus concluding with all dispatch our disputation and wishing each other a pleasant dinner.

If the very instructive Prussian General Lawbook had been in effect at that time,[66] the second part of the first Title regarding marriage would have done us no small service, in that although section 1 declares the main purpose of marriage to be the begetting and raising of children, section 2 comes to the following conclusion regarding *general* cases of the same nature: "A valid marriage can also be contracted for the purpose of mutual support alone." It really is too bad, though, that a single paragraph of this sort can behave so presumptuously and put an unblessed end to every further *responsum* down to the Day of Judgment—*responsa* which, as has been said, have in the State of Prussia already been on the way out for some time. Just between you and me: you will have noticed more than once from my review of the general *responsa* that I did not let the purpose of marriage go for as cheap a price in my debates with the theological faculties as I have here in the auditorium, where *Pater inter liberos* (the father among his children) is giving testimony.

But to come finally to a conclusion in this *responsum*, let me say that I consider everything to depend on the circumstances, and thus even if a eunuch wished to marry he could do so with impunity.[67] If a fortress capitulates, then it must not be taken by storm; if, however, nothing has been agreed upon before the wedding, then marriage and the precious duty which is bound up with it[68] would have to be interpreted in our own unhappy times as privileges in the narrow, rather than the broad, sense of the term.[69] This much is certain: that under these circumstances physicians would be more useful in marital contracts than lawyers; in the meantime, let us abide by the words "live and let live"—we will remain scribes and let the physicians continue with their prescribing and scribbling. Moreover, since when it comes to the last will and testament of these good doctors it is well known that one hand washes the other, then these required consultations certainly cannot do them any harm, but in fact will prove beneficial to any who know how to turn the system to advantage. Our own secrets were betrayed and bewrayed long ago when Caius Flavius and Sextus Aelius made the formalities of our court proceedings public,[70] and we consider merely that which contributes to our own peace of mind when we make friends for ourselves by means of the mammon of unrighteousness.[71] It seems that nowadays anybody who is involved in a legal dispute considers himself clever enough to take over the roles of prosecuting attorney and judge himself, and when he is forced during the natural course of legal proceedings to yield the case to others his own troubles are doubled: he apes the actions of the lawyers like children playing at soldiers, blathers constantly about the case, searches everywhere for new evidence, and generally winds up leading himself and everybody else on a wild goose chase.

You will probably be able to understand the entire matter of marriage somewhat better, gentlemen, if we take some examples from the consensual contract of buying and selling goods. In fact, people really ought to seek our services more often in matters of marriage in the sense that marriage is a first cousin to the concept of buying and selling and that the ancients *bought* their wives when they married, although it remains somewhat *in dubio* whether this particular contract had the advantage of being adhered to any more than others. The "act of recession" of the purchase (*actio redhibitoria*) can be invoked by the buyer against the seller when the latter sells a certain thing as perfect and without defect and a hidden defect is nonetheless discovered at a later time. The article is then returned and the buyer receives his money back. The *actio quanti minoris*, or "action for abatement of price," can likewise be invoked by the buyer against the seller who sells defective goods and is then willing to refund money to the seller only equal to the value of the damaged goods, and not the full purchase price. I would ask you not to leave out of consideration the age in which these actions were invoked in marriage contracts, however, if I am going to apply them to an analysis of the matter at hand. To be perfectly honest, though, what I would really like to see is a law which sets the statute of limitations on all our complaints at six months, so that we do not let the sun go down on our wrath.[72] The public would thereby have fewer legal disputes, the lawyers less money to lose at cards, and every other legal wolf in sheep's clothing (*vultur togatus*) fewer opportunities to deceive people.

The fiftieth and last question,[73] which I dealt with many years ago in as boring a fashion as the forty-ninth, now appears to me so critical and in such a different light that—since I have neither the strength nor weakness to speak in public about matters which frighten me in the dark, or to deny three times by day what I believed and feared the night before[74]—a certain unerring feeling on the one hand and my own fixed principles on the other have led me to answer this question without ever asking it, and in fact this simple method can often be so effective that the whole matter gains the appearance of having come up by chance and completely unintentionally. And I think this soft melody is much better suited to soothing the heart and mind, don't you? An ideal which requires a commentary is like wine mixed with water—it loses half its effect. The law of Lycurgus[75] that married couples at Lacedaemon should submit to each other's requests without question and meet only in secret in order to avoid the shame of being seen together—this law has both a psychological and an aesthetic application. If it is advisable to leave undrawn that curtain which even Nature herself has hung before the fountainhead of human morality; and if we would do well to watch an opera without being too inquisitive about the machinery which makes it all come about, and to applaud the actors and actresses without following them backstage or inquiring into their private lives because in each case the charm and power of attraction would be lost—then in addition to these metaphysical veils it follows that Nature has seen fit to place all the more deliberately a veil of over the physical realm as well. And what a noble veil it is! In the hope that the mere glimmer of a thought can have greater effect at this point than the bright noonday sun, I shall speak in proverbs here as well and not say exactly what I mean.

If due to unfortunate circumstances the farmer's first seeding fails to germinate, then he is obliged to rework his field and sow once again; and if the present and the future were not such an unequally matched couple that whenever it comes to a conflict of interest the present always emerges victorious, then husbands and wives would limit themselves even more than at present in their mutual demands on each other. But a stronger and more immediate sensation suppresses a weaker one; even if we were to investigate this assertion by taking examples from all the five senses we would still find it to be true in every case. "The five senses considered together" is a nice legal phrase and designates a kind of committee of five persons, none of whom presides over the others.

Whoever is hungry, eats; whoever is tired, sleeps; and only the common man feels, if not uniquely, then at least more strongly than the rest of us, the joy of knowing that every seven days there is a day of rest. There exist, on the other hand, certain fashionable types who always rest—except on Sunday, that is. Pleasure is the sweat of their brow,[76] and too much pleasure renders them insensitive to further pleasure. When they are annoyed and someone asks them why, they think in their hearts what that donna once said: *"Que voulez vous que je dise? Je n'aime pas les plaisirs innocens."*[77] Am I now beginning to answer before being asked myself? Beginning? I am nearly finished, and was just about to ask you to take to heart the comforting thought that works of love and works of necessity are both permitted on Sunday.

According to the Talmud, it was required of the scholar to recall his wedding-night vividly by re-celebrating it occasionally—at least once every two or three years. Academic teachers deserve the name *scholar* more than others not only in the sense that they are learned themselves, but also in that they make *others* learned as well, and in

125

comparison to the insignificant honoraria they get from their students, like the moon compared to the earth, give fourteen times more light than they receive. The gifts of an ICti Tiraquelli, who brought forth into the world every year both a spiritual and a bodily heir,[78] are not possessed by everyone, and whoever has them certainly does not need the encouragement of the Talmud. The curious thing about this is that, while this noble man pursued his handiwork a full thirty years (the favorite tenure of a lawyer), nobody has been able to determine which of these sixty Tiraquellian children had the advantage—those of the body or those of the soul. And what is even more remarkable, despite such unusually abundant physical and spiritual blessings, to my knowledge nothing of either of these two realms has lasted down to the present, although—let it be noted—the written word which has come into the world can never be written out again. Whoever writes, remains.

Just one more word concerning the wives of scholars, and I will put you out of your misery. This comes straight from the heart, and should go straight to the heart as well! And if you are beginning to think that this hour has gone on too long, pray keep in mind what is sometimes said of a long mile—that lovers must have measured it out.

Xanthippe[79] is generally considered to be the spiritual mother of all the wives of scholars, but if you feel she is perhaps undeserving of the pillory to which she has been sentenced, then I could recommend even more enthusiastically Hipparchia, the wife of His Serenity and Respectability the *Professoris philosophiae* Crates of Thebes,[80] who contrary to, and in spite of the last will of her Cynic philosopher bridegroom, remained faithful to him in memory, and when times got bad viewed the public streets through the glasses of his philosophy as a marriage bed.

While we are on the subject of the wives of scholars and learned men it will be worth our while, I think, to erect a monument to our own Leibniz, however far he might be removed from the aforementioned ICti Tiraquelli. When he first attempted to pursue his doctorate in Leipzig, he was (to the comfort of everyone facing a similar fate) rejected as a candidate. My source for this information, whom anyone is free to consult, is Louis de Jaucourt, who bases what he says on Fontenelle,[81] who himself places the guilt directly on the wife of the Dean of the law faculty. The twenty-year-old Leibniz seemed too young to the good lady (a rare occurrence!); nothing more or less than Leibniz's age persuaded this know-it-all faculty wife and her husband, who doubtless had washed his hands of the matter as quickly as any Pontius Pilate,[82] to cast the first stone,[83] and very possibly the keystone, in condemnation of him. An anecdote worth thinking about. It attains even more lustre if we consider the fact that Leibniz was certainly not dispossessed of his five senses, or even of Buffon's sixth sense[84]—senses which were strong enough to arouse in him an inclination to marry even in his fiftieth year. True, the object of his affections at that particular time did not exactly reject his candidacy as the Leipzig faculty had done many years before; nevertheless, the girl requested more time to think the matter over, perhaps in order to bind Leibniz to herself even more securely, and Leibniz himself—followed her example. What did the fifty-year-old suitor do? He decided to use this as a pretext to extract himself from the entire affair by maintaining that while marriage itself was a good thing, the philosopher and the scholar were required to do nothing more during their entire lives than simply *think* about the matter. Such was the consequence of her appeal for more time. Many scholars by profession who are not perpetual enlargers of their own empire[85] consider marriage in the same way as the common man his daily devotions: not as an impetus to action, but as an action in and of itself. They believe what Plinius[86] wrote to his wife, namely, that "she did not love him for his youth or his education, mere transitory merits, but for his honor." Golden words in silver bowls! Whether many others will have the honor of being equal to him in his belief in himself is a question which one doubtless could answer with less hesitation than my above-mentioned fiftieth, but which may nevertheless remain single, or unanswered, for entirely different reasons. A tried-and-true home remedy in such situations is not to be too curious and fall prey to the spirit of a Sylla, a Pompey, or a Claudius.[87] Let people sing the praises of their dear wives on the streets of the city, but may the husbands never hear of it, and cursed be the third parties who tell them! As in the case of Sylla, a husband can only hear such news from a friend, although the friend himself would do well not to disturb the gentle slumber of the man involved if he does not wish to engender an inward hatred against himself in the face of outward gratitude.

Anybody can take advantage of good fortune; to make use of misfortune, however, is the province of the wise. And who is not aware that sound is intensified to an extraordinary degree in both warm enclosed air and in air which is very cold? People who have learned to philosophize away such trivialities have come even further, and they are greatly aided in this by the circumstance that those who mock the loudest are the ones who unknowingly suffer the same fate. Scholars are in love with themselves; when they look into the mirror of their writings there is not the slightest chance they will forget what they look like. Even Hans Jakob himself was as if by a ghost so frightened and tormented by his own precious image that on account of this poltergeist he often could not tell up from down.[88] A scholar can rarely be brought to clear away the cobwebs (a fitting phrase!) in order to address his own domestic concerns, which are far too inconsequential to chain down a man who hardly occupies much of a place in this world anyway.

I hasten to my conclusion. There are people who are like bulls in a china shop when they ought to tread as softly as angels; who are like thunder and lightning when they should be gentle zephyrs; but we must recognize people by their fruits.[89] From shepherds have come kings; lawgivers have existed who could not read or write; generals, government ministers, or court favorites (who are one and the same thing) have often been brought into the world by means of an exalted: "Let there be!"[90] This is not the case with scholars, who have become what they are on their own. They can never be masters before they were apprentices, except a man be born of water and the spirit![91] Hail to those of you who are as yet unrecognized; hail to those whose generation was not worthy of them and who (as is almost always the case with us lawyers) from *necessity* believe in the powers of the world to come! Lord, strengthen them in their belief in the future!

Finally, may I request that the esteemed members of my audience no longer undertake the expense of providing musical entertainment in the evening for the benefit of my wife?

3

WHY MATRIMONY
IS CALLED HOLY

DR. MARTIN LUTHER says that marriage is a worldly affair and, like clothing, food, house, and possessions, subject to worldly authorities;[1] nevertheless it is a *holy* work. Just as nobody can relinquish his personality even for a time, much less abandon or sell it for a lifetime, so is marriage as well, whereby two persons of the opposite sex dedicate themselves to one another, exchange bodies and breathe their mutual souls into one another, a holy thing; and there is not the slightest doubt that marriage is a sort of spiritual order in which one takes an oath of faithfulness and self-restraint, to which is added in the woman's case an oath not of obedience—for in point of fact this expression goes too far[2]—but of absolute trust, which is to say one that is freely offered and thus even more firmly grounded. Obedience to the law, respect for one another—marriage is a contract based on mutual consent. Wherever the man buys his wife and is able to purchase as many as his pocketbook permits and his appetite desires, there obedience is his due—but the heart of a slave is all he receives. Love was ordained by Nature, marriage by reason; and if we wish to understand a sacrament as an action sanctioned by religious authority, then such a definition certainly applies to marriage. Since reason is first of all too weak to lead mankind itself, and furthermore more inclined to polemics than precepts, so that our desires outwit and deceive it with their rationalizations and doubts, was it not then a

129

well considered solution on Nature's part to provide us so amply with instincts and drives?

If there were no sex drive, the human race would long ago have ceased to exist, and without doubt there would be no marriages if our imagination were not so gracious as to continue to act the role of marriage broker for us. We honor the man who acts according to set principles—but we do not love him. We, and especially the fair sex as a means of honoring their patron saint Nature, wish for him to act according to his inclinations as well, inclinations arising from a specific continual stimulus but which likewise function as a mature and perfected motivating force themselves. Inclination and desire ought to be the visible means of motivation, whereby reason merely grants permission and pronounces its blessing. Inclination, like love, is blind; reason, however, is the optometrist from whom it, and everything else that is blind, receives the use of the eyesight of the soul. Reason is the salt without which no drive, even the sex drive itself, can be savored. Reason is the censor, experience the censor's edict; both can and must lead young men and women onto smooth paths when they enter the realm of love. Even at the commencement of those years called the "age of reflection"—which is often, however, really nothing of the kind in the sense that a sort of eternal fullness of youth replete with scenes of utter merriment hovers before even the most venerable candidate for marriage—censor and censor's edict can and must reveal to these gray-haired children the black book of miscarried marriages, place the mirror before them and leave it to them to decide either to give up their poorly organized plan or, with the permission of the authorities, to make some alteration in the order of things. As long as man can still reflect upon his inclination, can still separate it from himself and distinguish the outward from the inward man,[3] he will stumble to be sure, but not fall, and if he does fall, will not injure himself morally. All our drives taken together could be called the flesh, the outward man; likewise the principles on which we base the judgments of our reason we could call the spirit or the inward man. In this sense, marriage is such a good likeness of man—one could hardly steal a better one from a mirror—that it is in this state that he lives, moves, and has his being.[4] He as well consists of both body and soul and, insofar as it is right and just that we view marriage in the light of both reason and the senses, the inclinations of the flesh must also be justified by the principles on which we base the judgments of our reason. This is the sanctification without which no marriage can be truly happy, even if

130

it appears to be so in those first few weeks we call the honeymoon. The honeymoon is a kind of concubinage; is it not a terrible shame when an engaged couple enters marriage by way of this path?

But there is more. We are born as human beings, and reborn as citizens. One could call the first birth *being*, the second *living*. Thank goodness parents have not only the drives to procreate, but also the drives to bring about the welfare of their children. The children repay them these drives only in a spiritual sense with their thankfulness, which arises as a consequence of later reflection on their upbringing. Animals know only those other animals with which they are directly connected through need, and only as long as this bond lasts—they either feed, or feed upon, others. No other relationship exists among them, and the bond of physical nature extends no further than this; love among animals has reached its limit at this point. In mankind, love between the sexes and among relatives differs from the latter in terms of its capacity to endure and pass from generation to generation, although it does weaken in intensity to the degree that it extends in divergent directions from a central point. Thus animals know and love their young only until they are grown; the attachment of human parents to their children lasts not only as long as they live, it is transmitted to the grandchildren as well. I have stopped with the grandchildren on purpose, since if we go any further the relationships become cooler, perhaps from a feeling of respect for the highest stages of human life. Just ask yourself: would you kiss the hand of your old patriarch Adam? The *Jus canonicum* maintains somewhere that in the first generation it is the fire which is lost, in the second the air, in the third the water, and in the fourth the earth or the earthly part. If this were correct, the great-grandfather could marry his great-granddaughter without committing incest.

Animals very quickly become what they have been from the beginning and will be up to the end of their days; they are no different now than they were when they left Paradise or Noah's ark. Man, however, no longer looks like his former self; what one doesn't know, another does, and what one person cannot do, someone else can. We not only can inherit and bequeath earthly goods, but also spiritual ones; the latter through education, the former by means of that Last Will and Testament which civilized people, in accordance with their hope to live on past their death, hold so dear. Human beings come to maturity later than anything else living on the face of the earth; nevertheless, their powers and talents are so numerous, and moreover so exquisite, that education cannot cease when we are weaned from our mother's milk, and that milk which the Apostle refers to as the "sincere milk of the Word"[5] becomes an absolute necessity as well. Human beings should not only grow in their humanity, but also be educated as citizens of the state and the world. Whenever possible, the human race should gain through each of its members; in fact this can be said to be the goal of the race if it is not to remain a continual chaos, a disorderly horde of wild barbarians. Thus education sanctifies marriage and gives rise, as nothing else can, to virtue of such a high order that merely to behold it is a delight in itself.

Preservation, the theologians say, is the second creation; and nothing is truer than the kingly idea that *mutatis mutandis*[6] one ought to thank one's educator more than one's procreator. The main business of marriage is education, and in this respect marriages are sacred to the state and the world. When a child comes into the world it is nothing—but it can become anything. And what about you, O sacred body politic, do you need a hero, an executioner, a night watchman, a postilion; and you, O sacred soul of the world, do you desire a citizen of the world? Well, nothing is born for you, everything is a matter of education. We say that a nobleman is "born," and it is true that there are virtues which to a certain extent are inherited and merely require a bit of effort before they come to full bloom. Even scholarly learning can in a sense be passed on to one's children and children's children, and in general the apple never falls very far from the tree. Yet in fact things often take just the opposite turn, and many a nobleman has become what he is without having had truly noble parents or having been educated in genuinely noble fashion, but merely by virtue of having spent the requisite amount of time in an aristocratic cradle. Such was not the will of Nature, but of the state—and this latter will prevails. Only in the case of a hereditary monarchy, that is, in states where succession is *jure familiae*[7] hereditary, is the question of birth important for the state, and the ruling house can be proud of its birth whether it is educated or not. But just observe how much effort the greatest rulers expend on the education of their princes. Frederick the Great and Catherine the Great were so great as to stoop down to the little princes who were to become their successors. And since rulers ought to be educated mainly for the world at large and taught self-sacrifice in order that they will live for humanity and not themselves; since it is their duty to carry out what the wisest thinkers before and during their time taught and teach; and since not only the manner in which they conduct, but also express, themselves must bear ripe fruit and not just pretty flowers, there would thus be no greater prospect for posterity than if those who rule would personally hand over to their successors the code by means of which that great book we call the world can be deciphered. May I point out that such examples could prove extremely useful to those in a position of leadership by enabling them to bring to others' attention professions and positions for which they are well suited? Even though nobody ought to be educated according to the talents of his parents but with a view toward to his own particular physical and spiritual potential, does not Nature herself seem to favor a certain kind of family nobility in the same sense that bodily strength and weakness, spiritual health and sickness, are transmitted from generation to generation?

The precepts of religion and philosophy have no effect on us if the ground on which this good seed is to be sowed has not been prepared beforehand. This cultivation is called education. Every farmer must know his field; he cannot sow whatever he wants, but what his soil will grow, and woe to the hand which works at cross purposes with Nature! Education is a creative force in the same sense that poetry is—it does not create the material, but the forms; it does not produce the canvas and the paints, but the picture. The mother "educates" the child until it has seen the world for the first time, and either she or the nursemaid must educate it as long as it is still at the breast. I firmly believe that no one should replace the mother in the nursing process who is not also capable of educating the child. Women were the first educators of the human race. Eve even raised Adam; she helped bring him out of the infirmity of instinct to the use of free will and imparted to him thereby not only a knowledge of Nature, but of morality as well.[8] Does not this hieroglyph show us quite clearly what each mother must be to her child, since Eve too, herself a daughter of Nature, already was able to be this for Adam, the son of Nature?

If the fair sex truly does possess the heavenly privilege of heightening and sweetening human existence, of ennobling our sex and of developing our talents and rendering them useful, yet with regard to her children the mother is still not the only true church—the father, too, is responsible for their education, and not merely, as some would have us believe, that of the sons, but also, and I would like to say chiefly, of the daughters. Whoever has a father and mother must be educated by both of them, and nobody, neither the father nor the mother, can negotiate another father or mother for them in exchange for money or good words. Parents can make this business immeasurably easier on themselves if each of them takes upon himself or herself the division of labor appropriate for that person and then receives the satisfaction which comes with every improvement in the child's knowledge and behavior. Moreover, the mutual affection of the teacher and the pupil takes away at least half the effort. The mother can never be dispensed with in the education of the child; if the state, however, decides to make an exception of the father in this regard, then this is permitted by the highest tribunal of Nature only under the express condition that he nevertheless keep extremely careful watch over matters and be held personally responsible for any negligence and deficiency in their upbringing.

In our day, people have been more concerned about education than previously, and we have done well to begin to talk about this matter and circulate ideas, if only to keep from forgetting the well-nourished body for the impoverished soul. There was a time when people merely switched or caressed, hugged or scolded children and called this variation in treatment "education." But man is not called to the extremes of life, its funerals and marriage celebrations, but to the daily bread of ordinary existence and stability. Moreover, it is not only posterity which will reap benefits from this "chemical experimentation" in education; the advantage has already made itself visible in various places, and it is the particular nature of this affair that advantage either manifests itself *immediately*, or there simply is none. Since we each require a body in order to act, and mankind is born to act, then education demands the application of mouth, heart, word, deed, and truth. We become what we are through education; what we know, we owe to instruction. Each is as different from the other as having and being, and understanding and will are the province of the educator, just as memory is that of the teacher. Living languages are not actually learned, people are born and raised with them as with their mother's milk. Dead languages, on the other hand, are taught. The former languages are spoken, the latter merely read; the latter are called learned tongues, the former mother tongues. It is not right for us to have so discredited the word *"dressieren,"*[9] since it would in fact prove quite useful in providing insight into the underlying meaning of the word "education." In English, this word means "to dress," and could thus be used very nicely to illustrate the mechanical aspect of education; and anyone who lacked this ceremonial dress could quite rightly be addressed with the words: "Friend, how did you come in here?"[10] To be sure, it would be the most wonderful thing in the world if without the slightest effort whatsoever we could keep people spellbound merely by the use of words, or incite others to action merely by moving our lips. But people first learn to speak—that is, speak justly—through their actions. A military officer must himself know how to drill before he can command others on the drill field. There are people of high rank who have little idea what they are saying; to judge by their words, one would think they understood everything—in fact, they understand nothing. Whoever is inexperienced in the world and in their ingenious little deceptions will believe he hears in many of these boasters doers of the word as well, and privately admire them as highly competent and experienced people. "If there were just twelve of these, and beyond these twelve perhaps only seventy more in the entire world, how much further along humanity would be," the neophyte thinks and then proceeds to worship them. Young man, that highly experienced man is no more great than those people are holy who wrestle with God in their prayers, or those who, by dint of their previous exemplary behavior, have been found worthy of the honor of having their names stand on a roll of the martyrs of the Church and of sporting a halo, the greatest emblem of honor ever to be worn on the head of a human being. Your hero is merely prattling; he has no intellect, and his dead tones have lost all connection with truth and power. The babbling of his lips is but a mumbled rosary, a psalm in the mouth of a nun; he never tried to *do* anything in his life, and God preserve us from his experiments, for if he knows not what he is saying, how can he claim to know what he is doing?

Be that as it may, who *can* educate others then? That question is very much like asking who can be saved. "Become like little children"[11] is a maxim which, that awful notion of Original Sin notwithstanding, establishes beyond all shadow of doubt that education is not such a terribly difficult process, that our children are not really in such a bad way, and that everything depends on the method of approaching the child. Education is nothing more than the simple development of the natural powers and talents. True, the clergy maintain that man is merely a pupil undergoing instruction for the *next* world and in *this* world but a pilgrim or a stranger—or, as the bookkeepers call it, a "suspense account."[12] Nevertheless, we are not to become unworthy of the next world as a result of our actions in this world, and thus education should certainly be undertaken with an eye to the affairs of this world too, preparing the child not only to endure evil, but, what is infinitely more difficult, good as well—that is, the child should not be overly sensitive and should learn to enjoy all things through use of the powers of reason. If we raise a child as if it makes no difference which world he is born into, or which world he will live and die in, then we have forgotten that there are seasons and revolutions in the moral world as well, and that everything human remains subject to modification and fluctuation. Sufficient unto the day is the evil and the joy thereof.[13] Whoever teaches the child to command but not also to obey has spoiled him through neglect and has perhaps made a prince, a nobleman, a citizen, or a peasant out of him, but not a human being. Our yoke is not all easy and our burden not light;[14] only through self-restraint, the sweat of our brow, courage, respect for others and their rights, satisfaction with what we have, through renunciation of all those things our fantasy dangles before our eyes as necessities, and, in general, through the judicious enjoyment of pleasure—only through these does life become bearable and man not find the condition of being human to be strange and unfamiliar to him. Would you like more of the same sort of advice *ad hominem*?[15]

Books are merely poor copies of human beings. Even supposing they equalled humans in speaking, when it comes to actions we leave them far behind, and here, we know, is where experience must be our teacher. But in order to keep this extremely punctilious teacher from becoming too strict as it sometimes can, let us make the acquisition of experience easier for the child. Just look how hard he works to be active by constantly moving his hands and feet—how he strives for life! Continue to observe young children and you will soon become convinced that words are but an artifice and that we must not be weaned from Nature, the mother of us all, if she is not to abandon us, ignore us, or hand us over to the judgment of art, which in a certain sense could almost be described as a court of callousness and obduracy.

Has it escaped your notice that children people called *"Wunderkinder"* in their youth only seldom become mature people? They remain children and content themselves with being loved and praised within their circle, knowing something about everything, and nothing about life in general. If at every point of our life we are what we are supposed to be, then we cannot help but become what we are supposed to become. The entire highly acclaimed art of education can thus perhaps be summed up in this rule: arouse the child and the youth to action according to the limitations of their age and powers, and maintain and guide them in this activity, so that when they are grown they will be able to educate themselves. My dear friends, is it not really awfully presumptuous of us when we humans presume to predict the future from the present and a whole life from a couple of minutes? Has the person who is virtuous today been that way all his life? What changes more easily than man, a creature possessing understanding, will and reason—but the body of an animal? I beg of you, do not educate the child with a view to what he will be like as a youth, a man, or an old man, but with a view to the human being as a whole; show him methods by which he can educate himself, reveal to him principles which do not change. In certain cases, leave the child to his own devices at an early age, for soon you will have to be able to let him go his own way anyway, and what a shame it will be if he knows everything in the world but himself! Do not demand positive virtues from the child, but first of all strive to keep his soul pure and uncorrupted by base passions, and positive character traits will be awakened in him by themselves.

When we place the education of girls and boys on the same footing even in the very first years, the most important ones in the child's education, we are showing as little understanding of the creative aspect of education as when we keep them miles apart from each other. As long as the present circumstances remain the same for both sexes, both are required to learn obedience; yet if it is the case that the will of the girl absolutely must be broken, then the desires of the boy must only be impeded. As things stand now, the girl must learn to bear injustices with equanimity, the boy to avenge them, and both girls and boys must be taught to try to improve them. I submit we exaggerate this separation when we divide the children of the two sexes like sheep and goats, since that mental match-maker we know as the imagination is capable of causing all kinds of mischief thereby; I would also submit that both sexes are made up of human beings and that we should not—as if they were somehow not human—separate them from one another as we would melons from cucumbers and pumpkins, merely because in the garden it just so happens that the most delicious types of melons become inedible in later generations when all three are permitted to grow together. Thus man and woman should not resemble each other as one egg does another, but should bring about the harmony of the whole through individual variation.

Lycurgus appears to have derived his legal code, at least, from Mother Nature when he attempted to harden the five senses against a certain allurement which is often only alluring because people conceal it. When shadows are added to a picture, the outlines become clearer; modesty is the most artful deceiver; and through pauses, through monosyllabic words, we achieve our effect more than through exhausting phrases, no matter how pleasing they may sound. A thought broken off in the middle makes people think; a thought carried to its full extent tires them out halfway to the end. We would perhaps know nothing of desire if that so carefully arranged neckerchief did not say to us either (and I'm not sure which): "Thou shalt . . ." or "Thou shalt not covet."[16] I doubt that Lycurgus ever fulfilled his intention completely and permanently by recalling that paradisal innocence in which even a mere fig leaf serves as proof of the Fall of Man.[17] Opportunity makes the thief; habit becomes second nature, and Nature cannot be forced. If even weeds and vegetables are permitted to grow together, why not girls and boys? If we are all members of but a single Church, if we all wish to enter the same heaven someday, then we also have to learn to live together here on earth. Each sex is ennobled, educated, and made complete by the other. Lycurgus also wished to strengthen and invigorate the bodies of the girls through running, wrestling, and javelin throwing so that later on they would have less difficult births and bring stronger children into the world. But then again, what did Lycurgus not want!

Nevertheless, I am not writing a book on education here (although education and marriage are very closely related), and really intended only to pay tribute in this section to the rebirth of mankind I have been talking about—it is my heart which has made me so impassioned. How wonderful it would be if mankind would finally come of age, remove itself from the darkness into the light and then continue to tread the path of light! Even the oldest documents mankind possesses teach us what can result from the briefest period of neglect in the process of education. Just recall how Cain slew his brother Abel. What a sad thing for our poor first parents! I can never think of that story without saying a word of thanks to you, O philanthropic inventor of gunpowder, who, like all inventors, has had to endure so much criticism! Let us fire a salvo in salute to you for teaching us to kill human beings humanely, at least, and with style: we simply produce a cloud of smoke which keeps the murderer from seeing the blood of all the Abels around him and obstructs his view of heaven as well. But whoever can actually see heaven and his brother—and we are all brothers—whoever can then also lay a hand on his brother and defile himself with his brother's blood by committing murder is a savage and a Cain!

One more word in conclusion. It is the custom of the men to let both their valid and invalid reasons be known in high-sounding phrases, and then to let their light shine on the importance of adhering to this principle; in this regard the women, as in other cases as well, tend more to doing than to speaking. Hans Jakob himself, who, if I am not mistaken, has set the tone for the methods of education which seem to prevail in Germany these days, was so incapable of demonstrating the validity of his own theory that he placed his children in a foundling home (what a wonderful Philanthropinum![18]); and since he always got the worst of it with other people's children as well, are we being unfair if we say that he did not know how to educate children and that he betrayed and bartered away his own clever theories?

4

CONCERNING FAITHFULNESS
IN MARRIAGE

℮

Among Men

WHOEVER AMONG MY READERS happens to be a judge and would refuse to accept presents because that would violate your oath of office—do you know that you are committing perjury when you are unfaithful to your wife? Who forced you to enter the cloister of matrimony? Weren't you in the novitiate long enough? And once you did take the vow, why did you then stoop so low? Even if it were not a sin to have a couch to recline on in addition to your marriage bed, it would still be an irresponsible act because it runs contrary to the promise you once made. An honest man is as good as his word. Every contract must be kept holy, just as the freest man renders himself unworthy of the honor of freedom when he fails to be the slave of the oath he has taken. A legal partnership carries with it the right to sue one's partners and demand what is rightfully one's own. You belong rightfully to your wife, and if it is difficult for you to see flowers without picking them, to find beautiful children charming without loving them, then move into a house without a garden and try to establish such a close relationship between your heart and your head that this bond can neither be loosed nor severed. When she marries, a young woman gives her beauty as a sort of lifetime annuity, and how irresponsible it would be to enter into a contract of this kind (*contractum vitalitium*[1]) and then let the poor child starve afterwards! How harsh to cheat a woman out of the honor of her charms and every single thing in which she was permitted to—and did—take pride! I suppose it would help your case a bit if your wife herself had provided you with a passport for these little "side trips" of yours, or if she had even played the role of procuress in these debaucheries—but do you really think you could even justify yourself by that?

In such cases the state acts as intermediary, for marriage exists because of the state—or for the sake of the state. If a person fences off his property it is to signify that he makes no claim to anything outside his fences; and if it really is true that just as many girls are born as boys, then it would be nothing less than murder and robbery not to make do with but a single wife. But if it is in fact the case that more boys are born than girls, then you have good cause to thank heaven that you have a wife, and the European states have cause to protect rights within marriage in every way possible, and in this case to forbid extramarital affairs just as they do lotteries sponsored by other countries. People are the best product that the state can produce, and they are also the axle around which everything in the state revolves. The population of a state serves as a fortress against its neighbors and as an ammunition depot for its citizens, and no soil is so poor that it cannot nourish human beings. I said "human beings," because even if their hands can accomplish nothing they still have something which will bear fruit in the stoniest of soils, namely reason. The patron saint of marriage in the Protestant Church, the chosen vessel, allowed Landgrave Philip of Hessia to take a second wife, and those who differ with me and consider Melanchthon as rather less than a "chosen vessel" do an injustice to this pious Israelite, in whom there is no guile![2] In itself, the matter is not all that scandalous, although I would like to know who gave these men of the cloth I am referring to the power to decide in such cases, and by means of the magnifying glass of hermeneutics to find whatever they are looking for no matter how poor their eyes, while those who hold the Office of the Keys[3] can hardly spot anything even with perfect vision.

If a ruling prince has a barren wife and his country finds itself in dire straits because of this circumstance, there is one obvious solution to the matter. Whoever wields the power in the state can circumvent the law of succession by simply designating an heir; nonetheless, this bestowal of privilege must not take place on the basis of the sovereign's appetites and desires, but in accordance with the best interests of the state. Certain dishes—as well as "solecisms of gluttonous pleasure," as Lucian called extravagant delicacies in the realm of food and drink[4]—stimulate the appetite because people value them not for the way they taste, but for the difficulty encountered in obtaining them, and will search for them everywhere, from the Carpathian Mountains to the shores of the sea. In India there are classes of people ("Banyans") who eat only one type of food,[5] and when English sailors were reduced to eating only vegetables and plants they called this kind of fasting a "Banyan life" and such a meal a "Banyan dinner." Without a doubt these Indians are far less greedy and gluttonous than those who make a drama in five acts out of every meal and take the tongues, brains, milk, liver, and other highly desirable parts from countless animals, melt them down into a ragout, and then garnish this epigram with a thousand tempting broths and seasonings. If Noah, who was fortunately not far enough along in his knowledge of gastronomy to be aware of the effects of wine,[6] had any inkling of such a palate-tickling array of delicacies, he would have eaten up the entire animal kingdom by the end of his sixth meal, and the Lord only knows how we would have made it to this day.

Yet it is not merely the state alone which should encourage you to remain faithful in marriage, but your own domestic life as well. By bringing bastards into the world instead of sons and daughters, you are depriving your children of what the law has granted them and defaming your own name. Moreover, you will have to conceal these bastards from the whole world, your wife will come to detest them, and they will become the mortal enemies of each of your legitimate children. A man who looks down on his wife also scorns his children; he curses the circumstances which made him a father and this type of unnatural behavior soon becomes a habit of the worst possible kind. Passion merely has pleasure for its end and is but a passing need, a little walk for the exercise; in the case of marriage, this need is only a small concern in the face of other, more important matters, and when we take a walk, we want to get somewhere. If you merely wish to regard your lawfully wedded wife as an object of friendship, then you don't need another woman for that purpose; or, if you consider it necessary to have a woman for specific domestic duties, especially keeping your rooms clean and doing your laundry, then why don't you bring your old maiden aunt into the house?

It takes nothing more than everyday situations for a great mind to reveal itself; unusual circumstances raise even mediocre minds to a height unusual for them. Being faithful to one's wife and self-control in sexual matters are very common virtues; yet while we all walk around large stones in our path, it is the small ones that usually cause us to fall, and if you cannot rise to the level of a simple virtue, what will happen when you encounter a more difficult one?

It shows a great deal of astuteness on the part of a man when he is continually able to find something new in his wife. Like Glaucus and Diomedies,[7] you often wind up exchanging gold for lead when you are unfaithful; you obtain bodies, to be sure, but only imagine they are giving themselves to you willingly. Anyone who is supposed to be fasting deserves to be forgiven much more if he is seduced into breaking his vow by birds' nests, partridges, and pineapples rather than by pickled meat, and the women themselves more easily excuse us under similar circumstances than if they had been weighed in the balance with women of tarnished reputation. But how seldom is the seductress a Lais,[8] who in her time conquered the minds of all the philosophers and the heart of every hero! And even if she were—how did you come to know about her admirable qualities so well, since you were not supposed to look upon her with desire? "To forbid me to love," you join in saying with Knight Hudibras,[9] "is tantamount to telling my pulse to stop beating and my beard to stop growing." Perhaps, but don't you already have an object to love? And wouldn't having a lover in addition to her be the same as telling your powers of reason to stop functioning? Love is the master key which unlocks everything in human beings. And behold, you possess this master key in the form of your wife, and it is and remains a wise, a divine arrangement for a man and a woman to unite themselves with each other for life, even though a part of that couple should perhaps, as with any arrangement, suffer thereby. Thus, even in the best of worlds, hospitals are not a stone of stumbling and the gallows not an *argument ad hominem*. To be sure, when a youth of princely birth, who is accustomed to eating nothing but the rarest of foods, whose palate has been tickled by spices and seasonings, whose ear teased by Italian trills, and whose body covered by exquisite linen and robes of purple—when such a man now goes *ad sacra*,[10] that is, steps up to the marriage altar, then he believes himself to be bound less tightly than a strict interpretation of the rules would allow. But it has not always been thus; and are you guided by example or by laws, by exceptions or by rules? What if a woman's bosom, like a promissory note, loses its powers with the years; what if everything isn't so attractive to behold and so soft and fleshy to the touch—what of it? Those are merely childish playthings in comparison to the holy and honorable task which has for its goal nothing less than the creation of human beings and the imitation of God!

The ancient Romans took the liberty of separating human beings formally and legally into categories of people and things. But no human being is a thing, and it is even an injustice that our own often very legitimate way of expressing ourselves requires the use of the neuter article *"das"* for the noun *"Weib"* ["woman; wife"]. In German the word *"Frau"* ["woman"] is feminine, as is the word *"Männin"* ["virago; Amazon"]. But *"das* Weib" is the most wonderful expression of them all, and a word which has no equal in the honorable title "wife." The word *"Weib"* should be *generis feminini*.[11] Are not women bone of our bones and flesh of our flesh,[12] and—what is even more—spirit of our spirit? And yet they have so little freedom and voice regarding their own person that a legal contract similar to that of marriage would be considered *ipso jure*[13] null and void. Our services, insofar as they do not affect our person, can be rented, sold, or given away—but we can do none of these with our self, or even the tiniest bit of a finger or some other still more insignificant part of our bodies! Our self does not belong to us alone, but to the entire human race. We are all One; we are all God's! Man is never the means, but always the end; never the instrument, always the agent, acting upon his own free will; he is never the object, but always the subject of pleasure!

In marriage, two persons come together in order to find pleasure in each other: the woman wishes to be an "object" for the man, and her husband as well takes a legally binding oath to give himself to her. Since both parties are willingly lowering themselves to the level of "instruments," however, each of which is in turn played by the other, the two "null and voids" cancel each other out, and this one single contract for the enjoyment of another human being is permissible, necessary, and divinely wise. But what if this contract were valid only for a certain number of years? The business of marriage, at least, costs the man none of his ribs,[14] and he remains, if he is temperate, a *man* in the conjugal sense, often into ripe old age. His beloved wife, on the other hand, is often treated so harshly by the passage of time that very soon, especially if she is a blonde, it comes to the point where her place can hardly be found anymore.[15] That's exactly what happens, my dear husband! But just go and join the marriage chorus of the Moravian Brethren[16] and you will find that conjugal love is not a fire out of control, but rather a gentle flame.

If you have no children, then you have a wife who will keep her original form for a long time; if you have children, then through them you possess your wife as a young girl once again—that is, you retain the memory of her first blossoming into womanhood. Doesn't a healthy apple tree laden with fruit also have a kind of beauty of its own? Does it always have to be in bloom in order to charm and delight us? Doesn't the institution of marriage have both spring and autumn flowers, even if they aren't roses and lilies? And wasn't it you yourself who plucked the roses and lilies on the cheeks of your wife? And doesn't your wife represent a very special application of that biblical phrase: "Ye shall know them by their fruits"?

If there were such a thing as a market or an exchange for women, what would become of the two sexes and the race as a whole? The *votum castitatis*[17] of the Catholic clergy, which I am heartily against, could perhaps persuade me to think otherwise of it if in fact it merely intended out of hypocritical naivete to avoid the exploitation of human beings. It seems barbaric to us to eat the meat of animals which have a certain resemblance to man, or that of animals which are our pets, such as dogs, for example; and to eat human flesh—what an abomination! Who can fail to admire those who totally abstain from eating any meat whatsoever, and who would dismiss the rumor that the Patriarchs ate no meat before the Flood, the second Fall of Man![18] Since we are all completely convinced that nobody who is vigorous, hearty, and healthy is capable of fulfilling the *votum castitatis* in the strict sense, any affected superhuman behavior of this sort strikes us as mere sanctimoniousness. But you, my dear husband, can fulfill the humanly possible aspect of the vow of chastity with very little difficulty simply by being the husband of one wife.[19]

Elbert tells in one of his sermons of the Catharists in Switzerland,[20] a sect which insisted upon abstinence, that two men and two women would always lie in a single bed together so that one of the two could bear (very accurate) witness to the other's chastity. And do we not have other examples of great heroes of self-control from the past? In their day the minnesingers spent a night in the bed of their beloved not to practice courtly love, but to sing about it! This and other examples of exaggerated self-denial may also serve to convince you, my dear husband, just how much human beings are capable of in a positive sense. And the first man—didn't he also have only one wife? And shouldn't his example provide even stronger support for the Law,[21] since Nature was revealing her own will clearly in this matter at a time when there was a scarcity of human beings? Isn't there to be found in every sensitive soul, in every Sunday's child,[22] an image of perfection which finds its reflection in one's companion for life—or should find it, at least? Focus your powers of desire on this image, and if you have even one small spark of that creative power possessed by a happy imagination, you will need nothing more, and will find here, as in the pineapple, any sort of fruit you care to imagine.

According to Montaigne, marriage is " . . . *une religieuse liaison et dévote; le plaisir qu'on en tire, ce doit être un plaisir retenu, sérieux et mesuré, à quelque sévérité ce doit être une volonté aucunement prudente et consciencieuse.*"[23] Emperor Aelius Verus excused his extramarital affairs to his wife on the grounds that he was being conscientious, because marriage was an institution of honor and not of unbridled passion and debauchery— an excuse which amounts to clothing a pet sin in Christian garb, an Eulenspiegel-justification[24] not far removed from the kind of principles expressed in the comment: "I avoid strong drink and large groups of people, therefore I don't drink water or go to church." Who can deny that women are often led to unfaithfulness and debauchery by their own husbands when the latter treat them like prostitutes and allow themselves a kind of gross sensuality in their speech and behavior to them? Truly, everything depends on human reason, that faculty which limits the pleasure of mankind, but never destroys it. For a prudent enjoyment of the pleasures of this world is the true Philosopher's Stone,[25] and this stone is found nowhere else but in marriage.

Cures are generally unpleasant things, but you can elude these bodily rigors as well as those of the soul if you practice moderation and avoid all food and drink that can cause hunger and thirst. From the very beginning of his reign, the Emperor Augustus attempted, by means of harsh punishments and the granting of not insignificant privileges, to make better citizens out of his debauched Roman subjects by turning them into better and happier fathers of households. Nevertheless, in spite of his noble intention of bringing men back from error and foolishness, he was forced to work for nearly twenty years on his marriage laws, constantly strengthening or moderating them, before he even came close to attaining his goal. To fast and prepare oneself physically may also be excellent disciplinary measures in this case, although self-castigation, I have been told, sooner excites the Old Adam than subdues and represses him—and in any case, such measures fall under the rubric of the artificial and heroic, and would not be effective with every sort of person. Moderation works without fanfare and can be put to use as easily as our daily bread; it is far more effective and appropriate than all the exaggerations mentioned above, whereby we end up merely fleeing from our vice instead of smashing its lance and overcoming it with courage. Meaningful employment and industriousness could also be called goals in the conversion of mankind, and it can truly be said that a person who practices self-denial and moderation, especially when he has faith in himself and confidence in his aspirations, will conquer himself and the world with less effort than we would ever imagine. My dear husband, not a single one of these home remedies—nor the whole lot taken together—will ever be a cause of embarrassment to you, you can be sure of that!

If, however, you would prefer to learn from the experiences of others (for our own can be a harsh teacher, even if an infallible one), then take a moment to calculate the insults and abuse to which a husband exposes himself through his little stroll down Lover's Lane. Among women who share the same status as each other, but especially among those like Sarai and Hagar,[26] jealousy would kindle the flames of quarrels, strife, and eventually manslaughter. Would the daughters of the land consider it worth the trouble to preserve their virginity if they were often forced by necessity to divide up its reward in so unworthy a manner? And what can we expect from the general population in the face of such monopolies on women and misanthropic rights of first refusal? Only nobles and rich men will be able to amass such a harem, and while their excessive desires will prevent them from doing much or anything worthwhile in their lives, an extraordinary increase in the price of marriageable women will likewise exclude almost everybody else from the marriage market and confine them to nothing less than the wretched life of the cloister with its unnatural sins. Moreover, that strength of body and soul which makes us men what we are will also come out the loser in the sense that such a lack of moderation tends to weaken the intellect, which must then necessarily relinquish its control of the body, since it can no longer maintain it even if it wished to. Do I need to do more than merely mention the Turk to cite the most extreme case?

But take any people which practices polygamy—does it even deserve to be called a people? Or is it not sooner a chaos of humanity which will never amount to anything because the people at the helm will scarcely have the heart to overcome their lascivious arrogance and change a law to which they have given their complete consent? Behold, unfaithful husband, your wife is sighing over you and your daughter laughing at you. You are having an affair with Doris—but what if Damon[27] should do the same thing with your daughter? You are doing something which you would not want to happen anywhere, least of all in your own family. I personally would never marry the cousin or niece, for example, of a man who is constantly unfaithful, since he makes himself repeatedly guilty of the sin of usury by taking compound interest, that is, interest on top of interest. And what is even more unbelievable, this scoundrel is satisfying his lust under the sign of friendship while at the same time turning his house into a b——o and his family into wh——s! People believe that character defects run in the family; I for one believe—perhaps more than I have right to but for any number of reasons—that an inclination to sin can run in the family as well.

It is not incorrect to think that a woman can and will not get very far without a man even in the matter of virtue, for so many splendid virtues arise out of the domestic relationship that if marriages were not so frequent the spectacle of an utterly devoted love would be considered something extraordinary. There are also great numbers of married people with whom even angels could be invited to lodge and whom these angels themselves would behold with rapture. Mankind was not yet quite perfected in the noble figure of Adam of glorious memory, for Eve still had not been created, and it was through this *pair* that a single person came into being, and the two became one.[28] As I have already said, each sex exists to educate and ennoble the other. In a good marriage the man and the woman teach each other, and only a couple, the man and the woman together, constitute a complete human being. The choice of our friends reveals much about our friends; but the choice of our spouse reveals much more about us as men and women—providing, of course, that something other than pure physical attraction, which generally allows for little in the way of choice or sober reflection, was responsible for bringing about the marriage. In a marriage contracted solely on the basis of principles and without any particular inclination on the part of the partners for each other, experience has often taught us that love will come of itself, just as the rhyme does for the born poet who already has a poetic thought in mind. The happiest married couples are the worst at playing the part of lovers—yet the bond between each of them is all the stronger for it.

Even when they are very young, male and female children should not be separated from each other by too great a distance, and whoever

148

would separate men and women from each other, allegedly on the basis of legal grounds, has no idea what he is doing. Those peoples which lock up their women are antisocial and misanthropic—public places of amusement are known to them in name only. And can it be denied that we would have to be either gods or animals for solitude alone to have any attraction for us?[29] A society consisting solely of men is but half a society, and that of only women is utterly unbearable. If you men are segregating yourselves out of jealousy, then what you are failing to realize is that solitude, the soul-mate of our phantasy, is the true inventor of opportunity and often harbors as great an appetite for the forbidden as a distaste for the permissible. If you consider segregation as a means to make the best use of your time during the day and keep from letting a moment pass without some profit for the state, let me tell you that whoever then attempts to mix work and pleasure at social gatherings knows nothing about either work or pleasure. Soldiers in the field naturally constitute an exception to what we have been saying about separation, in the sense that they must needs be contemptuous of life and deny everything that reminds them of its great value and of the beauty of the world. If their wives were with them in the field, even if they were Amazons (straw is no defense against a fire), Nature would exert her rights, and the enemy would have a very easy time of it.

The idea that there might be something in the misfortune of our friends which, even though it brought us no particular pleasure, also failed to elicit our sympathy, has caused many people to shake their heads in dismay; yet if we weaken this idea to the point where we say that there might be something in the good fortune of our friends which depresses us, then the idea loses something of its awful harshness, to be sure—but not of its truth as well? Indeed, we do not need to look very far before—all the tedious expressions of condolence and good-luck wishes notwithstanding—we discover the snake hidden in the grass, and it is the surest test of a good marriage when the good fortune of one of the partners is the good fortune of the other, and when the misfortune of one is the misfortune of the other.

The remark of that alleged Frenchman[30] that people in Germany have their portraits painted too often redounds to the honor of my country in no small way. The writer in question is trying to force from this statement the French conclusion that people in Germany are too vain and proud, but the conclusion seems much more valid to me that love among married couples in Germany is still today more constant and heartfelt than in France, for most of the portraits are exchanged between husband and wife. The flood of German novels proves this as well, at least insofar as they stand on good terms with virtue and good manners and, in spite of their artistic defects, have no other moral failing than that they help to pass the time of day, or waste it, which is just as bad. But then how many people are there for whom their time in this world never hangs heavy on their hands? I almost believe that nobody in this case would cast the first stone.[31]

Any home in which the husband and wife take different routes to their love trysts will become desolate and eventually fall in upon itself, and the same fall is destined for entire states in which the marriages have begun to deviate from the purity of doctrine espoused by the First Church of Holy Matrimony. Even those peoples which kept their women as slaves sooner or later fell victims to their own slavery, and what is more, were utterly defeated by those states which treated their women humanely. That state which undertakes a revolution without taking into consideration the foremost of all points regarding the opposite sex and holy matrimony will never get very far.[32] How can a person expect to demonstrate humanity, goodness, and justice in his public life if he is foolish, unkind, or unjust in his own home? "For if a man know not how to rule his own house," Paul writes to Timothy, "how shall he take care of the Church of God?"[33] A man who extends his protection and support to his wife only so long as she maintains her feminine charms, who views her as a calendar with only a single year on it, and who then later divests her of all rights with respect to him while piously intoning that she has come under his authority and is therefore entitled to nothing less than his full love and devotion—such a man has a false idea of the rights of humanity and is doing harm to himself, his country, and the world! And the same is true for the man who honors the opposite sex by revealing his contempt for it (as the French do to us Germans), treading on the very flowers he had used to adorn himself when things were going well for him. He knows as little about what he wants, or at least is going about the whole matter as ineffectually as a person who constantly mocks fame in order to become famous for doing so, and who in fact secretly desires it but chooses to seek it in a different way, as Aretin and Arouet sought the favor of princes with whip in hand[34]—in other words, who is begging for alms with an unsheathed dagger.

Honor arising from contempt is the bitterest form of mockery, compared to which hate and persecution are but blessings![35] In fact,

I actually prefer the boorishness of the man who, when told during a storm at sea that his heaviest piece of baggage had to be thrown overboard, replied, "Here, take my wife." At least in a case like that we know straightway what kind of person we are dealing with.

Among Women

When a man is unfaithful, it is an injustice; when a woman is unfaithful, it is unnatural and godless. Polygamy is inadvisable; polyandry is one of the blackest depravities in the world. There is nothing easier than begetting children, but nothing is more difficult than raising them—and what a sacrilege it would be to burden a man with the raising of other people's children! Damage to purchased goods amounting to more than half their value automatically rescinds the purchase, yet even the slightest damage to marital fidelity ought to be enough to cancel the marriage. Consider, you wives who are unfaithful to your husbands, that those husbands, by courting and marrying you, were actually freeing you from the slavery in which you lived in the house of your parents! Women are manumitted by marriage and are duty-bound to perform for their liberators *operas officiales* (acts of kindness and love) for the rest of their lives. It is thus quite incorrect for a girl to speak of having lost her freedom through marriage, for freedom comes through marriage, and the husband loses his own at the same time. This idea is so natural that the custom of buying a father's daughters from him exists among very many peoples in the world, although by this means the daughters merely pass from a condition of greater slavery to a lesser one. Fifty shekels was the highest price to be paid for a slave according to the law of the Hebrews, and the father also received an equal amount for his daughter.[36] The Jews still possess remnants of this ancient custom in Solomon's proverb: "Many daughters bring great wealth."[37] The Romans had a type of marriage *per coëmtionem* (marriage through purchase), and the presents which engaged couples everywhere are accustomed to giving each other can be ascribed to this custom. Every woman should remain above reproach, the wife of a single husband; she must be true to her husband not merely because she has promised to be, but simply as a matter of course (*ipso jure*). Rules have exceptions, laws tolerate privileges; the laws of Nature allow for neither of these. A privilege from the law of Nature is more than a miracle, for God can perform miracles, but He cannot grant privileges from the law of Nature. It

151

is also true that privileges only serve to reveal the weakness of those who make the laws.

In a single year a man can beget three hundred and sixty-five children, and one more in a leap year; a woman, on the other hand can only bring a single child into the world during this time. Thus the excuses he can cite when he is unfaithful do not apply in the case of the woman.[38] "I can't fast," he could say, "my body just can't tolerate it. No meat for eight months!" Or, to quote another allegory: "It was simply a case of any port in a storm—my wife is ill"; or yet another: "I wanted to help my neighbor—he has no oxen to plow with." Now if a plague were to come over the land, I believe we can all agree that it would be our civic duty and patriotic privilege to bring more than one child per year into the world, especially if the plague had decimated the male population and the fields were lying fallow. But do we not stop taking medicine once it has taken effect? And show me the paragraph in Nature's law book where it states that we are required to sow countless times where we can reap but once!

These, then, are examples of what a man could say—what his reason might be for saying them is not my concern here. It is certain, however, that a man is bound chiefly by the state and his own maturely considered and clearly uttered word; the woman, on the other hand, is bound by Nature herself. This is also the reason the law grants to the man *ob justum dolorem*,[39] the terrible criminal and domestic right to murder his wife and the man involved when he catches them in the act of committing adultery; a woman, however, who comes upon her husband in the same situation is not permitted to take the same revenge. What is more harmful to the state than when its women become wanton and dissolute? They corrupt not only their own husbands, but at least one other man as well, and are murderers who have nothing to say in their defense. The *Swabian Mirror*[40] calls an adulteress a super-wh—e, and whether she *practices* adultery or merely commits it one time, she deserves this title and every other ugly appellation to boot. Do not you yourself despise that old crone of high station with a bosom like a whitewashed tomb[41] who still has the nerve to conduct sorties from behind those dilapidated walls? The whole city laughs at her, and even those who shortly will be doing the same thing now find it indecent for this woman to be squeezing the hand of some fop behind her husband's back—thus playing Blind Man's Bluff with him even though his eyes are not blindfolded? Is it not a venerable and well-established truth that of all the gods and goddesses Venus retains her trusty and beloved servants in her service longest of all—if they can no longer serve among the rank and file, they function as drillmasters for the latter. The veterans' hospital of this goddess is just about the most ludicrous thing anyone can imagine.

Truly, a woman would by her very nature have to be disposed to stubbornness and insensibility to prefer the flesh pots of Egypt[42] to domestic happiness. And woe to her who suffers the revenge of Nature! The residence of a lady of society is a continually open house; she lives as if she were out in the open air, and the sheer number and constant fluctuation of the guests relieves her of the responsibility of hospitality. She turns a respectable house into a hostel or foundling home for the fashionable; the guests at her parties are brought together more by accident than intention, and it is purely a matter of luck whether they pass their time pleasantly or prolong it unpleasantly. If the circle is too great, even the brightest sun in the heaven of hostesses cannot engender enough light and life to unite so many people to a single purpose and establish for them an atmosphere free from constraint— an atmosphere which in a smaller, more harmonious group of people causes all our cares to melt away; where our imagination, mood, and character are able to express themselves in actions and words; where the true reasons for the opinions we carry with us even in the most trivial circumstances of our daily life at court or in town are brought up from the depths of our souls and scrutinized—that is, where *in vino* (in wine) is truth. Circles which are too large either divide up into smaller ones, where jealousy, distrust, and small-town meddlesomeness prevail, or everything descends into utter chaos, and the excessive freedom introduces a kind of forced quality to social intercourse which is repugnant to all people of good breeding. In the final analysis such a so-called "open house" is similar to a wasteland devoid of cultivation and everywhere exposed to the depredations of the walker, the rider, and the wagon. Even in the world of the court, where the personalities differ from each other more by virtue of tints and hues than by primary colors, a certain humdrum atmosphere prevails which also lacks even the remotest sense of sociability. Wouldn't you agree, my dear lady, that the same seasonings which enliven a meal can also ruin it? O, we can do without so many things in life, once we have learned to form a true assessment of our own selves!

The wife of Ulysses, the Penelope of poetic renown, is depicted as clever as she is chaste, yet there is one feature of this image I do not like very much, which is why I would not recommend this particular subject for a ladies' picture gallery—namely, the fact that she is always painted as surrounded by a great number of admirers whom she is able to fend off by means of an artificial netting, but who nonetheless are still permitted to pay suit to her. A judge who refuses gifts is to my way of thinking far less noble than one who is not offered them in the first place, and even if none of these ladies ever grants a favorable *hearing* to one of her admirers, it is still not right (even putting the best construction on the matter) for her to *listen* to him or to accept his petitions. A fortress which is considering proposals for its surrender is already revealing a desire to surrender—it is just a matter of settling on the conditions; and a woman who yields her ear will defend her heart but weakly. Dripping water can make an indentation in the hardest stone, and a flattering word will find room tomorrow, if not today. It is not enough for the principal to remain intact—the last penny of interest is due the husband as well.

My dear lady, you have obviously given a great deal of thought to the limits of your faithfulness as a wife, and have come to some conclusions. "My husband is unfaithful, so why should I . . . ?"— "Why?" Because you are a woman and he is a man. Do you think you can bring your husband back onto the right path by being unfaithful as well? Or do you believe that just because he has made an unfortunate choice for himself, you are permitted to make an equally bad one for yourself? If your husband has already begun to wander and you have been fortunate enough to guide him back into your marriage you deserve to be admired more for this than when you first captivated him with charms as yet unfamiliar to him, directing his freedom of choice in such a way that it could not but fall upon you. The garland of flowers you carried on your wedding day as a sign of your chastity adorns you once again by virtue of your genuine understanding and wise judgment. Direct the coquetries reserved for your admirers to your husband, and decide for yourself that the honor for you is not in attracting admirers, but in having a husband. Carefully selected attire and a habit of personal cleanliness contribute a great deal in rendering a man constant, or to speak in non-technical terms, in keeping him faithful. White is the symbol of innocence; cleanliness could be considered the symbol of chastity; a clean dress proclaims a chaste woman, filthiness is the shop-sign of Venus Pandemos.[43] But women neglect these little tokens of thoughtfulness, just as do the Jews and Turks who are actually required by their religion to wash themselves. Perhaps the beard plays a role here, however, since even though the Poles, for example, merely tend to cultivate the merest trace of a beard, a certain disregard for cleanliness, comparatively speaking, seems to be a failing among them.

It is difficult to keep a husband constantly faithful and in love—or, to speak metaphorically, to surprise with a different sash or ribbon a man who has already seen all the clothes you own. On the other hand, nothing is easier than commandeering an entire regiment of admirers; and who would not let himself be recruited to serve under the banner of women, where one can serve so securely and well; who would not wish to dance without having to pay the piper?

Often it is the case that a woman brings her husband to the point where he leads her to her lover himself, and then she purloins the key from him in order to steal more comfortably. Meanwhile, Madame, are you absolutely sure in this *joyeuse entrée* of yours that sooner or later your lover will not pen his memoirs like Hans Jakob and reveal to one and all your love affairs even before the Day of Judgment? And women also should not think that we take no notice of their tricks and artifices, especially if they have been very subtly put into practice. We know full well that they believe themselves to be safest in undertakings too brazen for anyone to believe them capable of; nevertheless we perceive what they are up to, even if only indirectly, and often the methods they consider to be most effective are really the most transparent to us. The fear accompanying any act of foolishness betrays a heart that is not yet totally corrupt, and those self-righteous people who act as if they were above repentance are the most insufferable of all. Everybody is aware that when love begins to fade, a certain obliging civility enters to take its place, but since love without artifice is the very image of Nature herself, women are nowhere more easily betrayed than at this very point. Likewise the technique of enticing the lover through the husband is not unfamiliar to us, and even if the women in Germany are still far from being as gallant and sophisticated in this regard as those of Italy and France, German men, on the other hand, know how to spin intrigues with even more facility than their colleagues in either of those countries.

If I may request it of you, Madame, try to resist any inclination you may have to delve into secrets of a mystical nature, since such an inclination is not really an attribute of your sex anyway. Catherine the Great of Russia, who simply laughs folly right out of her country as it deserves rather than compromising her own majesty and that of her laws, mocked the Hermetic wisdom of alchemy in comedies[44] and was thereby able to suppress branches of the new Masonic lodges far more effectively than if she had banished them by law.

It is quite another matter, however, with regard to that particular trait of curiosity which disposes the opposite sex to take an interest in everything that is going on around them. True, the husband can never make use of this trait in his business dealings; nonetheless, in cases when he has shut himself off from the world and all that is in it, this attribute can occasionally prevent him from becoming a stranger in his own city or country and teach him to draw conclusions about that which he cannot do from that which he can. And you, my dear lady, who are able to read things before they are written and understand them before they are spoken, can do no harm whatsoever to your husband's reputation if you take the trouble to find out the latest news in your town and country.

The animals all sup at the table of Nature; man alone enjoys the perquisite of eating at a table by himself. The art of cooking is a human one which has as its goal the transformation of an animal need into a human one. Sexual attraction is less a human art, since it is also found in animals which are in the act of mating. Whether or not then that ingredient called reason actually does contain—as does, for example, Vitriolnaphtha[45]—the power to produce extreme cold, yet without this ingredient no true pleasure is possible, and mankind fails to acknowledge its superiority over the animal world when it does not attempt to ennoble every sensual pleasure and make every enjoyment longer lasting and more exquisite through the use of it. Let this superiority be the subject of your study, Madame, and its reward your daughter, who will resemble you in every way! Truly, I know of no greater honor for you than to have a daughter of whom it is said by others: "She is just like her mother!"

"My husband is grumpy and spends more time on his work than on me." — How ungrateful you are! The time that he sets aside for his business affairs is also in fact given over to you, for all his work is dedicated merely to supporting you at a level appropriate to your station; the honor which he receives from his work reflects on you when people say of you: "She is the wife of that fellow we were talking about who is so good at his job." And where do you get the idea that every day is a holiday and that you don't have a place at home in your own house? To do nothing is to do nothing good; whoever does nothing is offering his soul for sale after the manner of the open house mentioned above, which anyone with money can enter. Why do you cause your husband, who is already overburdened with the affairs of his work, to have to become involved in the policing of the home as well?

Egyptian women were not allowed to leave the home any other way except barefooted, in order to keep them home by means of this inconvenience, and the snail has been the coat of arms of women since the time of Apelles and throughout antiquity.[46] And now to conclude my refutation with a word of instruction: you know that societies in which a single party is held responsible for all damages are prohibited by the state, and that marriages are not excepted from this regulation—or at least shouldn't be! It is difficult to speak to young women of unpleasant things; I have noticed this in widows who treat their grown daughters not the way fathers would, but as admirers would treat them. But allow me, if you would, to change scenes at this point and say a few words to men on the same subject.

Some women believe that because their wealth has brought them the status of a man they ought then to be permitted to rule, and when their husbands refuse to vacate the throne on their behalf they seek to make other conquests. "After all, we've always had money," they say. That statement may be as good as the gold it is based on, yet the money a woman brings to her husband through marriage is such a minor matter that it scarcely deserves mention, and men who make something of it themselves deserve to be the lackeys of their wives. A man sells his own freedom in order to free his wife from slavery, and performs a deed thereby as great as that which we admire in the story of Damon and Pythias (which unfortunately, due to the intervention of a third party, Dionysius, does not exactly fit my metaphor for marriage).[47]

In legal circles the question has been asked as to whether young women—or, actually, unmarried women, since there is a great deal of difference between the two—were to be counted among the *personas miserabiles*,[48] and although this question generally is answered with a clear and straightforward "No," it is still very much a matter of the point of view from which one considers the question. In any case, I consider old maids to be the very foundation stones of our hospitals.[49] What we do not acquire by ourselves does not really belong to us— and what woman has earned her capital by herself? Either she inherited it or received it as a present. Everything really came from a man, and even if a woman brings capital to her husband through marriage, she is merely giving him that which came from his sex and already belonged to him by means of his membership in it. Among the Hebrews only the sons were the actual heirs—the daughters inherited only in the event of the unfortunate absence of sons. As proof that they were merely invested with this inheritance, moreover, they were required to marry a man from their own tribe.[50]

Women are often untrue in marriage for reasons which should cause them to beg daily for forgiveness from their husbands. "I have no children by him," they say.—My answer would be: "And why don't you have any children?" Read in the book of the Bible called The Wisdom of Solomon and you will find the lines: "It is better to be childless, provided one is virtuous."[51] In such cases the man is not nearly as often to blame; the dew is no help when the soil is rocky. Nevertheless it is widely accepted that women wish to have children because dandling is inborn for them. One can observe that a girl will play with her dolls much longer than her little brother, even though she is growing much more rapidly than he both intellectually and spiritually. If she prefers to play with male dolls, however, then one cannot later always look for the symbol of loyalty and honor on her ring finger—only time will tell what will happen in such cases. This kind of childish play, it seems to me, has greater appeal for the opposite sex than for our own because it is so closely bound up with another matter of greater importance to them. And could it not be said that the fair sex loves children so much because nothing on earth has been created so adept at using its tongue as a woman?

Marriages which are not childless have doubtless the best chance for being successful for a variety of reasons. It may be that the father is thereby faced with the necessity of working harder, and that all this hard work drives away evil thoughts; or that it is a result of the change which takes place in the house each time the mother herself is reborn in childbed; perhaps it is because the father finds in his daughters the image of his wife as she once stood so fresh and young before him, created out of his own rib—he Adam, and she Eve. Or it simply could be that children relieve the monotony of the marriage state. Speaking of children, moreover, it is not necessary for great minds always to have sons, and Shakespeare, that man after Nature's own heart, would not have become what he was if he had not had "merely" two daughters. A great man who has a son, however, takes great pains to leave laurels for him on the path to immortality. "He is my flesh and blood, and what is more, he bears my name," such a man thinks to himself. We can be sure that marriages which are blessed with children were made in heaven, and that husband and wife were meant for each other.

On the whole, the man who is a good lover can get away with most anything at home; this is the palladium which renders him invincible. The wife of such a man will put up with anything from him, even his love affairs, provided he does not spend any money doing it. Moreover, I ought to mention here that men who are impotent always seem to marry the prettiest women, and what they lose by way of the deed, they gain with their words. Whoever offers his wife empty flatteries is generally investing everything he has as regards both capital and interest, but a man who knows he is a *man* feels no need to use these stratagems, these tropes and figures of speech, because he has already made his statement by means of his *virility*. Widows snatch at him, as well as girls who are experienced with men; inexperienced girls who let themselves be deceived by flatterers end up complaining about their mistake and wearing the pants in the family, while their husbands, no matter how clever they are, remain forever barred from the throne. An entire treasury full of words is but an entire treasury filled with small change of little value; actions are coins of gold. True, we can at most believe only about half of what a young man in love says to his sweetheart, and thus nobody is taken aback when he lies and says to her, "I will give you anything you want." Everybody else appears shifty-eyed when they are lying, or they look at our nose as if they had lost their way and were looking for road signs, or squint as if the numbers on the clock were wrong. Primitive peoples act; civilized peoples speak; polished peoples sing.

But what can a man of weak constitution do in the case of impotence? If he can get his wife to enter into correspondence with a woman in a neighboring town he will have solved his problem; people love everything they have written. It ought to be considered a capital crime to draw up plans for projects in written form, for then they are rarely changed. People will defend their written statements, but their spoken words to a lesser extent, unless of course they are connected with a bet, a kind of intellectual duel which is the most fitting means of keeping uncontrolled tongues in check and putting an amicable end to every disputation. If you are able to induce your wife to write poetry, then even an Adonis could not seduce her and the only thing required of you will be the small obligation to listen to her verses and find them beautiful—that is the least a husband owes his wife. A woman poet would rather have one heir of the soul than ten bodily heirs. "Make me some children" is her way of saying "Help me to find a rhyme." The poets call some rhymes masculine, others feminine; and nothing could be more appropriate here than this harmless little circumstance. If your wife finds no enjoyment in correspondence, or if she has only learned how to write letters to persons of the opposite sex—then, poor fellow, in your affliction you might well set about acquiring a veritable Noah's Ark in miniature with every kind of animal, not forgetting the lap dogs; or buy yourself a garden and try to bring your wife into contact with Nature. People enjoy being unhappy when they are with others; alone they enjoy being happy. And if you are able to make Nature as alluring as she really is and to bind this couple together in true sisterly fashion, then you will have succeeded in securing yourself far better than if you were to attempt to pacify your dissatisfied partner by means of balls and concerts. Moreover, although these latter methods are the more usual ones, they are also the very worst and stand in the same relationship to the evils they are supposed to displace as oil to fire. When the wife of a man so afflicted plants a tulip, all is well in the home; but if she mentions that today is the festival of Lupercalia[52] (or, freely translated, today people will be giving parties), that tomorrow there will be a ball, the day after tomorrow a concert, and on Friday a comedy in the theater, then she is on the way to offering her charms for sale *publica auctionis lege*—that is, in incendiary fashion—and you, my dear husband, ought to consider either filing for a divorce or becoming a Socrates.[53]

And now just a pennyworth concerning the subject of jealousy, by means of which many people believe themselves able to safeguard their marriage—although with very little success. Jealousy creates a kind of spurious faithfulness; its antipode, indifference, brings about shamelessness, or, more elegantly expressed, the *cicisbeat*, or French gallantry. In this latter concept are coupled two unfortunate characteristics, fanaticism and obsession,[54] and even if jealousy does contribute to maintaining a sense of humility, the granting of a kind of dignified freedom does more to engender and strengthen marital faithfulness than either fanaticism or obsession possibly could. Treating women harshly makes them more submissive and their admirers all the more inflamed with passion. The more narrowly we limit the boundaries of the women, the farther they will stray once their feet have once begun to tread the wrong path. If perfectly innocent relationships are called crimes for them, then they will come to deny themselves nothing;

little intrigues will lead to greater ones, and women and lawyers will countenance anything until it becomes patently obvious that the exact opposite is true. All the worse for the poor women!

But when a woman has come to the point where she still feels herself to be alone even in the company of society; when she in fact has learned to utilize that society as a preparation for solitude and gradually begun to realize that she can be praised more fully not through flattery, but true respect—will she not then find her house and her husband more appealing than parties, balls, teas, and an entire army of lackeys committed to worshiping her? For her to shriek like an organ pipe when someone gets too close to her is hardly a mathematical proof of her faithfulness, and in fact a kind of dignified impertinence on her part will serve much better to render her indifferent to anything which might prove detrimental to her husband. Moreover, if she is permitted that well-ordered sense of freedom mentioned above, it will keep her from losing confidence in herself and in her own virtue—a consequence more important than we might presently imagine. To believe oneself to be virtuous and to be so in fact are two extraordinarily similar conditions. Where the appearance of vice prevails already, people make little or nothing of such vice; and where respectability is confined to words and gestures, it is generally refuted by works. Wherever there are many laws, then many people break the law. According to the Scriptures, the Law makes us sinners;[55] and fences merely tempt us to climb over them. Wherever there are many laws, one often chokes out the other, and none of them is obeyed. A virtue in need of a guard to stand over it has either already stopped being a virtue or will soon cease to be one. Anyway, who will oversee the overseer? Who will guard the guard? And why then do those fire-breathing conservatives among us wish to cast suspicion on a certain refinement in the relationships between men and women and declare themselves to be against any sort of tolerance within the marriage bond? Is it not a weakness inherent in both men and women that they demand that people fall in love with them without their wishing to reciprocate? Impetuous and inexperienced youth is easily misled by inviting glances with this design behind them, but more mature people who have valiantly served their years of apprenticeship in the world well know the true significance of those little pennants we perceive waving at us under such circumstances. Thus a mature man notices the loose blossoms heaving rhythmically on a woman's bosom merely out of politeness, even if it would be hard to deny that this sort of intentional negligence bestows on beauty its own special charm; likewise, the clever wife of the councillor alternates her glances between the ring of the council president and the graceful effects produced by the finger wearing that ring only because she wants to attain a six-week's vacation in the country for her devoted husband in order to find happiness in his arms alone.

Blessed are the pure in heart, for they can see God in Nature![56] It is only wise men and women who ever arrive—and generally later than sooner—at the conclusion that it is better to divert this mutual weakness I have been speaking of to the cause of respect and devotion. In this way coquetries—in the use of which, by the way, one can remain as true and honorable as in anything else, but which are the mere illusions and delusions of a foolish self-conceit and have much in common with the soap bubbles of children—are replaced by friendships of a special sort characterized by certain amenities which friendships between persons of the same sex can scarcely afford. If I may be permitted to give advice here, we should all withstand the desire to make others fall in love with us; opportunity makes for thieves, and the receiver of stolen goods is as bad as the thief. The eye which can look at a woman or a man without desire or invoking thoughts of adultery within the heart moves easily from person to person; conversely, the finer the twine, the more tightly we are bound.

Whoever honors that which he loves and lets reason and not passion guide his actions will only know jealousy from its advantageous side, employing it merely to add tang to the almost too monotonous flavor of love, so that it is no longer simply sweet, but resembles the noble wine of the Rhine. Whoever uses jealousy as a spice or a medicine will fare well. Is not intense love actually associated with physical pain, and the act of caressing often so vehement and passionate that it leaves marks and even scars; does it not thus seem that whatever is merely sweet is in fact insipid and insufferable? On the other hand, whoever purposely sets out to make that man or woman jealous who gave them grounds for jealousy in the first place has chosen the very worst cure possible.

Often it is with the most insignificant trifles that women make us happy, and just as in general it is the way a gift is given and not the gift itself which is most important, so a noble woman knows how to transform the innocent kiss she gives a male friend into a thing of such great value that in spite of her thriftiness in such matters she comes to be regarded as lavish with her favors. If you husbands choose to become angry at this, then it certainly cannot be described as a well-managed jealousy which is driving you to it, but blind envy, and this, like anger itself, can never lead to anything good. Anger, Seneca says, is like a collapsing building, which smashes itself to pieces in the act of crushing something else; and this applies to blind envy as well. No woman, by the way, considers her husband to be completely in his right mind when he becomes jealous, whether he has reason to be or not. Is it any wonder, then, when under such circumstances an unrequited lover takes the life of his sweetheart in a fit of jealousy, since it is his terrible envy which has driven him mad? Is it any wonder that if he cannot bring himself to allow any mortal to possess her, he has misgivings about entrusting her to the angels as well, even if it is not quite as certain as people might believe that all of these beings are *generis masculini*?

In situations where either of the two parties experiences a guilty conscience, the man is more cowardly than the woman; he will mince words when confronted with the deed, whereas the woman becomes angry when she is no longer able to extricate herself from the situation. Often it is the uncertainty as to the faithfulness of one's spouse which is worst of all, and I have seen people who felt happily relieved once they became certain of their husband's or wife's infidelity—in fact, they were even blessed by means of this curse, in the sense that they then convinced themselves they had the intelligence and will to give up their love for a person who was not worthy of it. Only that person is to be truly pitied who, tormented by suspicions and doubts, loves as deeply as ever in spite of everything, for how can we love a person who does not love us back, and how can we desire to experience pleasure with a person who reciprocates our advances with revulsion?

If I may be permitted one more remark at this point, let me just say that we men exaggerate our suspicions of the fair sex and perhaps bring them thereby to a knowledge of things they would not have been aware of without the help of our criticism, while at the same time it is only too frequently the case that we are content to remain angels of darkness all the while we are attempting to make angels of light out of our wives.

However crude and shallow the comment is that a woman becomes a saleable commodity as soon as the right buyer is found, this remark nevertheless is part and parcel of the usual affected rhetoric of the world of sophisticated men, to the extent that any man who makes such an assertion would have difficulty drumming up someone in his not insignificant circle of friends who would be able to bring himself to express embarrassment for it in his stead. But behold! A single princess of the theater puts to flight entire armies of men, makes rulers into slaves, and knocks wise men clean out of their philosophical saddles! People maintain with the utmost conviction that every fortress of the women is unassailable; are there men's fortresses which are invincible as well?

In answer to the question as to what sort of person makes the best ruler, a wise man of old once replied: "Whoever is master of himself." "For it is just as difficult," he added by way of explanation, "to reform a people whose leader manages his own life badly as it is to make straight the shadow of a walking-stick if the staff itself is crooked." Men! The crooked staff of authority by which you rule is in fact the cause of every burden which has been laid upon the women. Air is not seen, but felt; women should never use their chastity as a sort of cosmetic or perfume—it creates the suspicion that they have something to hide. It is said of people who praise themselves that they have bad neighbors. Are we not bad neighbors to women? And tell me, can they be blamed entirely if they seek justice for themselves and in doing so, as often happens in questions of justice, they stain their robe of righteousness?[57] It is not much of a compliment when it is said of a man that at least he is not a rogue—but what if even this distinction is a matter of dispute? "Je ne scay," Montaigne says, "si les exploits de César et d'Alexandre surpassent en rudesse la résolution d'une belle jeune femme nourrie à notre façon, se maintenant entière aux milieux de mille continuelles et fortes poursuites."[58] Whatever might be just in these reproaches is directly attributable to our injustice. Why do we exclude women from all occupations and means of employment? Why does the civil constitution not allow them a form of diversion through work or of activity through employment? The purest water is always artificially produced; in its natural state it is never completely pure, rainwater itself not excepted. Why do men present women with opportunities for going astray simply by virtue of their loveless behavior toward the latter? Eriphyle betrayed her husband Amphiaraus for the sake of a piece of jewelry;[59] and how many miserly men force their wives to borrow from their neighbors, who then take every opportunity to charge interest! Is it not the stinginess of men which drives some women to their passion for gambling, just because they cannot satisfy their need for adornment by any other means? A woman who gambles passionately and for high stakes will have difficulty resisting other temptations, and even dancing, which ordinarily offers a helping hand in affairs of the heart, is by far not so dangerous as a mania for gambling when it comes to bringing about the seduction of a woman. In the cultivation of honey a great deal depends upon the plants which grow where the nectar is collected; and negligence and ignorance of the soil can contribute to a bad harvest just as easily as the weather.

On German soil, because we are not able to joke about it and the *cicisbeat* has not come to be accepted among us, the consequence of marital unfaithfulness has generally been divorce. If this breach were the only ground for divorce, I would have no objection, but divorce has become such a matter of course that it might be of some use at this point to register a complaint about this sort of permissivenesss. Is it not extraordinary that a people which calls itself Christian and wishes with heart and soul to live up to that name would treat with such scorn a commandment of the Founder of Christianity which could not have been given more clearly—a commandment in which He, as every lawgiver should, merely brought to light a law which had already existed in Nature herself? Moses permitted divorce because of the Hebrews' hardness of heart, and if a man no longer considered it acceptable to have anything to do with his wife he was justified by law to send her away with an honorable certificate of divorce.[60] The poor wretch—that would have made it difficult for her to survive on anything other than alms! The Founder of the Christian religion condemned all manner of divorce except on the grounds of adultery,[61] and in fact this is really not divorce at all, but rather the public announcement of it and as such a mere formality, the act of adultery itself constituting the most obvious expression of divorce. And thus, this apparent exception notwithstanding, the rule remains: "What God hath joined together, let not man put asunder."[62]

My dear fellow, do you doubt these words? Either marriages must be kept holy and the marriage bed undefiled, or the human race will perish. The *begetting* of children is actually the least important thing among human beings, for tell me yourself, can a man and a woman ever come together and say, "Let us make man in our image, after our likeness"?[63] Only the raising and education of children creates an image which resembles us; procreation—can I say it often enough?—is the body in marriage, raising and education the soul. And since we cannot raise children unless both parents—the mother as well as the father—set about their work together, then it follows that adultery destroys the happiness of the children as well.

And if there were no such thing as marriage, where would we find our examples of conduct, of patience, and of hope—where the mirror of real human life?—"But who can live with someone who matches us about as well as a square peg a round hole?"—But you chose her, didn't you?—you, who could and should have first given some thought as to what would best have served your peace of mind! When she was still a bride, and in the first six weeks of your marriage she was the goddess of your heart, and you two were of one heart and soul. My dear fellow, should that same passion—now directed towards another—still be able to exert more influence over you than reason? The kind and gentle acts which stem from our basic beliefs as to what is right are perhaps not as captivating as those which derive from burning desire, but they enkindle in us more peace and happiness than anything arising from mere passion. Whoever cannot resist the temptation of novelty will quickly become bored even with the best woman in the world for a wife. And is there a position in the world which doesn't have its cross to bear? My friend, view these marital sufferings as an opportunity and a blessing given to you for your use in promoting virtue. Forgive, and you shall be forgiven; give, and it shall be given unto you;[64] practice becoming and being at home that which you are expected to be and become elsewhere in life. Problems in the home are difficult to bear, because they arise from circumstances we don't wish to reveal even to our closest friends, and because they deny us that small satisfaction of knowing that others are in the same boat along with us, since everyone upon leaving his house also leaves his domestic affairs behind and when at home takes care not to be surprised by visitors.

But why would you want to remain forever in grammar school when it comes to your education as a human being? We must learn to bear what we cannot change. Don't we all have to face death? Marriage is a school of higher learning; the formula for knowing yourself also includes knowledge of a woman if you wish to deserve the title of a student of human nature. Can there be a better time, place, and opportunity for this than in the household itself? You will doubtless recall, moreover, that there is a church which does not permit divorce, and when you reply in rebuttal that the clergy of that church are required to live in complete celibacy, then I would have to grant that you have a point. But you would also have to admit that my point would be well taken if I replied that your objection only refutes a single aspect of my argument, and not the most important one at that.

"But what can be done about most of our bad marriages, then?"—Do you wish to do wrong so that right may come of it? In countries where a divorce is easy to obtain it often happens that the divorced couple marry each other again, which is irrefutable proof of the fact that they had no idea what they were doing in the first place. Whoever marries a divorced woman is also committing adultery![65] This is particularly true when children are involved, because here the desire for novelty becomes a vice, whereas in most other cases it merely passes for foolishness; true in the sense that it sets a bad example; and true for many other reasons as well. Making divorce difficult is one of the most effective ways of preventing adultery. It is much easier to gather fruit from a tree along the open highway than from one that is fenced in, and the difficulty of attaining a thing weakens our appetite for it, as Aesop's fable of the fox and the grapes abundantly reveals. That law which forbids marriage between partners who have already divorced each other on the ground of adultery strikes at the heart of the problem[66]—it is just too bad that our friends who actually exercise legal authority in this matter have made such a mess of things.

Hard-hearted husbands! Is it your intention to soothe your consciences by having your wives consent to a divorce with a loud and vehement "Yes!"? But wasn't it you in the first place who brought them to the point of consent through your perpetual quarreling, your senseless affairs, through your shameful contempt for them and your low-minded stinginess? It would yield a great profit in terms of patience if in Protestant states divorced people were not allowed to marry again; yet this solution is not without its stones of stumbling and rocks of offense, which are hardly circumvented when we rule that only the party which has been divorced may not marry—or in this case remarry—that person who gave cause for the divorce in the first place by means of his or her illicit intercourse. If the former solution seems too severe, then this one is singularly unfortunate. Deception, caution, and cunning will transform the guilty party here into the innocent one, and without a doubt seductions and illicit affairs are more frequent when accompanied by a greater degree of secrecy— and in many respects more dangerous as well.

A home remedy for promoting faithfulness in marriage. There exist bodies which during a fixed period of time will always travel a constant distance, and whose speed is therefore always constant. What an excellent example for you husbands! If you follow this example, your life, like the movement of such bodies, will always be constant.

Or, my friends, do you prefer to envy those bodies which in every succeeding fixed period of time travel a greater distance than during the preceding period of time, whose speed thus increases or whose movement is accelerated? Or are you more attracted to those bodies which in successive fixed periods of time continually travel a shorter distance, whose speed decreases and whose movement is decelerated?

I have kept my word faithfully and addressed to the men alone a number of points which certainly might also have been of interest to the women. May I now direct to the hearts of the fair sex my suggestions for the practical application of my ideas by means of a quote from Seneca? "No woman is embarrassed by divorce any longer," he noted, "since some of the most fashionable women have begun to count their years not according to the number of senators, but by the number of husbands they have had." It should also be mentioned that women's clothes in Seneca's time were so thin and transparent that it would have been impossible for a beautiful woman to expose more of her charms to her lover in the course of a secret tryst than she had revealed to the general public already.[67] And in our own day? In England the chief magistrate used to have the women leave the courtroom during the course of a marriage trial dealing with delicate matters. The court usher would customarily open the door and call in a loud voice: "All women with chaste ears are requested to leave the room!" Faced with an atmosphere of confrontation such as this, even Lucretia[68] herself would not have left the room had she not been willing to incur the reproach of hypocrisy and lose more through her absence than she might gain. The women spectators generally could come to no better decision than to remain in the courtroom, and after a short interval wherein nobody left the room, the court usher would then shut the door with the words: "The women with chaste ears have now left the courtroom." My dear chief magistrate! "Unto the pure all things are pure,"[69] and in fact it is here not so much a question of pure ears, but of pure hearts. And if I may say so, they really ought to have gotten someone else as chief magistrate just to keep people from thinking they had hired a comedian for their theatrical performance. But I would ask again: "And in our own day?" In truth, I venture to say that it is the men, and not the women, who are responsible for most of the unhappy marriages today.

5

REGARDING AUTHORITY
IN MARRIAGE

Ｅ

IF THE *authority* in the household belongs to the man, then it is the
governing which falls to the woman; if the husband is Director of
the Household Judicial System, then she is Director of Police.[1] The
laws which prevail under these circumstances are grouped under the
heading domestic law, and domestic law breaks town law, town law
breaks provincial law, and provincial law breaks Imperial law.[2] People
accuse women of being power hungry—but who isn't? We are all
kings, priests, and prophets,[3] each in his own way. And yet it can be
assumed almost with certainty that women with all their majesty really
have nothing more in mind than to possess us and be loved by us.
All we have to do is belong to them. Those times are long past when
the husband had jurisdiction over life and limb, and when unfaithful
wives were subjected to the judgment of their husbands, almost as
if the shameless laws would have nothing to do with such a heinous
crime. The times, we, and the fair sex have all changed with the years.
What is there now to keep women from taking part in the exercise of
domestic authority in the household? The right of the stronger party
is no longer a convincing reason;[4] that statement made during the
wedding ceremony on which such great significance is placed, ". . .
and he shall rule over thee,"[5] can also be freely translated: ". . . and
he shall protect thee." We need only to recall the Chevalière d'Éon
and the great female rulers to come to the conclusion that it is the

fault of the stronger sex, and not the fair one, when now and again it happens that a woman rules without distinction in the household.

Since women, just like men, are human beings and since, therefore, equal rights are due to them as well, could there ever be enough proposals for putting both classes of people on the same footing? The mothers of our best people, who bore and raised the great and noble among us—are they forever to be repaid with the blackest ingratitude and treated no better than if they had fallen into the hands of "zeelverkooper,"[6] in the sense that, condemned to lifelong slavery, they are only happy or miserable depending on whether they are married to a good or bad man? Is the other class of mankind with all its admirable qualities to remain eternally in the cradle, forever entertained with children's toys and candy? Is it always to be the clay which is not permitted to ask its maker: "What are you doing with me?"[7] They are without true legal rights everywhere in the whole world! The clergymen say, "My *brothers . . .*"; and when we die we are said to be gathered to our *fathers*. At the time when printing presses were about to be set up for the first time in Constantinople the question was raised: "What will our copyists live on now?" And one can hardly imagine a stronger reaction than this if the question of improving the status of the other sex were also to come up for discussion.

Without a doubt, it is the notion that the man's duty is to protect, the woman's to please, which has held back the plan to send both boys and girls to a single school, and the present system is justified as long as the strict arrangement still exists whereby the man not only is expected to step into the breach in cases of emergency, but also is the only one to lead a public life. In the meantime, and while the public still continues to take no notice of the women, men should serve the state themselves and have their households served through their wives—for no man can serve two masters.[8] That in a political sense the expression *"to serve"* very often also means *"to give orders"* is better left unsaid, as well as the remark that our good friends the men really do sometimes manage the affairs of state in a pretty off-hand fashion. The more women work at being masculine and doing masculine things, the further they remove themselves from the authority they seek, in that this utterly unsuitable role robs them of so much time that they come off badly in everything. Whenever one free being requests help from another such free being, it does not enter into a condition of slavery with respect to the latter; rather it is the duty of the stronger to render this assistance. In fact, the weaker party assumes no debt whatsoever;

only the stronger takes one on. His creditor is Nature herself; and can he then regard her with distrust who has been so generous to him?

If the fair sex were just as strong as our own, what would have become of the world, and what would become of it in the future? Human beings have the honor and the dishonor, the good fortune and the misfortune, of being subject to their equals. Our Royal Highnesses are men just like their subjects, and in like manner the man, to whom generally the place of honor[9] in the household is due, is as little free of faults as his wife. And the wife can do nothing wiser in the face of the present situation than to reconcile herself to the times, especially for as long as those times remain hard. Do not the men—ostensibly to their advantage—sacrifice a good portion of their own human rights to the state? And who can swim against the stream? Men bear so many injustices for the sake of the state that women would do well to concentrate on the smaller evils in their own homes. If they remain women, they will be able to achieve everything by means of their gentleness and patience, so that it may be said of them in spirit and truth, "For when they are weak, then they are strong."[10] If men followed the path of gentleness and patience in their own professions, they would never attain their goals—nor should they attempt to by such means, for because they are strong it is incumbent on them to overcome through their strength alone; and yet, precisely because they are strong, they must also banish from their minds any desire to rule in the household. Whose wish is it that the woman should rule over the man? But neither should *she* be ruled by *him*. Is it not possible for people to live together, guided by the Holy Spirit of their own self-made laws, without having one among them raise his proud head and, by means of what he imagines to be his superior strength, change the order of things, preferring to ruin this order rather than follow it? Why do human beings, who rule themselves so poorly, so love to play lord and master over others, even though their security and peace of mind decrease in exact proportion to the extent they increase their power over others? At the time of Saturn,[11] there was neither lord nor servant, neither real[12] nor personal servitude. "There is no fear in love; but perfect love casteth out fear."[13]

The suggestion that the husband should be the regent, and Madame Prime Minister has much to recommend it—but is it advisable to acknowledge the requests of a Prime Minister so openly? I shall attempt to give the clearest explanation possible while avoiding all metaphors and similes. Men have permission to be defiant and stubborn, women must dissemble; men can assert what they hold to be true, women may merely offer their opinions; when worse comes to worst, men can laugh, women must cry. The virtue of humility—a virtue we are accustomed to treating as a weakness and would like very much to banish from those virtues presupposing strength and power—attains its complete and well-deserved superiority in the woman.

In order to answer the prize question,[14] "To whom belongs the authority in marriage?" without stepping on anyone's toes and still get to the heart of the matter, could we not reply with the answer "To reason"? Reason should in fact rule everywhere, even though cleverness often usurps her throne—it is probably not the most reasonable, but the cleverest people who everywhere rule over others. If even the weakest sovereign has a mistress who is not merely "loyal and beloved" but *discerning* and *judicious* as well, then his state is in good hands. Nobody, neither husband nor wife, is offended by the prize-winning answer "reason" because both of them rule together to the extent that they rule with reason.

If anyone wishes to object by replying that my casuistry fails to unravel the knot and merely cuts it in two, then I am prepared to give proof of my patience and bear this reproach with equanimity. Would to God that our casuists had always destroyed more questions than they had solved! The ability to teach a person also carries with it the authorization, or at least the conviction, of a right to do so; and if a ruler and teacher are really one and the same thing, or at least not much different from each other, then it can be said that teaching deserves the name only when it simultaneously aims for and achieves some kind of improvement. This being the case, it follows that even if the level of general prosperity (which under any circumstances is capricious and changeable, and based for the most part on usurpation) should happen to fall as a consequence of such improvement, mankind as a whole will nevertheless gain immeasurably, in the sense that the right both to teach and to rule (and that means more through love of one's neighbor than commands and prohibitions) belongs to anyone who, by virtue of wisdom and insight, is called, sanctified, or enlightened enough to do so. But what would happen if the situation were suddenly reversed and the subjects began to teach their masters? Would not the latter then still wish to be treated as human beings, and would they not be extremely unhappy if for all their majesty they were to lose their human dignity and be compelled to relinquish the thousands of little acts of kindness they had become accustomed to receiving from those former subjects? Or is one required to be arrogant and opinionated if one wishes to teach? Does not the Socratic method of teaching,[15] in which one never *seeks* an opportunity to learn, but merely utilizes those which occur naturally, have for its goal a teacher who gives less the appearance of a master than of one who appears to be learning through his teaching? Does it not remain the greatest virtue a government minister can have, to bring his sovereign to say what he himself would say? And should not every minister be responsible for that which his ruler does? But until our law-givers and our judges learn to moderate the shrill tone they have adopted, what are they but sounding brass and tinkling cymbals?[16]

If the authority in the household were set up after the manner of the examples mentioned above, who could be ashamed of being ruled in such a way? Do we not all make mistakes? And is it not the greatest mistake and the farthest thing from an improvement in the situation to try to convince oneself that one is *born* to teach? What a weak example words give when compared to examples and works! Deeds are the hermeneutics of words, and whoever teaches by means of good actions, whoever rules through noble deeds, is not far from the kingdom of God.

The opposite sex is weak—how can it command? It is born to cloak its requests in flattery—how can it scold? It is beautiful—how can it distort its facial features? The intellect of the women, which has so often triumphed over our own, stakes everything on words and can win anyone over—this intellect will never let them fall. And when we gaze at the stars and end up falling, it is women who help us up again; when we become lost in abstractions, it is women who guide us back onto the right path. They possess a practical reason, ours is a theoretical one.[17] Rousseau says that the woman has more understanding, the man more genius; the woman observes things and the man philosophizes about them. One might perhaps be tempted to content oneself with this sort of differentiation, even though the odes of the poetess Sappho[18] possess such a noble simplicity that hardly any male poet has ever surpassed her. But when Hans Jakob goes so far as to maintain that they do not love any of the arts or understand them; indeed, when he even denies that they possess any sort of genius whatsoever, then he will find it difficult to counter the charge of bias in his opinions—and in fact, now that we are in possession of his *Confessions*, the reasons for this bias can be accounted for very nicely.

Granted that quarreling and bickering constitute feminine weapons (the only ones we allow them and cannot take away), whose application more often merely exhausts than actually overcomes us; and granted that curiosity, credulity, envy, and delight at a rival's misfortune are their negative qualities, but which our own sex, unfortunately, also possesses in no small measure—do not the positive qualities of women also include a clever wit, patience, and a certain cosmopolitan love? Our own sex seems to reveal more love for the family name and for the fatherland. But do the women really have a fatherland? Are they not sooner obligated to sacrifice everything, even their name, to the new family into which they are received through marriage to their husbands?

In addition, their feelings are more heartfelt and immediate than our own, and while we, with all our exalted and profound reason, have to resort to faith in the end, women know how to turn a situation to their advantage by permitting reason *in optima forma* [19] to have her say and then turning straightway to the heart. The most important conversions have all been brought about by women. They are not inclined to public speaking, but are born to colloquize—an art wherein many people who could otherwise dance the night through are rendered unable to walk ten steps.

When, where, and how did women renounce their role in the affairs of state? [20] We all know that they are not about to give up their voice in the peoples' court. But the longer we dare to withhold from them so unjustly a voice and a place in everything having to do with the governing of the states and the nation, the more dissolute this sex will become as soon as the bonds of coercion and slavery have been torn asunder. One can already make the observation that the weak person tends to be more cruel; if we then use artificial means to render the weak person even weaker than God and Nature intended, who or what can hold back this person when he or she finally comes to power? This sex has very little if any belief in laws, because it was never invited to vote on them; nor does it put much stock in the tinseled grandiloquence of the great and wise among us men. Moreover, the notions they cherish regarding the obligation to render unto Caesar the things which are Caesar's and tribute to whom tribute is due [21] are almost unbelievable. Women realize better than we do that while wisdom and greatness eclipse or outshine the weaknesses of mankind, they do not put an end to them. They keep an exceedingly careful eye on the wise and the great in order to apprehend instantly any example of weakness garbed in grandeur and to bring the matter up later in the most mischievous way. If you want to hear the most impudent comments about the men who rule, about their body or soul, about the seven wise men of the land[22] and the seventy times seven administrative assistants under them, then go to the oracle of a bright and quick-witted woman, and she will pronounce her judgment and disperse justice just as freely as she will supply you with reasons to support her decisions. The spirit of revolution rests upon this sex.[23] Voltaire and Rousseau attended their school. The thought: "Academics are the monks of literature, the sciences, and the liberal arts," is the thought of a woman. A large number of the amorous intrigues of women in which they themselves become entangled arise not out of infatuation or love, but out of an inclination to dominate. They show that, despite all the oppression, they are not able to be brought down so far as to become entirely without will, and that they compensate for this by having the honor of leading kings and princes, ministers and wise men, clergymen and poets around in public bound in chains, and by confounding all theories by means of their practical approach to life until such time as they may show the world what their nature intended them to be!

If we examine history, we will find that even if women never actually occupied the seats of power themselves, nevertheless everything was governed through them and they managed to overcome every obstacle in attaining their intended goal by one means or another. Themistocles[24] had no qualms about admitting that his son governed all of Athens, in the sense that the will of his wife was the same as that of his son, and his own was that of his wife. The rule of the manly Roman women over the womanly Roman men can serve as an example for us here; and have not even the most depraved men always been ruled over more absolutely by their equally depraved mistresses than good men by their devoted wives, even though the Romans only granted to the women in general the most innocuous rights possible? That is precisely the reason, it seems to me, that the women were so powerful, and likewise precisely the reason, depending upon the time, the place, and the situation, why they still are so today. Caesonia and Drusilla had far more power over Caligula, and Messalina and Agrippina over Claudius, than the kind and good-natured Agrippina over Germanicus.[25] Given women's powerful inclination to goodness and their cosmopolitanism, we would stand to profit even more than they if we would but let them have their say. Occasionally one can

175

observe on a small scale their potential greatness on a much larger one. Thus, for example, in a recent parliamentary election in England, a certain duchess thought nothing of campaigning for a candidate by the name of Fox and bribing coal porters with kisses.

It might perhaps be worth the trouble here to deal with several objections with which the fair sex is often confronted and grant these legitimate obstacles within the marriage bond a sympathetic ear.— "Pregnancy and childbirth."—Yes, I thought as much. The laws declare that which will be so someday to be an already accomplished fact if it works to their advantage, and nothing is more just or wise than this particular practice. Terror, torment, and in fact all unexpected occurrences exert such a decided influence on pregnant women that we must take care to remove hundreds of objects from their path daily, even if the notion of "taking a fright" ought to be relegated to the status of an old wives' tale. But can we consider those to be reasons, my dear fellow, why Nature could have declared women incapable of governing? Doesn't His Excellency go the spa once a year? Aren't there also recesses during a courtroom trial? And won't women be able to deal with their pregnancies more easily than at present once their sex has taken on its new form? Every illness has deep respect for the well-founded excuse: "I don't have time to get sick!"; it only finds lodging in places where it is admitted and accepted, where it is cherished and protected. Doesn't women's irrepressible longing to govern mean anything to you? It even goes so far as to drive them to marry fools, just so that they may rule all the more securely on the basis of their husband's folly. But haven't you noticed that in general every woman takes extreme care to see that the intellect of her husband remains on an elevated plane? I am not quite sure why this is the case—perhaps it is a matter of paying homage to the intellect in general, or perhaps in spite of the overall protection accorded to the woman by the state, in the case of her husband she may count on no other special protection than that of the intellect, a kind of protection which is shared mutually between husband and wife.

"Women," one often hears, "are not suited for businesses of any kind—not even a needlework shop. The only exception might be a dressmaker's shop. Women can't measure pants for men,[26] and their imagination is altogether too strong for them to be able to cut men's shirts to fit. The cut is almost always wrong." But does making clothes have anything to do with governing? And have you never known women, my dear friend, who far outdistanced their husbands in the matter of making clothes? If I wouldn't be giving offense to the positions of honor decreed from on high and now occupied so "fittingly" by the men, I could name at least ten positions where the women would be in their element for every one where they would not. Take, just as a small example, the areas of finance and pharmaceutics— the latter discipline in particular being one for which women possess indisputable talent due to their own physical frailty. A doctor who is ailing himself makes the best kind of doctor; he knows how sick people really feel, and he will certainly not have any difficulty recognizing that *particular* enemy which is after his own life. I would almost say that it is improper for men to be treating the fair sex. It was a great doctor who once described the treatment of women's illnesses as a "disgrace to the medical profession." But let us now consider *sub rosa*[27] how things might have been in the very first ages of mankind.

It is obvious that in order to probe the original relationships between men and women in a state of nature and to determine their natural inclinations, talents, and needs, we cannot sail around the world gathering as examples barbarous peoples living outside the confines of normal social organizations, since in fact these are not natural men at all, but simply groups of humans who have degenerated from their original type due to the favorable or unfavorable influences of climate, soil, or other circumstances. Rather, we must imagine them just as they came from the hands of primeval and newly-created Nature, still in a state of innocence and leading a happy, animal-like existence, and as they then acquired for themselves a state of freedom and came to a knowledge of good and evil. Was it not Eve, according to the oldest documents of the human race, who brought about this most important of revolutions? If we could or would agree that love between the two sexes had already at the earliest period differentiated itself to an appreciable degree from the merely transient passions associated with brutish need and here and there developed into drives for well-being, companionship, or friendship, and thus into an association, a lasting relationship between men and women, then at this point at least the needs were too few and the means for fulfilling them too numerous for the man to hit upon the idea that he was somehow superior to his other half by dint of his ability to obtain food and provide protection for her during the six-weeks' period while she was recovering from childbirth, a period which in that golden age doubtless was set at six days and perhaps only encompassed the span of a mere six hours. Without a doubt, marriage was a relationship between equals until the time when mankind began to multiply and drive each other away from their lands, and until it became necessary to exert much greater effort and labor to feed themselves and defend themselves against wild animals—or against other men, which often resulted in even greater violence—and until various tribes began to infringe upon each others' hunting and fishing grounds and cultivated fields, a circumstance which then gave rise to feuds and the formation of confederations. It was at this point that the man gained dominion over his wife, whom he made subject to himself approximately in the same manner as the *"Majores Domus"* over the descendants of Chlodwig,[28] whereby dependency and aversion to hard physical labor engendered slavery—but, it seems to me, only for that period of time until reason was capable of both preventing and carrying out actions for which previously a strong arm had been the necessary requisite. In the face of this scarcity of necessities and the resulting greed for possessions (let these two circumstances, already mentioned above and to be taken up again later, serve as both a lesson and a comfort to the fair sex), women lost privileges. And is it not typical of mankind that Eve should now be subject to Adam and he the only head of the marital relationship and the master of his wife? But what does male domination go to prove other than that reason is still a long way from completely possessing its rights, and that women, therefore, are still in a house of bondage in Egypt and in the wilderness? Yet someday their land of Canaan will appear.[29]

Until then, Madame, have patience if you please, and although your dear husband might happen to have even less intellect than you, nevertheless deign to act toward him like a minister in the cabinet of an imbecilic ruler, who, although allowing nothing to happen without his sanction, sees to it that everything is placed before His Excellency to be signed. Otherwise, it might become possible once again for people to start bringing up that hypothetical question couched in such careful terms as to disguise the tyranny behind it—namely, the question as to whether it might not be good to forbid your sex all intellectual fire and water whatsoever in the form of reading and writing. Novels and love letters would lend the appearance of justification to what in effect would be bolted doors and border signs bearing the inscription: "This far and no further." Do you believe you will lose something by being patient? Those people are honored as heroes who are injured too severely by our laws; and this canonization remains their portion and inheritance.[30] Is not every clever wife capable of training her husband in such a way that he merely commands what the wife in fact wishes herself? This should be the true nature of all lawmaking. Wherever laws are made in some other way, it is the people who suffer. And in general it is a poor sort of cure when we attempt to help people along by means of legislation. Let us legislate that which people would do anyway without being ordered to; let us be satisfied to exhort where we now lay down the law amid thunder and lightning, and we will bring the human race farther than with the gallows and the rack. At present, women must keep silent in church[31] and cannot stand security for another person or accomplish anything without a man to serve as their guardian in the marriage relationship.[32] Indeed, before that second revolution of reason and blessed deliverance takes place when the fullness of time has come,[33] women can loosen the bonds in which they are now held only through virtuous conduct and faithfulness in marriage.

If the only guarantee for the men of their wives' faithfulness is a lack of opportunity, can they be blamed if they treat their wives like slaves? It also seems apparent, by the way, that historically whatever form of governance first prevailed in the household—that is, depending on whether the man was more or less head of it—later determined the system of government in the state as well, although with time the latter form of government came conversely to exert its own influence on the governance of the household, so that the man, with certain exceptions, is the monarch in his household in a monarchical state, and in aristocratic and democratic states has likewise taken on a role corresponding to these particular systems of government. To the credit of human reason it must be noted here that the dominance of the husband over his wife, even in monarchical states, is so far different from all other forms of dominance that the worst thing about it is the name. To be sure, women still have the legal right to claim mistreatment against men who tyrannize over them,[34] but this is really the least we can do for them. A person who oppresses a weaker person deserves universal contempt; whoever fights only against weaker opponents never deserves the title of *victor*, for from the duel to the bloodiest war the battle must be like a wager in which neither side knows at first who will gain the victory. For this reason it remains an unmistakable sign of a good heart to protect and defend women after the well-known manner of the chivalric knight. Wherever the tyranny of the man has made the woman into a rebel, everyone should want to come to her aid—here right even outlasts duty. The dominion of the husband over his wife must not be that of the lord over his manor, or of the

179

steward over his fields, but rather, in the words of a wise man of old, that of the soul over the body.[35] Marriage should be based on mutual consent between the marriage partners; harmony in marriage—even in the extended meaning of the phrase—can only be considered good.

It is hard to understand why there are no plans for an improvement in the status of women at a time when people are everywhere talking about human rights and the freedoms of citizens, since the need for this improvement should be obvious to everyone and, in respect to both culture and morality, would promote the public welfare of the state to a considerable degree. But when people speak of human rights, they mean nothing more than the rights of males and evade the issue by means of a *subintelligitur*,[36] which is a piece of roguishness not unlike that of the Augsburg Interim of 1548.[37] We once bought our wives; now they buy us. And surely it is time now to grant what is right to those who so often paid us on time and in cash—and sometimes even more than what was due! And which of you entered into marriage as into a relationship with a subordinate? Was not rather each of you at the time of your marriage the admirer, lover, and worshiper of your bride?

The domination of the husband in the marriage relationship is very closely related to the concept of paternal authority, and since neither in the marriage nor in the father-child partnership does any sort of contract form the basis for the distribution of rights as is—and can only be—the case with other partnerships, I would like merely to note here that parental rights are based on the duty of parents to raise their children. Nevertheless, parents may not be called to account for their children; they are not punished for not having utilized in proper fashion the power which Nature gave them. On the other hand, Nature has deliberately seen to it that parents automatically love their children and that children love their parents as a rule to the same degree that they have been well or poorly raised by them. Thus neither should any public institution interfere with this purely natural affair, nor should scholars give them any reason to, since in this way our natural freedom would be limited unnecessarily and political laws would surely make their way into the innermost chambers of our houses and our children's nurseries, ruining the most precious human relationships by their numerous artifices. The shame of having badly-raised children is punishment enough for their parents, and the love of parents for their children will accomplish more than all the laws and statutes in the world. That golden age to come, in which human laws will stand in the closest possible relation to natural ones, is not yet upon the horizon; and the hope of encountering legal officials who place importance on the honest and uncorrupted administration of such human-natural law is even farther in the distance.

Since the paternal and maternal authority depends on the parents' greater or lesser talent for raising children and the amount of time either the father or the mother can apply to this task, it seems to me that the question as to how paternal and maternal authority should stand in relation to each other, that is, whether one should be greater than the other, ought to be taken up and answered at this point, since it is not possible to establish general guidelines for this issue. If one considers that fathers are required to take to the field in order to shed blood in truly honorable fashion; that it is incumbent upon them to write a law or a prescription for the sickly state whereby in a neat and methodical way the often fundamentally sound constitution of the ailing body politic is corrupted and ruined; that they are often obliged, using all five methods of mathematical computation,[38] to levy a new tax, a tax which is all the more popular among the higher authorities because it immediately appeals to the stomach by plucking food from the mouths of the hungry, whereby the latter are thus assisted in acquiring the virtue of moderation; that they disperse right and justice among the people by couching perfectly clear matters in such learned gibberish that nobody except the royal officials themselves knows what to make of them; that they consider it their duty out of pure Christian love for the Lord to condemn their poor fellow men to the fires of eternal damnation for persisting in obdurate unbelief out of insufficient respect for human ordinances and institutions—now if one takes these highly important occupations into consideration, then it becomes obvious that as a rule the raising of the children will fall to the mother and that a part of the parental authority will need to be granted to her, by which means she will quietly and directly proceed to gain dominion over the entire household, because if the care of the green wood of the children is entrusted to her, what will become of the dry wood of the rest of the household without her care and management? In order to prevent future misfortunes, children must be forced to refrain from this or that foolish, dangerous, or indecent manner of behaving. This can hardly be accomplished without their experiencing some unpleasant sensations, and children will therefore stand to benefit more from that moderation and restraint which in general is sooner characteristic of their mothers than their much more severe fathers.

6

FOR THE BENEFIT
OF YOUNG MEN

❦

AS PROTAGORAS[1] WAS ASKED why he was giving his daughter in marriage to his bitterest enemy, he replied, "Because I couldn't give him anything worse." But then, maybe he had an obnoxious daughter! Democritus[2] took a small wife, although he himself was tall in stature. "I have chosen," he said, "the lesser of two evils." Solomon states, "Whoso findeth a wife findeth a good thing, and obtaineth favor of the Lord."[3] Now who is right, Protagoras, Democritus, or Solomon, the Wisest of the Wise?

It is hard not to marry; it is just as hard to be happily married. I do not believe that a single married man in the world is ever completely happy. He may be happy most of the time, but a day will come when he is not—but then where is the marriage which is perfectly harmonious? Getting married is like entering into a contract to purchase a house and not backing out even if a lightning bolt should demolish half of it or a storm damage the roof and a falling tile split your skull nearly in half; getting married is like chartering a merchant vessel whose cargo nobody will insure; getting married is like receiving an inheritance without ever having given any thought to how much it might be, or like exchanging large bills for pocket change; getting married is like trying to remove the pits after you have already eaten the cherries; getting married is like sleepwalking and not waking up until someone calls your name out loudly; getting married is like making a *glebae adscriptus*[4] out of a free man. The life of a married man is over long before he reaches the actual point of death; in fact, he ought to order his marriage bed and his cemetery plot on the very same day. Seldom will a man who gets married succeed any longer on his own; now he will have to buy his success with the virtue of his wife—and what is worse, the cemetery of love lies right next to the temple of Hymen.[5] Nearly all novels and comedies end with a marriage, since the eternal monotony of the married state affords no subjects worthy of such depiction. In several places in Germany, marrying is called "changing," and this is in fact true—marriage does change people. If the wife is ugly, then her husband comes to dislike her; if she is beautiful, then others like her as well; if she is rich, then he is poor, and poverty makes him dull-witted; if she is poor, then she eats him out of house and home; if she is clever, she wants to dominate; if dumb, then she does not know how to obey; if she is young, then people predict a sad fate for her when she turns twenty-five; if she is old, then she needs care; if she—whatever she might be, she is a woman, and that is enough.

Do you very often hear a man of reason talk seriously about love? He reports the status of his love life to his friend only briefly before he takes leave of him, and precisely at that point in the conversation where during the holiday season Easter, Christmas, or Whitsuntide greetings are conveyed come the words: "Oh, one more thing! I am engaged to be married!" Belfort confides to his friend Lovelace[6] that he has decided to mend his ways and get married, whereupon Lovelace replies sympathetically that he ought to carry out his plans in reverse order and begin with getting married, because he could then be certain not to miss any opportunity to regret what he has done, which would be the first step toward repentance and reform. And what should a person do? Do what you will, Socrates says, you will regret it no matter what. But what will a person regret the least—having married or not having married? Every person is naturally inclined to comfort and consequently has the calling to establish his own hearth and home—and a wife is the match without which no fire can be ignited.

When a house or country estate is offered for sale, people say that it is dilapidated, it has no wheat fields, it doesn't yield the usual interest for that part of the country, it has hidden defects; if it is then sold, then everyone wants it, and the buyer could make money by not keeping the estate or the house and selling it to somebody else. So it goes with girls as well. Before they are spoken for, there are no offers; once they are taken, then there are a hundred who say, ""Why didn't I notice her!" But the banns have already been published, and in order to comfort themselves, people open up a new chapter—they begin to slander and defame. But be of good cheer, my dear young people, a week after the wedding that will all be behind you. And since there are no perfect virtues here on earth, should you really be surprised that you won't ever be able to count on perfect happiness in this sublunary world anyway? What more should we ask for, really, than to be happy with our home?

But, you might ask, what about an occasional evening of pleasure outside the home? No, because we are rational beings, and it is first and foremost through education that the soul becomes what it can be. Prostitution has as a consequence a certain disdain for the human race, and whoever loses his respect for the latter is well on his way to becoming a wretched human being. I know of a country in which houses of prostitution are sanctioned by the state; yet is it a good idea to allow truly indecent behavior to be looked upon with favor and to grant public approval and legal authorization to an immoral mode of conduct that in fact condemns its own self to the darkness?[7] This admittedly easier and more convenient way of satisfying the sexual desire will lessen the number of marriages and create not bachelors, but dissipated men whose families are an abomination to them, just as they are to their families. And what about these unfortunate women? Do we wish to extinguish even that sense of shame already responsible for suffocating the feeling of natural motherly love toward a helpless and defenseless child and replace it with something worse—a sanctioned shamelessness which opens the door to every vice and degrading act known to man? Are we going to grant official recognition to a person who does not even consider herself worthy of the company of the members of her own sex? In this particular state I am talking about it is no longer a question of men and women meeting "in chambering and wantonness," but rather where "the works of the flesh are manifest."[8] People think they are going to make our wives and daughters safe from assault by means of such measures; but in fact is much more needed than all this publicity to arouse everyone's curiosity? I would not be surprised if sooner or later this privilege became indispensable in almost every home; at least it is conceivable that a man, his wife, his son and his daughter could meet each other some day in such a "house of good repute." Opportunities do not come about without the women of opportunity who toil in the service of Venus and make them

184

possible. The entire moral worth of a young woman is founded on her reputation as being "chaste and sober."[9] Once she has relinquished this advantage she has given herself up forever and can expect nothing more than contempt in return. We are born to be members of society; need and misery bind humans together more easily and firmly than prosperity and abundance. It was need which created societies in the past and still preserves them today. The first of all social groupings and relationships was marriage, and the politician is able to derive as much from that institution as a true poet of genius can draw from ancient Greece and Rome.

Why not a mistress? At the beginning of this century, Thomasius published a series of arguments concerning the legitimacy of concubinage.[10] Nevertheless, his disputation only dealt with this single institution, and was conducted on a very learned plane since neither party understood the other. Concubinage was tolerated among the Romans, but has been forbidden in more recent times. Now if we are just talking about temporary concubinage (*concubinatu temporaneo*), then I am against it, for the reason that the man then does not marry for years, and no woman can be leased out for such a long period of time. If mankind had no other capacities and no other duties than to satisfy its desires; if the state were only concerned with human beings and not with well-raised people; if marriage were just a factory for babies and not a sanctuary of morality; and finally, if Nature had given us hints in this regard by means of a disproportionate number of girls, then polygamy would perhaps have some justification in spite of the many doubts it raises. But neither polygamy, nor temporary concubinage, nor the leasing of women is allowed in this country because such institutions would naturally be accompanied by unfortunate consequences for the children, which are not the property of the parents alone, but belong to the entire community as well. Permanent concubinage[11] (*concubinatum perpetuum*), moreover, is hardly a trifling matter either—there is, after all, the solution offered by the *matrimonium ad legem Salicam*,[12] and if a man feels it necessary to give a Christian semblance to what we are accustomed to calling "willful cohabitation," then all he needs to do is send for a clergyman and give his mistress his left hand while he pays the preacher's fees with his right.

I beg your pardon—I must have been talking in my sleep again as in the first chapter. Now that I am awake, now that I see the women as they presently are, I could never advise anyone to take a mistress. A mistress has to be taught to dance, to play cards, and to do everything else that a wife already knew before she was married. A mistress has no other household goods outside her own person—and what sort of collateral is that? Goods which are sold for half price are generally damaged or, in the case of perishable foodstuffs, have been exposed to warm weather. A mistress is subject to no laws, since the entire arrangement is against the law. If she wishes to take up with another man, you cannot use legal means to bring about her return; she was not yours in the first place, and it was also a shame that you ever had to admit that you were hers. A certain procedure must be followed in everything, and if you cannot buy an estate or house, enter into a contract, give or bequeath something to anyone without observing already well-established rules, what makes you think that you can marry without following some sort of procedure? Pliny says that a ruler can give no more valid proof of his divinity than to bestow on his subjects a good successor; and do you wish to fulfill this divine duty by some path other than that of order and respectability? You desire the sister of Caius without the legal encumbrances; but what if Caius requested exactly the same arrangement with your sister? Some people make it their object to decline others as if they were adjectives and conjugate them like verbs; nevertheless they themselves want to have the honor—or bear the shame—of being like a particle in grammar which cannot be declined or conjugated. Aren't you trying to be like one of these particles? In the end, after you have been cut off from your relatives for twenty years, have sat in the corner of the church all this time, gone to confession with lowered eyes because everybody already knew what you had to confess; after years of having gone only to tragedies at the theater out of fear that you might find yourself and your situation being depicted in a comedy—in the end, when you've been through four lawsuits with the husband of your sister and bickered continuously with your brother, you will wind up doing what you dreaded anyway and on top of that having to give all sorts of presents to your relatives just so they will come to dine with you and say *"ma soeur"* to your "wife" when they leave. Husbands like you are in the same boat as Tarquin the Proud with his Sibylline Books: the amount of money with which he could have bought all nine books in the first place became in the end the purchase price of the three which were left over.[13]

If you have children, how it will hurt to have other children running alongside your coach who bear your features! In effect, you will be throwing your own image onto the rubbish heap, and people will know it: "The father of that boy," they will tell everyone, "lives in the house just to the right of the market square." That will hurt! What a heart-rending feeling it will be to want to kiss your own son and not be permitted to! Let's say you have him legitimized; is he then legitimized in his own eyes? In fact, the "Prohibition against Punishment"[14] will be the greatest punishment of all for him, and to be perfectly honest, can a legal action taken after the fact ever truly rectify an unjust one committed years before? The prince who decrees this on your behalf—if he could only confiscate the thoughts of your neighbors as well! And does his *"fiat as decreed"* have any validity outside the borders of his own country? The man who really raised your son still remains a cobbler, no matter whether his "son" now has noble ancestors or not. "What pretty hair," one lady whispers to another, and your legitimized son blushes, because he got it from his mother.

At a time when people still looked upon marriage as a yoke and a burden; when people were looking for a helper in marriage and the wife still bore the honorary title "helpmate," things stood well with this part of the Table of Duties,[15] and there were always men and women who desired to ease this already easy yoke and lighten this light burden[16] by uttering their vows with hand upraised and heart sincere and then being faithful to them. But since we have been letting these duties of marriage be carried out by maids, tutors, and governesses; since we have been taking away from the poor baby that bottle which Nature herself provided for it, just because its mother Her Ladyship the Countess does not wish to be forced to miss the ball—since then the remaining burdensome aspects of marriage have more or less disappeared and our wives now bear the title "marriage associates," it is true, although it seems to me that the idea of love within marriage has not gained very much by what I consider to be this lowering of the status of the woman.

"That is too high a price to pay for regret," says our friend Belfort the philosopher; and even if I don't possess the eloquence, my dear young friend, to persuade you to get married, at least I believe I have offered enough reasons to serve as a warning against taking a mistress, especially if you are a civilian. I have long considered it an honor when a girl of the lower class fell in love with one of us; a woman of the upper class, I felt, would *want* to have us as a husband. But I was wrong. A lower-class girl wants to become our mistress. O, the times! O, the manners![17] We are no longer in a position to show taste through our selection of a wife, and I must confess with a sigh that nowadays it is only the choice of one's mistress which is thought to reveal any taste. And who can refrain from crying out along with that Englishman: "O virtue, where hast thou hidden thyself?"

The distinction between ecclesiastical and civil marriages is now and always has been somewhat arbitrary, and if we consider marriage from the standpoint of its most essential aspect, that is, as a divine dispensation and a wise provision for man to enable him to rise above fleshly lusts and perceive his human self, his individuality, and his divine image, then the diference between ecclesiastical and civil marriage is only great enough to fill a few blank pages in the lawbooks. God joins together;[18] Nature fastens the marriage bond. It is a divine disposition; the state, in terms of either the sacred or profane order of things, has actually nothing to do with the matter—let it put off its shoes from its feet, for the place whereon it stands is holy ground.[19]

Nevertheless, since with the best of intentions we have prescribed certain ceremonies for the conclusion of a valid marriage whose fulfillment in any civilized country is not associated with any particular difficulty, then a young man of marriageable age would do well and wisely if he simply went to the town hall if in Holland and the church if in Germany and added the "Amen" to his "I do."[20] The German word for marriage [Ehe] comes from the Middle High German word "ê," meaning "law," and carries with it the implication of legality; an "Ewart" was formerly a priest who was a "warden" to the law.

Those of my readers who have no wish to get married can skip the rest of this chapter; those, however, who are firmly committed to entering the holy state of matrimony are now cordially invited to drink a cup of hot chocolate with me! I say "hot chocolate" because I have no desire to leave myself open to the criticism directed at Richardson's novel *Grandison*,[21] namely, that too much tea-drinking goes on in it. The words from which we are now going to seek edification are found in the Proverbs of Solomon, chapter 31, verses 10 to the end of the chapter:

> Who can find a virtuous woman? for her price is far above rubies. The heart of her husband doth safely trust in her, so that he shall have no need of spoil. She will do him good and not evil all the days of her life. She seeketh wool, and flax, and worketh willingly with her hands. She is like the merchants' ships; she bringeth her food from afar. She riseth also while it is yet night, and giveth meat to her household, and a portion to her maidens. She considereth a field, and buyeth it: with the fruit of her hands she planteth a vineyard. She girdeth her loins with strength, and strengtheneth her arms. She perceiveth that her merchandise is good: her candle goeth out not by night. She layeth her hands to the spindle, and her

hands hold the distaff. She stretcheth out her hand to the poor; yea, she reacheth forth her hands to the needy. She is not afraid of the snow for her household: for all her household are clothed with scarlet.22 She maketh herself coverings of tapestry; her clothing is silk and purple. Her husband is known in the gates, when he sitteth among the elders of the land. She maketh fine linen, and selleth it; and delivereth girdles unto the merchant. Strength and honour are her clothing; and she shall rejoice in time to come. She openeth her mouth with wisdom; and in her tongue is the law of kindness. She looketh well to the ways of her household, and eateth not the bread of idleness. Her children arise up, and call her blessed; her husband also, and he praiseth her. Many daughters have done virtuously, but thou excellest them all. Favour is deceitful, and beauty is vain: but a woman that feareth the LORD, she shall be praised. Give her of the fruit of her hands; and let her own works praise her in the gates.

Such an excellent description of a wife is really not any more to be expected from King Solomon than from the *Lex Papia Popaea*,23 which bears the names of two people who had neither wife nor children; nevertheless, precisely for this reason both sources are all the more instructive to me. Who can deny that marriages ease the burden of governing lands and people to an extraordinary degree, in the sense that the father and mother of the house hold an office not unlike that of a Justice of the Peace and as such benefit the state more than all governmental authority! Marriages keep people together and promote order, activity, and industriousness; they constitute the state; they are its image and the state itself in miniature. Whoever defends his own hearth defends the state indirectly as well; love for his own is the common man's love for his fatherland. How can anyone love the state he cannot see when he does not love his own hearth which he can see? If a man is married, he knows whom he is working for to attain those things which go beyond his own personal needs; and in fact, is marriage not unlike virtue in that it is honored inwardly even by those who disdain it before the world? The beginning of this chapter was probably torture for many of my readers, just as it was for me, but since there is nothing in the world which does not, like the Roman god Janus, have its two faces, then we have no choice but to do that which cannot be left undone.

If it were possible to tally the votes of the entire civilized world, it is apparent to me that the plurality would be for marriage, for the reason that the intermittent pleasures of sex, the ecstatic passions of man, tend to lead him to hold in contempt all his moral duties and noble principles, and that every person who gives in to excesses of this sort is ashamed of them. Does not all civilized and moral society find pleasure in a well-matched couple? They seem to be enjoying those simple pleasures which are a blessing only for uncorrupted spirits; we see in them that an ardent love, an affection which possesses all the exquisite pleasures of passion without permitting them to lead to debauchery, can result in a pleasure without lust which we would call, often without realizing the true power of this expression, a "heavenly pleasure." The bond of marriage exalts the soul; one would hardly expect, given our unceremonious, insignificant, and humble entry into this world, that the next world had much to offer us either. But in marriage lies a secret: more than we would care to believe, it appears to render probable the idea of the immortality of the soul in the sense that marriage, like godliness itself, contains the promise of life in this world and in the world to come.

Friend, that which brings advantages to the greater part of the human race is becoming a duty for you as well—go into the cloister of marriage! Just look how happy you will make the mother who bore you in pain, and your father is pleased with the thought of being able soon to celebrate the birthday which will make him a grandfather! The Creator has made you into a creator and placed His image upon you. Imagine what a joy it will be for you to be able to be addressed as "father"! One could describe joy as a loud public confession that we exist; with this in mind, try to form for yourself an idea of what it means to feel the joy which your children could bring you. After you have long ceased to exist there will still be sentient beings who thank heaven that you once existed; and truly, whoever leaves children behind will never cease to exist! *Matrimonium sic est honestum, ut humano generi videatur immortalitatem introducere.* ("Marriage is so honorable that the human race appears to owe its immortality to it.") Imagine the divine pleasure of seeing your children grow into adulthood. I call it "divine" because it was not too insignificant for the Creator, and because everything we are able say about it seems incomplete to me. The first days of the creation were a period of rearing wherein the Creator watched each of his created beings develop; and leaves, flowers, and fruits are too beautiful for the eye of God not to have seen that each of them was good. Just look, this divine pleasure is prepared for you—you will see them germinate, sprout, blossom, and then gradually ripen. Every observation a new gift! One birth will have ten others to follow in its wake.

To strengthen my argument, a word at this point from Dr. Martin Luther, the German who, as stout-hearted as he was, once became so overwhelmed at the thought that he was a husband that he was heard to say: "This humiliation of mine will cause joy among the angels and great displeasure in Hell." But a *little Luther* soon reconciled him to the idea, and Croesus[24] was a beggar compared to Dr. Martin Luther, the German!

I have noticed that even a hardened criminal is pure minded and sober on the day his wife reveals to him that she is pregnant and the day she is delivered of their child, and the name "father" which the son babbles on his lap sooner keeps him from returning to his criminal behavior than anything else, the fourth chapter of this treatise not excepted. If you have married with your heart and mind open, then the difficult places on the path you have chosen will become smooth; your wife will constantly be playing the other violin and no matter how badly out of tune your mood might be, she will bring it back into harmony again. Moreover, we tend to get indigestion less frequently if we sit at a table where women are seated—in fact, everything goes better for us. You will come to exude an aura of high-minded cheerfulness; and since a kind of fermentation—like that which produces the bubbles in champagne—is necessary in social intercourse, all social gatherings should be composed of the members of both sexes. Your wife feels your joys just as you do and doubles them— something even your best friend cannot do. She helps you overcome your sufferings while you are still repressing them in order to hide them from her. If each time after the birth of a child you reline the nest with down for her, everything will be like new once again; your hoary old age will be a bright winter day full of charm.

I praise your decision, my dear young fellow, to become a priest of matrimony, but be mindful of one thing before you allow yourself to be ordained—you will be dead for your friends the minute you step onto the carpet, and would do well as far as they are concerned to consider your last Will and Testament for them as you compensate your heart for their loss by the acquisition of a well-chosen wife.

A heart overflowing with emotion seeks out a friend, even if it has to find him on the street or at the fence; this is the reason we have marriage brokers and matchmakers. A man in love must have someone to tell it to; his feelings cannot find room enough in a single soul, and he needs another to lodge them all—in fact, he would really be happiest if he had a separate soul for every limb of his goddess' body. "It is not good that the man should be alone"[25] is thus his solution, and out of the necessity of having a woman to love arises the necessity of having a man to trust. This is the way love begins, especially first love. But how does it end? With the departure of the friend, for love is a spoiled child which always wants its way. "Friend," the bridegroom says on his wedding day to his confidant as they stand next to the bridal bed and he raises one side of the curtain, "as long as I am able to muster a single thought, I will think of our friendship. (The curtain falls back.) We must be sure to see each other every day. I know that the birth of love tends to spell the death of friendship, but thank God, we think differently." What a solemn way of saying good-by! Who would believe that after a time they are seeing each other only once a year—and that because they had the misfortune of being born on the same day. I say "misfortune," because otherwise they would be able to hold a funeral banquet for their friendship at least *twice* a year! The cause of all this is not very difficult to determine. Human beings customarily show more interest in a matter in which they act for the good of the body as a whole, and this interest constitutes in large part what people call "patriotism" (also known by the Germans as "*Gemeingeist*," by the English as "common spirit," and by the French as "*esprit de corps*"). When it comes to their own personal matters they show less interest. The treasurer of a public institution, otherwise stingy enough, virtually rewrites the definition of stinginess when he is serving in his public capacity. In fact, any artist commissioned to paint an allegory on niggardliness would do well to pick such a model in order to avoid being charged by his critics with exaggeration. Possessed themselves with a tendency to hoard, such people assume that everybody else wishes to do likewise; when it is a matter of a possible loss of money or an unnecessary and ill-considered expenditure, they consider the criticism which they would inflict upon themselves and then imagine that criticism multiplied many times by the mouths of others. If you apply this same phenomenon to the household situation, under normal circumstances you will find that what the patriot does in his country, the father does in his home. But please excuse this funeral sermon, my dear young man—you must understand that I, too, have lost many friends to this kind of death. Only yesterday I brought one of them to his grave; may God grant him a blessed peace!

The allegorical figures of virtue and sexual desire which appeared before Hercules were both women,[26] and one and the same thing can make us both happy and unhappy—it is entirely up to us to decide how we wish things to be. You can free yourself of everything much more easily than a woman can. True, a divorce is very easy to obtain in many countries, nevertheless, a divorced man is open to a great deal more scorn and criticism than we might believe. This is hardly ever the case with a divorced woman. People who should be free of prejudice think no differently in this regard than the common man, and what is the reason for this apparently groundless criticism? Nothing is more improper for a man to break his word, and people expect of him that he should sooner remain unhappy for the remainder of his life than to attempt to free himself from his wife. A noble man truly lives; a weak one only imagines that he does. The latter hovers between fear and hope, the former takes no thought for the morrow, for sufficient unto the day is the evil thereof.[27] Can we sleep in advance, or re-sleep a night in which we have failed to get any sleep? Can we wake in advance or after the fact? Whoever takes everything as it comes is wise; whoever attempts to use every second to his advantage can become as old as Methuselah—the oldest human being, I grant you, who ever lived, but of whom not a single thing he did during his 969 years of life was ever recorded.[28]

The longer laws retain their validity, the better they become, just as in the opinion of a certain excellent author, a story becomes all the more plausible the longer it passes from hand to hand and tongue to tongue. The longer we bear another's bad moods, the easier they are to bear; and is there any evil which has an existence unto itself? Man attributes existence to evil; man, the most impudent pretender to any throne, finds it hard to understand that things are merely evil when viewed from that particular standpoint from which he finds it in his interest to judge them. A miller sleeps his proud sleep even in his own mill,[29] and it is as dangerous to yell "Fire!" when nothing is burning as it is to set fire to something ourselves. A man should go forward and not turn back; he should overcome and not retreat. Feminine protestations of fear should be considered dishonorable in any man; he should act heroically and never plead. Women move us when they plead, just as they are victorious when they flee. A man who allows himself to be moved to pity through the pleas of another man is a born beggar no different from the man who is doing the pleading. Defiance, courage, and steadfastness are the arrows which wound a manly heart when a manly hand shoots them. I actually do not even like to take walks with people who turn around and go back the way they came—I would much rather walk with those people who return home by another route. It was a glorious but unnatural deed which the women of Sparta performed who permitted themselves to be executed in place of their husbands; the worst thing about our sex I can think of is that some husbands seek refuge behind the skirts of their wives. This is no different from the legendary fleeing Persian soldiers whose wives met them at the city gate, compelled them to hide under their skirts, and by means of this tactic gained the victory. An effeminate man is infinitely more unbearable than a mannish woman. He is something like the bat in that, as the common man says, he is neither fish nor fowl, neither cooked nor roasted. He doesn't belong *anywhere*, while a mannish woman on the other hand is merely not where *she* belongs.

There is hardly a more difficult thing for a father than to see evidence of this latter predisposition while his son is yet a child. Mothers themselves are dissatisfied with such sons as well, because after the death of their husbands they will seek protection from their sons and not be able to expect much or anything at all from them. If a father is uncertain as to the true nature of his son in this regard, he would do well when the child is about seven years old to take him to a fence which he can either climb over or crawl through (obviously, the father would give no instructions as to how to cross the fence, but let the child decide entirely on his own). If the child climbs over, he will become a man; if he crawls through, then the father should bemoan the fact that he is his son and let him become a yarn-weaver or a tailor, since according to an English proverb, it takes nine tailors to make a man. If, my esteemed friend, you would also like to know if your able son will gather his laurels in the field of prose or verse, here is my recipe: give him a bottle of medicine, sixty drops of which are to be taken every hour in any liquid he wishes. Let him measure the dose by himself. If he does it drop by drop, he will be a clipped-winged prosaist; if he pours it in and counts "one, two, three . . ." during this downpour, then he will be a poet. If he can eat right away with the same spoon into which he poured the medicine, then he could, if he and his publisher wanted to, write textbooks using the mathematical method (*methodo mathematica*) of instruction; if he cannot even look at this spoon for another twenty-four hours, then he will be a composer of songs; if even after six days he still cannot look at the spoon without a cold shudder, train him well in the poetic art and if you are lucky, he will become a Homer.

One further consideration regarding children born to parents who have been unfaithful to each other: the children are considered to be little more than bastards. The father, in fact, actually looks upon them as such, for when a man has once had cause to doubt his wife, then it also occurs to him that his little Leopold has blue eyes. "Blue eyes," he says. "That's right! ———— has blue eyes." Every time he sat down to dinner, Darius had a young boy call out to him, "Lord, think of the Athenians,"[30] and Leopold is in effect calling to his father time after time: "Lord, think of the men you know with blue eyes." It is altogether different with the women, since they are surer of their ground. And even when the man only halfway promises to better his ways, and immediately thereafter seals his promise by doing a good deed, namely by ————, the woman believes him completely.

Doctors seem to have better luck with their cures in hospitals for the poor than with men and women of importance; in the former case their method of treatment is simpler, in the latter they try to bring about the appearance of a cure through sham and pretense. In marriage we view usefulness, fairness, honor, and steadfastness as important, for marriage brings about a kind of pleasure which is less intense, to be sure, but which extends over matters of true and lasting significance, in the sense that mere sexual passion produces pleasures which are in reality seldom encountered, if only because its fire tends to consume, rather than merely warm. Whoever chooses, sometimes loses; and those marriages which are contracted after too much consideration are not nearly as likely to prove successful as those which almost seem to be fated. It is said that climbing up a hill backwards significantly reduces the effort; and too much reflection will only increase the number of people living in celibacy, even though this only rarely puts their lives on a heavenly course.[31]

Even when the fiancé follows his sweetheart everywhere she goes, constantly sings the praises of everything from the top of her head to the tips of her toes; even when dressed as Diogenes at the masked ball, he puts out the light[32] which he has allowed to shine in public all evening when they are finally alone—nonetheless, in spite of all this it seems to me to lie in the nature of things that burning passion cannot continue to crackle for long, and who does not know of examples where such passion proved to be of short duration after this overwhelming desire for each other finally led the couple to the altar? Excessive merriment renders us incapable of perceiving the true sources of pleasure; with every pleasure we sacrifice some of our energy, our position, our time, and ourselves. And since we are not called to follow our inclinations, but rather our principles, following these inclinations almost invariably results in feelings of uneasiness and annoyance. I can almost guarantee that soldiers' marriages among the English, for example, where the bridegroom gives himself to his bride to the accompaniment of a drumroll, often turn out better than other marital unions which were far more sentimentally conceived, intricately wrought, and widely praised. If the man is confident of his manhood, he would do well to give a friend the task of picking a wife for him, or merely to choose one by lot. A woman's inclinations in this respect are more general, or—how shall I describe it?—less definite and more instinctual than the man's. The opposite sex has been left with nothing more than a gentle, zephyr-like wish to be picked, and that would have been taken from them as well if it had been up to us. Thus, women are more indifferent with regard to the individual male; men, on the other hand, tend more easily to limit themselves to a certain woman. It is almost immaterial to women whether they get this one or that one; they permit themselves a choice and then make little use of this right to choose, because as a result of their allotment in life they have come to content themselves with the male sex in general—and should we allow them to put us to shame in this matter of selection?

Do not believe, my dear young man, that you are selling out love to marriage if you enter marriage without a great deal of hesitation—provided, of course, that when we speak of love we mean rational love. Our preferences and inclinations are nothing more than indications which must be guided by our reason. "To marry for love" generally means to unite oneself with a person on the basis of physical drives, without reflection and without any regard for the true and lasting happiness of a good marriage; love should be no more or less than a natural drive which happens to manifest itself in our minds and hearts. Nature has placed passions in us in order to bring us that much more quickly to our goal; and whoever attempts to put the blame on them and ascribe his own foolishness and stupidity to their account is committing a sin of malice against holy Nature herself. Did she not give us reason in order to bring the reins of passion not only under our control, but, where necessary, also to make them into our ally? As I said, our preferences, inclinations, and drives are merely hints—whoever rates them higher is confusing hundreds with thousands and making a grave miscalculation. A person can love without being "in love," and if this kind of love should seem heartless, it is nonetheless durable and long-lasting, as is everything over which reason is lord and master. Such love allows people to consider whether a single preference will coincide with the sum total of all our preferences; and one can love someone and still ask whether Miss Elizabeth has both money and good sense, or whether she knows how to run a kitchen and the like. Young man, in such transactions let your eyes be your business representative and the bearer of your authority—your reason, on the other hand, should remain the head of your firm and the source of that authority. There is more to the notion of loving and being rational at the same time than meets the eye among us mortals, and you may be inclined to think that the knack of doing this is reserved for the angels alone. Not so, my friend, for there they neither marry, nor are given in marriage, but are as the angels of God in heaven.[33] Reason is useful to all things; why should it not then manifest itself in the most noble of all things? And by the way, it ought to remain merely a matter of theological speculation as to whether on the Day of Judgment all women will have to be changed into men, since, as people suppose, the angels are all *generis masculini* and otherwise the Old Adam[34] might well begin to assert himself again.

If I only knew, my dear friend, what it actually is that you seem to be seeking so anxiously that I am almost tempted to say "in the sweat of thy face."[35] A wife? Nature has already taken care of that for you—and even if her upbringing might have spoiled your Miss Lottie a bit here and there, it only depends on you and your manly way of conducting yourself to bring her back to Nature again. A sex which is weak, in whose makeup there is little firmness and strength, can for the present, at least, not be expected to be completely without artifice; after all, how would matters stand if larger machines were needed to set the smaller ones in motion? Strictly speaking, the man is only physically stronger; otherwise the woman is stronger in almost every respect. Just observe carefully how women merely insist on a commitment from their husbands based on blind faith in them, and if now and again they incite the men to act magnanimously because of their weakness, nevertheless in more frequent, and I would almost say, more significant cases, they themselves demonstrate this very same magnanimity in the face of the harshness of their husbands. As soon as reason becomes a powerful force among the people and extends its benevolent influence to the fair sex as well—a sex which languishes now in a condition of slavery to men, where reason still counts for little or nothing—then how much more vigorous and robust the woman will be, not only in body, but in terms of her entire being.

People say that a pregnant woman has peculiar appetites, but these amount to nothing other than manifestations of a temporary inhibition of the privileges of superiority attributed to her by Nature, and which could not appear at a more appropriate time than now when she is able to count with assurance on the little sacrifices her overjoyed husband is willing to make for her in the fulfillment of these appetites. Under ordinary circumstances in fact the fair sex makes use of these privileges as often as it feels it can without fear of opposition—for example, on the very evening when the man intends to accompany his friend on a journey, read a paper at the Academy of Sciences, or wish His Excellency a happy birthday, Miss Doris decides she wants to take a walk with her sweetheart in the country. He is supposed to decline a medal and content himself with a flower, which of course she will have the inexpressible goodness to pin on his lapel herself. Nevertheless, whoever is in full possession of his rights must not deny himself these rights, and all these exaggerated ways of behaving will cease by themselves when we no longer continue to encroach upon the rights of the fair sex.

A melancholy temperament is excellently suited to providing stability within a friendship or anything else having to do with steadfastness and constancy. Thus, genuine tenderness often has melancholy as one of its ingredients and every lover, whether male or female, nowadays feels it is necessary to be melancholy in order to be fashionable. But why this strange ingredient in the recipe for love? Why not *devotion* as well, which for women, it seems to me, is frequently nothing more or less than a vague perception of a need onto which many other feelings can be grafted and which is also very well suited to support the burgeoning and blossoming of love? And the case can be reversed as well, for unrequited love has doubtless provided more sisters for the Order of the Devoted[36] than anything else. Devotion gives a special coloring to love: the nobler the goal, the greater the ardor, whose effect in this case is equivalent to a diploma from a school of beauty and cosmetology. And in any case the state of our own poor, dear melancholy one is not so monastically serious either (any more than in the theater, where the author even lets his characters die for our pleasure)—it is all just for appearance's sake. Who would paint a statue in order to make it appear more natural? Those two philosophers, Democritus and Heraclitus, of whom it is said the one was always laughing and the other crying,[37] were really nothing more than a couple of actors who had the honor of serving in comedies and tragedies respectively. Garrick[38] was equally adept at both roles, and so must anyone be who has aspirations of being a great actor on the world's stage. But why be an actor anyway?

To be honest, it is actually the theater-goer who has chosen the best part, and why do we need stage heroes and painted faces, when healthy unadulterated blood puts the most glorious red in our cheeks? I admit, my dear young fellow, that if you require of a woman that she possess *all* those characteristics which are prescribed as necessary by the most rigorous theories of marriage you will have trouble finding a wife. "A wife should be like a snail," one waggish loudmouth[39] has said,

> like a snail which loves its house and not like one which spends all its money on clothes; she should be like an echo—when you ask her something she should reply, and not like an echo which always has to have the last word or which passes on to others the thoughts her husband confided to her in a talkative moment; she should be like the clock in the town hall and move with the times; she ought to know how to divide up her time well and to use it wisely, and not be like a town hall clock which announces the news and then sees that it is spread all over town; she should be like a light which serves as a beacon to the entire household, lighting their way through her good example, and not like a light which would draw all eyes unto itself and which on festival days is placed in the window.

And how many other things should a woman be or not be, if one views the matter in the light of human wit or systems?

The chivalric system, for example, had its good points; but anyone wishing to marry now should be happy that system is no longer in effect either! The apprentice knight was taught to love God and women—"religion and *minne*"[40] were his watchwords. Virtue and love were not separated, and the love one served was a heroic one which repaid chivalric service with a chivalric reward, the guerdon of love. The lady was just as much a heroine as the knight was a hero. Women were exalted and yet sympathetic to the cares of others; their souls acquired a strength without becoming hardened in the process. And is not bravery a fire which, like love itself, must be kept burning? If I were ever to sanction any artificiality in matters of love, then it would be something along the lines of the chivalric code. It was sweet for a woman to subject herself to a proud and undefeated man, and just as flattering for the knight himself to elevate the goddess of his heart to the level of a true woman and connoisseur of his heroic worth. He paid homage to the intellect of his benefactress, she to his courage and strength; and from time immemorial a sinewy Hercules has counted for more than a dandified Narcissus.[41]

199

In this present glorious age we now realize that it is merely fear of shame which makes people brave; and thus, my friend, go now and consult with your head and your heart and make haste to marry according to your conscience and your own best advice, without being a slave either to pride, which would gladly unseat the passions and make itself ruler over them, or to the love of money, the root of all evil,[42] or to lasciviousness, that single passion more foolish and childish than all the others. From that moment when you finally decide to do it, be a man and have faith—provided you aren't one of those male lilies who neither toil nor spin,[43] but one who wants to work and can—that you will never lack for any good thing. Peter the Great once brought a hard-earned ruble and a piece of cheese to his wife, the Empress. "You see," he said, "I would have been able to provide for you even if I hadn't been the Emperor!" I don't know if a greater deed has ever been related concerning a ruling prince than this.

Marriage brings everything out of the realm of the genius down to the ruts and tracks of everyday life, and those who travel these paths are the truly blessed ones (*beati*), for only on the middle road can one gain experience in enduring life in all its points and particulars and in remaining true to oneself in every season—summer, fall, winter, or spring. If you who are so eager to marry have not yet figured this out for yourselves from what I have been preaching so plainly the last few pages, then allow me by means of a few practical suggestions to become more personal in my appeal and warn you not to harbor exaggerated hopes concerning your happiness at possessing a wife. Whoever never hopes, never has any need to despair either. Hope in and of itself really has no particular innate value, but it loses half of what it already possesses when we place our hopes in others instead of our own selves. Whoever hopes is frequently deceived, and even if he is not, there is still something about being disappointed that is utterly unspeakable, and keeps us from ever hoping again. If we have hoped and not been disappointed, the pleasure we feel upon attainment of what we hoped for straightaway permits other hopes to enter through the back door and occupies us with new things; disappointment, however, draws us away from everything else unto itself. It gives us pleasure to relish the fulfillment of hope, but hope itself is a pillow which makes both body and soul indolent; even heaven itself has no greater advantage over this miserable world. The lover is sorely plagued by his imagination; he sees everything as if through rose-colored glasses, and in his mind's eye he revels in the kind of pleasure which generally has a headache associated with its aftermath. The fly on the finger of his beloved rubbing its eyes with its front legs is only doing that in order to see the cambric covering on her hand all the better. What would a suitor not give to receive the God's penny,[44] the first kiss, or anything else even an hour sooner; what would he not give to be already at precisely that place toward which his rashness and haste are impelling him—and not merely out of love, either! The goddess becomes a wife, Adonis[45] an alderman, nectar becomes table-beer, the soul a body, and the rose turns into a rose-hip.

It really is not my intention to take away all your hopes, for this would amount to an act of plundering which would render you poor until the day you die; nor would it benefit me in the slightest. I am only speaking of exaggerated hope, the kind of hope we should never entertain concerning anything which is about to fall to our lot. The closer we are to something the less we ought to let our imagination run wild about it, and it almost seems as if the soul takes revenge on and punishes with contempt any object which has deceived it so completely. As a bridegroom the man tends to be a Sophocles, as a husband a Euripides. The former represented women in his dramas as pious and honorable, the latter as malicious; but it is in fact for his importance to the *husband* that we are often compelled to give Sophocles the nod in his depiction of women. "I portray women," he says, "as they should be—Euripides as they are."[46]

Plato prescribed that both men and women should appear naked when exercising in public,[47] and nothing is better suited for dampening the imagination and focusing our concentration on what we are doing than nakedness. It is not good for women to conceal their beauty—we should place our trust in their virtue and not their clothes. Yet it is even worse when they reveal their charms openly, thereby creating shadows which accentuate every outline as in the art of painting. As long as the wanderer sees nothing, he continues to go his way; but as soon as he catches sight of towers he gathers his strength and leaps forward, or at least begins to take longer strides, no matter how tired he has become. True, the young women themselves are in a bit of a fix here and often are at a loss to know what to do. They are not supposed to be making a choice themselves, but if they are not extremely subtle in their efforts at being *chosen*, they lose their good reputation and that old aunt named "marriage of convenience" begins to become eager and excited. To catch birds, you have to have birdlime; and it is really quite remarkable that young women are able to catch even experienced men with so much propriety and decorum. This subtlety and craftiness of theirs, however, is just one of those many rough spots which will need to be smoothed out before everything in society attains its complete roundness. There is no lack of lighthouses, and when you, good children, finally reach the port of your true calling, what a happy day that will be for you!

If, my dear young fellow, you have long wished to marry and now desire to take the first step, let it happen just as if you were taking a walk in the country, or doing anything else that requires very little preparation. The heavenly state of being a bridegroom is accompanied by the music of innumerable violins, and people about to be married exude a lust for life and live in Spanish castles;[48] all of creation performs a ballet for them, while the spheres provide the music.[49] They are exalted above the earthly context of things and everything follows a different course for them than for the rest of us sublunary creatures. Every consolation and comfort, nonetheless, must have conditions placed on it if it is not to be more than base deception, and everyone must build his own happiness if he wishes to be happy. I say "build" in order to indicate that it will take some work, and that it is really only our concern to see that things are *put together*—the stones, mortar, wood, and the other materials are all there already. How true was the answer of that wise man who replied to the question as to what the best and most beautiful kind of house was: "The soundest and most comfortable one!"

Among the characteristics which recommend a woman to us, beauty has precedence over them all. The midwives say of daughters: "A pretty child"; of boys they say: "A strong child." The woman's place of origin is paradise—no wonder she is pretty. Her soul and her body are similar to each other in that they are both merely beautiful. Read "beautiful" instead of "merely beautiful" in that last sentence—that was a typographical error! A woman who knows how to use this advantage provided to her by Nature can accomplish great things. She overcomes the greatest hero and the worst usurer,[50] and even the most learned scholar—if he has his glasses on. What person does not know that Hercules, who all by himself slew more heads of the Hydra than an entire regiment could, once disguised himself and took to spinning—all for the sake of a woman! (I have always wondered why it never occurred to some quarrelsome monarch to establish a regiment of such hydra-heads!) If you are hungry and chance to find yourself sitting at the table with a woman of uncommon beauty, then you will leave the table completely satisfied. Love satisfies our hunger; it can do anything but quench our thirst, and it seems to me that love and wine are two equally strong entities, neither of which has very much power over the other. "It is a disgrace to defeat men and then in turn be defeated by their women and followers," Alexander the Great once said with respect to the wife and daughter of Darius,[51] yet I consider this the greatest victory he ever attained.

All young women know that they are pretty—even those that are not *believe* they are. No man can remember his own features; if he has his portrait painted, he never knows whether it is a very good likeness or not. But a woman knows down to the very last hair. If we do in fact remember one of our own features without being aware of it, then we sense a kind of empathy with others who also have that feature, or even appear to have it. This even extends to the features of those who have been our friends in the past. For example, a generous man will often invite people to dinner who bear a resemblance to his deceased benefactor. "They are wonderful people," he will say afterward, "my house is always open to them." But neither he nor his wonderful guests have any idea why he is saying this. We speak of another person as "annoying," and the reason will actually lie in a certain facial expression our long-dead aunt used to make when we failed to find solace for our tears on her lap and went scurrying to our mother instead. In general, we love the people who resemble our own wet-nurse. People with an unpleasant face reveal constantly what the window of the soul[52] contributes to our sense of sociability and to our friendships. Such people have the fewest acquaintances, and the doors of their hearts are usually closed, just like the shutters on their windows. In spite of this, however, they are all the more thorough in their choice of friends, the more cheerful in that circle, and the more faithful in their relationships. May Heaven send me only friends who have the face of an idiot, and make my friend ———— even duller of expression than he already is!

I stated above that women are beautiful in soul and body; as a matter of information, however, it should also be mentioned that although women are not envious of those who are beautiful in soul, they are of those beautiful in body. Woman like to see beautiful souls,[53] and they can actually come to love them in our sex; in their own they merely tolerate them. But a young woman actually hates other girls who are just like her. A fop who proves an exception to the rule by taking

lessons in the art of knowing himself and memorizing his features will
often pursue a woman who resembles him and find her fleeing before
his advances. But when a mature and established man who is also very
much like her approaches her, she has no qualms about going out
with him.

It is a fortunate thing for a young man if he does not have a
girlish face. If he does, it will be difficult, if not impossible, to marry
a beautiful woman. No woman loves a man who looks like a woman,
or even a man who is considered pretty rather than handsome; in
fact, there is not a great deal of difference between the two. I have
noticed that very young girls do not like beards or moustaches; yet
one can almost precisely state the age when they will begin to favor
them. The best-looking men generally have ugly wives, and really
do not do a great deal better by other women either, for the reason
that more often than not they are in love with their own good looks,
and whoever loves himself too much has little or no time for others.
Actually, it is a kind of jealousy which women feel in the presence of a
man who is head over heels in love with his own person. The women
believe, moreover, that a man with a girlish face is not really a man,
and a pretty man is more than likely odious to them simply because
he is pretty. On the other hand, a man can even be ugly without
compromising his success with women; the only thing he must not do
is to exceed this privilege like Pellisson.[54]

With regard to their own sex, women have not the slightest idea of
what friendship is—they hate each other, because they hate everybody
who is beautiful and animated out of fear of competition. They do not
find it difficult to express admiration for female beauty carved in marble
or painted on canvas, as long as the originals are nowhere nearby, and
they can easily abide a truly ugly girl. "She is really quite pretty," they
will say, "and still she hasn't found anyone yet." It is obvious why
they say this: there is no finer way to praise themselves. They have
no objection whatsoever to any mythological figure except Madame
Venus—because she is prettier than they are.

I would also maintain, although merely for the sake of letting the
woman appeal the accusation immediately, that women possess no
particular feeling for art. They are only capable of judging Nature,
and in this judgment they err far less frequently than we men. A
feeling for description in literature, for expression in music lies within
their realm, insofar as it has to do with Nature and not art. We men
are more attuned to the practical application of things, they to their

introduction and reception. The first thought a person has about a matter, which we men often dismiss without good reason (since it is almost always the most correct one and comes from a resolute and unprejudiced soul not yet made hesitant by doubt), is their strong suit; they consider it to be a kind of inspiration and will recognize it from amid thousands of others if it was one of ours; if they happen to read it, they will exclaim: "Yes, that's perfect!" Everything belonging to the realm of the purely natural is their domain. People will smile at a learned woman (may Heaven preserve all who love it from such as these!) behind her back because they know whose heifers she has been plowing with. And what those people do who are in her circle—well, I am not one to tell tales out of school. Women ought to forego gladly all those theories which extend into the realm of the metaphysical and transcendental, and confine themselves merely to those which above all affect morality and human happiness.

A woman will write a better letter than a man; few of them, however, seem to have been called to the writing of literature, which requires a more creative impulse than letter writing. I am reluctant to mention here the tenth Muse, *mascula Sappho*, in this regard, perhaps because she threw herself off a cliff for the sake of Phaon.[55]

The body of a woman is beautiful in a purely *natural* way, that of a man is *artificially* beautiful. Thus, it needs to be mentioned here that women prefer tall men. A big chest, long fingers, and a masculine hand—a gladiator's hand—have an instant effect on them. Women who can hear pay no less attention to the sound of a man's voice, and with good reason I should think; in those years when Nature's fruits are ripening, one's voice can change in a single night—many a boy goes to bed a tenor and wakes up a bass. Since Nature has destined women to please others, they are permitted to use any means to accomplish this; thus, even a pretty girl may, if she pleases, wear ornaments and jewelry—but why overdo it? Moderation is the byword in personal adornment, and an ugly girl has to proceed as best she can. She can only deplore her fate, and often she pleases others only because they feel sorry for her. On the other hand, if she attempts to get the best of Nature by adorning herself in jewelry and beautiful clothes, people laugh at her. All the same, ugly women continually imagine that with every new dress the tailor has brought them a new face. I know a young woman who kept her house unpainted just like her face. "People will notice it better that way," she said, and in fact it actually looked better than if it had been painted. Rouge is the most abominable invention one can imagine, because it conceals the red of a woman's blush—next to that of a sunrise or sunset the most beautiful red in the world. In this regard, white people are better looking by far than black people; and in truth, whoever invented rouge must have been intending to do a service to those women who are beyond blushing. Nature wrote men's faces in Gothic script, women's in cursive; rouge obliterates all this, and we ask in vain: "Whose is this image and superscription?"[56]

My dear friend, I really can't hold it against you if you have an eye for beauty; but here is a bit of advice which you ought to preserve like a treasure of silver and guard like a piece of gold: do not marry the prettiest girl in town! After she is married, the prettiest girl begins to diminish in her husband's eyes, although in the eyes of all those who previously admired her she begins to gain in stature due to the constraints placed upon her by marriage. This circumstance tends to create certain atmospheric conditions which can be the cause of violent tempests, and I can't guarantee that a lightning bolt won't strike somewhere or somebody. A beautiful woman is better suited to be a mistress than a wife, in the sense that a mistress can be compared to the proverbial light under the bushel.[57] It isn't so difficult to get what the whole world wants, only to keep it.

I would like to close this section with a couple of observations. The first has to do with the test of beauty. A young woman will try everything possible to show off her beauty to the best advantage, and that is only fair and right; but when she attempts to conceal her natural faults she ends up insulting Nature and deceiving the man as well. In fact, she is deceiving herself most of all. Ladies, throw your corsets away, we don't want little wax dolls anyway! What would be the harm in taking off your armor? I know you are Christians and not Moslems, but take the example of the Turkish women as proof of the truth of what I am saying. If we find blue veins, teeth, and the color of healthy red cheeks lying on the night table, then might we not expect to find eyes, noses, and ears there, too? And what else can come of this besides a feeling of contempt? Even the slightest artistry a woman expends on her body leads us men as well from the path of Nature into gallantry. We trade their false coin for equally false coin of our own and come to believe we are permitted to deceive a person who we know has in mind to deceive us.

This kind of spurious beauty can be easily detected; there exists another, however, which is a little more difficult to detect, and for which I cannot exactly provide a rule of thumb. It is extremely important for a woman to have control of her facial expressions at all times. Women understand this art better than we do, and their physiognomy is also a far less secure mortgage than ours. Women are constantly on stage; the role they believe they play best is that of mixing with people. Her Ladyship the Countess is presently performing in a charming little bourgeois tragedy, while her Ladyship the Baroness is doing a wonderfully moving tragi-comedy and the latter's sister an out-and-out thigh-slapper—and so it goes. The usual ploy is a headache; hypochondria is a new invention which has lately won encores in London and bravos in Germany. Do not trust a woman's negligee— women give it the greatest attention because they know we assess their charms by means of it. I would put more trust in a woman's entire store of cosmetics than in her negligee. Moreover, do not trust her illnesses; she knows how to lie in bed in a very appealing way, and I would be willing to bet she is planning on dying very decorously as well. Madame will lie on her left side when she dies—it shows her face off to the best advantage. It is just about as difficult to tell anything while a woman is sleeping, especially if she happens to be dreaming about a man.

I would also like to add in passing that while the soul has rented the entire body for its use, it only lives on the upper floor—in fact, one could even say it peers out of the upper windows. You have probably noticed yourself that you can at times almost see it in a person's eyes. "The light of the body is the eye: if therefore thine eye be single, thy whole body shall be full of light. But if thine eye be evil, thy whole body shall be full of darkness."[58] Thus every great man has a way of looking which nobody else can duplicate. This "mark," which Nature herself stamped upon his face, outweighs all his physical advantages and in a special sense even makes a handsome man out of a Socrates.[59] Whoever possesses this mark knows that he has been singled out; at present he is merely not yet aware of the reason for this, for nothing is more unique than this mark. Monarchs have a certain specific character trait, but they have it in common, and one could maintain that they are in fact all alike: the nobility they represent is expressed in their faces. I am speaking of absolute rulers—of monarchs who, whether or not they are servants of their states, distinguish themselves from other servants in that they are never permitted to be clad in livery like valets and grooms. And kings who are *not* monarchs also have their own sign, which expresses itself in their gait. I have never had the honor of knowing Frederick the Great of Prussia, but I have heard from those who have that he has the mark of a *great man* in his eyes, and the mark of a *king* in his face. Women seldom have the mark of greatness in their eyes, rather that of beauty, amiability, of a certain kindness, a type of good-natured sympathy, a desire to please, and propriety.

A woman's face is like tombac[60]—it gleams and glistens, but lacks durability. Whatever grows quickly, also fades quickly; it is no wonder nothing becomes so dilapidated as quickly as their faces, since their souls refuse to yield anything to their bodies and grow just as quickly as the latter. The birth of a single child can often bring about terrible devastation in a woman, hardly leaving one stone on top of the other. The husband who has only had eyes for his wife's pretty face thereupon becomes a grass-widower, or something worse yet. But even if a woman loses something of her facial beauty, if she continues to think honorably and virtuously she does not stop being beautiful. The face is not always the shield of beauty, and while one can—to recall the quite fitting observation of a would-be wise man of our own age—look at a woman without loving her, it is not possible for us to possess her without adoring her.

Thus a wife often breathes the breath of life into her husband—she makes his learning and erudition come alive, and his resolution ripens to completion. Since the woman acts on a matter at the same time she is talking, or even thinking about it, here as well it could be said that one deed enkindles another. The eye retains its strength the longest, and it is not surprising that a young man will display special admiration for that particular feature of his beloved. Happy is the man whose sweetheart's eye tolerates impure colors as little as the sun! The sun reveals them in their impurity, and the sun-eye of his Doris can wither anyone who sins against her with even an immoral thought.

The most permanent charms a woman can possess are a delicate hand and a dainty foot. If it is beauty you are after, fall in love with either of these two and view her face as a present which one must accept as given. For me, the nails of the fingers are the most exquisitely beautiful thing of all, and it would depress me greatly if I had a wife who lost a fingernail during the course of our marriage.

It should perhaps be added here that the greatest attractive power of a young woman lies in her breasts. If surprised, a naked woman will cover her breasts with her hands first of all, even if other parts of her body might actually require it more. (This is because our glance reaches them first, and she hopes to prevent a landing on the mainland by concealing the coastline.) Those who do not know this from actual experience can learn about it from the fable of Diana and Actaeon.[61] Nature herself has declared the bosom to possess the greatest attractive powers and has, so to speak, placed it on the window sill as the best bread. Our hearts are especially inclined to this part of a woman's body, and this fancy is almost universal among us men. Nature also seems to appreciate our fondness for this especially beautiful feature, for here function has been combined with beauty and allurement. But, you might ask, does beauty even deserve the name if it makes so little secret of the necessity which has brought it about in the first place? Absolutely! Nature has no intention of creating anything for which no need exists and which merely serves as an object of universal pleasure—even though this latter emotion might well be interpreted as necessary. She prefers to leave this unprofitable business to art; *she* is not about to provide such a feast for our eyes and a joy to our hearts without calling attention to its practical advantages for us as well. In fact, she goes even further: the greater the number of useful ideas which can be derived from a thing of beauty; the more quickly and suddenly these practical ideas occur to us, the more highly we regard that thing. Nature tolerates no body without a soul; neither is she interested in setting any bad examples for the lazy. It is a truly wonderful feeling to comprehend a basic principle thoroughly and to remember precisely each of its constituent parts; and from the lofty perspective of such a principle there exists a view for the soul no expression is powerful enough to describe. Is it not true, for example, that even the most carnal of men finds the sight of a woman's breasts even more beautiful when he imagines a little baby being held close to them—even if this alluring bosom will never come to serve such a glorious purpose?

The most beautiful girls are to be found at the courts and in the large cities, since every beautiful girl in the entire country is drawn to these places in order to show herself off to greater advantage than in the provinces. If Nature had wanted to establish a portrait gallery of beautiful faces she would have had to look no further than the nearest prince's court, and one could almost say that she keeps a master list of all her most beautiful forms at the courts if it were not for the fact that her own creations are so simple and straightforward and the courts so well known for their artifices. It is also possible, by the way, that the women of an entire country could be ugly and the men universally handsome, for even if pure and healthy blood is the true basis for physical beauty, soul and disposition nevertheless exert an undeniable influence on beauty, and slavery is capable of turning the fair sex of an entire state into the ugly one.

What I have just said was in the nature of a poetic cupful on subject of beauty; the rest I prefer to state in drier prose. Above all things, one must be careful not to think either too well or too ill of a girl. People who have gained experience and not been content with the bonbons of popular literature and bon mots gleaned from books, but who have undertaken a pilgrimage among mankind and continue to make moral journeys around the world—such people realize that everything under the sun is imperfect, and it soothes and elevates the soul to know that out of this imperfection one day will come the true perfection we seek.[62] But how can we demand such perfection from the other sex if that perfection is of so little concern to the human race in general? Any idea not based in truth will reveal its shortcomings when brought into the abstract; and frailty—thy most natural expression is mankind.[63] The word *woman* is a free translation of the word *man*; it makes use of the original without binding itself to it, and it would be a good thing if every word in our language which expresses "loving" and "being loved" implied only the most refined feelings of morality, and little or nothing of sensuality. "For out of the abundance of the heart the mouth speaketh."[64] According to the report of one writer, who exaggerated the story in a very witty way, Queen Christina of Sweden is said to have maintained that she found a sort of sensual pleasure in the heated exchange of ideas;[65] and even if we knew nothing other than that after her blessed demise three thousand different dresses and gowns were found in her wardrobe, her life would still be a mirror, a ruler, and a guidepost for you, my dear young fellow. But don't forget that people like Queen Christina are a rarity, and that our own sex has very often wished to appear the way the other sex really is; that men have even gone so far as to make practical application of their ability to win women with words, although true eloquence is reserved only for those who are not involved emotionally; and that in fact we also know and admire women who, under the influence of Pythagoras' teachings, have brought all their valuables and feminine finery into the temple of Juno[66] in order to show by means of these home devotions that purity and domesticity are the true adornment of the fair sex.

It betrays no small degree of decadence in a people, I would maintain, when the men pay no attention to the opinions of their wives, for the braver and more civilized a people was in the past, the more it honored its women. And while I would admit that it is nothing less than the silliest kind of vanity which allows itself to rest on the fickle whims of a dictatorial woman, yet I consider that man a misogynist who insisted so self-righteously that with women *everything* is whim and nothing character—and this including their love, which is also but whim mixed with the spirit of coquetry and the desire to please. But are we ourselves not perfectly at home with our own whims, and is not the desire to please of great importance to us as well? Whoever wishes to please seeks to dominate, and do we not desire to be lords of creation? Do we not give every appearance of wishing to please women during the first half of our lives, merely in order to dominate them in the second? The accusation of that ancient writer, that women had arisen at an earlier time from a group of immoral and dissolute men, can also, with the strictest adherence to truth, be reversed to state that the men of former times must have been the worst examples of the female sex! And that writer of antiquity who called woman a monstrosity of Nature and yet married one was a great man.

Women are also accused of being too stingy merely because they tend to be whatever they are to a greater degree than the men; yet have not both in ancient and more recent times the most manifest traits of this particular vice been found among men—and men alone? Women are sooner thrifty than stingy, and they have often had to be so if the entire household was not to go to ruin. My friend, it is only a matter of having man and woman return to that relationship predestined for them by Nature, and I can guarantee that they will be one in heart and soul, and, by virtue of acquiring the feeling that each has what the other lacks, will attain the highest good marriage has to offer—a blessing I wish for them with all my heart!

Don't tell me, my dear friend, that there rarely has been anyone who treated the fair sex as gallantly as Homer did when he described his Penelope as so full of virtue and likewise equipped the others of her sex with noble and affectionate dispositions. But even if these descriptions are not drawn from Nature or from historically verifiable characters—yet are they not realistic in the poetic sense? And I would also imagine many of our own ladies and gentlemen are still quite satisfied with the portraits just as they are, since his figures lack the refinement which characterizes our own time, wherein we have saddled ourselves far more with physical and moral rules and regulations about which Homer knew little because he—to the everlasting good fortune of himself and his descriptions of female and even male characters—remained much closer to Nature. Our ladies have lost their halo, but at least they have kept a small nimbus. We develop our taste from women; they learn theirs from other women and not from us. Nor do they dress for us, but for each other. Friend, since your wife absolutely requires female company, try to guide her to such company as will, except in matters of taste and fashion, accustom her to something better in life. Even we are judged by the company we keep, and this is far more the case with women. If you have been able to convince your wife that he is the greatest slave and fool in the world who saddles himself with rules and regulations, then you will have chosen the winning number in the lottery of marriage. Master Adam was older than Miss Eve—do not choose a wife who is older than you. Women fade more quickly than we do—even though human life in general is but a flower in the field—and Shakespeare, that keen observer and portrayer of human nature, astutely says of them: "For women are as roses; whose fair flower, being once display'd, doth fall that very hour."[67]

The Apostle James was of the opinion that we *de facto* forget what manner of person we are immediately after having looked at ourselves in the mirror;[68] and although mirrors always reverse the image they reflect (the way fools answer the wisest questions), I still believe that it is not a bad idea to choose a life's partner with characteristics similar to ours. Eve had a rib from Adam. A calm, contented person will generally choose his own image and superscription; a headstrong and capricious one usually picks a person totally opposite in personality— he has whitish hair, and his wife has to have locks of a raven's hue. Experience teaches us that the more similar man and wife are, the longer they will remain happily married. When soul and heart are in accord, harmony in external matters is sure to follow. As a rule, we men would rather marry a girl who has led a secluded life; women, on the other hand, prefer a scoundrel or a rogue. The reason for this is that women believe they can convert their husbands after marriage, but the man despairs of any improvement in the female sex. They are probably both right in their own way; nevertheless, young man, if I may be permitted to give you a piece of advice, do not take a woman as your wife who has been kept quite secluded all her life, or who has been brought up to be exceptionally genteel and docile. I have always believed that in Italy, where couples now marry early merely in order to establish their own household, amorous intrigues come about especially because girls enter into society straight out of the cloister. Before one can look with disdain on the frivolities and vanities of this world, one must at least be able to call them by name.

In his youth, Augustine never gave a thought to anything resembling his *Civitas Dei*,[69] and people who have been around a bit in the world have no qualms about living in the country. Even if a girl has listened to the worthless blandishments of some foppish carnival pitchman only a couple of times, she will yearn for a play of the better sort; but if she has never had any opportunity to experience these enticements firsthand, she thinks there is something to them and will often become unfaithful simply out of curiosity. "If only he had meant what he said," she says then, and is unable to keep the tears from flowing. Pretty girls are like goods offered for sale *a vista*; congenial ones, on the other hand, are offered *a uso*.[70] A virtuous girl only half as pretty deserves a better man than a more beautiful girl of the flashier sort. The latter girl will be unfaithful in marriage either with her soul or her body and become, depending upon which of these two paths she takes, either a religious fanatic or a prostitute. What a pair of sisters that is! And do not imagine that a religious fanatic would be easier to live with than a prostitute. With the latter you would at least get a good day once in a while—you would never get fat married to the former. "Husband!" she screams, not even hesitating to throw the contents of the Holy Book up to her spouse, "Husband, you Parthian and Mede and Elamite, you dweller in Mesopotamia and in Judea and Cappadocia, in Pontus and Asia, Phrygia and Pamphilia, in Egypt and in the parts of Libya about Cyrene, and stranger of Rome; you Jew and proselyte, Cretan and Arab!" And then she makes a pious face, looks toward heaven and intones very softly: "Acts, Chapter 2, Verses 9 to 11."

But no matter how reluctant I am to recommend a hypocrite to you, I am equally as hesitant to endorse a freethinker. Nothing is more detestable than a girl who speaks out against her church. Such girls have a tendency to superstition, and the only ideas which inspire respect in them are religious concepts which have been "purified," as they say. All young women have an inclination to free thinking within the religion into which they were born; for the great minds among us men this often takes on the form of hypocrisy. The greater and loftier our thoughts are, the more we tend to doubt what mediocre minds believe, and to accept as true what the common man believes. The nobility goes about poorly dressed, the farmer likewise; the upper- and lower-middle classes dress in splendor and continually seek to outdo each other. If a member of one of these latter groups happens to be a businessman, he might choose lace; if a scholar, embroidery; or, if he is a governmental official, braid on his uniform—but splendor is splendor. Intellects which border on the great are secret mockers; those in the lower-middle class of intellects, who stand in the same relation to mediocre minds as the latter to great minds, consider religion as nothing more than a pair of boots to be put on in bad weather. Great minds who write against religion have in fact done it against their own convictions. It can always be taken for granted that great men believe in ghosts—or are at least afraid of them.

Since I have already begged your indulgence before, I would just like to add a couple of snippets to what I have said above. No great mind can ever add very well. The other species of humans do better, but in fact almost everybody constantly adds incorrectly. Whoever is a master calculator in his youth will never be an original inventor, a Newton, Copernicus, or a Leibniz.

Everything beautiful belongs to the realm of the women, and consequently this also includes wit. A witty remark is like ready cash with them, and its value is determined by the laughter at the table. Thus women usually find it quite comfortable to sit in the seat of the scornful.[71] Nevertheless, even though they must never approach too closely to the temple of religion with their mockery, or even its outer courtyard,[72] there is a vast field of topics open to their wit in everyday life. Wit is, after all, but a summer dress; truth can be worn at any time of year. A woman without religion will also be a woman without a husband.

I believe that when it comes to learning languages, women will go much farther than we men. They all begin studying them at the same time as their brothers, and then it is almost too late. Women all like to talk; a great man is quiet. Even a man gifted with linguistic talent would rather learn his Greek vocabulary by himself in a corner than converse with anyone at a social gathering. True, there are a few clowns among the men who are witty and keep the rest of us entertained; yet soul and body cannot both digest at the same time. We reproach people for reading while they eat, but if they read only trivial things it can hardly be any more harmful than when a great genius occasionally holds forth at a dinner party. The wine soon begins to enrapture him, but without his realizing it his body slowly succumbs to fatigue. Yet his soul is beside itself, and even during sleep refuses to be quieted, for a soul once set aflame will never allow the body a moment's rest—it keeps on dreaming thoughts. Unfortunately for the poor genius, everything falls on poor soil and bears no fruit. When a man's powers of judgment and his wit enter into competition with each other, his

For the Benefit of Young Men

memory is affected the most. A genius sows thoughts; mediocre minds sitting at the same table catch the grains as they fall, fertilize them and make them bring forth a harvest—which they later peddle as their own. Whenever a genius becomes inspired to speak at length, he ought to have a bookkeeper for his thoughts nearby. In short, whoever talks much cannot always talk well; nevertheless, you can count on the fact that any *woman* who does not speak is dull-witted. No woman can write a letter without a postscript; if she has been able to get away with only two, she has been concise, and downright laconic if only one is present. "All right," said Lady ———, in whose presence I once took the liberty of making this remark, "my next letter will refute your statement." I was curious; but after her signature there appeared the question: "Isn't this a letter without a postscript?" and then after that: "Who won the bet, you or me?" The cause of this habit lies in one of their own typical postscripts: "I'm sorry to have written so much but I didn't have much time." In fact, people generally end a long letter with the statement: "I have to close now. I'm in a hurry . . ."

If you are about to make your Easter confession and have a rather porous memory, go and curse the old woman who sells apples down in front of the town hall; or if you want to take the matter a little further you could ask your mother-in-law whether what people are saying about her is true, namely, that before she married your late father-in-law she. . . . Listen to her, and then go, wretched and heavy laden, and relate all of this piously to your Father Confessor. Our human passions, even those which render us men speechless, never seem to keep the women from talking—and if they do, then at least their suffering speaks eloquently for them. "Before long," writes a woman trapped in an unhappy marriage to her sister,

> before long I will cease to exist. I forgive my murderer; may God forgive him as well! I have wept a thousand tears over him, and as much reason as I have to despise him, I still wish—have pity on me for saying this—to die in his arms. You won't be able to read this letter. Everything is running together. Perhaps it's the last one I'll ever write to you. When you write back, don't forget to tell me whether I can get that lace for the price they quoted to us. Also, dear sister, would you be so kind as to send my necklace—I'm sure the jeweler will have been able to set the stone by now. Out here in the country the weather has been bad. May God have mercy on my soul!

So it is with their anger as well. Indeed, even while expressing the tenderest feelings of love, they still talk—even if only in monosyllables. They are ashamed to sigh, and yet it is in their nature to do

215

so; we on the other hand are ashamed to cry and would rather sigh, although nothing is more improper than for a male to sigh. When things become truly tragic, then tears are for men and sighs for women. If we are rational people at all, we can hardly keep from laughing at the sighs of a man, and the tears of a woman leave us unmoved. But if we see a man crying there is immediately a tear in our own eye—it is almost as if the entire sex were crying in sympathy. The tear of a man is but a mite offered as a sacrifice for his feelings;[73] when women weep they are so far from exhausting their supply of tears that no matter how copious their offerings, they are still hardly exerting themselves. What the spendthrift gives away is of little value, because it does not cost him anything himself.

Those who speak slowly are in the habit of keeping a tight rein on their thoughts; they seldom tumble and even more seldom hurt themselves thereby. To think and then to fail to express the thought because one can find no words to express it, even though it often seems to linger on the tip of the tongue—that is the way of the wise; to speak without saying anything is the custom at court; to say what one means is the manner of sincere people and children; and to say more than one knows and understands is the fashion of fools. The wise man seldom says what he has done, and never what he intends to do; moreover, he never prefaces his remarks. The fop tells us what he has done and what he intends to do; you can ask him about anything and his stock of answers is never diminished—in fact, anything can be had in quantity from him if you are merely willing to overlook the quality of his products.

Flora, even if in life an archwh——e, deified her wealth;[74] and for this reason flowers still today are able to bring good fortune to men who are not embarrassed to make use of them. If I thought that you, my good friend, would also do the same as Flora if you were in debt and make money the Dulcinea of your heart—why, then I must honestly say I would have nothing more to do with you.

Whenever you encounter a family in which the parents have been able to raise only a single daughter, pass them by, since she will surely turn out to be spoiled. The more children in a family, the better they have been raised. I would also like to note quickly that you should never marry while traveling. Constantine the Great, for example, absolved from punishment all cases of adultery involving girls working at country inns. While traveling we are all in love, and at certain ages in a man's life he can hardly pass by the gates of another city without taking a wife. It could be that we are able to sense somehow that we are drawing ever closer to the natural state of things, and, if I may be so bold as to say so, beginning to breathe the healthful air of Nature—or perhaps it is a newfound cheerfulness in our disposition which exerts this influence over us. Thus it is often the case that the girls in country inns become pregnant without the blessing of the priest, for the women who work in such establishments have to possess a great deal of morality to be able to resist seduction. Travelers seldom become ill, and it is even rarer for newlyweds to die—the emotions sustain even weak constitutions. But when the trip is over and you have already slept in the nuptial bed, then there is not much more I can do to save you.

I would also advise you, my dear young friend, not to marry someone who is too closely related to you. In the primitive state I would be permitted to marry anyone with whom I am capable of having children except my mother and grandmother. It ought to be noted that even my great-grandmother and her mother would not be excluded from this group, although it seems to me that I would owe them too much respect to be able to get to know them so intimately. It is not difficult to understand why it is considered an abomination in civilized society to marry one's closest relative, however, for if this were not the case, a young unmarried sister would soon find herself pregnant by virtue of her naturally close association with her brother. It may well be that the truth of this situation has now become second nature to us, since we only rarely encounter happily married people who are also closely related to each other. And when they are unhappy, nobody cares to contribute to their happiness, because the way everyone else looks at it, they brought on their problems themselves. Generally, however, such marriages only come about when they are made necessary by a too-intimate relationship within an already existing association of people, and this necessity is never accepted without anger and resentment. In my own country I would not permit those persons to marry who are free to kiss each other in public; in other countries one might have to establish different regulations.

These are the cardinal points with respect to marriages among persons too closely related to each other; I could, nonetheless, add a point regarding a political interpretation, namely, to keep individual families from becoming too powerful, and a philosophical one, that is, to bring about a better stock of people among the population as a whole. The argument which has been passed down to us from the Church Fathers and is also applied in this situation—to wit, that feelings of love should not be allowed to burn so hot that they burst into flames of passion—is not well founded, for it is written: " . . . a man [shall] leave his father and mother, and shall cleave unto his wife; and they shall be one flesh."[75] And Moses' laws of marriage nowadays amount to nothing more than a schedule of fees for the theological faculties which the Catholics, because of their spiritual affinity for such things, have even seen fit to supply with supplements and appendices.

So, my dear young friend, you want to know still more about the fair sex? Very well. It certainly can't make your path to marriage more difficult; whether easier or not, is up to you. *Our* powers of concentration tend to be diffused and dispersed when we observe other human beings—we are constantly distracted by this or that thing which has captured a greater or lesser part of our interest for the moment. The fair sex almost always directs its attention to the entire appearance of the person. If you were to seek eyewitness accounts out of a group of young women as to this or that particular facial feature or other details, for example, they will have missed them; but if you want that person life-size before you—why, there he stands. We are assuming here, of course, that such women are not in love with the object of their description. *Our* recollections of an event to which we were all witness are universally at variance with one another, the degree of variance depending upon the time interval and the circumstances. Women's recollections vary little from each other, and it is less necessary in their case to gather a collection of witnesses. They are extraordinarily inclined to hypotheses, and when men would rather not testify about an event rather than report incorrectly, women act no more uneasy about the matter than they in fact are; they hold nothing back and say whatever occurs to them without concerning themselves whether it is relevant or not. By means of their noble candor they can in many cases give explanations for the behavior of people which men for sheer timidity would never be able to attempt.

The parenthetical remarks they so like to make serve merely to animate their narrations; if they do not render the story any clearer, they at least divert us in a most pleasing way. In many respects they are more faint-hearted, but in others more courageous than the male sex. They attain their most significant victories through negotiations behind closed doors, rather than on the field of battle. They drive away the bitterness of death more easily than we do, and thus do not like to hear bells. They are also much less interested in the world after death than we men, perhaps because we are better acquainted with the pleasures of the mind—or think we are—and because we are accustomed to honoring ourselves by placing greater emphasis on our own being and existence. "Perhaps they die so peacefully just because their charms have also passed away," you might ask.—No, also in the prime of life. That is when a young woman in childbed alternately presses her child and his father to her bosom, for as a rule the death of women is only a kind of sleep. Why should I deny it?—they have less on their hearts and consciences, and whoever first called death a form of sleep surely took this metaphor from a dying woman.

Dissimulation? True, they are not exactly inexperienced at this audacious art form, but have there ever been actors among the women who were the equals of Garrick, Baron, and Roscius?[76] It was said of Tiberius[77]—*the* Tiberius no less—that "the powers of his body finally left him—all but that of dissimulation." We know better how to put more into what we write than they do; women grasp better the true sense of things: for example, an allegorical interpretation does not readily occur to them, while we, on the other hand, are not averse to cabalistic exegeses. We are more in need of instruction than the opposite sex, which is better adapted to educating itself. If we almost universally need some sort of revelation, the other sex much prefers to see with the aid of Nature's light. They will, in their own good time, most certainly catch up to us in everything; once this happens, we will never be in a position to overtake them again.

A woman seldom acts as if she knows more than she is saying; she has no use for common sayings translated from various tongues or for elegant phrases and rhetorical devices—everything she says simply rolls off the tip of her tongue. Of plagiarism she knows nothing. Women steal hearts and nothing more (I am speaking here of a kind of decorous purloining, of course). When they learn something, they begin at the beginning; we do it like some scholars I know who thumb, run, or jump through everything; perhaps this is because we are more easily distracted than women, who tend to concentrate intensely on the matter at hand. We work more, but accomplish less than they do; and if it ever came down to an Olympic competition between the sexes, I bet they would beat us in every event. We men, like the Pharisees of old, are inclined to strain at gnats and swallow camels;[78] the opposite sex will less often fail to find the middle road. Our rules are as lame as our allegories; theirs are better grounded and more firmly founded. We often burn the candle at both ends; they would rather remain in the dark than to proceed so uneconomically. We are like Machiavelli, whom Frederick the Great, that great seer and prophet, refuted in all seriousness; like Machiavelli, who long had people wondering whether he was serious or merely making a very sophisticated and elegant joke.[79] For women, laughter is an infallible touchstone of truth; we are still looking for the Philosophers' Stone. It is said that they are not as good at abstract thinking, but I doubt this—how often have they not struck some Goliath of a philosophical system with a single one of their snowballs and caused it to fall dead to the ground?—"Their efforts are less concentrated, and they don't work together as well as we do."—That may be because of their situation; and our own sex—what association was ever firm and indissoluble with us? What oath was ever unbreakable? Judas betrayed and sold out his Lord and Master for thirty pieces of silver; Rousseau did likewise to Apollo for the honor of an academic prize,[80] and I could easily provide even more examples of the fact that our own sex has not exactly distinguished itself in the realm of loyalty and faith. No fixed and permanent bond can ever be established unless men and women are in union with one another—if you want an obvious example of this, just look at the Freemasons or the Moravian Brethren.

Young man, have no fear of women's inclination to fashion. Would you have them be like the Turkish women in that regard—enervated by years of despotism? Whether your wife remains true in heart and mind will depend on your wisdom alone, and a woman's love of adornment will subside after she is married. Thus the combination brought about by the attractive powers of the two bodies for each other often takes up less room than the two bodies occupied singly. Whatever all those histrionic poets might have babbled, and all those many novelists may have criticized, about love is not nearly as important as the personal experiences which can be gained from a single case of true love traveling on the path to marriage. Even fops and dandies, those fluid bodies whose various parts all hang together by means of the weakest of forces—even they become solid if their parts are brought into closer proximity to each other, and a high-minded young woman can bring about transformations in such cases which are nothing short of creative, or better still, which are natural.

It is perhaps not entirely inappropriate to draw a parallel here between that quality in Nature which we call "brittle"[81] and the kind of affected prudery we sometimes encounter in the female sex. If a body is considered to be brittle when, upon the separation of certain

of its parts from one another, other parts not immediately involved in
the separation break off as well, can we not also apply the same term
to a girl who feigns embarrassment at the most innocent jest and who
thus treats a respectable young man concerned with the good of her
soul as slanderously as if he were some sort of rogue who only had
eyes for her physical charms? If it also seems apparent to you that a
coy or prudish girl of your acquaintance is either a spoiled child or
one without any upbringing whatsoever, or what is even worse, that
she is a hypocrite peddling sour wine under the guise of sweet, then
I would advise you, my good fellow, not to approach any closer to
her, for whether you win or lose her, you have neither gained nor
lost much.

Finally—I say this not because I have said everything, but because
I do not wish to say more—finally, look for a girl who is a virgin.
Virginity is the May of the year, the blossom on the tree, the morning
of the day, and in the face of beauty and freshness what can prevail?
Virginity is such a delicate matter that one can hardly talk about
it; a girl runs the risk of coming too close to the subject even by
mentioning the word, and there is hardly a word which can inflame
the passions like this one. Thus the high priest of the Hebrews was
required unconditionally to marry a virgin,[82] and the Archbishops of
the Greek Orthodox Church still retain this high-priestly privilege—
although I am not sure any longer, given the corrupt times we live in,
whether to call this privilege a "weal" or "woe," an *odiosum* or *favorabile*.
True, there are laws which declare marriage to a wh——e to be the
keys to heaven, but in fact Nature contradicts these statutes, and I
will never be able to understand how anyone can justify paying the
same price for something which has already been worn as he would
pay if it were new. It is said that "Fruits which the birds have already
savored taste the sweetest"—however, this does not hold true for girls.
There is, moreover, a bit of bitterness to the most sublime pleasures,
the most subtle sweetness has a little pain to it, and an old wine is
always somewhat tart to the taste.

"Whoever knowingly marries a wh——e is either a scoundrel or
wishes to become one," another more reasonable and natural saying
declares, and nothing is more certain than that a man who disregards
this point is capable of the most despicable acts possible. Nothing is
more just than for the laws to prohibit the wearing of a bridal veil to
women who have been raped.[83] Moreover, to marry a person regarded
by everyone else as possessing a dubious reputation is likewise the

straight path to becoming a scoundrel; actually it is more a matter of what a woman appears to be than what she is. The subtleties of the Hebrews in this regard were compelled to place very strict limits on that particular pleasure which normally has very little fear associated with it, and in fact appears to require a sort of bold audacity.[84] It is true that nothing else was able to preserve chastity so effectively—but what good is chastity if one cannot enjoy the fruits of it to the fullest extent and when one is forced first to peel the apple one would simply like to bite into as it is?

That well-known law of Lycurgus which stipulated that married couples in Lacedaemon ought to come together only clandestinely not only kept the wives new and fresh for their husbands, but also hindered certain preliminary activities which tend to dampen desire in such situations.[85] But much is lost of the original spirit of a text in translation, and I wonder if I might not be permitted here to put this difference between the original and its translation into practical application? Since a law similar to that of Lycurgus is no longer suitable for our times, let me urge you, my dear husband, to recall certain memories using your powers of imagination which will enable you to bring about a much more heartfelt and profound pleasure than perhaps has recently been the case. Every description is more pleasing than the object being described itself. That which is displeasing and dull, the merely physical, falls away and we begin to imagine the object spiritually, as if our entire soul were focused on it. In particular, those things which touch us deeply must come entirely from the soul and not be based merely on previously derived opinions. Just look—I am giving you some acceptable means for achieving new stimuli in respect to that certain pleasure—stimuli which, in the final analysis, will benefit you in more than one way.

There is not one in ten thousand of us who would wish to imitate the ancient Cynic philosophers and make the public streets into a bridal chamber; a public examination of any kind is nothing but a public shaming, whereby even the cleverest person becomes filled with terror and panic. Even Roman law—although it can be said to have paid homage to natural law in the same sense as Christianity did to philosophy—contains nothing regarding the necessity for a proof of virginity, and if one wished to maintain that what we call the "Morgengabe," namely, the gift of the bridegroom to the bride on the day after their marriage, has always been viewed among the Germans as a kind of finder's reward, that is, as a present for finding one's bride to be a virgin, then this argument as well is fraught with every possible kind of difficulty, one of them being, for example, the fact that the same gift was also given to widows. Our ancestors had no need of bothering themselves about something which was simply a matter of course to them, and I fail to see why they should have been obliged to pay for it. The laws do not permit the man to receive a *Morgengabe,* and I would bet a hundred to one that no husband-to-be would ever ask me why. It would be a crime to be like Montaigne and not even be able to count to three,[86] or to assert that Adam, just as he sinned for all mankind, also married for all mankind. Surely there still exist groves of myrtles untouched by every wind which blows, and surely there still exist honorable women who are more than they seem, who avoid not only splendor but also the pretense of it, and who, even if some degree of pretense can still be found in them, nevertheless pretend to be less than they really are. But then why must we pretend at all?

And now, my dear young fellow, farewell! Great joy is often the harbinger of bad news; a certain anxiety the sign of a happy event to come, although faint-heartedness is actually an emotion unbecoming to any male heart; whatever is not begun with courage, enthusiasm, and love, walks crabwise; and even if too much courage can sometimes lead us astray, to dare is to win, to dare is to lose, and fortune favors the brave! You would not be the first to tread the path leading to matrimony, nor would you be the last—so what is there to keep you from it now? People who think evil have two enemies: their conscience and their own convictions; good people display a certain consciousness of the correct path to follow even in times of crisis—and behold, your path has already been hallowed by Nature herself. To fail because we lack some knowledge which could easily be attained, or to give up in the face of obstacles we could overcome without difficulty is not much better than doing evil intentionally; whoever *is* not what he *can* be is merely deluding himself. We wish to experience human joys, and must therefore suffer as human beings; shadow is as important to a painting as light; whoever fails to use what he has will sooner or later lose what he needs. A book we borrow is more quickly read, but one from our own library no more than an arm's length away is what brings us true and lasting pleasure—and the early bird gets the worm. By marrying we set ourselves o'f from the world, and it has been rightly said: "Love not the world, neither the things that are in the world."[87] It is a poor consolation to know that a good chess player still can win even after

223

his queen has been captured, and that it is difficult to tell from a tulip blossom whether it has just bloomed this morning for the first time, or has bloomed before. On the other hand, a good reputation, a rational upbringing, and virtuous mothers whose morality does not derive from legislation—these are what afford a sure guarantee for a happy choice in a bride.

7

For Girls

A MAN HAS various jobs: to go to war, to become a citizen; to serve as town councillor; in my case, to write on marriage, etc. At this particular time a woman has but one: to get married. Your life's plan has thus already been made, my dear girl, although this is something it will take a thousand men their entire lives to accomplish! Only the means are up to you; yet no matter how little is left for you to do yourself, it is nevertheless still your duty to perform your vocation honorably.

Some girls hope to captivate by leading a life of seclusion, others by a kind of compliance which unfortunately often gets out of hand. The latter stand with their wares displayed as if they were in the open market and have no compunction about offering them to every passerby, just so that not a single item of their stock, as the business people call it, will remain on the shelves unsold. It is true that "when fools go to market the shopkeepers rejoice"; but also that these good children often can bankrupt a merchant because being in business means taking risks, and whoever takes risks wins less frequently than he loses.

If I were to give advice on this matter to young girls who were also very pretty, I would advise them, if their mothers lived in seclusion and were regarded by all as solitary people, to show themselves at the window once in a while. If on the other hand your mother, my dear girl, is a ———, then you must live in exaggerated tranquility; if she begins talking to the man next door, read a devotional book; if

225

she is going to a masquerade ball, then develop a headache; if she is listening in on your conversation, then say to your male friend: "If you only knew how much I regret it, but I really mustn't . . ." A mother who is a ———— will gladly sacrifice her daughter, provided there is some profit to be had, and only occasionally is her grown son in a position to do anything about it.

A father, even if he is a free thinker,[1] likes to see his wife and daughter praying. And if your suitor turns up his nose at your father's indiscretions, then cry a little bit and leave the matter at that. It is perhaps the safest stratagem for a girl to live in seclusion; nonetheless, this is a stratagem like any other and has about the same rate of success. Whoever is smart will choose to marry a cheerful and independent girl over one who is not. A girl who is completely independent is like a flower in the meadow—she blooms for every wanderer who has the desire to stop and take a closer look. If she already has a suitor, she can be compared to a flower in a garden with a wall around it, and it is her suitor who has the key to the gate. If, however, she is married, she is a flower in a vase in the parlor, and her aroma is meant for her husband alone. I have noticed quite often that girls who through hypocrisy have won the main battle and thereby gained themselves a husband still skirmish under the same banner even after they have married. Whoever would control his passions according to the dictates of reason must subordinate them to civility and not anger, for just as anger cannot replace what we lose in strength, since in fact we become even weaker when we yield to it, so also does a girl who uses force and hypocrisy lower herself in the eyes of anyone who truly knows human nature.

There are speakers whose speeches do not seem to have been written for the minds of their listeners (or for their immortal souls either, for that matter); and that certain bearing, those pious airs which are meant to assure us that the dear young girl in question knows nothing of the profane notion that there are two sexes other than what she has read in the Bible—that sort of behavior is much more odious than if an ingenuous young girl occasionally is happy and in good spirits even if she runs the risk of contradicting the decrees of her worried mother. Neither the heathens of old nor the Israelites were much at proselytizing. Since their localized religion was limited to customs and ceremonies in which they plied the divinity with food and drink in turn for mere temporal benefits, the extent of participation of the true believers in these ancient religions would have diminished day by day if they had gone out to the highways and byways to invite people to come to their ceremonies.[2] So it often is with girls, especially when at a certain age and at times when they are together as equals they disdain the institution of marriage with their mouths, but honor it in their hearts. But when the time has finally come and they have drawn their lot, they become all too eager to find a husband for every one of their playmates in a single evening's work. That sort of petty and everyday dissimulation—whereby every young man, I might add, knows the score precisely—may be excused in the fair sex without anyone needing to make a formal accusation of hypocrisy.

Most of the gifts which Nature bestows upon her favorites are not like legal documents and promissory notes which are valid over a long period of time; they are more like certificates of prepayment for goods which do not come into our possession until after many years. To this category belong common sense and good judgment. Whoever possesses good judgment has in it a faculty adapted to the acquisition of every possible skill; whoever has common sense possesses a soul of this kind. Beauty, however, is a gift of Nature which expires after a specific period of time, a present which must be paid for immediately and with cash. Beauty is like a sword: whoever does not know how to use it will end up hurting himself, and a beautiful girl often finds happiness in a marriage later than one who is not. The former is admired, and yet who really knows whether while being admired she in turn secretly admires others herself! If a pretty girl is prudish, she frightens people off; it she is not, then people question her virtue.

A pretty girl who appears unaware of her beauty becomes all the more beautiful on account of this; she would do well, however, if on festive occasions she did not dress like a trollop but always quite simply, never neglecting the accomplishments and skills required of her sex. In doing this she will enjoy the benefits of her beauty without the difficulties which accompany it, and will not need a father of great wealth or noble heritage in order to find a husband who is both—she will be able to make her own choice out of a phalanx of youthful suitors. If she is from a good house and has money to boot, she would do well to view these as rare coins to be used only in the case of emergency.

A girl who is not pretty must not despair, however. "Beauty," states a philosophic poet, "lies not in the color of a maiden's cheeks, but in the eyes of her lover." How true! Beauty is not a characteristic appended to an object, but that which lies in the very soul of whoever perceives it;

thus we all see collectively, but everyone sees differently. Beauty is like a banquet prepared only for display on which the eye can feast after the stomach has been completely satisfied. Goodness of heart, a mild countenance, and a thousand other things will compensate for beauty, and just as it is a comfort to know that there is no book so bad that it cannot serve a purpose somewhere, so you should never consider yourself completely without powers of attraction. Invest the talent that you have,[3] but in such a way that you do not charge excessive interest, for that would be unfair, given the fact that your resources are not the best and you cannot exactly behave like a capitalist under the circumstances. If you are poor, then learn to manage the affairs of the house well; if rich, then learn music. A pretty hand on the lute often surpasses the prettiest face; a dainty foot on the dance floor outshines the most engaging eyes, and nothing can resist a full bosom. It is my humble opinion that no girl is completely ugly, and if there should exist one who came close to deserving this reproach, I believe nonetheless that if she were to apply even her meager talents well, she could still lay claim to the affections of a forty-year-old man, and marriages of that sort are often happier than those where both parties are but children.

It can serve as a warning to beautiful women, and as a comfort to those less beautiful, that while Paris gave the apple to the most beautiful of the three women, namely Venus, it was also another beautiful woman, Helen of Troy, who turned out to be the cause of disaster for so many people.[4] But in order for us to arrive at an even closer agreement on the subject of beauty at this point, let me just stop here for a moment and back up a little—a technique which I hope will not work to your disadvantage. Your sex is weak and infirm in comparison to ours, and in fact one could not incorrectly assert that you die a little bit each day. Since we find among many animals that the female is smaller by a fifth and about a quarter weaker than the male, it is not surprising, then, that the woman is ill with disorders of a gynecological sort about a fifth of her life. It might even be said that women have much of the good and bad about them that characterizes sick people in general. But why do we not then set about restoring them to health? A role in the affairs of the state suited to them would, I should hope, serve them well in this regard—they would become healthy at the very hour it was granted. If one were to hold back even the most capable young man as if he were a child, he would never give up his childish ways and would retain all of the good and bad aspects of his childhood into his life as an adult. But release the little Hercules from paternal authority and in but a short time he will reveal himself as the man he is. And before their own release from bondage comes about, I would like to offer the young women the following well-intentioned advice: even though according to our present constitution you are not now *active* citizens or allowed to attain that status, nevertheless show yourselves to be true *passive* citizens of the state and even in your Egyptian exile[5] never forget that your destiny is the same as that of mankind in general, and that you will have ample opportunity to make yourselves visible by means of your particular destiny as wives, mothers, rulers of the household, and passive citizens of the state. I have already commiserated with the fair sex on account of its depressing relationship with society, a relationship wherein it finds itself in such a condition of dependence that the state only addresses it through men, as God spoke to the Israelites through Moses—indeed, that the state appears to women to be less a moral human being than merely a moral man. That assassin who once told his partner that their assigned victims were to be "two people—or, if you like, one and a half, a man and a woman" was expressing an assassin's view of things which none of us, if we are not in fact bent on murder, ever ought to become guilty of, unless it would be to give wider circulation to an academic joke about some dissertation attempting to prove, after the manner of the Scholastics, that "women are not people,"[6] or that "women will never get to heaven," since, according to the Revelation of St. John there was a "silence in heaven about the space of half an hour,"[7] and women would never be able to keep quiet for so long.

In what I have already stated I have often taken the liberty, although without becoming a traitor to my own sex, of suggesting means for lifting this burden of oppression which is as insulting as it is tiresome and undeserved, and which never existed before the Fall—but of lifting it gradually and not heroically. And since I have also retained the privilege of repeating myself occasionally in this little marriage book of mine, permit me one last time to assure you women again that once you have freed yourselves from the bonds in which your immature appetites, vanity, and thirst for conquest presently restrain you, you will then, by means of the continuous application of your sex's native diligence to the simple tasks of providing for others' souls and bodies, be in a position to invigorate, strengthen, and finally to establish your own sex once and for all. Your sex is noble in and of itself, and only through purity of heart, modesty, and chastity will you ever attain that propriety and godliness which serves better to adorn you than anything else and helps you acquire a kind of beauty neither fashion nor sophistication can supply, but which is rather the gift of a good conscience and rigorous self-examination. Nature has revealed her respect for the human race by not forcing anything upon us and giving us free rein, and the King of the Earth is also king over himself. It was not she who made the female sex beautiful, it was to make itself beautiful. There are women who, if I may put it this way, because of their obvious natural beauty excite interest wherever they may be; nevertheless, the impression they make is but short-lived. They overwhelm, but do not captivate us, and usually the most beautiful of them remain old maids—irrefutable proof that in addition to natural beauty there is another beauty which far surpasses the former and which through its lack of guile lends purely natural beauty a permanence not even sickness can destroy. Helen of Troy was still enchanting men at an age when women in Italy and France, as well as in Germany, are considered to be well past their prime. To this can be added a way of attiring oneself which harmonizes so nobly with the face and the body that it appears to intermingle, so to speak, with every facial expression and gesture and seems so individualistic that it gives every appearance of being inborn in the person who knows how to choose it well, even though its main elements, at least, tend to correspond to the national style of dress—a style, by the way, which hardly implies a kind of national costume slavishly adhered to by all and determined by what is currently the fashion in Paris, but one in which climate and national character play a significant role.

If the criteria of propriety and decorum are adhered to and everything is treated *medice* and *modice*,[8] I am certainly not against the modest emphasizing of the more beautiful parts and proportions of the body. Among people everywhere a certain type of ceremonial law has been introduced and found acceptance, a certain silent agreement as to what is permissible in terms of external appearance, and this is often more sacred to them than their own moral law. This is an area, moreover, in which the fair sex really need not attempt bold strokes of genius, or even the introduction of new ideas. It is also seldom if ever the case that one girl alone is the first one to introduce a new fashion—she often confers in council with at least one other person (the queen with the crown princess) as to whether, for example, the ribbon this year is supposed to be pinned on the right side or the left.

Propriety surpasses all beauty; women are like a brightly polished mirror which can be dimmed by the slightest breath. They can allow themselves nothing but the most strictly adhered-to code of behavior in public, and a girl must not *think*, or a woman *say*, what a man, even a respectable one, may *do* without hesitation. Thus, for example, a girl must consider the matter longer than a man when she wishes to give a present, and she can never give money directly. The enemy of propriety—as the palladium of virtue—and the adversary of beauty itself is fashion, ruling with an iron scepter and making the freest nation into a slave. Even if nowadays it is beginning to encounter some opposition in the free states,[9] sooner or later it will exercise dominion over them as well, just as England, along with the rest of the civilized world, now receives its instructions in matters of fashion from France.

My dear children, if you promise to soothe the ruffled feathers of my critics I would like to mention in passing that fashion engenders a kind of uniform which causes our young men and women to look like the members of two separate military regiments—a uniform which does nothing to enhance the figure of either sex and make it more pleasing, but merely allows us to prove that we belong to the fashionable world and know what currently happens to pass for trump in it. This manner of living causes us to be honored not for having done anything honorable, but because we belong to that particular group of people who have given each other their word to honor one another—an honor of the sort which, both for the bestower and the recipient, is really no honor at all! And what has been the net effect of these very important circumstances? Fashion surpasses everything; it rules in life and in death, and makes known its respect of persons even into the next world through the act of beatification. It is too bad that this ruins every chance for us to have and display good taste, for it is with great reluctance that fashion has left even the very little room to maneuver which still remains to us—about as much, in fact, as prisoners are allowed in which to catch a breath of fresh air and get some exercise.

But use the little room to maneuver you do have, my good children, until finally everyone begins to realize what a tyrant fashion has become! Do not scorn those who take the liberty of contradicting this despot in small ways, and try yourself, by using a ribbon which complements your face, or other such provisional means, to keep a couple of back doors open until you dare to defy publicly the infallibility of this Holy See which has been established in Paris. Resist with all your might every law of fashion which offends propriety and exposes it to ridicule, and you will be richly rewarded for it. In all matters be true to Nature unto death; the radiance emitted by art, as dazzling as it may be, can never procure for you that dignity befitting you and which you deserve. A Turkish ambassador once replied to the question as to his opinion of the ladies at court: "Sorry—I'm no judge of painting."[10]

Even that erudition by means of which our own sex makes its fortune or loses it; wherein we rack our brains attempting, for the most part through writing, to make a name for ourselves above all others—that is, for the present at least, not your affair either. On the other hand, there are skills and kinds of knowledge you can acquire which are useful and not merely impressive. Do not behold the sunset in the poet, but in Nature herself; do not forget, for the trills and moving passages of the singer gurgling away on his sonorous aria, the song of the nightingale; and seek to apply everything you learn to the domestic sphere in a practical way. To be perfectly frank, it is also true to say that you must not cease being pretty in order to please and not make it your object to bowl us over with your Latin and Greek. As a matter of fact, you yourselves do not really believe that book learning is the pinnacle of human wisdom, in that your own practical wisdom so often gains the victory over all manner of scholarly erudition; and—to return to a previous theme—why would you want your melancholy to throw those very social relations off key which you yourselves tend to render so harmonious? The realm of wisdom and of the graces is open to you, and it can be said of you that you are the very image and reflection of Nature, and in fact that we have in you—if you avoid seeking art and artifice—the very embodiment of Nature herself. I do not know whether it is a hard and fast rule that the people in any given place talk most about the best preacher, least about the best woman, and frequently about the best girls, although never without respect; but I do know that that particular intellect which people call agreeable and loving; which one obtains less from books than from experience; which can be transformed without difficulty into words and deeds; and which a teacher of more recent times maintained that we cannot define, simply because we never encounter any more or less of it in others than in ourselves—I do know that this intellect is the true feminine one. If your ear becomes too sensitive from Italian music, the racket of the children's playroom will be intolerable for you. Nature is not your main textbook, it is your entire library, and by means of it you are far better able to read other people than we are. You read and understand the most famous scholar as soon as he steps out of his study and into society, and without that fear which much sooner comes over us in the presence of such men before we come to know them more intimately, especially when they are not quick-witted by nature or do not let their wit shine in public. Since you well know that heroes pay homage to you and even Field Marshal Hercules contrived out of love for you to prevent anybody from withstanding you, so that even to attempt it would be to commit a sin against Nature and a greater loss for him than gain,[11] you thus approach the hero and the scholar with an ingenuousness that is as amiable as it is admirable. In your eyes only the noble, virtuous man is of importance, and only for him do you show veneration.

You always understand just what you are saying, since you make a special effort to put all your thoughts into words—an endeavor in which you reveal an extraordinary dexterity, often in combination with a power and vigorousness of expression. The Greeks popularized the arts and sciences, the Egyptians concealed them; you are in this respect born Greeks, destined to draw the highest lot in the apportionment of expressive powers and to render things tangible through words where the scholar can only conjure up spirits. You breathe a living soul into everything; whoever hears you and has good sense will listen to what you say. Your first thoughts about a matter—which we, as I have already noted, place no trust in because we think them unworthy— are, if they represent the sincere reflection of your mind and heart, a little treasure trove in themselves, because you are accustomed to thinking simply, nobly, and naturally, and to expressing yourselves in the same way, and because you hate whatever is bombastic and unnecessarily complicated. Good for you that you view all knowledge as mere piecework if it cannot be put to use and are only satisfied with yourselves when you are able to do something more effectively than you were able to say it—that is, when you do more than you say! Your capacity for doing things is such that you must necessarily also talk more than our sex in doing so, and I will take up your defense whenever you are accused of talking too much—when it comes to talking it would take at least ten women and twenty girls to equal a single one of our fops. And if someone wished to counter this argument by bringing up the women of the lower classes, I would reply that even here it is very often only a matter of their wanting to keep active. In people of this sort words come very close to being actions; and in fact words often outdo actions if we judge them by their consequences, so that it is right to demand that we be held responsible for every harmful word we utter. May I also take this opportunity to digress a little and ask you to enunciate every letter precisely and clearly and not let yourselves be frightened off by the letter "r," or even another less harsh consonant? Perhaps your example will bring some men with affected speech to think the better of it.

I am not asking that you take a Domitian-like joy in swatting flies,[12] but should a mosquito bite you, take no notice of it—this way you might help some poor sentimentalist or fop recover his strength. The kind of engagement the Doge of Venice enters into every year on Ascension Day[13] is not for you, and it is right and proper even for old maids to embrace enthusiastically the offer to enter into the sacred state of matrimony, for whoever conceives of a nun—that is, a female monk—as a blossom on the tree of the Church has failed to bear in mind that blossoms without fruit are little better than leaves, and that fruit trees which bear no fruit merely take up space. "If I speak with the tongues of men and of angels," writes the Apostle Paul, "but do not have love (to be sure, he is talking about a different kind of love, nevertheless, this passage can be applied without irreverence to married love as well), I have become a noisy gong or a clanging cymbal. And if I have the gift of prophesy, and know all mysteries and all knowledge; and if I have all faith, so as to remove mountains, but do not have love, I am nothing."[14]

Men die for the fatherland, women live for it. The former destroy families by their wars and unfortunately also by plans and arrangements which are not well thought out; the latter preserve them. Frankly speaking, if women maintained the household as poorly as men the state, what would have become of the so-called civilized world? You cannot and must not forget that you have been destined to be mothers and managers of the entire household, and every skill and bit of knowledge having to do with those two things can be of use to you. You are as little required to be a professional cook as a professional cleaning woman; nevertheless, in order to keep your husbands at home you will have to know how to cook and dress attractively—but also in both cases simply, effortlessly, and naturally, always remaining free from the slavery of other people's opinions. Is it a discredit to the fair sex that it is able to cook fish better than Lucullus' best chef?[15] I believe there are certain aspects of food preparation which not only do not dishonor the feminine hand, but which in fact render it more beautiful.

Moreover, experience and the development of household skills not only give women practical experience, but protect them from the frivolous yearning for distraction and amusement which seeks peace everywhere and never finds it. And most of the kinds of needlework women do today take so little of their time that the work of the state, which even at its most demanding can be accomplished with half of one's brain on vacation, will be very welcome to them when the fullness of time has come.[16]

Now that we have finished with these preliminary remarks, you will be able to see for yourselves that the desire of people to marry is the most natural one of all, and that you would now do well to look around for a good man. The thoughts and feelings of a great soul and noble heart are slumbering within you; seek out men, therefore, who are capable of appreciating this, men of principle who, even if they can be counted on less to grant you a freedom based on your own inclinations than one of a more regulated nature, are nevertheless much to be preferred to a reed which is driven back and forth by the wind, to a namby-pamby little fellow with fancies which are never more than passing. What do you want with a man who is always at either flood- or ebb-tide, who lies at your feet and then ignores you, alternately weeps and laughs, becomes angry and then resents it, is despondent and dauntless, all depending on whether the weather is bad or good, or whether things are going poorly or well between him and His Excellency? Not everything which passes for a principle truly is one; the more tempting the promises sound, the less likely they are to be kept. Nevertheless I am not recommending a man to you who merely *talks* about principles, but about one who *has* them, not one who lets his light shine in words, but in works.[17] No man can be judged by a thousand things he says or a few things he does; in emotional situations, at times when they receive unexpected news, especially good news, we can often comprehend others at single glance, and this is the reason why prudent people are careful not to reveal themselves in such situations.

What kind of husbands do you want, girls? Do you want a soldier? A good choice, I should think! The fair sex needs protection and loves people who have heart. A girl likes it when men fight over her, and views the scar on the face of her suitor as a kind of medal which she has presented to him. I say "a girl," and exclude in this case experienced coquettes and flirts, who actually try to establish peace between their suitors when they threaten to break each other's neck out of jealousy merely because these coquettes have a need for more than just one of those Humble and Obedient Servants of theirs. They are no longer served—in the words of one of those mistresses herself, uttered on the occasion of a duel taking place beneath her very balcony—by iron, only by gold.

A sex which cannot and should not defend itself will as a rule side with people who are decisive. Here we encounter one of the reasons why the soldier, called to a profession demanding courage, generally enjoys success with young women. Yet a girl who takes a soldier for a husband also takes on the requirements of his profession, and when one looks at the matter from the side of Lycurgan Law,[18] which demanded of the soldier the vow of poverty and forbade him all pomp and luxury in weapons and possessions, even as the consequence of plundering a defeated enemy, how can one help but honor a discipline whose only intention is simplicity and inner fortitude?

There are, of course, also *foppish* soldiers who lay more stress on the visible than the invisible; who make every effort to see that their beautiful clothes are never stained by blood; and who bear arms not for the sake of a just war, but for a loathsome desire to plunder, not out of a noble sense of honor, but for their own worthless motives. The good life enervates a man's courage, and from time immemorial those soldiers have been the bravest who had to make do with poor fare. They considered their life as nothing—and why in fact *should* they have pampered through the delights of food and drink that body which they were so eager to sacrifice for their fatherland in order to win for themselves the crown of life or a fame which lived on after their death, and thus become worthy of a hero's life or death for fatherland and for right? Now, when there exist leaders in many armies whom Lucullus would not have refused had they invited him to one of their meals in camp; now, when many a general of those truly heroic days of yore would view the everyday meal of a common soldier as a victory feast and think himself celebrating a banquet at the table of his host—now (just to get myself out of this the best way possible) we must live and let live. A pampered and coddled enemy who make it the first law of their preparation for war to live splendidly amid the pleasures of life; who permit themselves every comfort even down to a Soubisian field library,[19] will necessarily forfeit their last ounce of courage when they come face-to-face with an army reduced to the barest necessities, and when the last of their hopes, that of making themselves richer, vanishes before their eyes. It is only this latter hope, by the way, which can bring the most spoiled of soldiers temporarily to a kind of courage, since the greedy enemy soldier is attracted to the spoils of war, and even the enemy's most cowardly soldier will not allow a little danger to keep him from enjoying the fruits of his labors in return for but a short period of inconvenience.

As long as the destiny of women consists in nothing more than making the lives of men happier and more glorious; as long as so little thought is given to a wise use of the powers which Nature has given them, and we spend so much time and effort trying instead to render them powerless; as long as we view the women as the common folk do the stars, that is, merely as little lanterns in the sky, is it then advisable for military heroes to marry? When they have finally brought themselves to the point of being able to expose their own dear and carefully cultivated lives to danger, will they not then still attempt to safeguard them for the sake of their precious wives at home? Is it not possible that women could actually serve as an encouragement to the enemy? "If we win, our booty will be beautiful women," they think. A hero can indeed love his wife, but his horse and weapons must share this love; he can feel, but he must act as if he felt nothing. This situation is made all the worse by the fact that women already have had to make do with the mere *melody* of feeling, having found it easier to do without the text which accompanies it. They are satisfied if we only act as if we were feeling; they pretend, and can also put up with our own pretending. (Their pretending comes from pride, ours often from an angry heart, and even more often from bad habit.) May I also take this opportunity to give honorable mention to the French hero Richelieu,[20] who, when finally exhausted from his amorous conquests, still had the vanity to send his empty coach to the doors of all the gallant women he had had the honor of courting in his better days; and may I also express my uncertainty as to whether one ought sooner to forgive him or the ladies for this empty coach? In every case, the question as to why girls are so attracted to soldiers receives the same unfortunate answer: because they believe that by virtue of the uniform they have married the entire regiment (I am referring here, of course, to the corps of officers).

What would become of the human race in the end if soldiers were absolutely forbidden to marry, since our rulers can never think of anything but war even in times of lasting peace? In addition to defensive wars, which nobody who has been attacked would seek to avoid, an offensive war, whether for punishment of a foe or the retaking of lost land, can break out at any moment. Finding justification in such cases amounts to the easiest deduction in the world, since nobody questions the legitimacy of any war if it is in the least bit advisable, and when the growing power of a neighboring country and the resulting change in the balance of power makes it likely. Under these circumstances one is forced as usual to make a virtue of necessity and wink not just once, but twice at soldiers' marriages. But once the other sex begins to participate actively instead of enduring passively; once it is convinced that human beings who are equipped with reason and freedom *can* do something when they *want* to; once it is placed in a better position through improvement in its status to work with its own hands and become independent, then the question "marry a soldier?" will no longer require careful consideration. Human life itself is a kind of soldier's life—why should the woman only take part in the Platonic[21] and not the real republic? As soon as they are found worthy of the honor of being human beings, there will no longer be any doubt in this regard. And even if a soldier's life is hard—how much material is in it for providing happiness! How it broadens the mind! And even to end one's life quickly and gently amid the fifes and drums and in the course of fulfilling the duties of one's profession, as a master over the circumstances one has at least accepted personally and feels to be serving the cause of right, without having to be subject to all the miseries of fever, gout, or disease—how sweet it must be!

It is true, of course, that I have commanders and officers more in mind here than common soldiers; and it does seem to me as if there are additional supporting reasons for making marriage difficult for the common soldier, as much as I have been wont to defend the general populace elsewhere in my essay. The armies which countries are forced to maintain in these recent calamitous times are too large for the pay of a common soldier to be able to keep up with the needs of more than a single stomach. A brief moment in which instinct puts to flight all doubts is enough to get the marriage knot tied; yet this happy moment is mother to a thousand miserable ones, and nothing is more certain than that the child who must experience the misery of this world already in its mother's womb will bear traces of this experience when it is born. I believe that a person can tell instantly just by looking at one of these needy children, if I may call them that, that it would rather have stayed home than come.

Most parents will tend to love a frail child more than a strong one, for along with the natural love for a newborn and the later love for the antics of a young child comes a kind of sympathy which causes people to coddle and pamper a weak child to the point where it becomes a harder burden for the state to bear than for itself. It is expecting a lot for such children—who can never become more than half human beings by the time they reach their majority—ever to attain anything resembling true humanity in their lives. To be sure, that law would be perhaps a little too harsh which would prevent us from attempting for the sake of the republic to make weak children an exception to the rules for educating children, but is not a quick death far easier than an eternal captivity?

A certain knight-errant (Johannes Leyser[22]) who adopted false names and advocated polygamy, even though he never took a wife himself, once attempted to cloak his principles with, among others, this particular saying: "A curse on him who is slack in doing the Lord's work!"[23] Now if this saying could be secularized to fit our discussion it would find an even more appropriate location here, for what I have been saying all along concerning parents who merely start to work on children without being able to carry out the plan finds its most precise application in the case of the common soldier. It is more tolerable for a man not to touch his "Kunigunde,"—like Heinrich II, who thereby earned the sobriquet "Heinrich the Holy"[24]—than to have branches without sap, leaves without fruit, or children without life. A learned man seldom has learned sons; but a common soldier is even less likely to produce more soldiers. With regard to this point I could describe in greater detail the conditions in three armies with which I am familiar, but I am only writing for people who read not merely the lines in front of them, but what lies between them as well—too much light hurts the eyes, and nothing is more common than for coppersmiths to go deaf.

If, therefore, after having weighed all the arguments against each other, we conclude that we cannot in fact deprive the common soldier of the joys of the married state[25] without running the risk of committing the cruelty of causing disproportionately more disorder than is presently the case—if this is so, do we not then still have to think of some means of mitigating this evil? Yet could not such means, as things often tend to go with political remedies, be worse than the evil itself or, by correcting a smaller problem, bring about a larger one? True, with respect to soldiers' marriages, the state gains little in quantity and even less in the quality of its members; nevertheless such marriages are necessary for the sake of morality. And if the soldier's wife takes on the duties of an Amazon and the state sets aside something for each of the children, who then can forbid the soldier from establishing his own nursery? And why, without compromising his situation, can he not be made more useful to the state in peacetime than he presently is? Agricultural labor, for example, will hardly cause him to be overpaid for his work or cradle him in the lap of luxury, two things to be feared (in the minds of some state economists) if he were to be allowed to ply any of the middle-class trades in the city. For, they say, aside from the fact that thereby all order in the city would be destroyed, and that the difference—still very necessary—between townspeople and soldiers, according to which the latter are sustained and the former provide the sustenance, would disappear by itself, would not the townspeople also soon be worse off than the soldiers? And what can be expected from the soldiers themselves, made soft by the flesh-pots of the city, by parties and other comforts of life, when they finally have to take to the field? Will they ever be able to be used as anything more than a national guard? Or, on the other hand, would we prefer to harken back to the time when countries did not keep standing armies, when every citizen was a born soldier and even if he was capable of rendering more necessary or useful service to the state under ordinary circumstances could scarcely restrain himself from enlisting his services as a soldier for short periods of time? St. Paul writes, "No man that warreth entangleth himself with the affairs of this life,"[26] and St. John the Baptist proclaimed the watchword: "Do violence to no man, neither accuse any falsely and be content with your wages"[27]—which is as much as to say: do not become involved in the affairs of everyday life, for no man can serve two masters.[28] What were the Janizaries[29] when they were merely soldiers, and what have they become, now that they are tradesmen of the middle class? All their courage is gone, and they cannot even defend their own flesh-pots. Whoever would attribute their lack of vigor to a lack of tactics is mistaken; they would not even be able to hold off an undisciplined army.

There you have it, my pretty children—a sure sign of my devotion to you, a devotion which has led me to accommodate myself to the present Articles of War[30] and let me be enlisted as a writer in the service of the soldier, although not in order to defend you, but to let you receive from this side as well the justice you deserve.

Which of you will have an academic for a husband? You would, my dear vivacious girl? Well then, act as if you were ignorant. Don't read anything, and if you are accustomed to reading already, act as if you weren't. Just listen; if you have to talk, tell him stories and all sorts of silly stuff. The latest town gossip can't hurt, but there ought to be something grotesque about it. Play a children's song and sing monotonously: "My mother has ge——ese."[31] But I know for a fact that you are as little likely to take an astronomer for a husband as a night watchman[32]—so, just between us, why are you considering an academic anyway?

If you are looking for a man who enjoys displaying his wealth, then marry someone without money who will be able to earn it without a great deal of effort. Of course, if earning money should for some reason become more difficult for people of this sort, they tend to become stingy, and if a person has once paid homage to this idol, he will come to sacrifice everything to it, even an inheritance. In general, however, it is better to marry someone who can become rich than one who already is—hard-earned money is better than inherited money. But be sure you look to your dowager's estate while he is still alive, otherwise you will become the laughingstock of the town after his death.

Do you want a man of rank? I feel sorry for you; even the fastest colors fade in the sun. It is not only the Keys of Peter[33] which cause people to go about bent over until they finally possess them—everyone who seeks something adopts this attitude of servility. A man who is conscious of his own merit considers it unnecessary for others to bestow honors on him, as well as improper to attempt to gain advantage by doing so; an ambitious man crawls before those in authority and regards everyone who is equal to him, including his own wife, as wards entrusted to him, and those who are not equal he treats as slaves. If a countess should happen to take notice of him, he can refuse her nothing; to please a princess he would hang himself.

A rich man? A girl who marries a young man for his money reduces herself to the level of a concubine; if she marries a rich old man she winds up selling her services as a maid. Children destroy everything; people advanced in years, that is, aged children, *keep* everything and by doing so try to make it last forever. Even in a palace you would only live in one room; the remaining ones would be for other people. If you were rich, who would be responsible for keeping you from becoming either a miser or a spendthrift? In the former case, you would spend all your time guarding your money, in the latter, you would eventually have to go begging. Often it takes only the slightest change in circumstances to bring about a change in one's temperament, so that as quickly as consumption changes to dropsy, a skinflint can turn into a spendthrift.

Do you want a poet? That is a strange question, I know. I really have nothing against marrying poets, but please believe me, in marriage a healthy prose is always better than poetry. Difficulties in love affairs bring poets into the world, but poetry and the *Zona temperata* where the land of military victories and the begetting of children is located do not suit each other very well. A poet lives, hovers, and exists in the realm of the imagination, and marriage is expressly calculated to clip imagination's wings and bring us back to earth. The story of Pygmalion, who fell in love with a statue, and Narcissus, who fell in love with himself, are hardly recommendations for people who feel their purpose on earth is to employ their imagination. Poetry is like alchemy, which renders metals more noble. If the man of poetic talent writes good verse, you know he only has a sweetheart; he could not write a successful poem about his wife unless it were on the occasion of her death. But the wife of a poet would be wrong to be jealous of her husband, for without the ability to spread the wings of his imagination he is completely inert and nothing but a poetaster; he must be moved like the sick men at the Pool of Bethesda;[34] he must have a sweetheart, or at least have one in mind; he fails to recall the most familiar facts, and even loses the power over his mother tongue when he has not been set aflame—but once he has got the feel of his poetry again, even the most ordinary tasks of his chosen profession are accomplished with ease. Why, my dear Frau Poet, would you want to obligate him to ride without spurs and spend a whole day on a stretch he could otherwise cover in an hour? To write prose is to travel by *coach*—sometimes with a six-horse team, sometimes with four horses, sometimes with two, now in a covered wagon, now in an open one, occasionally even in a carriage; poetry rides on *horseback*. Often a person can accomplish wonders as a rider without schooling, although some training, even if it is no more than learning by imitation, is nearly unavoidable. Whoever cannot count syllables and keep a tight rein on his meter will never be able to win his spurs, however talented he may be. Some say that these gentlemen ought to climb into the gondola of a hot-air balloon if their horse won't rear high enough for them; but without question, Pegasus would have to take offense at that sort of poetic license, would he not? And Pegasus and Bucephalus[35] yoked together, no matter who was driving the carriage—what a ride that would be! But just between us, Madame, all of those alleged acts of unfaithfulness of that darling of the Nine Sisters,[36] namely your dear husband, no matter how awful they might appear on paper, are, when it comes right down to it—sheer poetry.

If you want to lead a truly happy life, then marry a nobleman who lives on his own—if possible—independent estate and who has good taste to boot, even if like the storks he spends his winters in the neighboring town. (If he lacks good taste, he is nothing but a farmer, and if he is in service to the king, then he won't belong to you alone.) You will be for him the most beautiful portrait of Nature: the winter will mirror your pregnancies and the spring your return to the world of society; and as little as he is likely to become tired of *Nature*, just as little need you fear that this sad fate could ever befall *you*. I do not wish to pursue this point further in order to avoid revealing myself. Nevertheless, I cannot conceal the wish that my dear friend J—— may someday be able to lead a happy life at the hand of a husband who is worthy of her, far from the noise of the court and the city, so that when my hour has come I may be present there to have her close my eyes in death.

In general, I believe that couples who are in love should live in the country, and geniuses should live in the city. A genius in the country becomes rusticated as soon as he spends any time there; he is too much shamed by Nature for his artistic powers to have any effect. A loving couple, on the other hand, will not waste time thinking about Nature but grasp it with their hands—not read, but see. The passions are at home in solitude—here is where they begin, here they come to maturity. In the city, one drive enervates another, one thought the other, and a person is neither cold nor hot;[37] people express themselves politely and elegantly, but only because they must constantly be aware of how they might devise a new turn of phrase or give a different twist to the most mundane of matters. A lady well over sixty is considered there to be in the blossom of her youth simply because she happens to be a princess, and the Count is the wittiest and most polite man in the world merely because he is wearing a star. At important places, people coin new words and introduce new styles of clothing. And these two things are so closely bound together that a well-turned phrase in everyday life presupposes equally well-wrought clothes— seldom will a person in shabby clothes express himself well. In the solitude of the country people spend time thinking. "It takes a healthy soul," says a certain worldly-wise man who is also an excellent human being, "for one to truly appreciate the charm of country life," and this is no different from what Juvenal and the Christian community sing with the words: "a pure soul and a clear conscience."[38] I should add here, however, that the body must be healthy as well. Hospitals and doctors belong in the cities, where one out of seven houses is a hospital, whether it has a sign on it or not. To put it succinctly, large cities are a kind of purgatory for lovers, a mere stopover for the high-minded, a mortuary for philosophers, an auditorium for would-be wits, and for doctors ("*dat Galenus opes*"[39]) either a lazaretto or a goldmine.

By the way, my dear children, as long as it is still "today" and you are still single, rejoice and be happy! The seclusion to which you have been accustomed by others ought not to be a time of monastic confinement, but should prepare you for the outside world in which you are to play no small role later on. You have no need to cast your glance downward, but can choose the man you love, the man to whom you feel called, freely and honorably with your own eyes, almost haughtily rejecting the insipid and foppish conceits which weak-headed and weak-hearted admirers would force upon you, while the burning bush[40] of your wit compels them now to approach you with deference and respect. Yet a good host is neither prodigal nor niggardly, but entertains his guests simply and respectably, and thus I would advise you, my good children, to be somewhat economical with your wit even before you have chosen your young man and when you are not yet required to observe certain rules of decorum. I know very well that you are familiar with love games and riddles we ourselves could hardly solve, or would wish to; that even when the question "Could she be the one?" has barely crossed our mind it does not go unperceived by you; that you can guess the secret love of the Stoic even when he not only keeps tight reins on his lips, but has placed his thoughts under oath as well.[41] When the Quaker attempts to disguise his feelings and begins to sigh about the turn events have been taking recently, you know for a fact this sigh was really meant for you, and it is the spirit of love, the guardian spirit of your sex, which reveals to you such inklings from afar. Do not let these love-thoughts pass by duty-free; urge those who are so taciturn to make their declaration openly. On the other hand, why torment people who respect you wholeheartedly and who would reveal it to you so unreservedly? Deny them any hope in an honorable way, and reject them quickly if you cannot or will not encourage or fulfill them! Whoever gives quickly, gives doubly; and whoever refuses quickly is doing a good deed even in refusing. Whoever does not know how to give even before he is asked, is an unjust steward;[42] and indeed, you possess in full measure the talent for guiding matters in such a way that whoever you refuse is never forced into the embarrassing position of having to beg. And if your heart is firm, do not leave the one you *truly* love in uncertainty! The longer you burden him with your tyranny, the more he deserves his chairmanship after he is your husband. Whoever has many friends really has none, merely many enviers; and when too many lovers worship you, you are often faced with the dilemma of not being able to find a single one who really loves you and is worthy of your own love and gratitude.

From that moment when your heart first says "Yes," then let this Yes shine before men[43] and be as true to your sweetheart now as you would if he were your husband—for in your heart and soul he already is. If you call this a sacrifice, then you have no idea what duty really is. This may be a difficult statement to take—perhaps doubly so because it is continually being repeated. At this point I cannot help addressing one of your former playmates, who was married six years ago today amid hearty congratulations from all sides: your self-praise, my dear Madame, "Haven't I been true to my husband?" hardly has the smell of roses about it—in fact, I would be hard pressed to think of anything more insufferable even though I am such an admirer of marital fidelity that without bragging I can safely say I have devoted a whole chapter to it. You extol your marital fidelity? Why not that you eat, drink, and sleep as well? Isn't it in fact your most natural duty of all—and one closely bound up with the world, the nature of things, and your own well-being—to remain true to your husband? Or would you tithe with that coin only sporadically, in order to permit yourself little departures from fairness, good will, and compatibility in your marriage as the occasion suits you? Your marital fidelity should come as a matter of course, and you must in addition be agreeable, of a domestic disposition, tidy, a mother to your children, an overseer to the domestic servants, and a wife to your husband. Nevertheless, that fidelity which you consider to be so important and which has served you so well up to now can also at times become so tedious that he would actually be much happier with a coquettish, disloyal, or even unfaithful wife than with you if in spite of your faithfulness you are proud, jealous, argumentative, miserly, or extravagant in your ways. There is an expression—not uncommon in German—which runs like this: "She is a woman of the Seventh Petition,"[44] and is used to designate not an unfaithful woman, but one who makes her husband's life intolerable despite her marital fidelity. And since Luther also includes a "pious spouse" in his commentary on "our daily bread" in the Lord's Prayer,[45] then it follows that among the evils we are to be delivered from in the Seventh Petition must be included all manner of impious spouses, and among a hundred other types as well those who in spite of their rock-solid fidelity in marriage *still* manage to bring their husbands to the brink of despair. May I also at this point, since I have already brought up the perhaps inconvenient subject of the Seventh Petition, request married couples who love each other, as well as brides- and bridegrooms-to-be, to refrain from public expressions of tenderness, passionate caresses or fiery kisses? Nothing inspires rival lovers and gallants more who here and everywhere "worm their way into homes and gain control of weak-willed women."[46] Nothing awakens sleeping desires more inappropriately and causes greater annoyance; nothing is more unseemly to watch; and it is even possible for this lack of self-control to do more harm than gossip itself.

I will hasten now to a tender farewell. Whoever advises a youth not to marry may have his reasons; those who warn girls against marriage know not what they do,[47] for if marriage should someday become completely outmoded, men would lose much thereby, but women everything. It is perhaps for this reason that marriage is called *matrimonium* and not *patrimonium*. If you attack or criticize the *female sex*, then you provide food for thought and others will ponder what you say; but just try and speak out against *marriage*, and immediately the atmosphere changes completely: everything that is feminine is suddenly seething with indignation and you might as well be dead. The case of Héloïse does not suffice here as proof to the contrary, for while I am fully aware that she was against marriage to Abélard, the kind of fanaticism involved in that relationship does not pertain to the point in question. Girls love showy weddings and view them as a kind of festival of roses which they deserve because of their virtue; their mothers also lay a just claim to one of the roses from the bridal wreath of their daughters because they raised them so well.

Women suffer, we act; we are, they are becoming; we create, they are the chaos from which everything can be made; they hope, we fulfill; they wish, we grant their wishes. A woman is a comma, a man, a period; with the latter you know where you stand, with the former you must keep on reading. Women also have time to experience the emotions brought about by good and bad times in marriage; men are merely distracted by them. Because of a false report concerning the death of his son, Thales threw Solon from the top of a mountain into a deep valley, thereby making a father out of a philosopher.[48] And consider for yourselves: does marriage not often bring about untimely pauses in our business dealings, and does it really harmonize, especially in its present state, with the seriousness and uninterrupted diligence required by our official duties? Without question, it contains more scenes meant for girls than for us; nonetheless, it is no less an honor for a masculine soul to say: "I, too, am a human being, and cannot and will not deny anything that is human." Thus King Agesilaus rode on a hobby horse with his children for the sake of a wager, and Heinrich IV, that truly original monarch, even let his children ride on his own back.[49]

Roman law permitted a girl whose fiancé had been absent for a period of three years to marry someone else, in order that she would not lose valuable time when she was of marriageable age; and in truth, my dear children, nothing passes so quickly as this golden age. We men advance more slowly and thus do not get out of breath so quickly. A male lives simply in the first years of his life until he is fifteen; that is his Year of Jubilee[50] after which he finally begins to count his years; nevertheless, he never really learns his own birthday by heart until he sets up housekeeping himself. Even the most capable of your brothers, my dear girls, lags far behind you in terms of strength of soul before you reach the age of twenty. This is your equinox, and the days of your soul begin to diminish in length after that, for Nature has destined you to become mothers. With your bodies you are to praise her and enrich the state. Everything living ripens to a certain point and then begins to wither; if he had not been immortal, Adam would have died of ecstasy when he first beheld Nature in this fully ripe state at its creation. It is not the pear that has fallen to the ground which is ripe, but that which is about to fall; and blessed is the man who is able to harvest such a girl!

Just one more thing in passing. Whatever blooms quickly also fades quickly. A fruit from the greenhouse cannot approach one from the hand of Nature in taste and appearance, although the former is sooner ripe. Wine and women often work diligently hand in hand, the drink being the artifice some girls use when on the spur of the moment they happen to have need of a man. All they have to do is touch the hand of a young man as if by accident and sparks begin to fly—the tip of her little finger is enough to electrify his whole body. Of course, no one can guarantee whether his love will outlast the effects of the wine. If this method is not for you, then proceed like Nature herself, who takes neither giant steps nor crawls, but who approaches her goal gradually.

Woe to the girl who enters the state of marriage because she wishes to sleep with other men! I know for a fact that many a girl marries because her new husband has a good-looking brother, or because he is at his board meeting every day from three to five, or because she needs a blind for her extramarital affairs. I also know that children from these affairs nonetheless call her husband their father, and that everyone considers him to be that as well, for it is only right that the children not bear the burden for the misdeeds of their mother. But woe to the mother who thus uses the law as a cloak for her wanton behavior! Girls, marry because your mothers married, and be what you can and should be: women and wives! Whoever speaks well of me and my book on marriage does me an honor; yet whoever would speak well of my wife would do as much harm to her as if he were to speak evil of her. People say that water is best about which nothing more needs to be said—either good or bad—than that it is water. *Fiat applicatio!*[51] Plato thanked the gods for having had the good fortune to be born at Socrates' time; and if this little reminder wouldn't be taken as rudeness, I would say that you have reason to say this about your husbands as well. The thanks which the Divinity requires from you consists in your virtuous conduct, and it is to this that I challenge you in your marriages. Be not only true to your husbands, but give neither them nor anyone else the opportunity to think that you aren't completely faithful; the one harms them—and you yourself—as much as the other. If your husbands are jealous, they will assign a bodyguard to you, add watchman upon watchman, sentry upon sentry, will try to become an Argus[52] (although they still won't be able to keep from falling asleep occasionally) and end up spending time and money they could have made better use of elsewhere. Lepidus was shamed to death by the unfaithfulness of his wife,[53] and even if a Lepidus appears on the scene about as regularly as a Lucretia[54] (who, just between us, might well have stabbed herself to death even a bit *sooner*), it is still the case that even a husband who is not jealous at all must necessarily be displeased with the unseemly conduct of his wife, since his status among others is reduced by half, people doubt his sanity if he doesn't let it show that he notices, and they make a fool out of him as soon as he admits that he does. If he is a judge, people appeal his sentences; if a soldier, they question his courage; if a minister in charge of finances, then everybody tries to cheat the king. I would almost bet that most robberies take place as a consequence of adulterous acts. "Whoever cannot keep track of his wife," others think, "must be easy to steal from." Under normal circumstances, the woman loses little or nothing through the unfaithfulness of her husband; people feel sorry for her if she is jealous, and respect and admire her if she is not. And who would not rather be respected than pitied?

Let the Temple of Janus[55] in your house remain continually under lock and key, and make your peace with everyone. You stand only to lose through arguments and grudging acceptance; you ought to seek to overcome everything that is odious to you by submitting to it. Let the raising of your children be what keeps you busy; your sons must receive from your tutelage a sensitive heart, and your daughters should turn out just like you. It is a mistake for us to think of our youthful years only as a time for faith, and our mature ones only as a time of action. Even the most insignificant games of children can lead to great actions later on, and it is your duty take notice of these, bring them to the attention of your husband, and together with him make a judgment as to this or that particular talent or inclination of your children. This is a duty which will be accompanied by the greatest pleasure for you. The games we play, even as adults, reveal our true passions; a wise enemy cannot enlist the services of a better spy than those provided by a simple game. The happiest players are, in the final analysis, those who have nothing to lose; often the winners are unhappier than the losers, for our soul is, if I may express myself thus, clad only in a dressing-gown when we are at play, and will not take offense at many things it would find insulting if it were fully dressed.

Games should not be children's pastimes, but their work, so that in later years other work will seem like a game to them. It is thus to be hoped that someday a great mind will be able to become like a child once again and reform the games of our children along these lines. A few of our boys' games have excellent potential for this; those of the girls are almost universally useless and would have to be invented anew.

As long as these remain mere wishes, however, then those of you who are mothers—try to do as much as you can! Consider carefully your own upbringing and apply it especially to your daughters, avoiding the mistakes and retaining what was good. The continuation of the family name is not a factor with a girl, and from the point of view of the father she may be viewed much in the way of capital one withholds from one's heirs and uses to purchase a canonicate. There are people who have enlisted private tutors for children at a time when their mothers were still pregnant with them, but I consider such tutors just as unnecessary during pregnancy as before. It is, however, up to the mothers to begin the instruction of their children while the latter are still infants, and thus not to become guilty of the serious crime of having neglected them in any way. They must then continue this instruction by means of gestures and actions during the time before their children learn to read, and in this way the first words the children speak will be a sacrifice which the Deity Himself would look upon with favor,[56] and the memory of their mother's teachings will remain with them as a constant companion throughout their life.

To my way of thinking, the moralists among us are much too strict regarding the question of nursing when they refuse to allow a wet-nurse under any circumstances; one ought not to think only of the child in such cases, but also of the mother. What took place in the past cannot necessarily continue into the future because times change, and we change with them. Our own ladies have now become so refined that they would kill both themselves and their children if they were to begin to force things in this matter. As long as they can still bear children themselves, we should excuse them if they want to keep wet-nurses. Jupiter's wet-nurse was a goat,[57] and even if he did have the singular honor of becoming Jupiter himself, who is to say whether, given the well-known wanton disposition of this particular four-footed animal, Jupiter's exceedingly strong inclination toward the fair sex might not be traced to the milk he received from his wet-nurse?

What I said above notwithstanding, I know two types of people who could be very dangerous to the state even though no one is afraid of them: wet-nurses and barbers. A victim might perhaps taste the poison in a communion wafer; a dagger must be drawn before it can be used; but a barber has the capacity to commit the subtlest type of assassination. Either only the most respectable people ought to be enlisted for this trade, or it ought to be abolished completely. As far as the wet-nurse is concerned, she has a thousand opportunities to exchange one child for another, and I would bet that this has actually happened times too numerous to count. I once knew a count who looked so much like his wet-nurse—the daughter of a local church organist—that everybody would have taken him for her son had he not been lying in the cradle of a count. The cradle is the only proof of noble ancestry, and a wet-nurse loves her own child more than that of another—the rest you can imagine for yourself. Mothers lose in every respect through the use of a wet-nurse. Just look around you—that estate owner who lives in splendor and luxury and lets his own mother languish in poverty? A wet-nurse suckled him.

If time still lies heavy on your hands, then I should point out that the management of the household staff also belongs to your department, and in this particular case you will find it necessary to maintain a gentle and quiet disposition. If a woman strikes another woman, she is common and vulgar; if she hits a man, however, she is something even worse. All violent passions disfigure the woman—they distort the soft contours of her face, and without question, violent actions on the part of a woman make her ridiculous in the eyes of others. Among our ancestors it was the function of women to mete out the prizes for victory in tournaments, and in the most ancient times women led the victor back into his home city with dancing, music, and songs of praise. The daughter of Jephthah came out to meet her father the general with timbrels and dances after his victory over the Ammonites;[58] and after their victory over the Philistines, women streamed out of all the cities of Israel, singing and dancing to musical instruments, in order to meet King Saul and David, the victor over Goliath. The text of this heroic hymn ran: "Saul hath slain his thousands, and David his ten thousands."[59]

The woman's role on such occasions is only to distribute rewards—but in doing this they become the kings, and the men are merely ministers. Men punish, women can mitigate the punishment or even revoke it. Somebody once told me an anecdote about Frederick the Great of Prussia which I can only describe as exquisite. The government of one of the provinces once condemned an unruly citizen to life imprisonment on the grounds that he had insulted God, the King, and the government. "God will forgive him for it," wrote the King under this sentence, "and I forgive him as well; but because he has attacked my government, let him be sentenced to three years imprisonment at ——— (the name of the prison in that particular province)." This little story has too many different applications for me to confine myself to just one, but it is perhaps worth noting in this context that in spite of women's decrees regarding mitigation of the sentence mentioned above, the actual carrying out of the punishment is reserved for men.

As a pastime and for pleasure, I would suggest music; you are gentle, and the instruments you play must be so as well, if they are to accompany your true nature. To play an instrument which screeches and to smoke a pipe are equally improper for a woman. Vocal music is your field, and we should be excluded from it entirely. It was a great man—Aristotle, if I am not mistaken—who replied to the question as to what he thought of music that Jupiter himself neither sang nor played an instrument. When Themistocles[60] was once urged to play something on the zither, he replied, "I cannot play any instruments, but I am able to make a great state out of an insignificant one." When a male sings, he is either a castrato, a Frenchman, or a fop; and whenever I see a man giving lessons in singing it is the same to me as watching soft-boiled eggs being cooked.[61] The gentler instruments are not really for us either, just military music. Men, blow on trumpets, beat on drums, but let the women play the piano and the lute!

Whoever lacks the gift of brevity had better take the trouble to make himself clear. I am speaking of course of the rule, but where is the rule without exception? And who can and will look askance if a man sings out in a bass voice when in a moment of inexpressible joy his usual gait is transformed into a kind of dance—something which is said to have happened to the royal prophet David upon the return of the Ark of the Covenant[62]—and the speech of his mouth raises itself to the harmony of a song? Whoever is not satisfied with this declaration of honor, let him weigh the wisdom of the precept: "Whatever you are doing, remember the end that awaits you"—by which the author means your destiny, the plans you have made for your future, the ideal state you wish for yourself in your reflective moments—"and you will never go wrong."[63]

My dear girls, I now wish to take leave of you the way we do from a friend we love; we slip away and wish in our hearts: all the best to him! And all the best to you as well!

8

Widowers and Widows

𝓔

THE EAGERNESS WITH which men as well as women enter into a second, or if luck would have it, a third marriage nowadays confirms the notion that things must not be as bad with the institution of marriage as we have been led to believe. I know a language in which, according to a popular proverb, that man is to be considered happy "whose horses all turn out to be good ones and whose wives all die on him." One can also find people who, simply because every day is filled with joy and luxury for them, long for tragedy in their lives and for whom their widower's and widow's tears become tears of rapture by bringing something piquant into their everyday existence and turning it into a holiday of sorts.

Euripides himself, who certainly was no apologist for the fair sex, decided to marry again. Such a second marriage often takes place under the assumption that it would be a shame to do something only halfway, even if it had been a foolish thing in the first place. "If luck would have it," I said above, for some people simply take it for granted that they will marry three, four, and even five times, and marriage for them is nothing more than a means to acquire wealth. "It should take about forty years," they say to themselves, "in three or four years she will die, and then I'll marry her sister—each one thirty thousand Talers, *facit*[1] sixty thousand, and so on." The women are not much better about this themselves, and often an Abishag the Shunamite will marry an old David[2] and sell herself as a reading glass,

253

a bedpan, or even a bedwarmer merely in order later on to honor the old man's day of death annually in the arms of some dissolute paramour. It is quite true that these marriages depend a good deal on luck, and that one can often lose with the very best of cards. But even when a person wins, what is really gained beyond something that he or she is ashamed of, or should be? Every bit of luck we experience ought to humble us, for it is an act of generosity bestowed on us which we have not deserved. "He was lucky" is another way of saying "He didn't deserve it." Whoever is convinced that even if he were to venture into deep caverns and abysses where the light of the sun and the moon were never seen his own personal providential star would appear to guide him out of the depths—what does that person need in life? Certainly not the rule: "dwell in the land and verily thou shalt be fed."[3]

According to law, the man as well as the woman is permitted to marry again upon the death of the spouse, for death ends the union and, providing that no promises were made or written into the will beforehand, it is left to the surviving party to do whatever he or she considers best. If the man dies without having added provisions of this sort to his will, then his wife may honor his memory by wearing black only the number of months required by the country in which she lives, as long as it does not exceed nine. The man, however, must be free even to dispense with the mourning period altogether, because in his case it merely serves the function of appeasing his own heart and has no other justification whatsoever. There are also laws which grant a dispensation to the woman and in all Christian innocence give her the right to remarry immediately, even if she has promised her husband to remain a widow the rest of her life. But why, then, does she take her husband's possessions? Certainly not because he has promised them to her? "Yes," people argue, "the promise to remain a widow all one's life is an unnatural one." Well, I find it a lot more unnatural to let a wife have possessions who denounces my name and who removes the diamonds from the frame of my portrait and then puts it up for auction! It is different, of course, when a husband fails to leave his wife enough to live on, since in that case she is left to her own devices. Likewise, the craftiness and mockery of that question of the Sadducees: "Therefore in the resurrection whose wife shall she be of the seven? For they all had her"[4] is exposed for what it is and answered just as all such questions should be answered. In spirit and in truth[5] the questioned man replied: "In the resurrection they neither marry, nor are given in marriage."[6] Thus, from this perspective as well, nothing stands in the way of widowers and widows.

For a widower there often exist reasons why he cannot be faulted for remarrying: for example, surviving children and his business affairs often require the presence of a woman in the house. And since opportunity makes the thief, he would rather take a wife of his own than be tempted to steal the wife of another. After all, he thinks, he has paid for the whole business once already, why not reap some benefit from it? True, friend, but you know yourself that half-brothers and half-sisters are born to hate each other. The concept of "single proles" [*unio prolium*[7]] may have its uses but it is not in a position to eradicate this seed of enmity[8] completely. Just look, your first-born son is in tears because your second wife has also presented you with a first-born son, and you can be sure that these two boys will someday form two armed camps and turn your house into a field of battle. It should be obvious which side your wife will be on, and I also know whose side you will be on in the end. But remember how tenderly you embraced your late wife when your first son, the beginning of your strength,[9] first called you "Daddy"? She died a heroine's death, for she died in childbed after she had been victorious in battle four times and gained for you—what a blessing!—four sons. Just keep in mind, if you believe in heaven and a reunion of the Good in that place, that she is someday going to ask you about her children! You can hardly expect to escape without reproach when accounts of the heart are settled in the next world if she finds out you have put her children on the debit side of the ledger. At least attempt meanwhile to be just to everyone concerned, which unfortunately is about all you can do anyway. Where children of two marriages are in the house together it is rare that any good comes of it. Jealousy, persecution, miserliness, and all possible vices are bred under such conditions, and without your even being aware of it your children will be drawn so far away from the notion of brotherly love that they will treat even their own natural siblings as half-brothers and half-sisters.

Among the ancient Israelites it was a matter of common agreement that the true first-born son was the first son of the father, and not the mother;[10] and although this privilege could not be taken from him, nevertheless I believe that he had to give way to the first fruit of the second wife of his father often enough. History is full of examples of stepmothers who have perpetrated the most wanton acts of cruelty in order to place their own sons upon the throne, and what royal stepmothers have done for thrones, common stepmothers have done for farms. The magic used by Olympias to render her stepson Aridaeus unfit for the throne in order that her son Alexander might ascend to it is a matter on which stepmothers have always rather prided themselves, since otherwise the world would have had no Curtius, no marvelous answer of Diogenes: "Yes, . . . that you stand out of my sun a little" to Alexander's question as to whether he lacked anything, and for that matter, no Alexander the Great himself.[11] Every stepmother considers her children to be Alexanders as well and tries to charm her husband into agreement, so that in the end he begins to believe it, too—thus on this particular point they can be said to have achieved rather spectacular success. A man must love the children of his second marriage doubly: first as a father, and second, in order to do his wife a favor. If he has had three wives and children by all three, then as a general rule both father and stepmother strongly favor the children of the first marriage over those of the second; the father, because he has come to know them better and feels guilty for having treated the children of his first wife so harshly without cause merely in order to please his late second wife; the stepmother because she believes that her husband has forgotten his first wife more than he has the second—since nothing loses its power so quickly than the memory of a departed person. Moreover, she has now become, at least with regard to the children of the first marriage, a *stepmother* herself. All marriages would gain immeasurably if people were not allowed to marry more than once. They would become solemn events, just as death is solemn because we only die once; and to be perfectly honest the second marriage is really only a sort of adultery anyway—a single case if one marries a young girl, a double one when someone marries a widow. This is the reason the *poenae secundarum nuptiarium*[12] were valid even among peoples which were otherwise quite concerned about increasing their population.

A young husband who loved his wife and saw her suffering in childbed once began a heart-rending letter to the family physician of the noble house to which he belonged begging the doctor to come over and help before his wife died. At the very moment he finished it his wife actually died and he sent the letter by express courier with the note: "My wife has already passed away; Your Excellency need not concern yourself about the matter any more." The young husband's grief was genuine, for even the purest kind has something of the comical about it. One is almost tempted to say that without this characteristic our grief is a little suspicious. Whoever never forgets himself in his grief is not truly afflicted, and in turn, every outbreak of true passion leaves us open to become the butt of others' jokes. Passions are always excessive in their expression, and even in cases of extraordinary joy or happiness one would do well to sequester oneself for a while, until the sun had ceased to shine quite so brightly. I know that even for the best of you the loss of your wife is not too different from hitting your elbow on a hard object: you experience a sudden severe pain, but one which quickly subsides. Do not mourn the loss of your deceased wife even as others which have no hope,[13] but dedicate to her and the children you shared a memory which will never die.

You widowers will notice that I am not able here to provide actual reasons for not remarrying, but merely a motivation or two, and that for the most part even these do not apply if your first wife has not left you with children. But whoever is in a position to look for reasons in matters such as this will invariably do so, no matter what they might turn out to be. So, if you want my opinion—and I feel I owe you this much at least—take your time and don't rush into anything. Are you aware that your second choice will draw a great deal more attention than the first, and that others will require proof from you that you've become wiser through the misfortune, or more circumspect through the happiness of your first marriage? It is unfortunately the case that happiness tends not to make us wise and contented, but foolish and discontented. People say that there is no better way to determine the prevailing mood of a city than by what is playing at its theaters. The proportion of tragedy to comedy in the theaters will be the same for everyday life within the town itself, and anyone wishing to be a popular member of its social circles—not a lofty goal, to be sure—is duty bound to partake of this medium if he wishes to have any success in his endeavor. In point of fact, my dear widower, if you find yourself contemplating a second marriage, your situation is hardly different than if you were presenting both a tragedy and a comedy at the same time—wait a bit and see which one prevails. Don't believe you can disregard the judgment of the world completely, for consider that your late wife is involved in the matter as well, and thus that you can't take offense at the opinions and the sympathy of those who knew you both. It is our duty, moreover, to take only as much from the world as we put back into it, and in this exchange not to overreach ourselves to the detriment of the world. Wouldn't it be unfair (the case is hardly unusual) to demand more than we deserve; to take more out than we put in; and to measure others with a different measuring stick than we measure ourselves? It is the nature of things that this exchange will maintain itself in a state of equilibrium—as we grow in that which is good, the good which is due to us increases in like manner. Or, friend widower, do you wish to honor freedom of expression in writing and speaking as the palladium of the Enlightenment and the guardian angel of virtue, all the while making an official exception of your own worthy and estimable self? Everyone must be able to say and write whatever he thinks if we are to avoid a kind of deformity of the intellect, the most beautiful of God's gifts and the daily bread of mankind; and which of us lives by earthly bread alone?[14] And shouldn't we do to others what we would have them do to us?[15] The easiest way—and that which has proven most effective—to reconcile yourself with the shadow of your late wife and with the world is to choose a wife who is similar to, or even exactly like your first wife—for example, her sister or one of her close relatives. Then all is as it should be, and you will have put everything back into its former place, even as far as your close circle of friends is concerned. And—what is no small matter—you will not be giving up the memory of your first wife, for she will now have been transformed into a friend.

Nothing is more respectable for a widow than for her to remain in that state for the rest of her life and not to move the widow-bench,[16] or I might say, have it reupholstered, should she be counseled to do so by the courts. A woman who takes off her dress takes off her modesty, and this could especially be said of her mourning dress. Has she not lost a husband, and is this loss not worth mourning eternally? The French of the *ancien régime* maintained that their king never died, because at the very moment of his death the Dauphin became king. Widows, your husbands die even less than this when you know how to keep their memory alive and present continuously, to call them back with a sort of Platonic love, and to find them once again in the image of the children they have left behind; this is a type of spiritual communication which raises a widow to the level of the angels. As Leonidas was marching off to his hero's death he bound his wife by oath to marry a man who could make her into the happy mother of children who would resemble himself—a course of action we can readily excuse him for under the circumstances.

If, on the other hand, you as a widow already have children and other children should then come along to the joy of those of your first marriage, then, my dear widow, accuse death itself of being the adulterous party; follow the path I have cleared for the widower and be assured that it is less difficult to bear pain than joy. Nobody ever died so easily, or at least so suddenly, from pain as from overwhelming and unexpected joy. And finally I would suggest to you, especially if you are still not disinclined to tread the path of marriage once again, not to mourn your dead husband as those who have no hope. Heed rather the well-intentioned advice which declares of a wise woman that she exercise vigilance over her honor not only during the festival of Bacchus,[17] but that she take care to moderate the violent emotions which accompany her in time of grief, as well—not by foregoing sympathetic words and caresses from others, as some people believe, but merely by avoiding any hint of impropriety. The great majority of people may attribute such power and might to external things, but the kingdom of God lies *within* us![18]

The Apostle Paul, who makes some very good points regarding the disposition of widows, would require young widows—when they get into the habit of idleness and wandering about from house to house, becoming not only idlers, but gossips and busybodies as well, saying things which they ought not to—to marry, to have children, to manage their households, and, it should be noted, to give their "adversary" (an expression which young widows under the care of a guardian would not fail to interpret as a curator, an uncle, or someone of that ilk) "none occasion to . . . speak reproachfully."[19]

I am against all pre-nuptial contracts and agreements; during the course of the marriage people get used to holding back something for themselves, and what at first is true only for one's treasure later becomes true for the heart as well.[20] "*Ubi tu Cajus ego Caja*"[21] answered the Roman bride when she was asked who was knocking at her bridegroom's door: she was to be the mistress where he was the master. Contracts are especially objectionable in unexpectedly long and drawn-out bankruptcy proceedings, for example, where money has to be borrowed from the capital funds of the wife so that the couple can continue, by virtue of this "unrighteous mammon"[22] and subsequent to the deduction of the usual ten percent for court costs, to enjoy the good life if not during, then at least after the weeks taken up by the proceedings—weeks which, by the way, it is said often more closely resemble Daniel's weeks of seven years[23] rather than the customary ones of seven days' duration.

If one of the marriage partners dies, then nobody has a greater right to his or her wealth than the surviving spouse. I myself, however, would deny to a widow who remarries everything she had or would have received from her first husband—including the lifetime annuity the legal authorities grant her;[24] and to be perfectly honest, she ought to be satisfied with that in the sense that now everything has been laid aside which could at any moment remind her of her ingratitude. "A widow, however, in the full sense," Paul writes to his son Timothy, "is one who is alone in the world," and he ordains that if a widow wishes to be included in the list of those who are supported by the Church, she must be the widow of only a single husband.[25] The number of benevolent institutions and foundations set up expressly for them indicates the extent to which widows could count upon the charity of others, and the suffering they endure seems to capture our imagination more strongly than that which accompanies sickness and much other human misery.

The entire ancient world had an aversion to remarriage by widows; among the heathen Greeks considerable time had to pass before it became even somewhat acceptable for a widow to enter into a second marriage. Pausanias says of Perseus' daughter Gorgophone that "After the death of her first husband Perieres, this ruler married Oebalus, and she is the first widow to have remarried, for previous to this it was an inviolable custom that every woman who had lost her husband had to spend the rest of her days as a widow."[26]

Among the Israelites the high priest was not permitted to marry a widow; and, although according to Mosaic Law the other priests were not required to observe this commandment as carefully, it appears that later on even they too were still somewhat restricted in this regard.[27] Nowadays men often seem to prefer widows to unmarried girls, although if widows are in fact interested in remarrying they really ought not to be permitted to until all the unmarried girls in the surrounding area have been provided for. The Greek Orthodox Church, in which priests are forbidden to marry a second time, deserves favorable mention here—after the death of his wife the priest must then either enter the cloister or resign his priestly office. Such a state of affairs would quite naturally induce both husbands and wives to trouble themselves to care for each other and make each other's lives enjoyable, and if this particular church's priestly law were made universal it would doubtless serve to put our own marriages on a better footing as well. The Montanists disapproved of remarriage, and one of the Church Fathers, Athenagoras, considered the second marriage to be a sort of respectable adultery.[28] Now, however, people seem to believe that two of anything is twice as good as one, and that the first marriage merely serves, like Pre-Justinian law, an educational function (*usus dogmaticus*). Not every woman, on the other hand, is a *Praefica*[29] at the death-bed of her husband. Lamentations mixed with tears may perhaps stem from a very real source; nevertheless, it is no different for women than it usually is for anyone who agonizes at the bed of a friend who then suddenly recovers: we become annoyed with ourselves if we find we have suffered in vain. Who can prepare a feast and not get angry if the guests fail to come?[30]

Soon after the funeral, signs of spring begin to appear in the features of the widow; as the occasion allows, her face begins to take on a smoother, more scrubbed look, and milady, her bout of seasickness now valiantly overcome and no longer facing any legal hindrances to deter her, prepares to set sail once again. She is familiar with the bed of honor—not reserved only for the dying—and has no need of the consolation and encouragement which many a young girl requires at this decisive time. Unfortunately, it is often the case that the veil women wear in memory of their husbands is so transparent that it could easily be taken for a net with which to catch their second husband. They treat the period of mourning very much the way they treat their six-weeks' confinement after childbirth, to be shortened or prolonged depending upon their physical needs and the external circumstances. On the whole, the mourning clothes worn by widows are much like the wreaths displayed by wine sellers to show that their wines have not gone bad—or, to put it another way, the most seductive way of dressing and using cosmetics is a tactic still readily accessible to them. For this reason, notaries, clergymen, and others who continually deal with cases of death, almost always marry persons in mourning— the heart of the notary melts like the wax he uses for his seal, and the good Reverend takes to sighing himself instead of comforting the bereaved. The unhappy face of a young woman already has something triumphant about it; it is hardly any surprise to see it also well set off by the black of mourning!

What is a widow, it could be asked, besides a half-effaced painting, a patched dress, a warmed-up meal, a wig instead of one's own hair, a tulip which has lost its petals and can no longer close itself? But one could also answer: keep your foolish and useless questions to yourself, because you know they just cause arguments. One might also say that the second husband is in a position to see even without the gift of prophecy just what lies in store for him after his death,[31] and that also in this life he will have to give up all claim to the memory of the original angelic beauty of a woman and continually be faced with the fact that someone before him received the blessing of the first-born.[32] But to this one could reply that "seeing counts more than hearing,"[33] and since so many marriages for which widows laid the cornerstone are now thriving and flourishing, why such rigid intolerance? Honor pays the gambler's debts, but miserliness would let his own brother starve to death. In truth, morality should only be preached to those with pure hearts, since it is better suited to ennoble than to reform. I would now like to add a few more links to the chain of reasoning in my sermon with the hope this time of rendering it more beautiful, rather than stronger.

Annia[34] replied in the following way to the question as to why she did not wish to marry a second time: "If I got a good man, then I wouldn't wish to live in fear of losing him; if I got a bad one, I would act quite foolishly, since I once had a good one." One could add to this that even if she had had a bad first husband, the second marriage would not have helped anything. If her second husband turned out to be a good man, then she would come to regret that she had wasted her best years, the best morsels of the feast, on a bad man and only had—depending upon the season—the rowen left over for her beloved second husband; and how she would have worried about losing *him*! But if the second husband were bad as well, then the outcome would be obvious. In any case, if I could not do otherwise, I would choose a widow over a girl whose fiancé had deserted her or died, since with the former, at least, one knows precisely what one is dealing with.

It takes something of a good heart and memory for a woman to maintain the true sentiments of widowhood and render her faithfulness to her former husband indomitable, even if nobody among the living will ever demand an account of her actions. It is her memory, her religion, and her imagination, strengthened by their constant association with ideas from daily life, which must give vigor to these sentiments and render her late husband immortal—not a mummy or an urn full of ashes. The recollection of shared joys has an effect on us to the same degree as the pain we feel when we witness the misfortune of other people. Artemisia[35] drank the ashes of her husband in order to unite herself with him in death. "Wherever my king is, there is my kingdom," said Isabella, the wife of Christian, the exiled King of Denmark,[36] when given the opportunity to remain in a country which was no longer her country without the presence of her husband. And

Valeria[37] replied to the question as to why she had not remarried: "Because my Servius lives with me now and will always live with me." Behold, *there* are a couple of excellent portraits for the walls of your widow's cell! And if you have just a bit more space, have a portrait done of the dying Arria as she says to her husband, "Paete, it doesn't hurt,"[38] or of some Indian women, who consider it an honor to be burned on a funeral-pyre with their beloved husbands.

And while we are talking about painting, why not order a portrait for your oldest daughter of a woman whose story, it is said, reaches back to the beginning of the fourteenth century in the Electorate of Brandenburg, although another place and age are traditionally assigned to it; in truth, however, such a tale deserves to be told again and again. As the story goes, an enemy soldier was once about to rape a girl—or, since I can't stand this word, commit an indecent act *cum effractione*[39] with her; or, if you will, take her by force. "Let me go," she said, "love me in the right way and I will show you miracles. Here is a salve which will serve as a pledge of my own love—whoever uses it will never die."—"Not even by a sword?"—"Not by a thousand swords." What could be of greater interest to a soldier than a salve which makes a person like iron! She applied a little to her lily-white neck. "And now," she said, "I will prove to you that it works." He drew his sword and—her head lay at his feet.

You may dispute, O mounted maiden Europa,[40] as to whether this splendid story was only born a single time or whether it has had many births in different places, just as people once quarreled about the birthplace of Homer. Nevertheless, the mere heartfelt wish that it could have happened a number of times is enough to reflect honor on you. Lucretia, you are but a hired mourner, a mere actress in comparison to a Grace of this sort, whose ashes deserve to be venerated by pilgrims from distant lands. May she rest in peace!

The custom of dying along with one's spouse is perhaps not unworthy of a brief postscript at this point. I would gladly admit that religious fanaticism and pride have been in the past and still are the motivation for self-sacrifices of this kind, sacrifices which actually could be said to have become the rule in India. Yet the observation has also been made that death can be tempting and even inviting when we have lost a spouse, a friend, or a relative. And if the pain we suffer at the death of a loved one did not itself have something sweet about it, the idea of dying along with someone else might have found many adherents among lovers of both sexes. People tend to give up on life when they lose a person who was irreplaceable to them; they have suffered the loss of half of their entire being—what good is the half which remains? This would be even more readily apparent in the case of the opposite sex if it were not able to accustom itself to viewing death more easily than our own.[41] It is difficult for us men to be witness to human beings entering into this world and departing from it; women, on the other hand, reveal themselves to be so steadfast under such circumstances that these actually serve to bring out a certain majestic strength in them which imparts courage to us men as well. It should be made a requirement for everybody to be present at at least *one* birth and three deaths; perhaps this preventive medicine could help us avoid many of the foolish and hurtful acts we commit without thinking during the time when our spouse, our friend, or our relative is still with us here on earth. After all, isn't it considered a good idea to bring a horse into close contact with an object it has shied away from until the horse finally becomes accustomed to it? That there is such a thing as dying *gradually* along with a loved one—which could also be called following them in death because it takes place over an extended period of time—needs no further mention here.

The one difficulty which could prove to be an obstacle for this particular chapter comes from our own laws; yet whoever does nothing more than obey the laws really has done very little. Laws render us punishable not only in a monarchical state—where there are actually no laws but a monarch, because he himself constitutes a monopoly with regard to the laws—but in aristocratic and democratic states as well, where it is the letter of the law which kills;[42] yet while these laws make us susceptible to punishment, they never degrade us. There are, however, certain improprieties which, although they have never even been considered worthy of a footnote, nevertheless often debase those who commit them more than a transgression against an entire chapter in one of our law books. When we avoid them they give us more honor than if we kept ten chapters, and if the committing of these indecencies is not expressly forbidden by Nature, then our honor is all the greater. Whoever keeps the law of the land is a citizen; whoever observes the laws of Nature is a human being; whoever does more than this is a human being in a higher sense, just as whoever overcomes himself is a hero.

CONCLUSION

THE WEDDING NIGHT and the first chapter of a book are as similar to each other as a father and an author—if not more so. A smart midwife does not begin to count the days after a birth until nine have passed;[1] and if an author begins to calculate his royalties as soon as he has finished the first chapter he will end up bankrupt unless the publisher decides to relieve him of the financial responsibility, which hardly ever occurs, since even if the book should turn out to be excellent, the only tributes he is likely to receive will be in the form of frankincense and myrrh, depending on whether the critics are favorably or unfavorably disposed to him, whereas with other, shall we say more *formal* offerings, gold is less frequently omitted.

I would bet that of a thousand beginnings to a book we never see a single one. Just between you and me, in my case I have already crossed out four Introductions, and frankly the present one is not safe for a moment while it is still in its father's hands. Of all the ages of man, childhood is the most dangerous; most people, like most books, die as children, I would say—that is, if I wanted to sin against my own allegory and talk gibberish, or even commit adultery against it, for in truth, metaphors are like the marriage bed: one cannot simply jump from one into another. *Nihil est frigidius quam lex cum prologo.*[2] But what is valid for a law—namely, that it absolutely must remain unprefaced—does not always hold true for a book. "Go up," cried the little children

265

to the prophet, "go up, thou bald head;"[3] and one would indeed do well to put something on one's head and, as we say, "cover" oneself; the hat is a sign of freedom.

"The beginning is hard, the middle is satisfying, and the end is fun," the teachers tell their pupils when they begin to teach them the five declinations and four conjugations in Latin, and everyone, even clergymen (if not sooner, then at least at the close of the Church year) maintain that all is well that ends well. Solomon considers the end of a matter to be better than the beginning.[4] These circumstances, especially the latter one, ought to give me pause. Nevertheless, I am so little daunted that I would still have courage enough to restore for my readers the above-mentioned four Introductions had I not, after having crossed them out, immediately torn them up and thrown them out the window into the garden, from where they scattered to the four winds—although, as it then seemed to me in my paternal pride, in such a way that each piece of an Introduction remained attached to the others and that each Introduction itself laid claim to a particular part of the world, where they are probably doing at least as much good as the present treatise will when it is finally published.

I would like to impart one idea in particular from this yoked team of Introductions for the reason that it will prove useful to me in the present Conclusion. Soon after the "English Diogenes"[5] had embarked upon his sentimental journey, all of Germany began hitching up the horses too, and even if a good many people remained continually underway and never did reach their precise destination, at least now and again someone would come close. Without question, it is this universal desire to travel which is at fault in my having imagined the author and his reader at the beginning of my treatise as a couple of travelers meeting each other for the first time at a stagecoach stop. "Where are you headed?" — "I'm going to ————." — "Excellent, let's travel together!" These words have such a power of attraction that magnet and iron do not unite as quickly as the hearts of these two people. The trunks are closed, the hearts are opened; the two tell each other their life stories up to the point of their meeting, as usual over a cup of bad coffee, at the stagecoach stop; and although this occurrence is well known to both, each of them wants to relate it again himself. They interrupt each other ten or more times until they can agree on which of them ought to tell the story they both already know. Even if occasionally time hung heavy on their hands or they had a bad road and felt every bump along the way, nevertheless near the end of the trip they shake hands and, upon Christian acknowledgement of the sentiment that man's journey through life is not a hair's breadth better, wish each other equally good company for the rest of the trip, or even express the wish to meet again; and when they finally arrive at ————— all filled with such wishes, they part exchanging the valedictory "Your humble Servant" and go their own way.

These were approximately the thoughts I had expressed in even better form in Introduction *sub Nro. III* which, if I am not mistaken, was my favorite and blew off to the east somewhere. I noted there that the one difference between an author and a reader is that only the author speaks and it is more difficult to listen openly and sincerely than to do all the speaking.

To the question "Where are you going?" a military chaplain astride a horse of his general he could not control was once heard to give the answer: "Wherever God and my horse wish to go." Since I have now, albeit with the greatest difficulty, reached the conclusion of my work, I am admittedly safe from this question—but certainly not from the question: "Where have you come from?" And to make matters worse, I would a thousand times rather be asked the question "To where?" than "From where?" I can take comfort from the thought that at least some of my readers will say "Your humble Servant" and go their own separate ways, and I am beholden to these for their own good heart with an equally good one; nobody can do anything about a restive horse and a road full of ruts. Good friends, wherever you may be and whether male or female, you who have not found fault with the places where we have tarried a while and have not thought me a vagabond just because I travel incognito;[6] good friends, to you I say: may Heaven someday send you a better traveling companion and better horses and a better road—no, *better* is not enough, may you receive the *best* of these!

To keep you better from being blinded by mere appearances, however, be on the lookout for that syllogistic sand which can fall on your clothes and get into your eyes. I would also advise you not to entrust yourself completely to that traveling companion of a different stripe who rides through nothing but fields filled with flowers and blooming bushes and calls his horses "swans"—at least be sure you don't stop with him for the night anywhere! To be sure, he will talk of temples and the like, but bring you then to some wretched inn where you will be hard pressed to find any gods or goddesses, for how would they ever get there? The waitress serving coffee there was not seduced, she did the seducing herself, and the object of her affection was no prince, but a shopkeeper's clerk. Her father with the silvery hair who is thought to resemble old Anchises[7] stole money from the city treasury and is now here in exile filtering coffee. The road itself may be beautiful, but what good is it to travel constantly and never reach your destination?

It would hurt me unbearably if *you*, dear soul, were to find in this treatise a single word which made you angry. I would commit to the flames any chapter of this with pleasure if that would keep from troubling anyone in the world, for it would be infinitely preferable to me to publish this with only seven—the number of colors in the spectrum—chapters rather than eight, if there should be anything in one of them which annoyed you. You can take comfort in the fact that it is least of all my intention to force my opinion upon anybody; as long as people can still ask "Why?" someone is still free to answer "Because." Socrates spoke socratically; I have written "matrimonially," and occasionally had to speak figuratively or in proverbs in order to serve as a spokesman for simplicity and an advocate of its rights. Do not authors often preserve the truth by writing fiction? High-sounding words and billowing banners attract attention, and there are people who are not deaf but merely have uncircumcised ears[8]—people to whom one must speak loudly, not softly, if they are to hear anything at all. And may they hear indeed! Many of my noisiest blasts were meant for them, and for that I trust people of a gentler nature will forgive me.

Poetry and marriage, by the way, serve to join things together which otherwise would never be united. Thus in my book, too, humor and seriousness are intertwined; and if on the wedding day, the first holy day of the institution of marriage, the hard words "What therefore God hath joined together, let not man put asunder";[9] the priestly blessing; the hymn "Now thank we all our God"; and then an English, Polish, French, and German dance all seem to get along very nicely together, I felt it would cause no difficulty in my treatise if the warp of my fabric were seriousness and the woof humor.

Whatever displeases you, good soul, do not hesitate to blame on the humor, for while one must not spread lies in the guise of jokes, a mistake contained in a joke can be forgiven sooner, because it does the least harm. I speak the truth when I say I mean no harm to anyone, but on the other hand I do not exactly cover my mouth in my treatise when I yawn, or say "Gesundheit" when my neighbor sneezes. I am not offended by many things for which other people are accustomed to saying "Excuse me," or, if they are highly educated, *"Salva venia,"* and I am of the opinion that anything which is natural cannot be harmful. I let everything grow the way Nature intended it to, and do not keep my trees under the threat of the shears. *"Naturalia non sunt turpia,"*[10] the priest intoned when the owner of the lands rented by the Church—a man who knew no Latin but knew what worked to his advantage better than his Latin-speaking ecclesiastical steward— attempted to demand the monthly rent in money instead of grain in order to be free of the vicissitudes of an agricultural economy. At any rate, everyone ought to be convinced of the necessity not of cutting off branches, but merely of bending them back now and then in order to break, if I may express myself so, the obstinacy of their growth pattern and open up new paths for them, thereby justifying Mother Nature over the imagination of reasoning man, her favorite of all the created beings.

Rules give interpretations in cases where Nature, as the *summus imperans,*[11] remains obscure. If only heaven would grant us a *legalis interpretatio,*[12] and we could receive *authenticae* or *usuales*[13] from this Supreme Authority! But now, since our interpretations are but *doctrinales,*[14] we ought perhaps not be so strict about things. After all, even if we open a window, we're still in the study! I am aware that there is almost as great a difference between *thinking* and *saying* as between *knowing* and *doing,* and could perhaps have expressed myself more appropriately had I been accustomed to meditating on the meanings of those words which enjoy "miller's rights"[15] with me: whatever comes first, I take first. It seems to me people already have enough on their hands when it comes to dealing with thoughts, and who has not had to cope with the jealousy these thoughts express the instant one attempts to put in a good word for words? But what of the thoughts themselves? It is true that I could have thought differently at some points, and I cannot help it if people accuse me of being myopic in some places and presbyopic in others; anyway, who is safe from all misfortune? Whoever has a noticeable blemish on his face—and there are said to be many people in this category—generally has all the better ears for it; and if there are apocryphal books in the Bible, then people should be able to tolerate apocryphal thoughts in my treatise. People who remove spots from clothes have to make a living, too, and if they are given a chance to show their skill on this treatise I will be truly indebted to them—as long as they do not proceed with their usual carelessness and remove the color along with the spots. I do not even ask for the appearance of infallibility; otherwise I would have been able to sew together some of those conclusions of mine which up to now have never known the need of a needle.

A little pebble hardly makes the water murky, and I would think it a good thing to have thrown at the target even if one had missed. Cannot a person be considered to be at least half an inventor whose errors give another the opportunity to invent something? Or, does not that person who tears down the old Gothic structure[16] also play a part in the construction of a new building, even if he is not able to carry away every bit of rubble himself? Even if making porcelain is hardly the same as making gold, can a person not find some satisfaction at least if he invents porcelain while trying to make gold?[17] Also my enemies will have to admit that I have shown myself to be neither a follower of Lamech nor a panegyrist for the Emperor Charles V, who only ate and ———— once a day,[18] but that I have rather shown my repugnance for all forms of unfaithfulness. What is more despicable than a butterfly which flutters from one flower to another, or a deer which runs from forest to forest? On the other hand, who would want to follow the philosophy of Thomas Brown[19] and require people to bear children the way trees bear fruit; who would idolize Theophrastus,[20] whose idea is even more ridiculous than Brown's, or that minter of false coin, Diogenes of Sinope?[21] For even if Troy had never been burned or Priam sacrificed on the altar of Jupiter;[22] even if the cacophony of voices which would have been raised in protest if Nature had thought it advisable to adopt another method for propagating the human race had been a thousand, or even a thousand thousand times less harsh, the advantages accruing from this new method would never have made up for the loss we would have suffered. For I declare hereby and on the basis of what I have just said that love is the very pulse of Nature, and when everything is undertaken with this circumstance—whose means are pleasure and whose end is utility—in mind, then I will have attained the most important of my wishes, which was nothing more or less than to trace for those inclined to marry the shortest path to the fulfillment of their desires and their years of servitude, or, to put it more correctly, their years of idolatry.

Certain kinds of caresses which the fair sex receives from us will never cease to take place, simply because Nature herself confirms them in the behavior of the animals, which dally before they enjoy and play before matters become serious. Nature herself thus seems given over to a kind of gallantry as long as the way of all flesh[23] is not overlooked thereby, a way which in our case is the path to holy matrimony. That which we call eating and drinking for enjoyment could be equated with gallantry in love. This kind of gallantry, while it often appears otherwise, derives from a good heart and a noble aim; and if that proud wisdom which stubbornly stands upright and bends neither neck nor knee[24] cannot bring itself to say a good word for such gallantry, then at least none who is truly wise will join such company. If I may be permitted to say it, our souls, too, desire to become wedded to one another—and this even before it comes to a physical union; our souls as well wish to take part in these physical pleasures and be invited to the wedding. I suppose this participation is something akin to people of means and influence being entertained by their servants.

This natural gallantry is as far removed from the kind which rules the world as heaven is from earth, and I wish with all my heart that the latter would be banned along with all its trappings forever! To *wish* to serve and to *have to* serve are two different things; and when the opposite sex finally achieves those rights which were so unfairly taken away from it—rights which the sex itself must first come to yearn for with all its heart—then everything else will come of itself. The hierarchy of Christianity was only devised in order to lay at rest the accusation that Christians not only shared their possessions but were also of one blood with each other; and if I have not exactly divorced what God has joined together, I have nevertheless been a stern judge of the mutual responsibilities and rights within the marriage bond, and I believe I deserve as little criticism in this matter as one should level, for example, at the statutes governing the payment of bills when they are being strictly held to by the government in order to maintain the credit standing of the country on a sound footing.

If anyone wishes further proof of my attempt to restore this mutual attraction of the sexes to its ancient rights, I believe I can confidently refer him to the previous eight chapters, and the fair sex can have no great complaint about what I have done on this score at least. I have simply maintained that there is an Old Eve to go along with the Old Adam;[25] and in truth, to view the fair sex from this standpoint is to reveal the standard whose proper application will enable us to avoid most of the errors committed in marriage. Who would not prefer fruit growing on trees to that which has been glued on? If I have written neither *interveniente uxore nostra*[26]—a phrase we so often find in the old documents—nor, like Justinian, asked a Theodora[27] for her advice, I have nevertheless been a strong defender of the rights and privileges

271

of women. I no longer believe what people believed at one time, namely, *iis divinum quid inesse*[28]—their human qualities adorn them too much for that. And if I have disdained silliness and jokes, which are unbecoming to any masculine soul; if I have maintained that fashion and rules of propriety are the most merciless tax collectors (not to say companions in sin) there are, to the extent that no tyrant is able to exact so harsh a tribute from us; if I have told the members of court as frankly as possible to their faces that their knowledge of the world is being gleaned only from a highly corrupt circle and from among a very questionable class of people, and that they are hurting women more by the distrust with which they treat them in every relationship than by their rash judgments and hastily formed opinions; then, it seems to me, I have drawn from a fountain whose purity would satisfy anyone who would be so good as to dip into its water with an uncontaminated container. I am convinced that righteous women, far from lending an ear to blandishments and flatteries, utterly reject anything that has the appearance of hypocrisy about it; yet along with this precise delineation of their collective merits I have not ignored their failings, although these must be attributed more to their present situation than to any sort of "original sin" supposedly inherent in their sex.

Just as there are novels which seek to engage their readers in a more noble way than by means of improbable occurrences and bizarre, complicated turns of plot, so also, it is to be hoped, the other half of the human race, realizing that the most valued possessions of mankind, virtue and wisdom, cannot be attained other than through struggle and strife, will upon closer examination of its present condition gladly exchange its present *empty* honor for the advantages of *true* honor and among other things also be willing to trade mere sense impressions, those flowers cut off from their roots which are here today and gone tomorrow, for *principles* which, like trees, defy the onslaughts of wind and weather. In this sense as well, those writers will find a place on our dressing-tables who are not simply satisfied with speaking of emotions but are able to evoke them in us, and who advance their readers words which the latter would immediately be able to repay with interest in actions if these writers were accustomed to drawing such a rate of interest from their capital.

A *Terrae filius* (man of lowly birth), that is, an author without name and family pedigree, can often give a better account of himself than a well-known writer who is announced by heralds and rides into combat amid the astonished gasps and applause of the audience. Moreover, I encourage anyone to offer proof that I have caused any harm through my anonymity, even for the sake of a greater good. A public writer lives in public works of the spirit, just as there are people who live in public works of the flesh—although I am not sure which of the two bears the heavier burden of criticism. The spirit is invisible—thus one ought not to censure those first in the spirit, the writers, for their invisibility; is there not an Invisible Church, of which all good people are members? How much differently would I have had to speak to the world of the women if I had been required to open my visor! My intentions were good, and the means were as pure as when I sought to raise the status of the fair sex by recommending the technique of self-abasement. Self-glorification and self-hate flow from one and the same source, namely pride, and it is really only through a feeling of self-confidence that mankind attains the worth it deserves. And what do women have to fear if, when they decide to make use of their rights, they proceed as delicately and agreeably as that defendant of old who submitted his appeal to a decision of the court presided over by King Philip of Macedonia—a decision rendered first at a time when the King, like Homer,[29] had dozed off briefly during the proceedings (as judges not infrequently do)—to the King once he had *awakened* again? Would their appeal not then be being made from one well-informed "Papal" authority to an even better-informed one? And to tell the truth, if we were to renounce our insistence on Papal Infallibility and the alleged "natural" guardianship with respect to the fair sex, our own sex would be much better off as well.

Human beings tend more frequently to invent things which facilitate the pursuit of pastimes and pleasure than those which satisfy needs, and one can daily observe instances during the planning of buildings and parks, for example, where consideration is given to the necessities of life only after people have given thought to their pleasure. Often with perfectly good intentions we feel constrained to pay more attention to that which is less necessary, if only because we feel needs will always manifest themselves. But sometimes our anxiety over gambling debts, so to speak, leads us to forget the creditor who once helped us in time of need, and who perhaps incurred financial burdens himself in doing so. And does not our neglect of the opposite sex reveal how easily that which is useful and necessary can be overlooked in our preoccupation with playthings? What a wise first step this sex would be taking if it would renounce those titles which fail to do it justice! Wife and mother—these are appellations of honor which are due them with full right. In Germany the common people call a woman "*Mutter*" or "*Mütterchen*,"[30] and no woman over fifty ought to be called otherwise; in contrast, the very appropriate ellipsis "*Mann*" for "*Ehemann*" is used for the husband, even if he is a man nearing seventy. A woman who, like her Patron Saint Mother Nature, travels life's road without adornment; who loves the man who has left father and mother for her and has been united to her;[31] who is chaste and has no time for the cloister-vice of gossip and who administers justice to her soul as harshly as she polices her heart—such a woman is a gift of God, a true heaven for the earth.

To those who are now beginning to think that I failed to touch upon certain themes which others would have considered essential to a treatise such as this, I would reply that the outline of my plan for its execution would have suffered too many gaps and contortions thereby. The extent to which the two facts are related that Plato banned the poets from his republic[32] and that he himself failed to marry might have been just as valid a theme for a fruitful investigation as the relationships among devotion, service to love, and bravery, the three vows to which the errant, or better said, the inerrant knights of medieval times swore their allegiance. If I had taken up these themes I would perhaps have been able to add a few more pages to my treatise, but I fear I would then sooner have been found guilty of unappreciated verbosity than appreciated for my brevity. And yet I cannot refrain from requesting "that every one of you should know how to possess his vessel in sanctification and honor"[33] in order that you may "glorify God in your body and in your spirit, which are God's."[34]

You are aware how highly I regard faithfulness in marriage for both wife and husband; may I suggest that women especially limit their strongest declarations to the words "Upon my honor!"?[35] If this declaration first arises from our heart, how powerfully will it then proceed to the hearts of others! I have also expressed the wish, moreover, that the state not become involved in domestic affairs. And may I call once again to mind that custom of the ancients whereby the father brought his newborn child to a public place, called the "*Lesche*" (λεσχη), where the child was then examined? If it was considered worthy of being educated and becoming a citizen of the state, and if it was found to be strong and healthy, then it remained alive; otherwise it was condemned to the pit, called the *Apothetae*. If one takes the freedom and joy in raising a child away from the parents, and if the state does more than *discreetly* guide the rearing of children, then the size of the population as a whole will begin to experience a drastic decline. To be sure, whoever has the fewest needs is—to put new trim on an old dress, so to speak—closest to the angels; nevertheless, for a population to grow it needs an overabundance of goods, although such an overabundance can also serve to limit growth in the long run. Add, sagacious reader, the word *freedom* to *overabundance*, and you will understand me perfectly.

May I also be allowed to note that every day is a life in miniature and that it is especially within the marriage bond that this is the case? In the morning we live for the state, in the evening for ourselves; in the morning we are citizens, in the evening human beings. Even at noon, although the day is already beginning to wane, it is difficult to achieve a feeling of real human warmth before the fifth glass, especially if the glasses are rather on the smallish size. The newspaper report on the death of someone we love affects us deeply when we receive it in the morning, but it does not overwhelm us; if we are told of such a death in the evening, we cannot sleep the entire night. If we listen to chamber music in the morning, it annoys us to the same extent that it entertains us in the evening. When it is evening, feeling, sympathy, and reflection prevail. In the north for just this reason we ought to have the best minds, the greatest people, and the happiest marriages—why then is this not the case?

And one more point: you must still remember, gentlemen, that you come to Nature only through women; it is she who calls your attention to the tree in front of your window weeping voluptuously in the fullness of its blossoms; and what do you really see without her guidance? Women, on the other hand, come into contact with the state only through men—that is, until their hour has finally come.

Yet how much more it would take to finish the task if I had wanted to amplify more than just indicate, to dig into matters instead of merely touching upon them! I could then have worked out, for example, the actual difference between love and sexual appetite, a topic for which I have only given the faintest outlines. It would also have been easy to put on a puppet show with the title "Not All that Glitters Is Gold," or "A Disputation Between Reason and the Senses"; then you would have seen how Her Ladyship Reason herself, even if she is permitted to pass judgment in every court of appeal, still fares no better in the end than the Polish courts, which do not permit execution as a punishment. "Reason is no more or less than a compass—it only shows us the way," I could have remarked had I had the opportunity, and what could I have provided in addition to this bar of silver—from which others might have minted their coins—if I had also wanted to write on the subject of marriage *de lucro captando* and not merely *de damno vitando!*[36] Moreover, it would not have taken extraordinary powers of discernment to answer the question as to whether the queen is also a subject of the king. Nor would it have been difficult to render a judgment in the matter of Besser vs. Leibniz, concerning the point as to whether Anna of Bretagne committed adultery when the Count of Nassau under authority of the Emperor Maximilian took a place next to her in bed wearing a full suit of armor.[37] And whoever would ask the question whether a daughter is justified in offering her body for sale *sub hasta*,[38] if thereby her father could be saved from disgrace or death, simply has no concept of the art of questioning, for it is not the person, but only the situation which it is within our power to judge. Furthermore, the recent essay contest question on the topic: "Who should be given preference, a man's child, his mother, or his wife, when only one of them can be saved?" only seems more important than it is, and I would not hesitate to answer it by saying: his wife, for even if the child owes its life to him, and he himself his own life to his mother, it is to his wife that he owes the most. If, on the other hand, the similar hypothetical question were asked: "Which daughter is acting more in accordance with her duty, the one who gives up her father for her lover, or the one who gives up her lover for her father?" then, in conformity to the above-mentioned basic principles, I would not hesitate a moment to assert that it is the father who would have to be preserved.

I have written to defend the honor of the household and domestic concerns, and thus had no intention of baking fine bread, but rather merely of serving up some home-baked philosophy. I have no desire whatsoever to make tame animals wild and wild ones tame—I am too great a friend of Nature for that. Whatever is supposed to be eaten cold ought not be placed in the sun, and who would store a nice bowl of beef soup in the ice-house?

Much in this treatise is written for the benefit of my countrymen. A prophet is not without honor but in his own country;[39] in his home town they even let him starve to death, although if it is a question of dying of thirst the treatment is not quite so cruel. Since I am no prophet, I have not concerned myself with anybody else than my beloved *German* fatherland, which as far as marriage is concerned exists in a fairly comfortable relationship with Nature. I am very much in favor of people traveling, as *Nro. III* shows; but they also must come home again, they must travel in order to learn to appreciate their native country. Perhaps it is easier for people to die in a foreign country because death is welcome to an abandoned heart. That lawmaker[40] who died away from his homeland in order to render his laws immortal was looking out for himself as much as he was his compatriots. People need to live where they are born. "For the cause of the fatherland nothing is so sweet as . . ."—sharpening my pens;[41] for without even taking into account my other meager labors, I have already sharpened six on this treatise alone. Voltaire is said to have remarked *"Je donnerais cent ans d'immortalité pour une bonne digestion"*;[42] truly a very high price! Happy is the man who cannot do business like that, for I believe I can say with all honesty that my treatise is limited far too much to a single climate and nationality to be able to seek its fortune on foreign soil.

A Frenchman—I am as convinced of this as I am that this treatise is not printed in Greek letters[43]—a Frenchman would, if he were to happen to read this work (for he certainly would never *want* to) would take me for an idiot in matters of love; an Italian for a pilgrim; and the Englishman, otherwise a close cousin to us—well, in matters of love we are not exactly of the same familial line, he being descended from the mother's side, we from the father's. He is the slave of his wife, just as we, by the grace of God, are the masters of ours. Perhaps this is because he is conscious of the advantage he enjoys from his greater and more important freedom outside the house as compared to us, so that he considers it unnecessary to make such an issue of it at home.

At this point I would like to take a "Spanish minute"[44] to mention a suggestion with which I am not in complete agreement. One proposer of new projects is of the opinion "that it would be good to give everybody in Germany his own freedom of choice; one court could thus become English, the next French, and another Spanish. Germany itself, however, would lose nothing by this tolerance, provided that— and what could be more certain—it also possessed a uniqueness of its own, for then its own seed would in time be persuaded to sprout, grow, and bear fruit. We would then no longer be compelled to fence in a piece of forest or pasture land and shout to the passers-by: 'Look— an original German garden!' or serve our boarders English meat in a French sauce." Thus far the proposer of projects. If he should— as I almost think he will—be banished from the country, then let us nevertheless continue to grant to French and English books in the original and in translation the privileges customarily accorded to guests in our German lands—provided, of course, that these are not mere trash. We should only refuse to allow Germans to Gallicize or Anglicize German things; such products, whose very nature prevents us from understanding what to make of them, should be banned. Put the screws to them! And if—although it will rarely happen—they should still be able to put up a fight without their thumbs, then let us be more severe, be Brutuses, and pass and carry out the death sentence, if that is what it takes for us to be *German*!

As far as my own little marriage catechism is concerned, I would be happy to see it undergo torture at the hands of the critics and watch every chapter torn asunder by glowing pincers if it is found to be of foreign manufacture—although I do not think this will be the case. If it is condemned in court and hanged everywhere on the gallows, I will shake the hands of the people who do it. I will cover my eyes with my hat and say: "There where my book is being hanged they are hanging a thief; the mob is right to lynch him, and woe to the forger!" Let people ban him and declare him to be an outlaw, take away his goods and chattels, house and home—it is only what he deserves. If my book fails or falls short, let anyone do what he wants with it, and I will merely consider myself fortunate that the rights of guardianship which are specifically applied to people[45] do not also apply to me. But—I must stop writing, and nearly reached for the inkwell again instead of the blotter.

Finally—I believe I have said this word several times already, although this time I know it is for the last time—it is well known that clergymen in the Protestant church, especially in the country, where people in this regard are still somewhat more "protestant," need to be married if they wish to have the complete confidence of their beloved congregations, whereas the priests of another, and likewise Christian church, view marriage as a sacrament and yet must possess naturally, or at least are required to acquire the gift of abstemiousness or of living the life of a eunuch.[46] It should be apparent from this consensus among Christians that it is not absolutely necessary for me to be married, and whether I am or not is thus a question I would politely request my public not to pursue.

Plato's *Phaedon* had the effect on one person that he drowned himself because of it;[47] and if I were to discover that because of my treatise even one single young man had decided to make a girl happy, I do not know how I as an author could be any happier! If I were able, however, to lead couple after couple out of my book the way Father Noah brought all the animals into the ark, or even to be able to contribute something to improving the status of that other so important and honorable half of the human race, then my joy would be beyond measure. Perhaps the time will come some day when we will not spoil pure reason with laws; when we will know no other worth than that of humanity; when we will not spend our time learning how to be happy, but how to be worthy of happiness; and when the kingdom of God shall come and we shall be His people.[48]

So fare well—and not just goodby for now, for it is sooner possible that we will never see each other again than that we will. Again, fare you well!

Just a couple of words to those critical readers—both those who are permitted to baptize without exorcism and those who are not[49]—who have attacked my treatise with their lead pencils and perhaps in the heat of the moment simultaneously scored the paper with the fingernail of the index finger of their right hand. I would almost say they were *lying in ambush* with regard to the above-mentioned Introduction *sub Nro.* III if I weren't afraid to have to add a *Nota bene* because of the use of this phrase. Do not act, my dear fellows, so that it may later be said of you: " . . . they are dead which sought the young child's life."[50] If you wish to lord it over this work and demand that every unnecessary word give an account of itself, then remember that even rulers do not retain their *jura in,* but rather *circa sacra.*[51]

True, if one can maintain that the spendthrift is no more than a subject of the usurer, and the miser a slave to himself, then in fact too rich a diet is harmful to both body and soul. But why should I water down everything I serve? Only when we adulterate the gifts of God or use them wrongly do we enter into sin; we have only reached the point of excess when the parts begin to assume the effect of the whole.

And a last voluntary confession: that I have made no judgments *sub- et obreptio,*[52] and that I will accept with pleasure that verdict which a competent judge will pronounce who does not bend the law or judge me instead of my treatise. This judge and friend will easily be able to convince himself that I would have been compelled to abrogate the very essence of this work—a work which has already been seeking its fortune or misfortune in the world for some time now—and replace it with another if I had wished to proceed differently *in formali* and *materiali*[53] in these later editions of the book.[54] To those who would withhold the greater portion of their opinion simply because they do not know my name—to these Asmodae[55] I would merely like to say that *no one* has ever seen the passport wherein my name, nationality, and place of origin are revealed.

NOTES

CHAPTER 1

1. Cf. Gen 1:28; cf. Isaiah 8:14. Unless otherwise noted, all citations are from the King James version of the Bible.

2. Lat. *pubes*, "capable of becoming a father"; *virilis*, "manly."

3. "Never does nature say one thing, wisdom another."

4. "A wife, so to speak."

5. Cf. Luke 15:18–19.

6. Cf. James 1:17.

7. Hippel is referring to Jean-Jacques Rousseau.

8. Cf. Mark 12:42–44.

9. A reference to the anecdote in Cicero's *De oratore*, book 2, sec. 68 in which a certain Nasica called at the house of the poet Ennius and was told by the maid that the latter was not at home, although he perceived that the poet was in fact within. When Ennius next called upon Nasica, Nasica shouted from within the house that he was not at home. When Ennius replied that he refused to believe such a thing because he recognized Nasica's voice, the latter replied that Ennius was an insolent fellow, for Nasica had been compelled to believe Ennius' servant when he had called on the poet, and now the poet did not believe him when he stated himself that he was not at home. Editions two and three of Hippel's book have "*un*roman fiction"; the first edition does not include the passage.

10. One of the chief tenets of the philosophy of Cynicism founded by Diogenes was that mankind should reduce its wants to the most natural standards, thereby avoiding the corruption of civilization.

11. In Greek mythology, it was foretold to Acrisius of Argos that his daughter Danae would bear a son who would later kill him. Acrisius thus imprisoned Danae

in a bronze chamber half underground, where Zeus either took pity on the maid (according to Hippel's unnamed interpreter) or, in the more traditional version, took a fancy to her, and, in either case, impregnated her by means of a shower of gold. The son born to this union was Perseus, who in the end did (accidentally) kill Acrisius.

12. Dulcinea was Don Quixote's beloved, perceived and adored in idealistic fashion by the knight, but for everyone else the object of reproach.

13. That state was Hippel's own, Prussia.

14. "Pious memory!"

15. Luther, in his interpretation of the Fourth Petition of the Lord's Prayer ("Give us this day our daily bread") in his *Small Catechism*, assigns a broad range of meanings to the term "daily bread," including "food, drink, clothing, shoes, hearth and home, land, livestock, money, goods, a pious spouse, pious children, pious servants, pious and loyal rulers, good weather, peace, good health, propriety, honor, good friends, loyal neighbors, and the like."

16. The *venia aetatis* was a privilege granted to a minor by the emperor allowing him to be considered as having attained his majority before the age of twenty-five if the honorable life he had led up to that time endorsed such a privilege. In the later empire, the *venia aetatis* was granted to women over eighteen and men over twenty.

17. The Law of the Byzantine emperor Anastasius I (circa A.D. 430–518) was directed against usurers; the Justinian Code was the body of Roman law compiled and annotated at the command of the emperor Justinian (A.D. 483–565).

18. See Aristotle, *Politics*, Book 7, sec. 16, 1335 a29 (Aristotle actually states that a man ought to marry in his thirty-*seventh* year), and Plato, *Laws*, 721b–d and 774a–b.

19. A Greek king and hero, famous for his defense of Thermopylae against the Persian army, at which battle he was slain in 480 B.C.

20. Cf. Deut. 23:1.

21. Anak was a giant, the founder of the Anakim people. Cf. Numbers 13:33 and Deut. 1:28.

22. Although it is not clear from the text, Hippel apparently intends the reference to "future criticism" to be applied to the parents of the illegitimate children only.

23. Molech was the god of the Ammonites, to whom human sacrifices were offered. Cf. Leviticus 18:21 and 20:2–3.

24. Hippel is apparently writing from first-hand experience here, a circumstance made even clearer by the fact that after he left home for Königsberg he exhibited utter indifference to his parents up to the time of their deaths, and did not return to Gerdauen for the funeral of either of them. In the words of Hippel's biographer, "neither his parents nor his less gifted and also less difficult brother [had] understood him" during his later childhood (Kohnen, *Hippel*, 23).

25. Genesis 49:3.

26. In the eighteenth century, the verb used here ("*anwerben*") had both the meaning "to recruit a soldier for military service" and "to sue for a woman's hand in marriage." It no longer has the latter meaning.

27. "Local clergymen and lawyers."

28. In early Germanic law, the father's guardianship over his children was seen as ending not with the attainment of their majority, but with their departure from the paternal household, which generally occurred upon their marriage. Hippel's reference to the parents thus appears to be a play on the idea that they are "debtors" not only

in the sense that they lose money in paying for the wedding, but that they lose their child as well, whose status changes from that of a ward of his parents to one who is merely "counseled" by them. The new husband in this sense is a "creditor" in that he gains not only a bride, but also his own emancipation. This emancipation did not apply to the woman, however, who went from the mundium (guardianship) of her father to that of her new husband.

29. Jonathan Swift maintained a questionable relationship for years with Esther Johnson, the illegitimate daughter of his patron, Sir William Temple. Swift referred to her as "Stella" and married her in 1716. From 1714 on he was also involved in a relationship with the daughter of a Dutch businessman, Esther Vanhomring, whom he called "Banassa." Both of these relationships were said to have been strictly platonic.

30. Matt. 26:41.

31. A body of military monks under whose auspices a hospital and church were founded in Jerusalem. It reached its military peak in the twelfth century; in the sixteenth century it was given possession of Malta, which it ruled until 1798. In 1812 it was also established as an order for the German nobility, and in 1852 the King of Prussia revived that branch of the order called the Mark of Brandenburg, thereby recognizing it as a separate order—hence the use of the Maltese cross as an insignia by the German military in World War I.

32. This same figure appears in all four editions, and it is difficult to understand how Hippel arrives at the figure forty-five unless one calculates *seven* children for Laura and her unfortunate lover.

33. "Bloody" Mary, Queen of England from 1553–58, lost Calais to the French in 1558.

34. Generally referred to as the *Jus vitae necisque*—the power of life and death. In early times this was the right a father had over his wife and children, as well as over his slaves. His right to punish them also included the death penalty. This power was abolished by the Roman emperor Valentinian I (A.D. 321–75).

35. During the seventeenth and eighteenth centuries it was the custom in Italy for a young unmarried aristocrat to act as escort and companion ("cicisbeo") to a married noblewoman during the temporary absence of her husband. As one might well imagine, this practice not infrequently resulted in adulterous relationships.

36. The *votum consultativum* is the power to have an advisory voice in a matter; the *fidele consilium* conveys the right to make a decision in matters regarding doctrine.

37. Also called the *Dominium ex jure Quiritium*, this term referred to the ownership which a Roman citizen might have of things which according to the *jus civile* (*jus Quiritium*) were permitted to be owned. This permission apparently was not originally intended to include the ownership of children by their parents, however.

38. Hippel is speaking of the law found in the "Book of General Laws for the Prussian States" (1791). This law is repeated in the "Prussian General [or Territorial] Code" (1792–94), part 2, title 1, sec. 68. For an account of both these works, see the Introduction to the present work.

39. In the German language of the eighteenth century, a young unmarried woman was referred to as a "*Frauenzimmer.*" This word is apparently derived from a sixteenth-century collective term referring to all the women in the women's part of the house.

40. Hippel has "*Viel Kinder, viel Paternoster*"; the more common version of the proverb is "*Viel Kinder, viel Segen,*" which is the version used in the translation.

41. The Ubiquitarians were a group of Lutheran theologians who held that since Christ was omnipresent, his body was everywhere, especially in the bread of the Eucharist. Priapus was the son of Bacchus (Dionysus) and Venus (Aphrodite). He was regarded as the promoter of fertility in Greek and Roman life, and for this reason is often represented in statuary with an erect phallus.

42. "An argument to the man," i.e., in logic, an argument which attacks one's opponent personally instead of his arguments.

43. Hippel appears to be referring to the lantern as a symbol for intellectual enlightenment and liberty in the sense that the phrase *"les aristocrates à la lanterne"* became one of the rallying cries of the French Revolution, when many a nobleman met his end hanging from just such an object of "illumination."

44. Cf. The Wisdom of Solomon, 14:26.

45. Cf. Gen. 2:23.

46. Cf. Matt. 25:18 and Luke 19:20.

47. I.e., "The Book of General Laws for the Prussian States," published in 1791 (see part IV of the Introduction to the present work).

48. "With good reason."

49. Hippel's own case, of course, is no exception, although the reader finds only a small hint in the very last chapter of the book that the writer in fact might not be married.

50. Gottfried Wilhelm Leibniz (1646–1716) is still celebrated as one of the last universal geniuses. Like Hippel himself, he entered the university at fifteen and by the age of twenty had already received the degree Doctor of Laws (Hippel's illustrative anecdote regarding the circumstances of Leibniz's failure to obtain the degree earlier is related in chapter 2 of the present work). Leibniz is now acknowledged—along with Newton, who discovered the principle independently—as the inventor of differential and integral calculus; in philosophy, he is recognized as the originator of the theory of monads. In addition, he served the Elector of Mainz and the Duke of Braunschweig-Lüneburg in a literary and diplomatic capacity.

51. Hippel often uses the more prosaic German version of Rousseau's name (Hans Jakob = Jean-Jacques) to poke fun at the Swiss reformer's boorishness and insensitivity to others in the face of his overweening social aspirations. On Rousseau's relationship with Thérèse Levasseur, see the Introduction to this work, part III.

52. As Hippel will maintain in chapter 7 when he offers advice to girls on the possible choice of a poet for a husband, the poet invariably finds his poetic wings clipped when he exchanges his idealized conception of love for the everyday reality of matrimony.

53. Cf. Judges 16 and 1 Kings 11.

54. Cf. Gen. 6:12 and 1:26.

55. Cf. Matt. 6:24.

56. Cf. Matt. 22:20.

57. Cf. Gen. 7–8 and Jude 1:21.

58. Matt. 12:49.

59. "Whether we want to or not."

60. Cf. Exodus 12:8 and Matt. 13:8.

61. Cf. Luke 6:40.

62. A legal expression meaning "with unfettered [authority]."

63. As related in the Book of Susanna and Daniel in the Apocrypha, two elderly judges begin to lust after the chaste Susanna after they became aware of her great beauty. One day they confront her in a private garden where she has been bathing and demand that she do their will. She refuses, and screams so loud that other people come running, whereupon the judges bear false witness against her, saying that they surprised her with her lover in the garden. She is sentenced to death, but just in time a young man named Daniel comes to her rescue and tricks the judges into revealing that they have purjured themselves, whereupon it is they who receive the death penalty.

64. The state Hippel is referring to is France. His attitude toward the French Revolution was positive at first in that he lauded the restoration of privileges to the disenfranchised, but he later deplored the needless sacrifice of some of the best minds in France to the guillotine, and his initial sympathy turned to hatred of the Revolution because of its excesses. For more information, see Joseph Kohnen, "Hippel und die französische Revolution," in *Festschrift für Albert Schneider*, ed. Fernand Hoffmann and Joseph Kohnen (Luxemburg: Centre Universitaire, 1992), 107–20.

65. Cf. Matt. 5:37.

66. I.e., by his bourgeois name. In fact, the actual Duke of Orleans during this period, Louis Philippe Joseph, had been a member of the Constituent Assembly from 1789–91, and was at the time of the publication of Hippel's book a Montagnard delegate to the Convention. A sympathizer during the Revolution, he had renounced his title, assumed the name of "Philippe Égalité," and voted for the death of the king. He was executed on 6 November 1793 upon the accession of the Jacobins to power in the Convention.

67. Deut. 5:6.

68. Probably Antigonus Gonatas, who was king of Macedon from 277–39 B.C. Cleanthes (ca. 300–ca. 220 B.C.) was a Stoic philosopher who is said to have earned his living in Athens by means of work as a day laborer.

69. The gods of Epicurus, like everything else in the Epicurean philosophy, consisted of atoms. They were and always had been in a state of pure happiness, and had no part in the laborious creation of the world. Likewise, since the governing of the world would interfere with their happiness, Epicurus conceived of them as having no influence whatsoever on its affairs.

70. I.e., the Roman Catholic Church.

71. In the Roman Empire, parents of several children enjoyed certain privileges due to legislation (the *Lex Julia et Papia Poppaea* later mentioned by Hippel) introduced during the Augustan age. Fathers thus might claim exemption from certain public expenditures and from the guardianship of others' children which they were required under certain circumstances to assume. Hippel does not mention it here, but the most important application of the *Jus liberorum* concerned women, for according to this law a freeborn woman with three children and a freed woman with four children were declared free from the guardianship (*tutela mulierum*) to which women were usually subject, and had a right of succession to the inheritance of their children.

72. Cf. Gen. 30.

73. Gen. 30:3 (New International Version).

74. Cf. Gen. 16:1–3.

75. Hippel's meaning in this case can perhaps be more clearly understood if one compares the present text with the uncut version of the first edition: "It is thus only

just to reward women for their children. They can truly be as proud of such deeds as of victories. Historians should write about these deeds for posterity, and apply to them as well the true saying that whoever loses his life for his country can never die."

76. Luke 12:20.

77. Such marriages, otherwise called "morganatic marriages," (matrimonium ad morganaticam) were contracted under Germanic law by men of royal or noble families with women who were commoners. The children of these marriages were considered legitimate, but neither they nor the wife acquired any rights to the rank or possessions of the husband. The word "morganatic" is actually a medieval Latin corruption of the Germanic word morkankepa (modern German: Morgengabe), the term for the husband's gift to the wife on the morning after their wedding—in this case, the only thing received by the bride who elects to enter into such a marriage.

78. Gen. 21:10.

79. Cf. Exodus 22:22; Deut.10:18; 24:17; 27:19; Job 22:9; 24:3; Psalm 68:5; 94:6; 109:9; 146:9; Isaiah 1:23; 10:2; Jeremiah 7:6; 22:3; Ezekiel 22:7; Zechariah 7:10; Malachi 3:5; James 1:27.

80. Cf. Gen. 25:34.

81. Although Montaigne is undisputably Hippel's favorite essayist, he here pokes fun at the former's rather tasteless description of his personal habits in Book 15 of his autobiobraphy:

> Both kings and philosophers go to stool, and ladies too. They, for their part, must maintain discretion; but as a simple private individual, I enjoy a natural dispensation. . . . So I will say of this action that a man should set for it a fixed hour in the evening, and force himself by habit to stick to it, as I have done. He should not chain himself, as has been my wont in my declining years, to the convenience of any one place or seat, nor make it troublesome by long and dilatory sitting. Where, but in foul offices, are cleanliness and dispatch more necessary? Of all the actions of nature, this is the one I am most unwilling to be interrupted. I have seen many soldiers troubled by irregularity of the bowels, but mine and I never fail to keep their appointment, which is immediately upon leaping out of bed—unless illness or importunate business interferes. (Michel de Montaigne, Autobiography, ed. and trans. Marvin Lowenthal [New York: Random House, n.d.], 132–33)

Mademoiselle de Gourney is Marie de Gournay le Jars, Montaigne's woman friend and companion whom he idolizes in chapter 20 of his autobiography, and who published the first complete edition of his essays in 1595.

82. According to Günter de Bruyn in his edition of the first edition of Hippel's book on marriage, this sentence is to be understood in the enlightened sense that a misalliance is an intolerable alternative because the woman is never equal in birth to the man (Theodor Gottlieb von Hippel, Über die Ehe, ed. Günter de Bruyn [Berlin: Der Morgen, 1979], 107). Moreover, if the term misalliance (the "disparagium" of Roman law) is extended here to cover the full range of its meaning, then such an arrangement is intolerable also because the status of the lower-born party cannot be changed for the better under any circumstances, and thus marriage in general can never work to the benefit of the woman.

83. *Contubernium* was a permanent union resembling marriage between slaves, or between a master and his female slave; *matrimonium, nuptiae,* and *conjugium* were all terms used to describe marriage at various times during the empire and bore very little legal distinction among them; *matrimonium in specie* referred to marriage "in appearance" (cohabitation with a free woman who had not been a prostitute); *connubium* referred to the legal capacity of a man to enter into marriage.

84. The right to contract a marriage recognized by law.

85. Generally called the *Lex Julia et Papia Poppaea* (see also note 71, above), this law of Augustus (A.D. 9), along with his *Lex Julia et maritandis ordinibus* (18 B.C.), dealt with a number of problems connected with marriage.

86. "The bastards are worth more than those who are legitimate."

87. Cf. Exodus 20:5 and 34:7.

88. The sign which the beleaguered residents of a town or castle gave by means of drums or trumpets when they wished to capitulate.

89. A Roman rhetorician and historian who lived in the first part of the first century A.D. Almost nothing is known of him except that he published a collection of acts and sayings of orators, philosophers, and statesmen for the use of rhetoricians.

90. Charles Geneviève d'Éon de Beaumont (1728–1810), generally known as Chevalier d'Éon, was a French diplomat and secret agent of Louis XV. He served the king at the court of the Empress Elizabeth from 1755 to 1760 (where Hippel doubtless came to hear of him on his visit there in 1761), and later in London. From the time of his youth onward it was said of him that he was really a woman. Involved in a legal dispute later in his life, he declared in court that he was a woman in order to avoid the embarrassment of submitting to having his sex determined by examination, and lived from 1777 to 1785 in women's clothes in Paris. Hippel cites him in *On Improving the Status of Women* as a woman of merit, as does Mary Wollstonecraft in her treatise *A Vindication of the Rights of Woman* (chapter 4). Both writers were unaware of d'Éon's true sex, which was not conclusively established until his death in 1810.

91. Cf. 2 Cor. 11:14.

92. Minerva had no mother, but according to Greek mythology sprang full-grown and fully armed from the head of Zeus alone. In the earliest accounts of her in the *Iliad*, she was a fierce warrior-goddess, but in later classical times came to be known as the patroness of all the arts and trades, where she guided women in sewing, spinning, weaving and the like, and men in the turmoil of war.

93. Elizabeth Charlotte, Duchess of Orleans, was a Palatine (German) princess born at Heidelberg in 1652. She later became the second wife of Philip, Duke of Orleans, the brother of Louis XIV of France. Her published letters are important for the cultural history of the period; she died at St. Cloud, France, in 1722.

94. The Marie Germain in question did not exactly become a man through jumping. The anecdote, as related by Montaigne in his *Essays* (book 1, chap. 20), actually runs as follows: "Myself passing by Vitry le François, I saw a man the bishop of Soissons had, in confirmation, called Germain, whom all the inhabitants of the place had known to be a girl till two-and-twenty years of age, called Marie. He was, at the time of my being there, very full of beard, old, and not married. He told us, that by straining himself in a leap his male instruments came out; and the girls of that place have, to this day, a song, wherein they advise one another not to take too great strides, for fear of being turned into men, as Marie Germain was" (trans. Cotton).

95. Worn almost constantly by the woman of the eighteenth century, both *inside* and outside the house.

96. A fascinating, albeit literary, example of the misery caused by the mismanagement of the household by some husbands during this period is provided by Goethe in his *Sorrows of Young Werther*, letter of 11 July 1771. Here an elderly wife admits on her deathbed to her miserly husband that she was forced to steal from the cash box of their business in order to make ends meet in the household because the husband did not once change the amount of her allotment of seven Gulden a week during their entire married life, in spite of the growing expenses caused by the birth of numerous children. This poignant deathbed admission is extracted from her only because she fears her successor will have to endure her new husband's reproaches for not being as economical as his first wife.

97. Cf. Plato, *Symposium*, 190d–191d.

98. Cf. Gen. 2:18, 20.

99. Cf. Luke 9:48.

100. Athena is the Greek goddess of wisdom; *phronasis*, defined by Aristotle as practical wisdom, and *sophia*, called theoretical wisdom by him, are both feminine Greek nouns. "Sophie" was a popular German woman's name during the period.

101. Prometheus is famous in Greek mythology for having stolen fire from the gods and given it to mankind.

CHAPTER 2

1. Ulpianus was a celebrated Roman jurist of Phoenician descent, murdered about A.D. 228. He wrote many commentaries and other legal works, and extracts from these works constitute fully a third of the *Digest* of Justinian later discussed by Hippel.

2. A reference to the German proverb "Bart und Mantel machen den Philosophen nicht" ("A beard and cloak do not make a philosopher").

3. A *"Legulejus"* was a lawyer who adhered strictly to the letter, while ignoring entirely the spirit, of the law. Cf. Cicero, *De oratore*, book 1, sec. 55.

4. Since a master craftsman was required first to become a citizen of the city in which he lived, such a sign would be redundant, and, as such, amount to over-advertising or "quackery."

5. *Salva venia dupondii*: newcomers, as, for example, *freshmen*, in academic terminology.

6. "Considered in a formal sense."

7. In fact, in the Justinian Code the *Digest* and the *Pandects* are generally considered synonymous and refer to a collection of Roman civil laws made up of the decisions of various lawyers to which the Emperor gave the force and authority of law. This compilation is the most important of the body of Roman civil law, and consists of fifty books, a circumstance upon which Hippel later plays in this chapter with his fifty questions.

8. *Authenticae* are portions of laws found in the *Novellae* (*Novels*), which are themselves collections of laws in the Justinian codex.

9. Christian Wolff (1679–1754) was a German philosopher whose controversial life and works made him one of the most popular writers and speakers of the day. His philosophy is essentially a systematization and slight modification of Leibniz's ideas, which he tried to popularize by lecturing at the University of Halle in German instead

of the customary Latin. Wolff defined philosophy as the science of the possible and viewed it as embracing the entire field of human knowledge. His attempts to base theological truths on evidence of mathematical certitude brought the charge of atheism upon him from his colleagues, and may be what Hippel is referring to with his remark that Wolff "incorrectly" assessed the realms of the possible and impossible.

10. An institute is a systematic statement of the law in a single and complete work, as distinguished from a mere compilation or collection (a pandect or digest). The *Institutes* of Justinian, to which Hippel frequently refers here, provide the best example of such a work.

11. Cf. Gen. 30:31–43.

12. According to Greek legend, an oracle had declared to the people of Phrygia that a king would come to them riding in a cart, and, as the peasant Gordius appeared to them by accident in such a manner, he was declared king. His cart and the yoke of his oxen he dedicated to Zeus at Gordium. Later an oracle declared that whoever should untie the knot of the yoke would rule over Asia. Alexander the Great cut the knot in half with his sword.

13. In theological terms, the "external practice of the Christian faith" ("*äußerlicher Gottesdienst*") consists of prayer in its various forms, the reading and contemplation of the word of God, teaching and evangelizing, the singing of hymns, and participation in the sacraments.

14. I.e., at the Pharisees, as the keepers of the Law.

15. Cf. Matt. 20:1–16.

16. "A controversy concluded with the judgment of a judge."

17. Plutarch ascribes this saying to Plato, but it has also been ascribed to Pythagoras, Thales, Socrates, and others. Juvenal (*Satires*, book 11, sec. 27) states that this precept descended from heaven.

18. "Note this well."

19. Cf. 1 Cor. 15:43.

20. I.e., the *Institutes* of Justinian, the basis for the Roman law in effect in Germany at the time (see also note 10).

21. Literally, "It is wrong to speak without law once right itself has been consulted."

22. Cf. John 11:9 and Psalm 8:20.

23. By means of the cabinet order of this date, Frederick the Great's *Ministre chef de Justice*, Count Johann Heinrich Kasimir von Carmer (1721–1801) was ordered to prepare a set of court rules and a codification of the laws of Prussia in German. The result of this was that many smaller courts were abolished or unified under a single rubric. On 26 April 1781 the new court and procedural rules became law, as the first part of the *Corpus Juris Fridericianum*. For more information on this unification of Prussian law under Carmer, see Walther Hubatsch, *Frederick the Great of Prussia: Absolutism and Administration*, trans. Patrick Doran (London: Thames and Hudson, 1975), 217–20.

24. I.e., his thunderbolts.

25. Cf. Matt. 21:18–19.

26. "You are abandoning people for paintings."

27. I.e., judicial (legal) separation.

28. Cf. Matt. 19:6.

29. Cf. Matt. 13:24–30.

30. The German expression used here by Hippel in all four editions ("*Soll man fügen?*") is very ambiguous, and the interpretation given here represents the best guess of the translator based on the general meaning of *fügen* ("to join") and the context which follows the statement.

31. A statement to the effect that the master has no need of the apprentice's work.

32. "Right off the bat."

33. 1 Cor. 7:9.

34. Cf. John 6: 5–14.

35. In ancient worship, an Adytum was a sacred place which might be entered only at certain times and by certain people, as for example priests performing rites. In general, it was the most sacred part of any place of worship. Mystagogues were priests, especially in the early Church, who presented candidates for initiation into the sacred mysteries.

36. Jacques Étienne (1754–99) and Joseph Michel (1740–1810) Montgolfier were the inventors of the hot air balloon, which was first tested at Annonay in 1782 and then demonstrated before the French court at Versailles on 19 September 1783. It was one of the sensations of the eighteenth century.

37. All three were well-known naturalists of the period. Peter van Muschenbroeck (1692–1761) was professor of physics and mathematics at the University of Leyden; Albrecht von Haller (1708–77) taught physiology at the University of Göttingen and simultaneously wrote poetry celebrating the beauties of nature, particularly the Alps; Johann Friedrich Blumenbach (1752–1840) was professor of anatomy and physiology at Göttingen.

38. "Keep your hands away from the table" (for fear of getting shocked).

39. Cf. Gen. 1:28.

40. In paintings and statuary, Justice was represented as wearing a blindfold in order to show that she was no respecter of persons.

41. I.e., the ass.

42. The church is the Roman Catholic Church, and those who say this of it are obviously its detractors.

43. Cf. Mark 12:31 and Galatians 5:14.

44. "Specifically"; "in a particular sense."

45. "In question."

46. Cf. Gen. 2:24.

47. Johann Gottlieb Heineccius (1681–1741) was a well-known German jurist of the period. He was professor of philosophy and later law at the University of Halle, and the author of numerous legal texts, including *Elementa juris civilis* and *Historia juris civilis*.

48. "The most beautiful appearance of sequestration." Sequestration was the depositing of property disputed by two parties with a third party, who was called in Roman law a *sequester*. This third party was a depositee and his liability was the same as in the case of a normal deposit, the difference being that the *sequester* was considered possessor of the property and protected by the laws of possession. Hippel is here stating that Heineccius considers marriage to be a form (albeit the most "beautiful" one) of sequestration, wherein the husband becomes the *sequester* of the wife's property after marriage, the actual possessor of everything previously owned by her.

49. Cf. Leviticus 18: 1–20; 20:11–12, 17–21.

50. See note 97, chap. 1.

51. The Council of Trent was an ecumenical council held at Trent in Tyrol from 1545 to 1563 which condemned the main tenets of the Reformation regarding the Bible, original sin, and justification. The Augsburg Confession is the chief Lutheran creed, prepared by Luther's friend Melanchthon and read before the Diet of Augsburg in 1530.

52. Cf. 1 Cor. 7:3–5.

53. A "legal response," i.e., a legal brief.

54. Cf. 2 Cor. 10:5.

55. Origen, along with Augustine, one of the two most influential of the Church fathers, was most likely born at Alexandria around A.D. 185 and died at Tyre, probably in 253. He is credited with creating the dogmatic of the Church and laying the foundation of the scientific criticism of the Old and New Testaments. Hippel is here referring specifically to the fact that Origen mutilated himself as a young man in order to free himself from the lusts of the flesh. While Hippel attributes this act to Origen's great piety, it is known that he came to regret this rash act in later life.

56. Hippel is alluding to the Jesuits and their founder, Ignatius of Loyola.

57. Cf. Deut. 23:1.

58. Cf. Leviticus 22:17–25.

59. Eunuchs are those who by mutilation or operation have been rendered incapable of procreating; "spados" is the more general term referring to those who are incapable of procreating for any reason whatsoever.

60. Cf. Matt. 19:12.

61. In Roman legal terminology, the *Traditio* referred to the transfer of ownership from the owner to the transferee. The usual *Traditio* required a just cause because it was based on an obligatory relationship between owner and transferee. Here the argument seems to be whether the just cause can be considered as merely one of a number of "symbolic things" ("*symbolica*") which can be dispensed with because of the unusual nature of the case.

62. Peter Abélard was born near Nantes, France in 1079 and died in 1142. While Abélard is notable as one of the founders of scholastic theology, it is his relationship with his pupil Héloïse (1101–64), one of the most famous love stories of all time, to which the lawyers are indirectly referring. Héloïse was a niece of Fulbert, canon of Notre Dame. During the course of her instruction the two fell in love and he became her seducer. After the birth of their child, Abélard proposed a secret marriage to which Héloïse only reluctantly agreed because she was concerned about the future of Abélard's career. Even after it had been performed, she denied the marriage and retired to a convent. When Fulbert heard of the affair, he inflicted a mutilation on Abélard's sexual organs out of revenge. Abélard later became a monk, and Héloïse took the veil.

63. Cf. 2 Kings 20:18.

64. Cf. Matt. 3:9.

65. Cf. Psalm 68:6. The English version is from the Bible translation of Luther, which Hippel is quoting here. English translations of the Bible unanimously interpret this verse (Psalm 68:7 in the German) as meaning "give the lonely a home."

66. Hippel is speaking of the "Book of General Laws for the Prussian States" of 1791.

67. This sentence is less elliptical, and thus clearer, in the first edition and gives credence to the interpretation that Hippel is still talking about eunuchs here.

68. I.e., the sexual, not the procreative, act.

69. The first edition has "interpreted not as privileges in the narrow, but in the broadest possible sense of the term."

70. Cneius (not Caius) Flavius was an early writer on Roman law. Although knowledge of the law of his time was confined to the patricians and pontiffs, he obtained possession of the forms and technicalities relating to its practice and published them in a collection known as the *Jus Flavanium*; in A.D. 449 Sextus Aelius wrote a work entitled *Commentarii* in which he provided an exegesis of various texts in Roman law with notations regarding the procedures for submitting and handling a legal complaint.

71. Cf. Luke 16:9.

72. Cf. Ephesians 4:26.

73. As noted in the Introduction, the "fifty questions" allegedly treated by the lecturer in this chapter correspond to the fifty books of the Justinian Code. We know from the first edition of Hippel's book on marriage that the fiftieth question deals with the frequency of sexual intercourse in marriage ("How often?" he had asked in italicized letters in that edition), but by the time of the fourth edition Hippel's early boldness in linguistic matters had been replaced by a reserve bordering on prudery which made it difficult for the reader unfamiliar with the earlier editions to know what he was driving at.

74. Cf. Luke 22:33–34, 54–62.

75. Lycurgus was a Spartan legislator and the traditional author of the laws and institutions of Sparta. He is thought to have lived in the 9th century B.C.

76. Cf. Gen. 3:19 (New International Version).

77. "What do you want me to say? I am not fond of innocent pleasures."

78. Little is known of ICti Tiraquelli other than that a single work of this medieval legal writer, his *Semestria*, remains from what must have been, according to Hippel's information, a very prolific career.

79. The wife of Socrates, whose name has become a byword for the ill-tempered wife.

80. Hipparchia, the wife of Crates of Thebes (lived about 320 B.C.), was referred to by Diogenes Laertes as "the female philosopher." She had become so enamored of the Cynic philosophy and of Crates that she threatened to commit suicide unless he married her. Although marriage was excluded as a rule from that philosophical system because of its interference with the role of the philosopher as a messenger of the gods, the two married and enjoyed one of the rare love matches in the history of philosophy. Hipparchia, wearing the garb of the Cynic, went everywhere with Crates, and was without doubt a true representative of his philosophical principles. But because of the liberal sexual mores of this philosophic school—according to Menander, Crates himself claimed that he gave his daughter in marriage for a month on trial—Hipparchia became the model for those numerous examples of unfettered sexual morality associated with Crates' school (of which most, if not all, were apocryphal in nature).

81. Louis de Jaucourt was a French *chevalier* and the author of many medical writings. In addition to these, he penned a biography of Leibniz (*La vie de M. de Leibniz*), translated into German in 1757. De Jaucourt died about 1680. Bernard le

Bovier de Fontenelle (1657–1757), the nephew of Corneille, was a French lawyer, philosopher, poet, and miscellaneous writer. His *Éloges des académiciens*, of which one contains a piece on Leibniz, were written from 1699–1740.

82. Cf. Matt. 27:19–24.

83. Cf. John 8:7.

84. Hippel is referring to the sex drive. In 1749, Georges-Louis Leclerc, Comte de Buffon (1707–88), had caused something of a sensation with his "Adam in Eden" passage contained in an essay *Des Sens en général*, itself a part of his "Natural History of Man" in the second and third volumes of the monumental *Histoire Naturelle*. In this passage, a newly-created Adam, after discovering the existence and function of each of his five senses one by one, falls asleep only to waken shortly thereafter next to the woman who has meanwhile been created out of his rib. In exploring this new being with his hand, he finds a new sense awakened in him. In the words of a modern interpretation, Buffon, by means of this text, traces "Adam's ultimate assurance of the reality of his own identity to the first awakening of his sexuality, following the discovery of Eve at his side, sexuality conceived in broadly idealistic terms as a supreme impulse toward giving, a desire for the total surrender of self" (Otis E. Fellows and Stephen F. Millikin, *Buffon* [New York: Twayne, 1972], 129).

85. A play on the words *"Semper Augustus"* ("Perpetual enlarger of the Empire"), a title of Roman emperors from the time of Diocletian on.

86. Caius Plinius Caecilius Secundus, frequently called Pliny the Younger (A.D. 62–113), was married twice, the second time to Calpurnia, granddaughter of Calpurnius Fabatus, and an accomplished woman in her own right. She was considerably younger than her husband, who recorded her kind attentions to him in his *Epistolae* (letters). The quotation here is not in a letter to his wife, but *about* her in a letter to Hispulla; cf. *Epistolae*, 4, 19.

87. According to Plutarch and Cicero, each of these Roman rulers was the object of public rumors of unfaithfulness on the part of his wife—Sylla (Lucius Cornelius Sulla, 138–78 B.C.) because of his second wife Metella; Pompey (Cneius Pompeius Magnus, 106–48 B.C.) on account of his wife Mucia, who dishonored his bed in his absence; and Claudius (Tiberius Claudius Drusus Nero Germanicus, 10 B.C.–A.D. 54) by his third wife, the infamous Valeria Messalina, whose spectacular acts of unfaithfulness actually led her to contract a public marriage with one Caius Silus while Claudius was away from Rome. She was later executed for this deed.

88. This is probably a reference to Rousseau's often histrionic self-revelations in the *Confessions*, of which the following provides an excellent example: "My passions are extremely violent; while under their influence, nothing can equal my impetuosity; I am an absolute stranger with regard to descretion, respect, fear, or decorum; rude, saucy, violent, and intrepid: no shame can stop, no danger intimidate me. My mind is frequently so engrossed by a single object, that beyond it the whole world is not worth a thought; this is the enthusiasm of a moment, the next, perhaps, I am plunged in a state of annihilation. Take me in my moments of tranquility, I am indolence and timidity itself; a word to speak, the least trifle to perform, appear an intolerable labor; everything alarms and terrifies me; the very buzzing of a fly will make me shudder; I am so subdued by fear and shame, that I would gladly shield myself from mortal view" (book 1; trans. Ed. Hedouin).

89. Cf. Matt. 7:16.

90. Cf. Gen. 1.

91. Cf. John 3:5.

CHAPTER 3

1. Cf. the Introduction to Luther's *Traubüchlein* in his *Kleiner Catechismus* (*Small Catechism*).

2. In the first edition of Hippel's book, the second sentence of this chapter reads as follows: "Two people who dedicate their bodies to each other to the exclusion of all others are in fact performing a holy act, and there can be no doubt that marriage is a kind of spiritual order in which one takes an oath of faithfulness and self-restraint, to which is added the oath of obedience in the case of the women."

3. Cf. Romans 7:22.

4. Cf. Acts 17:28.

5. 1 Peter 2:2.

6. "With the necessary changes being made."

7. "According to the laws governing the family."

8. For Hippel's arguments regarding his assertion here, see *On Improving the Status of Women*, 64–65.

9. Generally used in Hippel's time with the meanings of "to train" animals and "to drill" in the military sense.

10. Matt. 22:12 (New American Standard Bible).

11. Cf. Luke 18:17.

12. A temporary holding account used by bookkeepers and accountants pending a further decision regarding the circumstances of the account.

13. Cf. Matt. 6:34.

14. Cf. Matt. 11:30.

15. "To the man" (i.e., personal; concerning one's own interests).

16. Cf. Exodus 20:17.

17. Cf. Gen. 3:7.

18. A reference to the model school called the Philanthropin, founded by the German teacher and educational reformer Johann Berend Basedow (1723–90) at Dessau in 1774. Basedow put into practice in the Philanthropin the educational principles regarding primary education which he had advocated in his *Elementarwerk* ("Elements of Education") of 1774.

CHAPTER 4

1. "Contract for life."

2. Philip I, "The Magnanimous" (1504–63), Landgrave of Hessia, was permitted in 1540 by the two leaders of the Protestant Reformation, Luther and Melanchthon, to take a second wife in addition to his first wife, a Saxon princess. On the term "chosen vessel," cf. Acts 9:15.

3. So-called by Luther in his *Small Catechism* to refer to the power of the Church to preach, administer the sacraments, and to forgive sins; thus, it here refers to the officials, especially the clergy, of the Church in general. Cf. also Matt. 16:19.

4. Lucian (A.D. 120–200) was a celebrated Greek satirist and humorist who in numerous literary works attacked the religious beliefs of his time, earning for him the sobriquet "The Blasphemer." This citation is from his *Nigrinus*, 31.

5. The name "Banyans" was used in Hippel's time to designate a class of the Vaisya caste in India, the caste of the merchants. Hippel's description is based somewhat on popular lore concerning this class; perhaps it is more accurate to state that they eat no meat.

6. Cf. Genesis 9:20–27.

7. Glaucus was a Lycian prince who assisted Priam in the Trojan war. He was connected to Diomedes by ties of hospitality, and when the two encountered each other on the field of battle, they abstained from fighting and exchanged arms with one another. This amounted to an exchange of gold for bronze, however, and not lead.

8. The name of two Greek courtesans famous for their beauty, one of whom lived in the fourth, the other in the fifth century B.C.

9. The hero of *Hudibras*, a heroic-comic poem (pub. 1663–78) satirizing Puritanism, by the English author Samuel Butler (1612–80).

10. "To the sacred thing or place."

11. "Of the feminine gender."

12. Cf. Gen. 2:23.

13. "By the law itself."

14. Cf. Gen. 2:21–24.

15. Cf. Rev. 12:8.

16. The name "Moravian Brethren" is often applied to the Christian denomination whose official name is the *Unitas Fratrum*, or United Brethren. This group traces its roots back to John Hus (ca. 1369–1415), but had to be reorganized after centuries of persecution at Herrnhut, Germany in 1722 (hence the popular German designation "*Herrnhuter*"). Pietistic in orientation, the Moravians stress a gentle demeanor, good works as the fruit of the Holy Spirit, and continual self-examination. In the eighteenth century, single young men and women in Moravian communities lived separately in dormitory-like structures until marriage.

17. "Vow of chastity."

18. Cf. Gen. 1:30, 3:18.

19. Cf. 1 Timothy 3:2; Titus 1:6.

20. The name "Catharist" ("puritan") has been applied to various bodies or sects at different periods, especially the Novations of the third century and the antisacerdotal sects (Albigenses, etc.) in the south of France and in the piedmont regions of Switzerland and Italy in the twelfth century. They differed greatly among themselves in doctrine and in the degree of their opposition to the Church of Rome, but agreed in denying its supreme authority.

21. I.e., the Mosaic Law.

22. A child born on Sunday has always been considered in popular lore to be especially blessed. Cf. the "Mother Goose" rhyme in English:

> Monday's child is fair of face,
> Tuesday's child is full of grace,
> Wednesday's child is full of woe,
> Thursday's child has far to go,
> Friday's child is loving and giving,
> Saturday's child works hard for a living,

And the child that is born on the Sabbath day
Is bonny and blithe, and good and gay."

23. "[Marriage] is a religious and devout union; the pleasure which one derives from it should be a reserved, serious, and measured one; viewed rigorously, it must be understood as a kind of prudent and conscientious desire."

24. Till Eulenspiegel (died 1350) became the popular symbol of the arch rogue due to his exploits in northern Germany during the Middle Ages. When questioned as to why he behaved as he did, his answer always served to mock the authorities, exposing their hypocrisy and small-mindedness.

25. The "stone" sought by the alchemists of the Middle Ages, thought variously to provide ultimate knowledge or eternal life, heal any wound, or change base metals into gold.

26. Cf. Genesis 16.

27. Common Greek names used generically in this sense.

28. Cf. Matt. 19:5–6.

29. A sly thrust at Johann Georg Zimmermann, one of Hippel's intellectual adversaries and the author of a very popular and influential four-volume work entitled *Über die Einsamkeit* ("On Solitude"), published in 1755 and revised in 1784–85. Cf. also notes 19 and 38 of the Introduction to the present work.

30. I.e., Rousseau, who actually came from the French-speaking part of Switzerland but in the *Confessions* makes no secret of his preference for the taste and culture of France.

31. Cf. John 8:7.

32. The reference is to France. See also Part III of the Introduction to the present work.

33. 1 Timothy 3:5.

34. "Aretin" is Pietro Aretino, an Italian writer of satirical sonnets and comedies, who was born at Arezzo, Italy in 1492 and died in Venice in 1556. In his day he was referred to as "The Scourge of Princes." "Arouet" is François Marie Arouet, better known by his assumed name, Voltaire, whose verbal and written sallies directed against his patron Frederick the Great were the subject of widely circulated anecdotes in the eighteenth century.

35. Cf. 1 Peter 3:7 and Colossians 3:19.

36. On the law regarding slaves, see Lev. 25:50–52. Hippel is presumably basing the sum of fifty shekels as the price for a wife on Deut. 22:28–29, but those verses do not necessarily constitute proof of his assertion. In fact, during biblical times the dowry could be in the form of money, jewelry, or services rendered (cf. e.g., Gen. 24:22–23 or 1 Sam. 18:25), and it was not until later times that the nature and size of the dowry became fixed.

37. Proverbs 31:29 (in Luther's German version only).

38. This same argument is taken up and expanded upon by the philosopher Arthur Schopenhauer (very possibly under Hippel's influence) in his essay "The Metaphysics of Physical Love":

That an instinct, directed absolutely to what is to be produced [i.e., a child] underlies all sexual love, will obtain complete certainty from more detailed analysis;

we cannot therefore omit this. First of all, it is not out of place to mention here that by nature man is inclined to inconstancy in love, woman to constancy. The man's love diminishes perceptibly from the moment it has obtained satisfaction; almost every other woman charms him more than the one he already possesses; he longs for variety. On the other hand, the woman's love increases from that very moment. This is a consequence of nature's aim, which is directed to the maintenance, and thus the greatest possible increase, of the species. The man can easily beget over a hundred children in a year, if there are that number of women available; on the other hand, no matter with how many men, the woman could bring into the world only one child in a year (apart from twin births). The man, therefore, always looks around for other women; the woman, on the contrary, cleaves firmly to the one man; for nature urges her, instinctively and without reflection, to retain the nourisher and supporter of future offspring. Accordingly, conjugal fidelity for the man is artificial, for the woman natural; and so adultery on the part of the woman is much less pardonable than on the part of the man, both objectively on account of the consequences and subjectively on account of its being unnatural. (*The World as Will and Representation,* tr. E. F. J. Payne, vol. 2 [New York: Dover, 1966], 542)

39. "By virtue of [having suffered] legitimate distress."

40. The *"Schwabenspiegel"* was a compilation of law brought together by an unknown author in the thirteenth century which attained great authority in southern Germany. It was based to a great extent on the *"Sachsenspiegel"* ("Saxon Mirror").

41. Cf. Matt. 23:27 (New International Version).

42. Cf. Exodus 16:3.

43. "Pandemos" ("Common to all the people") was a surname of Aphrodite (Venus) and in this case refers to the purely sexual side of her nature.

44. Catherine II ("the Great") wrote three comedies, *"Der Betrüger,"* ("The Confidence Man"), *"Der Verblendete,"* ("The Deluded Man"), and *"Der sibirische Schaman,"* ("The Siberian Shaman"), published in 1788 under the larger title *Drei Lustspiele wider Schwärmerei und Aberglauben,* ("Three Comedies Against Fanaticism and Superstition"). These were published by Nicolai in Berlin and Stettin and appear to have been written originally in German and published only in Germany.

45. This is sulphuric ether (known by the alchemists as *Naphtha sulphurici*), a highly volatile, mobile, and inflammable liquid which does in fact have the power to produce cold by virtue of its extremely rapid evaporation, and was used in Hippel's time to numb skin before minor surgery. The modern international name of this compound is diethylether.

46. The most celebrated of the Greek painters, a contemporary and friend of Alexander the Great (356–323 B.C.), and the only painter whom Alexander would permit to paint his portrait. His most famous work, often considered the best painting of antiquity, is the "Venus Anadyomene," or "Venus rising out of the Sea."

47. Damon was a follower of Pythagoras and friend of Phintias (not Pythias). When Phintias was condemned to death by Dionysius I of Syracuse for plotting against the king, he asked for temporary leave to settle his affairs, promising to find a friend who would stand in his stead until he returned. To his surprise, Damon offered to be put to death instead of his friend, should he fail to return. Phintias arrived at the last

minute to save Damon, and Dionysius was so struck by this instance of friendship that he pardoned the criminal and requested to be admitted as a third into their bond of brotherhood.

48. "Persons deserving pity" (because of age or infirmity). In Roman law, such persons were granted certain privileges in proceedings before the imperial court.

49. Because they were not eligible to inherit money from their parents or a husband, older women who had never married were often forced to enter homes for the aged ("hospitals") when their sex guardianship under a married brother ceased with his death.

50. Cf. Numbers 27:7–8, 36:5–10.

51. Cf. The Wisdom of Solomon 4:1.

52. A festival celebrated on 15 February in honor of Lupercus, an ancient Italian divinity whom the Romans sometimes identified with the Arcadian Pan.

53. I.e., learning to live with a shrewish wife, in the sense that Socrates' wife, Xanthippe, was proverbial in ancient times for her bad humor.

54. Hippel is here breaking down the German word for jealousy, "Eifersucht" into its component parts, "Eifer," ("zealousness" or "fanaticism") and "Sucht" ("obsession" or "mania").

55. Cf. Romans 3:20, 7:7.

56. A modification of the beatitude found in Matt. 5:8.

57. Cf. Isaiah 61:10.

58. "I don't know if the exploits of Caesar and Alexander surpass in severity and fierceness the resolution of a pretty young woman brought up according to our fashion who keeps herself unsullied among a thousand continuous and vigorous pleadings from suitors."

59. In Greek mythology, Eriphyle was induced to persuade her husband to join in the expedition of the "Seven against Thebes" by means of the splendid necklace of Harmonia, which Polynices had given her.

60. Cf. Deut. 24:1; Matt. 19:8; and Mark 10:2–5.

61. Cf. Matt. 5:31–32, 19:9.

62. Matt. 19:6.

63. Gen. 1:26.

64. Cf. Luke 6:37–38.

65. Cf. Matt. 5:32, 19:9.

66. A Prussian law of the period presumably based on Deut. 24:1–4.

67. Hippel is speaking of the vestes coae, often mentioned by Roman authors. Cf., for example, Horace, Satires, 1, 2, 101.

68. The wife of Tarquinius Collatinus, famed in antiquity for her virtue and beauty. Inflamed with passion for her, Sextus, son of King Tarquinius of Rome, forced her to yield to his advances after she had entertained him as a kinsman. Upon informing her husband and father of the deed, Lucretia took her own life out of shame and despair. Her body was then carried to Rome, where all the classes of the people rose up in anger and demanded that the king be deposed and banished (510 B.C.). Sextus was later murdered by the friends of others he himself had put to death.

69. Titus 1:15.

CHAPTER 5

1. The German terms used by Hippel are *"Präsident von der Hausjustiz"* and *"Polizei-präsident."*

2. During the late fifteenth and early sixteenth centuries the *"Corpus Juris Civilis"* (that is, the law of the ancient Roman empire) became fixed as the legal system under which justice was administered in the German states. This development was known as the "Reception" of Roman law. This Reception, however, resulted in a great deal of confusion as to the nature of the law in cases where Roman law failed to address specific problems. As a result, many of the ancient Germanic private laws were permitted to exist side by side with Roman law, and were used as the basis for deciding cases not specifically dealt with by the "alien" Roman law. It was later decided in many states to give native rules of law precedence over alien law, which was administered for the most part in the larger territorial courts and in the courts of the Holy Roman Empire. Thus it gradually became recognized that the more special law took precedence over the more general law. In this predominance of local and special law the persistent decentralization of German law found its clearest expression. For further information, see Rudolf Huebner, *A History of Germanic Private Law*, trans. Francis S. Philbrick (Boston: Little, Brown, 1918), 22–23.

3. I.e., as Christians we are followers and imitators of Christ, who was prophet, priest, and king (cf. the Epistle to the Hebrews).

4. On the question of the dominance of men based on their strength, see chapter 2 of Hippel's *On Improving the Status of Women*.

5. Gen. 3:16. This verse is also quoted by Luther in his version of the marriage service contained in the *"Traubüchlein"* section of the *Small Catechism*.

6. "Peddler of souls"—the Dutch word often used for slave dealers.

7. Cf. Jeremiah 18:1–6.

8. Cf. Matt. 6:24.

9. In Hippel's version, "the place at the right hand." On this place as a seat of honor, cf. Psalm 110:1 and Matt. 20:21.

10. Cf. 2 Corinthians 12:10.

11. The Romans imagined the time of their ancient god Saturn to have been a golden age of universal happiness.

12. In the feudal (and later in the adopted Roman) system of law, "real" servitude was that form of bondage which resided with the user of a thing (as for example, land) only while the user held it and not with the person himself.

13. 1 John 4:18.

14. During the Enlightenment it was customary for academic institutions to offer a prize of money for the best solution in essay form to difficult social and intellectual problems of the day.

15. In the Socratic method known to us though Plato's dialogues, the teacher brings a single pupil or disciple (at most several) to the recognition of certain truths by means of a series of carefully stated questions leading indirectly, but inevitably to the correct answer.

16. Cf. 1 Cor. 13:1.

17. Hippel means these terms very much in Kant's sense as they were defined in his *Critique of Pure Reason* and *Critique of Practical Reason*.

18. A Greek lyric poet who flourished about 600 B.C. She appears to have been the center of a women's literary society, most of whose members were her pupils in poetry, fashion, and gallantry. Her poetry, which has come down to us in the fragments of nine books, had in classical times and still possesses today the undisputed mark of genius.

19. "In [her] best form."

20. Hippel attempts to answer this question at length in chapters 3 and 4 of *On Improving the Status of Women*.

21. Cf. Matt. 22:21 and Romans 13:7.

22. Probably a reference to the seven rulers of German states known as "Electors" (*Kurfürsten*), who were empowered to choose the Holy Roman Emperor.

23. In chapter 2 of *On Improving the Status of Women*, Hippel declares that the impetus for the "revolution of reason" which separated mankind from all other animals came from Eve (woman) rather than Adam (man).

24. Themistocles (died ca. 460 B.C.), the famous Athenian statesman and commander, after leading the populace of his city to victory over the Persians and developing its naval power, was ostracized from that city about 470, in part because his ostentation and boastfulness (exemplified here by Hippel's anecdote) offended the Athenian sense of democracy.

25. The Roman emperor Caligula (A.D. 12–41) was legendary in classical times for his capriciousness and brutality; his marriages were hastily contracted and speedily dissolved, and the only woman who truly exercised power over him was his last wife, Caesonia. On Messalina's behavior as the wife of Claudius, see note 87 to chapter 2 of this work. Germanicus was one of the greatest of the Roman generals, who conducted three campaigns against the Germans, the last of which in A.D. 16 was completely successful. Germanicus and Agrippina had nine children, including the emperor Caligula and Agrippina, the mother of Nero.

26. On the suitability of women as tailors and seamstresses, see *On Improving the Status of Women,* chapter 5.

27. "In secret"; "confidentially."

28. The *"Majores Domus"* (sing. *Major Domo*) were the men, often called stewards, who had charge of the royal households of the Frankish kings in France and Germany in the seventh and eighth centuries.

29. Cf. Exodus 13:3 and the Book of Joshua.

30. Cf. Gen. 31:14.

31. Cf. 1 Cor. 14:34.

32. On sex-guardianship in marriage, see Part IV of the Introduction to this work.

33. Cf. Gal. 4:4.

34. This right, known as the *"Sävitien-Klage,"* was granted to women by canonical, not civil law and permitted a woman to sue for divorce on the grounds of severe mistreatment by her husband.

35. Cf. Plato, *The Republic*, 353b; 353e; 440b; and 441e. This line appears in precisely the same form in all four editions of Hippel's book on marriage.

36. "It is taken for granted [that women's rights are not included under this heading]."

37. The Interim was a provisional arrangement for the settlement of religious disagreements between Roman Catholics and Protestants during the Reformation

period pending a definitive settlement by a church council. There were three interims, the first in Regensburg in 1541, the third in Leipzig in 1548. The second interim, to which Hippel is referring here, was unpopular with the Protestants and thus not adhered to by many of them. Religious toleration was finally secured for Lutherans at the Peace of Passau in 1552.

38. Arithmetic, algebra, geometry, trigonometry, and calculus.

CHAPTER 6

1. A philosopher of Abdera (481–411 B.C.). Protagoras was a contemporary of Socrates and the founder of the philosophical school known as Sophism. He was driven out of Athens on charges of atheism, and his work "On the Gods" was publicly burned. He is the author of the well-known maxim "Man is the measure of all things."

2. A Greek philosopher (460–357 B.C.) from Abdera nicknamed "The Laughing Philosopher" because of his cheerful disposition and his ridicule of the follies of men. According to tradition, he put his eyes out in order to be less distracted in his philosophical speculations. In his system of ethics, Democritus considered the acquisition of peace of mind the ultimate end of all human action.

3. Proverbs 18:22.

4. "Attached to the soil" (i.e., a serf or bondman)

5. The Greek god of marriage.

6. The main characters in Samuel Richardson's popular eighteenth-century novel *Clarissa* (see Part III of the Introduction to the present work).

7. Cf. Romans 13:9, 12.

8. Romans 13:13 and Gal. 5:19.

9. Cf. Titus 2:4–5.

10. Christian Thomasius (1655–1728) was one of the most learned and prolific legal scholars of the Enlightenment period. He came early under the influence of the writings of the legal authorities Hugo Grotius and Samuel Pufendorf (see Part III of the Introduction to this work), and began his study of law at Leipzig in 1681. In an attempt to free politics and jurisprudence from the control of theology and to bring them into close contact with the everyday world, he published and lectured in German instead of Latin. His views on legal matters were considered heretical, and this along with his sharply satirical criticisms of the pedantry of the scholars of the period forced him to flee to Halle. There he was instrumental in founding the university (1694), where he became professor of law. He served in this capacity the rest of his life, becoming one of the most esteemed teachers of the university and later its director. The work Hippel refers to here is Thomasius' *Dissertatio inauguralis juridica de concubinatu, i.e., Von dem Unehelichen Beischlaf*, published in Halle in 1713. The respondent with whom Thomasius conducted his disputation in this case was another legal scholar, Erhardus Julius Kiechel.

11. A permanent monogamous union of a man and woman not legally married. It differed from marriage by virtue of the lack of *affectio maritalis* (conjugal affection, which presumed the intent of living as husband and wife and procreating legitimate children), and *honor matrimonii* (the social dignity of a woman living with a man in a legitimate marriage). Such a relationship bore no legal consequences. Hippel here uses the German word *"Kebsehe,"* a word also used by Luther in describing such marriages in his translation of the Bible (cf. Gen. 22:24; 25:6; 35:22; 36:12, etc.).

12. "Matrimony according to Salic Law." According to the common law of the Salic Franks, codified about A.D. 500 under Chlodwig, marriages contracted by persons of high noble birth with those not of equal rank were, even up to Hippel's time, not considered perfectly valid and, technically speaking, fell into the category of misalliances (see note 82 to chapter 1, above). The lower-born woman, in particular, acquired neither the name nor the arms of the man, nor further claims to property. The children issuing from such a marriage followed the "worse" ("ärgere") hand and were likewise excluded from the rights and property of the house, as well as, in reigning princely houses, from succession to the throne. When the consequences of misalliances were contractually regulated and the claims of the wife and children thus assured, such marriages were given the name "left-handed," or "morganatic marriages" (see note 77 to chapter 1, above), hence Hippel's reference to the left hand.

13. The Sibylline Books reputedly contained the oracles of the Sibyls, certain women in ancient mythology reputed to possess special powers of divination and intercession with the gods. Of these the most celebrated was the Cumaean Sibyl who, according to the story, appeared before Tarquin the Proud offering him nine books for sale. He refused to buy them, whereupon she burned three and offered him the remaining six at the original price. When he again refused, she destroyed three more and offered the three which remained at the price she had asked for nine. Tarquin, astonished at this behavior, then bought the remaining three books, which were found to contain directions as to the worship of the gods and the policy of the Romans. These books were kept with great care at Rome and from time to time consulted by the oracle-keepers under the direction of the senate.

14. The "Prohibition against Punishment," whereby illegitimate children were protected against punishment or unfavorable treatment at the hands of the law, grew out of the adoption in Germany of the *Legitimatio per rescriptum principis* of Roman law around A.D. 1100. According to this privilege, a child born in concubinage was to be considered legitimate, as if it had been born in a valid marriage (*justae nuptiae*). This privilege was granted at the request of the father if the mother was already dead or not considered worthy to be married. At first this was granted only by the Holy Roman Emperor, but individual German rulers later exercised this privilege personally (hence Hippel's reference to "the prince who decrees this on your behalf"); in part they conveyed the right of its exercise to others. In some cases it was actually included in the office of ruling noblemen.

15. "The Table of Duties" ("*Die Haus Tafel etlicher Spruche*") for all walks of life, including husbands, wives, parents, and children, is found in Luther's *Small Catechism*.

16. Cf. Matt. 11:30.

17. "*O tempora! O mores!*" (Cicero, "Against Catiline," 1, 1, 2).

18. Cf. Matt. 19:6.

19. Cf. Exodus 3:5.

20. Whether or not a couple chose to be married in a church ceremony as well, in Holland during this period a civil ceremony at the town hall was the only legal means of contracting a valid marriage.

21. *The History of Sir Charles Grandison*, an extremely popular novel of the period, published in 1753 by the English novelist Samuel Richardson (1689–1761), a favorite writer of Hippel's.

22. The New English Bible corrects this line to read: "wrapped in two cloaks."

23. On this important marital legislation see notes 71 and 85 to chapter 1. The fact that the two consuls who introduced this legislation in A.D. 9, M. Papius Mutilus and C. Popaeus Sabinus, were indeed unmarried is recorded in Dion Cassius' (A.D. 155–after 230) history of Rome, 56, 10.

24. A king of Lydia in the sixth century B.C. legendary for his wealth.

25. Gen. 2:18.

26. The choice was between the allegorical female figures of Vice (associated with ease) and Virtue (associated with hardship). This story apparently first appears as a parable told by Prodicus of Ceos (a contemporary of Socrates) and recounted by Xenophon, *Memorabilia*, 2, 21–34 and Cicero, *De officiis*, 1, 118.

27. Matt. 6:34.

28. Cf. Gen. 5:25–27.

29. A variation by Hippel on the German proverb *"Wenn die Mühle stehen bleibt, wacht der Müller auf"* ("When the mill-wheel stops, the miller wakes up"), which carries more or less the same connotation as the English proverb "If it isn't broken, don't fix it."

30. Darius (521–485 B.C.) was king of Persia and father of Xerxes. In 501, the Ionian Greeks under Darius' rule revolted; they were assisted by the Athenians, who burned Sardis and thus provoked the hostility of Darius. He invaded Greece, but lost a great deal of his naval force off Mount Athos, and was finally defeated by the Athenians at Marathon. Darius died before he could execute his plan of subduing Greece, and the war was continued by Xerxes.

31. Cf. Matt. 19:10–12.

32. According to legend, Diogenes the Cynic (412–323 B.C.) spent much time wandering about with a lantern in his hand looking for a man whom he could call truly wise.

33. Cf. Matt. 22:30.

34. Cf., for example, Rom. 6:6; Eph. 4:22; and Col. 3:9.

35. Gen. 3:19.

36. Although not officially an order as such, the devotees (in modern parlance, nuns or deaconesses) were known for their piety, religious fervor, and ministry to the sick and oppressed.

37. On Democritus, see note 2 to chapter 6. Heraclitus was born at Ephesus about 535, and died there about 475 B.C. He was reckoned as a member of the Ionian school and considered fire to be the primary form of all matter—but by fire he meant a substance not essentially different from air. At the end of his life he became a complete recluse, living only on herbs.

38. David Garrick (1717–79) was a famous English actor of the period known for his versatility, his range extending from Hamlet to the extremes of low and light comedy.

39. The quips comparing woman to a snail and a town clock, as well as the comment in chapter 7 (also found in *On Improving the Status of Women*) that women will not be found in heaven because they cannot maintain the necessary half-hour's silence described in the Book of Revelation, originated with none other than Immanuel Kant. It is most probable that Hippel himself heard these comments at a social gathering at which Kant was present (See J. H. W. Stuckenberg, *The Life of Immanuel Kant* [1882; New York: University Press of America, 1986], 187). Kant's views on marriage are found in his *Metaphysische Anfangsgründe der Rechtslehre* ("Metaphysical Elements of a

Legal Science," his *Anthropologie*, and his book *Betrachtungen über das Gefühl des Schönen und Erhabenen* ("Observations on the Sense of the Beautiful and Sublime").

40. *"Minne"* was the Middle High German word for courtly love in medieval times.

41. In Greek mythology, Narcissus was a beautiful youth entirely without feeling for others. One of his rejected lovers prayed to Nemesis to punish him for his unfeeling heart. Nemesis caused Narcissus to see his own image reflected in a fountain and become enamored of it. Because he could not approach the object of his love, however, he gradually pined away until he died, and his corpse was then metamorphosed into the flower which bears his name.

42. Cf. 1 Timothy 6:10.

43. Cf. Matt. 6:28.

44. Money given previous to the conclusion of a transaction indicating one's seriousness regarding its completion; a handsel.

45. In the mythology of Greece, a beautiful youth beloved of Venus. After Adonis died of a wound, the grief of the goddess at the loss of her favorite was so great that the gods of the underworld allowed him to spend six months each year with her upon the earth.

46. Although Aristophanes has Euripides describe himself as a realist in his comedy *The Frogs*, the description of Sophocles as an idealist is derived from ancient tradition, rather than Sophocles' own utterances about himself. The treatment of women in the plays of both authors here referred to by Hippel is most clearly evident in their treatment of the Electra theme, and in Sophocles' play *Women of Thracis*.

47. Cf. Plato, *The Republic*, 452b.

48. I.e,. fairytale castles.

49. The ancient Pythagorean philosophers of Greece believed that the movement of the heavenly bodies created a kind of divine music.

50. A reference to the usurer Shylock who is defeated by the eloquence of Portia in Shakespeare's *Merchant of Venice*.

51. After his defeat on the plains of Issus, the mother, wife, and children of the Persian king Darius III (reigned 336–30 B.C.) fell into the hands of his vanquisher, Alexander the Great (356–23). Alexander treated them with the utmost delicacy and respect, and appears to have been favorably influenced by their beauty and the attainments of their culture. In 325, after the death of Darius and in an attempt to form his European and Asiatic subjects into one people, Alexander took Barsine, the eldest daughter of Darius, as his second wife, and ordered the adoption of numerous Asiatic customs for himself and his generals.

52. Cf. Luke 11:34–36.

53. German: *"Schöne Seelen."* This philosophical term has a long tradition extending back to Plato; through the influence of such writers as Shaftesbury, Richardson, Rousseau, Wieland, and Goethe, it reached the height of fashion in the eighteenth century. Schiller gives perhaps the most detailed definition in his essay "On Grace and Dignity" (1793), in which he calls that soul beautiful and noble which has achieved a full and harmonious equilibrium between moral sensitivity and sense perceptions.

54. Paul Pellisson-Fontanier (1624–93), a cardinal in the Roman Catholic church and the chief biographer of Louis XIV, was so disfigured by smallpox in his youth that he was considered one of the ugliest men of his age.

55. The Greek poet Sappho (see note 18, chapter 5) was, according to the traditional story, so in love with Phaon that she gave herself the title *"mascula Sappho"* ("Sappho, the masculine one") and threw herself off the Leucadian rock when her love was not requited. This story appears to have been the invention of later times, however, and the mention of the Leucadian rock only a metaphor taken from an expiatory rite connected with the worship of Apollo, which seems to have been a common poetic image. The name of Phaon occurs in none of Sappho's poems.

56. Matt 22:20.

57. Cf. Matt. 5:15.

58. Matt. 6:22–23.

59. According to legend, Socrates, although his body was handsome and powerfully built, possessed a homely face.

60. An alloy of zinc and copper.

61. According to the mythology of Greece, Actaeon, the great hunter, entered a grotto after a hard day's hunting in order to cool himself in the spring therein. Unknown to him, this was the goddess Diana's favorite bathing place, and he came upon her at the very moment when she had let fall her garments and stood naked at the water's edge. Greatly offended, she flung water into his face and as the drops fell upon him he was changed into a stag, both inwardly and outwardly. He thus suddenly knew cowardice for the first time and fled from the scene. His own dogs pursued him and he was finally torn to pieces by them on Mount Cithaeron.

62. Cf. 1 Cor. 13:9–10.

63. This is a modified version of Shakespeare's line in *Hamlet* (Act 1, scene 2), "Frailty, thy name is woman!"

64. Matt. 12:34.

65. Christina, Queen of Sweden from 1644 to 1654, became queen-elect at the age of six. She was a major force in bringing about the Peace of Westphalia, which ended the Thirty Years' War. Highly cultured and devoted to learning, she was known as the Minerva of the North. Her beneficent rule saw the founding of the first Swedish newspaper and the first nation-wide school ordinance. New privileges were granted to the towns; and manufacturing, trades, and mining also made great strides during her reign. Having secured the election of her cousin Charles Gustavus as her successor, she abdicated the throne in 1654. Later, she embraced the Roman Catholic faith and eventually settled in Rome, where she became a patroness of the arts and the friend of four popes. A militant protector of personal freedom as well, she espoused the cause of the Jews in Rome until her death in that city in 1689.

66. The Greek philosopher Pythagoras (flourished 540–510 B.C.) gained during his lifetime a great number of adherents to his views, chiefly of the noble and wealthy classes. Three hundred of these were formed into a sort of select club, bound by a vow to Pythagoras and each other, for the purpose of cultivating the religious and ascetic observances developed by their master, and of studying his religious and philosophical theories. Juno was the queen of heaven, sometimes known as the female Jupiter, who was worshiped as the protector of the female sex.

67. Shakespeare, *Twelfth Night*, Act 2, scene 4.

68. Cf. James 1:23–24.

69. This work of St. Augustine (A.D. 354–430), actually entitled *De Civitate Dei* (*On the City of God*), was written between 413 and 426. It was intended as a great

apologetic treatise in vindication of Christianity in which the Christian Church is conceived as arising in the form of a new civic order on the crumbling ruins of the Roman empire.

70. "A vista" was a business term meaning "upon visual examination"; "a uso" meant "after a trial use."

71. Cf. Psalm 1:1.

72. Cf. Psalm 84:2, 10; 96:8.

73. Cf. Mark 12:42–44.

74. Flora was the Roman goddess of flowers and spring. Later Roman writers, with the intention of bringing Roman religion into disrepute, maintained she was a courtesan who had accumulated a large property and bequeathed it to the Roman people in return for being honored with the annual festival of the Floralia.

75. Gen. 2:24. Cf. also Matt. 19:5 and Eph. 5:31.

76. On Garrick, see note 38 of this chapter. Michel Baron (1653–1729) was the most famous French actor of the *ancien régime*; Roscius was a great Roman actor, the friend of Cicero and his teacher in declamation.

77. Tiberius Claudius Nero Caesar (42 B.C.–A.D. 37), Emperor of Rome A.D. 14–37, and known in the later years of his reign for affecting a pious regard for external appearances while indulging in the depravities of lust and cruelty in private.

78. Cf. Matt. 23:24.

79. Niccolo Machiavelli (1469–1527) was a celebrated Italian statesman and writer, chiefly known for his treatise on government entitled *Il Principe (The Prince)*, completed in 1513. This work is a study of the founding and maintenance of a state, and of the character and policy of a successful despotic ruler. *The Prince* reflects the unscrupulousness of Italian politics of the day, and the motive for its composition has long been the subject of dispute. In his *Anti-Macchiavell* of 1740, published for him by Voltaire, Frederick the Great attempted to refute the ideas of the Italian statesman with a more humane concept of ruling drawn from his own experience and the philosophy of the Enlightenment.

80. In his first winning entry for one of the academic essay contests of the day (in this case, awarded by the academy at Dijon), Rousseau had replied negatively to the question as to whether the sciences had contributed anything to the advancement and improvement of humanity; Hippel is here referring to intellectual endeavor as representing the "Apollonian" side of mankind.

81. The German word *"spröde"* means both "brittle" and, when applied to people, "coy" and "prudish."

82. For the requirement of priests, cf. Leviticus 21:7; for high priests, cf. Lev. 21:13–15.

83. By this sentence Hippel does not mean that a woman who has been raped should not marry at all, merely that she should not be married wearing the symbol of virginity (the bridal veil).

84. Cf. Numbers 5:11–31 and Deut. 22:13–29.

85. Lycurgus (7th century B.C.) was a Spartan legislator and the traditional author of the laws and institutions of Sparta. On the laws described here by Hippel, see Plutarch, "The Life of Lycurgus," 14–16.

86. Probably a reference to the following lines in an essay by Montaigne entitled "On the Education of Children": "there is not a boy of the lowest form in a school,

that may not pretend to be wiser than I, who am not able to examine him in his first lesson, which if I am at any time forced upon, I am necessitated, in my own defense, to ask him, unaptly enough, some universal questions, such as may serve to try his natural understanding; a lesson as strange and unknown to him, as his is to me" (trans. Cotton).

87. 1 John 2:15.

CHAPTER 7

1. The German designation for those who in England were called "Deists," adherents of the theological doctrine that God was the Great Clockmaker who set the world in motion but then remained aloof from human affairs—and thus that prayers directed to Him would be ineffectual.

2. Cf. Luke 14:23.

3. Cf. Luke 19:12–26.

4. In Greek mythology, Paris was the son of Priam and Hecuba and an exceedingly handsome shepherd. He was drawn into the arguments of the gods at the wedding of Peleus and Thetis, to which all the gods were invited except Eris (Strife). Enraged at her exclusion, she threw a golden apple among the guests with the inscription "To the fairest," whereupon Juno, Venus, and Minerva each claimed the apple for herself. Jupiter ordered Mercury to take the goddesses to Paris and let him decide among the three. While Juno and Minerva promised him great glory if he would choose them, Venus promised him the fairest woman in the world for his wife. Paris decided in favor of Venus and, depending upon the accounts, she either gave to him or allowed him to abduct Helen of Troy, thus bringing about the Trojan War.

5. Cf. the Book of Exodus.

6. This argument, based on the assumption that women have no souls because they lack the powers of human reason identified with the soul, gained some popularity during the Enlightenment. Typical of this genre is Timothy Constant's (pseudonym?) *An Essay to Prove Women Have No Souls* ([London]: Sold by A. Dodd, [1714]).

7. This witticism, based on a passage in the Book of Revelation in the Bible (Rev. 8:1), can be traced precisely to the philosopher Immanuel Kant himself (see note 39, chap. 6 above), who enjoyed the company of women, but did not think them capable of great intellectual attainments.

8. *"Medice"* means here "according to prescription"; *"modice"* is used with the meaning "moderately."

9. The free (city-)states in Germany, which were not ruled by a king, bishop, or the Holy Roman Emperor, were thus less subject to the whims of courtly fashion and attempted to maintain more independence in matters of dress.

10. This anecdote also appears in Hippel's *On Improving the Status of Women* (110).

11. Probably a reference to Hercules' fight with the centaur Nessus. After committing an accidental murder, Hercules was forced to go into exile as a punishment. Upon coming to the river Evenus, Hercules gave his wife Deianeira to Nessus in order for him to ferry her across. When the centaur attempted to abduct her, Hercules heard her screams and shot an arrow through the heart of Nissus. The dying centaur then called to Deianeira to take his blood with her, which would be a love potion strong enough to keep Hercules from ever looking at another woman.

12. The Roman emperor Domitian (T. Flavius Domitianus Augustus, reigned A.D. 81–96) was well known for his delight in the sufferings and misfortunes of others, which led him to indulge in strange pastimes, of which the one described here is a good example.

13. A symbolic ceremony existing since the Middle Ages in which the Doge entered into marriage every year with the sea, the source of all Venice's wealth and power.

14. 1 Cor. 13:1–2 (New American Standard Bible).

15. A Roman general (110–57 B.C.) who, after achieving fame as a warrior, devoted his later life to displays of luxury, and was known especially for his feasts, which were celebrated on a scale of inordinate magnificence. He is thought to have introduced cherries into Italy, and on one occasion a single supper in his great hall is said to have cost fifty thousand denarii.

16. Cf. Mark 1:15 and Gal. 4:4.

17. Cf. Matt. 5:16.

18. Most of what we know of the laws of Lycurgus is recorded in Plutarch's "Life of Lycurgus" in his *Lives*. See also note 85 to chapter 6 of the present work.

19. Benjamin de Rohan, Seigneur de Soubise (1583–1642), was a French commander known for his learning. He was one of the Huguenot leaders in the wars of 1621–29, and led the heroic but unsuccessful defense of La Rochelle in 1627–28.

20. Armand Jean du Plessis, Duke of Richelieu and Cardinal of the Roman Catholic Church (1585–1642), was a celebrated French statesman and the principal minister of Louis XIII. He was noted in his day for his numerous love affairs, later described with embellishments in his well-known memoirs.

21. A reference to Plato's *Republic*, in which the ideal (city-)state is discussed and the conclusion reached that "no practice or calling in the life of the city belongs to woman as woman, or to man as man, but the various natures are dispersed among both sexes alike; by nature the woman has a share in all practices, and so has man, but in all the woman is rather weaker than man" (455d–e, trans. W. H. D. Rouse).

22. Johannes Leyser (1631–84) was a pastor in Schulpforta, Germany, and later a chaplain in the service of the Danish king. He defended polygamy in such writings as *Discursus de polygamia, Discursus politicus de polygamia*, and *Polygamia truimphatrix cum nobis*. The radical nature of these publications caused them to be banned in Copenhagen and resulted in the persecution of Leyser himself.

23. Jeremiah 48:10 (The New English Bible).

24. Heinrich II (972–1024), Emperor of the Holy Roman Empire (1002–24), was nicknamed "The Holy" because of his actions and demeanor. According to legend, his wife Kunigunde, a princess of Luxembourg, disproved a charge of marital infidelity by passing unhurt through an ordeal of fire. Both were later canonized by the Roman Catholic Church.

25. In Hippel's day the army, including the enlisted ranks, consisted of professional soldiers who remained in that profession their entire life. Whether enlisted men were permitted to marry depended on the laws of the particular state they served.

26. 2 Tim. 2:4.

27. Luke 3:14.

28. Cf. Matt. 6:24.

29. The Janizaries were captured Christian children who, when grown, were forced to serve in the infantry of the Turkish army. After the Peace of Karlowitz (1699) they were permitted to marry and ply a trade. They were not allowed to let their "holy" field kettle (flesh-pot) fall into enemy hands.

30. The code of laws governing the conduct of the members of the military forces of a particular country in time of war and peace.

31. Since the possession of geese was the sign of a stable prosperity, Hippel probably means here that the girl should lovingly chide her learned husband with this childish and repetitive taunt into devoting more time to providing a living for his family.

32. The night watchman stood on the lowest rung of the social ladder.

33. When Pope Sixtus V was still a cardinal, he was sickly and walked with a pronounced stoop, which led others to say of him that he was "looking for the keys of St. Peter" (cf. Matt. 16:19).

34. Cf. John 5:2–9.

35. Pegasus is the fabled winged horse of classical mythology; Bucephalus was the horse of Alexander the Great, which no one was able to break except the youthful Alexander himself, and which carried him through his Asiatic campaigns.

36. In earlier classical times, the nine goddesses of song known as the Muses, and according to later writers, the divinites presiding over the different kinds of poetry, and over the arts and sciences.

37. Cf. Rev. 3:15–16.

38. This is probably a reference to the well-known phrase *"Mens sana in corpora sano"* ("a sound mind in a healthy body") of the Roman rhetorician and poet Juvenal (A.D. 60–140), found in his *Satires*, 10, 357.

39. "Always give credit to Galen." Claudius Galenus (A.D. 130–ca. 200) was a renowned Greek physician and writer, long considered the supreme authority in medical science.

40. Cf. Exodus 3:2–4.

41. The Stoic philosophers, followers of Zeno who founded the sect about 308 B.C., taught that men should be free from passion, unmoved by grief or joy, and submit without complaint to the unavoidable necessity according to which all things are governed.

42. Cf. Luke 16:1–8.

43. Cf. Matt. 5:16.

44. According to Luther's catechism, the Seventh Petition of the Lord's Prayer is "but deliver us from evil."

45. See Luther's commentary to the Fourth Petition of the Lord's Prayer in his *Small Catechism*.

46. 2 Timothy 3:6 (New International Version).

47. Cf. Luke 23:34.

48. According to the account in Plutarch's life of Solon, Thales (640–546 B.C.), the Greek philosopher and mathematician, was entertaining Solon (638–559 B.C.), the famous Athenian lawgiver, at his home in Miletus when the latter expressed wonder that the philosopher did not marry and raise a family. Thales gave no immediate answer to this, but later instructed a messenger to say that he had just come from Athens where the funeral of a young man had been attended by the whole city. As

Solon questioned the stranger further about the funeral, it became clear to him that the young man who had died was none other than his son, whereupon Solon began to beat his head in anguish and despair. Thales then took him by the hand and said, "These things which strike down so firm a man as Solon, kept me from marriage and from having children; but take courage, my good friend, for not a word of what has been told you is true" (trans. Langhorne).

49. Agesilaus was king of Sparta from 399 to 361 B.C. and as a general contributed significantly to the reputation of that city as a great military power. The anecdote is found in Plutarch's life of Agesilaus. Heinrich IV (1050–1106), Holy Roman Emperor, is chiefly known for his disputes with Pope Gregory VII over the question of the primacy of the secular state over the Church. After having been called to Rome to answer charges of sacrilege and oppression, Heinrich, in a fit of anger, deposed Gregory. Gregory retorted by excommunicating Heinrich who thereupon, in one of the most significant incidents of the Middle Ages, was forced to do penance before Gregory at Canossa in 1077, thereby restoring at least temporarily the supreme authority of the Church.

50. Among the ancient Hebrews, every fiftieth year was a jubilee year of general celebration. Cf. Leviticus 25:8–14.

51. "Let this be put into application."

52. In Greek mythology, Argus was surnamed *Panoptes*, "the all-seeing," because he had a hundred eyes. Juno appointed him as guardian of the cow into which Io had been transformed, but Mercury slew Argus after he had lulled him to sleep by means of the sweet notes of a flute.

53. Marcus Aemilius Lepidus (died about 77 B.C.) was the father of Lepidus the triumvir. He was consul in 78 B.C. and attempted to rescind the laws of Sulla, but was opposed in this by Catulus and Pompey. The next year he marched against Rome, but was defeated by them in the Campus Martius and forced to take flight. He died shortly afterward of sorrow, said to have been increased by the discovery of his wife's infidelity.

54. Cf. note 68 to chapter 4 of the present work.

55. The Roman divinity Janus was the porter of heaven, and thus bore the surnames *Patulcus*, "the opener," and *Clusius*, "the shutter." On earth he was the guardian deity of gates, and thus is commonly represented with two heads, because every door looks both ways. In this capacity he is depicted as well with a key in his left hand, and a staff or scepter in his right.

56. Cf. Gen. 4:3–5 (New International Version).

57. According to the mythology of the Greeks, for untold ages before the time of the Olympian gods, Cronus (Saturn) was the lord of the universe along with his wife, Rhea. When Cronus learned that one of his children was destined to overthrow his rule, he swallowed every one of them as soon as they were born in an attempt to alter this prophecy. When Rhea bore Zeus, her sixth child, she had him secretly carried off to Crete and gave her husband a great stone wrapped in swaddling clothes to swallow. In Crete Zeus was nursed by a goat in the absence of his mother.

58. Cf. Judges 11:34.

59. Cf. 1 Samuel 18:6–7.

60. The incident is related at the beginning of Plutarch's "Life of Themistocles."

61. Typical of the contradiction between Hippel's life and this sort of statement in his writings is the fact that he loved to sing the old hymns in church and was greatly moved by them. According to Kohnen (*Hippel*, 143), Hippel "often had himself informed on Saturday night as to the hymns which were to be sung in church the next morning. He then sang them while accompanying himself on the piano, whereby he not infrequently broke out in tears. And yet he was never a lover of the art of music."

62. Cf. 2 Samuel 6:12–14.

63. Ecclesiasticus (Jesus Sirach) 7:36.

CHAPTER 8

1. "A total of."

2. Cf. 1 Kings 1:1–4.

3. Psalm 37:3.

4. Matt. 22:28.

5. Cf. John 4:24.

6. Matt. 22:30.

7. Called in German the "*Einkindschaft*," this law dates back to old Franconian law and has to do with the creation of a "single proles," or single family, by virtue of agreements made immediately before the contraction of a second marriage. Such agreements took place between the children of the first marriage and the spouses of the new marriage, and made the children of the first marriage the legal equals of the children expected of the second marriage. This was accomplished by having the first children renounce their rights to the property of the first marriage in favor of the spouses of the second marriage, and in turn having these first children substituted by the spouses in the position of actual children of the second marriage. The "Prussian General [or Territorial] Code" of 1794 made such agreements obligatory in that state.

8. Cf. Gen. 3:15.

9. Cf. Gen. 49:3.

10. Cf., for example, Gen. 25:1–6 and Deut. 21:15–17.

11. Aridaeus was the half-brother of Alexander the Great, the son of Philip of Macedonia and a female dancer, Philinna of Larissa. Aridaeus was an imbicile, although it has not been determined whether this was due to Olympias' "magic" (poison?) or a hereditary defect. He was nevertheless thus prevented from becoming king during Alexander's lifetime. Upon the death of Alexander (323 B.C.), Aridaeus was proclaimed king in the name of Philip. When his wife Eurydice attempted to attain supreme power in Macedonia, she and her husband were taken prisoner by Olympias and put to death. Quintus Rufus Curtius was a Roman historian living at the time of Claudius, the author of a partially extant biography of Alexander.

12. The *poenae secundarum nuptiarum* were penalties imposed upon people who married a second time. From the time of Constantine (that is, from the period of the Christianization of the Roman Empire), imperial legislation became unfavorable to second marriages; it imposed upon both men and women who entered into such contracts various restrictions of a financial nature in favor of children born of the first marriage.

13. Cf. 1 Thess. 4:13.

14. Cf. Matt. 4:4.

15. Cf. Matt. 7:12 (New International Version).

16. The "widow-bench" refers to that share which a widow was allowed of her husband's estate, besides her jointure; thus,"to move the widow-bench" was a common expression for "to marry again."

17. The Dionysian festivals in honor of Bacchus, the god of wine, were a time of wild celebration throughout ancient Greece, during which licentiousness was the order of the day. Many women as well as men are known to have taken part in the orgiastic rites on Mount Parnassus and elsewhere.

18. Cf. Luke 17:21.

19. 1 Timothy 5:13–14.

20. Cf. Matt. 6:21.

21. Caia was the faithful wife of Tarquinius Priscus, in Roman legendary history the fifth king of Rome (reigned 616–578 B.C.). The quotation is here used to mean, "Where you are the master, I am the mistress and supervisor of the household." In fact, the ceremony in which this question was asked by the man and the set reply was given by the woman was part of the traditional marriage ceremony, and took place precisely at the point where the bridegroom's threshold was crossed.

22. Cf. Luke 16:9.

23. Cf. Daniel 9:24–27. In this prophecy each week is to be understood as a period of seven years; thus the 70 weeks of verse 24 total 490 years.

24. Along with a small lifetime annuity from the state and what she inherited from her husband (depending on whether the husband had left surviving children), the wife in all Germanic lands in Hippel's time and before received the right for life to live on and enjoy the proceeds from the land of her dead husband. This right was revoked, however, if she married a second time.

25. 1 Timothy 5:5 (New English Bible). On widows remaining single, cf. 1 Timothy 5:9.

26. Pausanias (lived in the 2nd century A.D.) was a noted Greek geographer and writer on art. This statement is found in his *Guide to Greece*, 2, 21, 8.

27. Cf. Leviticus 21:13–15

28. The Montanists were a sect of the Christian Church, now extinct, founded during the second century A.D. by Montanus of Phrygia. They practiced religious asceticism, believed in the immediate approach of the Second Coming of Christ, and in the establishment of the heavenly Jerusalem at Pepuza in Phrygia. Athenagoras (born about A.D. 176) was a Greek Platonist philosopher and Christian, the author of an apology or intercession on behalf of Christians addressed to the Roman emperors Marcus Aurelius and Commodus.

29. A *"Praefica"* was a woman hired to mourn at Roman funerals.

30. Cf. Luke 14:15–24.

31. I.e., that his wife will remarry just as quickly as she did after the death of her first husband.

32. Cf., for example, Gen. 25:29–34.

33. This was a legal maxim at the time having to do with the validity of contracts. Thus, a visible (written) contract was considered to have precedence over an oral contract.

34. Upon the death of her husband, the Roman Emperor Lucullus Aurelius Verus, in 169 A.D., Lucilla Annia (born about 147) was compelled by the Emperor Marcus Aurelius to marry Claudius Pompeianus, a favorite of the Emperor.

35. Artemisia was both the sister and wife of the Carian prince Mausolus, as well as his successor (reigned 352–350 B.C.). She is renowned in history for her extraordinary grief at the death of her husband, and is said to have mixed his ashes in her daily drink. She built a monument at Halicarnassus to celebrate his memory, the famous *Mausoleum*, regarded as one of the Seven Wonders of the World and whose name now has become the generic term for any splendid sepulchral monument.

36. Christian II (1481–1559), King of Denmark (1513–23), married Isabella, sister of the Holy Roman Emperor Charles V in 1515. In his domestic policy he allied himself with the middle classes and attempted to strengthen royal authority at the expense of the nobility and the Church. This resulted in a rebellion and his exile from the country. He was deposed in 1523.

37. This is more than likely a reference to Galeria Valeria, daughter of Diocletian and Prisca, who married the Emperor Galerus Valerius Maximianus in A.D. 292. Upon his death of *morbidus pediculosis* in 311, she went into mourning and later rejected the repeated proposals of his successor Maximinus who, as a consequence, stripped her of her possessions and banished her into exile along with her mother. She was later executed by Licinius in 315.

38. According to Pliny, Caecina Paetus was condemned to death in A.D. 42 for being privy to a conspiracy against the Emperor Claudius. When he hesitated to kill himself at the Emperor's command, his wife Arria stabbed herself and handed him the dagger with the words: *"Paete, non dolet"* ("Paete, it doesn't hurt"). This anecdote appears in chapter 2 of Hippel's *On Improving the Status of Women*, as well.

39. "Along with burglary."

40. The maiden Europa is often depicted in paintings as riding on a bull (actually the god Zeus transformed into animal form).

41. The theme of death as it relates to women is developed more fully in chapter 5 of *On Improving the Status of Women*.

42. Cf. 2 Corinthians 3:6.

CONCLUSION

1. The number nine played in Hippel's time and even later a significant role in various superstitions connected with childbirth. In this case, the first nine days after parturition were considered to be especially critical for mother and child.

2. "Nothing is more abhorrent than a law with a preface."

3. 2 Kings 2:22–24.

4. Cf. Ecclesiastes 7:8.

5. Laurence Sterne (1713–68), an English humorous novelist known especially for his *The Life and Opinion of Tristram Shandy* (1760–67) and *A Sentimental Journey Through France and Italy* (1768), both of which exerted such an influence on Hippel's fiction that he is often referred to as "The German Sterne."

6. A reference to Hippel's anonymous authorship.

7. Anchises was a legendary hero from the royal house of Troy. In beauty he was thought to equal the gods; he was beloved by Venus, by whom he became the father of Aeneas. Warned by the goddess never to reveal Aeneas' true mother, he nevertheless boasted of his relationship with her and was punished with blindness (or, in some versions of the legend, lameness) for the rest of his life.

8. Cf. Jeremiah 6:10 and Acts 7:51.

9. Matt. 19:6.

10. "That which is natural is not sinful."

11. "Supreme authority."

12. "A legal interpretation."

13. The *"Authenticae"* are a collection of 134 novels (*"Novellae"*), or decrees, promulgated by Justinian between A.D. 535 and 556, after the publication of the second edition of his Code. *Usuales* are common laws based on nature.

14. "Laws based on doctrine," i.e., on reason.

15. A reference to the old German legal maxim *"Wer zuerst kommt, mahlt zuerst"* ["Whoever comes first, mills first"] dating from the time of the legal code known as the *"Sachsenspiegel"* (ca. 1225).

16. In the "enlightened" period in which Hippel lived, the symmetrical Georgian and Neo-classical architectural styles were considered far more beautiful than the overwrought Gothic style dating from medieval times.

17. Johann Friedrich Böttcher (1682–1719), an alchemist in the service of Augustus the Strong, King of Saxony, invented hard-paste porcelain as a direct consequence of experiments in the vitrification by heat of clays and rocks, and as an indirect consequence of his attempts to turn base metals into gold. The incident is mentioned in chapter 7 of *On Improving the Status of Women*.

18. Cf. Gen. 4:18–24. Lamech is here referred to as the father of polygamy. Charles V (1519–56) was Holy Roman Emperor during Luther's time. By the mention of these two persons Hippel appears to be claiming to tread a middle path between licentiousness and asceticism.

19. Sir Thomas Browne (not Brown) (1605–82), a celebrated English physician and writer, is now known chiefly for his *Religio medici* (1643) and the ethereal speculations which characterize his work *Urnburial*, in which he reflects on the transitoriness of human existence and on the signs and symbols of mortality.

20. Now known as the father of pharmaceutical chemistry and chemotherapy, the medieval alchemist Theophrastus Bombastus von Hohenheim (1493–1541), otherwise known as Paracelsus, was much ridiculed during the Enlightenment for his visionary and theosophic form of philosophy.

21. I.e., the Cynic philosopher who was born at Sinope about 412 B.C. The father of Diogenes was once accused of counterfeiting and banned from Sinope. On Diogenes, see chapter 1, note 10 of this work.

22. Priam(us) was the king of Troy at the time of the Trojan war. When the Greeks landed on the Trojan coast, Priam was already advanced in years. As the Greeks entered the city, the aged king put on his armor and was about to engage the enemy, but was persuaded by Hecuba to take refuge with her and her daughters as a suppliant at the altar of Jupiter. While he was there his son Polites, pursued by Achilles' son Pyrrhus, rushed to the temple and died at the feet of his father. Priam then hurled his spear at Pyrrhus, but was ineffective in combating him and was soon killed by the latter before the eyes of his wife and daughters.

23. Cf. Gen. 6:12–13.

24. Cf. 1 Cor. 1:19–21.

25. Cf. Romans 5:13–14.

26. "On behalf of our wife." Since the woman was under the sex-guardianship of her husband, it was necessary for the man to represent his spouse in trials and judicial proceedings.

27. Theodora, the wife of the Byzantine Emperor Justinian, grew up in poverty in the streets of Constantinople. She later became an actress and courtesan, and was elevated by Justinian to the patrician class so that they might be married. She exercised a powerful influence on the administration of the affairs of state, and in A.D. 532 persuaded Justinian to quell a riot of the powerful circus factions in Constantinople with force. She died in 548.

28. "That [women] possess something of the divine." This is part of a line from section 8 of Tacitus' *Germania*, in which the writer describes the high regard in which the women of the ancient Germanic tribes were held by the men. The passage reads in full: "They even suppose somewhat of sanctity and prescience to be inherent in the female sex; and therefore neither despise their counsels, nor disregard their responses. We have beheld, in the reign of Vespasian, Veleda, long reverenced by many as a deity. Aurima, moreover, and several others, were formerly held in equal veneration, but not with a servile flattery, nor as though they made them goddesses" (Oxford translation).

29. Cf. Horace, *Ars Poetica*, 358–60: "and yet I also feel aggrieved, whenever good Homer 'nods,' but when a work is long, a drowsy mood may well creep over it" (trans. Fairclough).

30. "Mother" or "little mother."

31. Cf. Matt. 19:5 (New International Version).

32. Plato, *The Republic*, 607a.

33. 1 Thessalonians 4:4.

34. 1 Corinthians 6:20.

35. Although the expression used here (*"bei meiner Treue"*) is generally translated "Upon my honor," the word *"Treue"* carries a greater connotation of faithfulness and fidelity in marriage than the English word "honor."

36. "In the interest of seizing gain"; "in the interest of avoiding loss."

37. Presumably this incident took place at some time after Maximilian (Holy Roman Emperor, 1493–1519) had become engaged to Anna of Bretagne, and was designed to keep Maximilian's "possession" intact until the marriage ceremony could be performed. It was to prove fruitless, however, when Charles VIII of France broke off his contract of marriage with Maximilian's daughter and took this same Anna of Bretagne, who was already *per procura* engaged to Maximilian, as his own wife instead. As a consequence of this action war broke out, with England and Spain siding with Maximilian against Charles. On Leibniz, see note 50 to chapter 1. "Besser" is Johann von Besser (1654–1729), Master of Ceremonies and poet at the court of Brandenburg, whose collected works were first published in 1711. The debate mentioned by Hippel caused quite a stir among the social circles of Berlin during the early part of the eighteenth century, and represented to the public at large the ultimate in pedantic legal nitpicking.

38. "Under the spear." This expression is derived from the custom in Roman times of indicating by means of an extended spear the designated place for a public auction or sale and the authority of the government to hold such a sale.

39. Cf. Mark 6:4.

40. Hippel is referring to the Spartan lawmaker Lycurgus (see note 75 of chapter 2).

41. Hippel here alters for humorous effect the statement of Horace (*Odes*, 3, 2, 13) *"Dulce et decorum est pro patria mori"* ("It is sweet to die for the fatherland").

42. "I would give a hundred years of immortality for a good digestion."

43. In the first two editions, printed with German letters (i.e., in *Fraktur*), Hippel had written: "I am as convinced of this as I am that this treatise is printed in German letters." The second two editions were printed with Latin type, presumably in an attempt to attract an international audience for the book—Hippel's remarks concerning its appeal in other countries notwithstanding.

44. That is, a short while.

45. On the institution of sex-guardianship, see Part IV of the Introduction to the present work.

46. Cf. Matt. 19:12.

47. The Latin poet Cicero (106–43 B.C.) mentions in his work *Tusculanarum Disputationum* (5, 34, 84) an epigram of Callimachus directed at Cleombrotos of Ambracia, according to which the latter threw himself into the sea upon reading this Platonic dialogue—not for the reason that he wished to escape his sufferings, but so that he might exchange this life for a better one.

48. Cf. Mark 1:15 and Leviticus 26:12.

49. I.e., both Protestant and Roman Catholic readers.

50. Matt. 2:20.

51. I.e., "remember that even rulers do not retain their jurisdiction explicitly, but rather implicitly from holy things."

52. "By means of deceptive reasoning."

53. "In terms of the form [and] content."

54. I.e., in the 1792 and present (1793) editions of the work.

55. Cf. Tobit 3:8 and 6:15 ("Asmodae" is here used humorously for "wicked marriage demons").

INDEX

Abélard, Peter, 291n62
Academics, 240–41
Acrisius of Argos, 281n11
Actaeon, 305n61
Action vs. faith, 249
"Adam in Eden" (Leclerc), 293n84
Adonis, 201, 304n45
Adultery. *See* Fidelity
Adytum, 290n35
Aelius, Sextus, 123
Agesilaus (king), 247, 310n49
Alexander the Great, 289n12, 304n51, 311n11
Anastasius I, 282n17
Anchises, 313n7
Animals vs. human beings, 131
Anna of Bretagne, 276, 315n37
Antonius Caracalla, 97
Apelles, 157, 297n46
Aretino, Pietro, 296n34
Argus, 310n52
Aridaeus, 256, 311n11
Aristotle, 60n69, 74
Arouet, François Marie. *See* Voltaire.
Arria, 263, 313n37
Artemisia, 262, 313n35
Ascetic movements, 33

Astell, Mary, 37–39
Athenagoras, 260
Augsburg Confession, 291n51
Augsburg Interim of 1548, 180
Augustine, 213, 305n69

Bachelors. *See* Single people
"Banyans," 142, 295n5
Baron, Michel, 306n76
Basedow, Johann Berend, 294n18
Beauty, 202–12, 227–30
Besser vs. Leibniz, 276
Blumenbach, Johann Friedrich, 290n37
Böttcher, Johann Friedrich, 314n17
Breasts, 208
Britain: discussions on marriage in, 34; laws of, 99; parliamentary elections in, 176. *See also* English
Browne, Thomas, 270, 314n19
Bucephalus, 242, 309n35
Bullinger, Heinrich, 34
Butler, Samuel, 295n9

Caecina Paetus, 263, 313n37
Caia, 259, 312n21
Caligula, 300n25
Carmer, Johann Heinrich Kasimir von, 289n23